TENNIS:
A Professional Guide

TENNIS

A PROFESSIONAL GUIDE

by
United States Professional
Tennis Association

KODANSHA INTERNATIONAL
Tokyo, New York, San Francisco
Distributed by
Harper & Row Publishers, Inc.

Distributed in the United States by Kodansha International/USA Ltd.,
through Harper & Row Publishers, Inc., 10 East 53 Street, New York,
New York 10022.

Published by Kodansha International Ltd., 12–21, Otowa 2-chome,
Bunkyo-ku, Tokyo 112 and Kodansha International/USA Ltd., 10 East 53
Street, New York, New York 10022 and the Hearst Building, 5 Third
Street, Suite 430, San Francisco, California 94103.

Designed by Dana Levy, Perpetua Press/Editorial Co-ordinator Hiroshi Unno

Printed in Japan
First Edition, 1984
Library of Congress Cataloging in Publication Data
Main entry under title:
Tennis; a professional guide.
    1. Tennis—Addresses, essays, lectures. 2. Tennis—
Study and teaching—Addresses, essays, lectures.
1. United States Professional Tennis Association.
GV995.T413 1984   796.342′07   84-846
ISBN 0-87011-682-7

Contents

PART II

PART III

SEIKO
an enthusiastic supporter of tennis and other sports,
is proud to collaborate with the
United States Professional Tennis Association (USPTA)
in the publication of
TENNIS: A Professional Guide.

Introduction

The top professional players of tennis—the Lavers, Borgs, Connorses, and McEnroes—have always been the most visible practitioners of the game. But the top players need an organized, cohesive, knowledgeable group of teaching professionals working at the grass-roots levels to keep interest in tennis high, and to provide the champions of the future with the tools they need to succeed.

Just as the top professional players gained recognition and credibility through the formation of the Association of Tennis Professionals (ATP), so professional tennis teachers have benefitted from the increasing growth and prestige of the United States Professional Tennis Association (USPTA). Higher certification standards and ever increasing seminars, academies, conventions, and teaching conferences have lifted the quantity and quality of teaching professionals to the highest level ever. As a result, I predict that American players will actually increase their dominance of professional tennis in future years.

To be able to say "I am a USPTA pro" is important to tennis instructors and coaches today. *Tennis: A Professional Guide* is one more valuable way in which the USPTA contributes educationally to its members and to the tennis community.

JACK KRAMER

Foreword

As President of the United States Professional Tennis Association (USPTA), it is a great pleasure to be able to dedicate this tennis manual to the players, coaches, spectators, and participants throughout the tennis world.

During the past decade, tennis recorded an unprecedented growth throughout the U.S. This growth is now being reflected throughout the world as more people are coaching, playing, and generally enjoying this wonderful lifetime sport. The USPTA is the oldest and largest non-profit tennis association in the world, made up of the finest certified teaching professionals. Our objectives are twofold: 1) to create and stimulate a greater awareness in the game of tennis, and 2) to upgrade the standards of the teaching profession. In the past we have accomplished these goals through educational seminars, academies, and workshops throughout the world.

Thanks to the support and cooperation of Seiko, we are now able to crystallize the thoughts and methods of some of the finest teaching minds in the game today by offering you this manual. I am sure you will benefit and enjoy the keen insight of the USPTA professionals who have shared their knowledge with you. This is a book by professionals, dedicated to you, the most demanding and enthusiastic tennis public the world has ever known.

Yours for Better Tennis,
BILL TYM
President, USPTA

Preface

Most tennis players and teaching professionals are of the opinion that there is no *ONE* correct way to hit a tennis ball, or to play the game of tennis. The profusion of playing styles and techniques among today's top professionals supports that opinion. But how, then, does one learn to play tennis as well as one's potential allows?

The answer, at least partially, is in these pages. Do not adhere blindly to one teacher, one system, one way of playing or hitting. Study what each of these teachers and/or players has to say, compare what you learn with other books, other methods, other teachers, and decide for yourself what fits you best.

The best teachers are the ones who bring out your best. They don't try to make every player play the exact same way. In keeping with the philosophy that there are many excellent ways to play tennis, Seiko and the United States Professional Tennis Association (USPTA) offer you the knowledge and wisdom of 24 outstanding tennis teaching professionals. All but two of the 27 authors (Dr. Haas and Dr. Nirschl) are members of the USPTA, an association of almost 4000 teachers. Every USPTA member is required to pass a two-day certification examination that tests a candidate's knowledge and skills in the areas of playing, teaching, and management. In addition to the certification test, which is an education in itself, USPTA professionals partake of numerous educational opportunities each year, ranging from local professional tournaments to sectional academies, national conventions, and tennis teaching conferences.

Among the authors included here, you will find a few world champions, some great coaches, four past presidents of the USPTA, and five USPTA Professionals of the Year. Together, these authors represent the very best of the tennis teaching profession. I hope you enjoy them.

SEAN SLOANE
Editor

PART I

1

History of
Professional Tennis

Although tennis has been played as a game for its entire existence, modern tennis may, perhaps, be better known and understood as a sport, especially in the U.S. The crucial event that caused tennis to become both game and sport was the 1968 decision of the International Lawn Tennis Federation (ILTF) to open Wimbledon and other tournaments to both amateurs and professionals.

Prior to 1968, tennis was considered an amateur game, today it may be more sport than game. The Association of Tennis Professionals (ATP) and the United States Professional Tennis Association (USPTA) exist today as visible proof of the proliferation of tennis professionals since 1968. Begun in 1972, with a membership of 43 and no voice in the development of the sport, the ATP today numbers over 360 members and has gained tremendous visibility and power in tennis. Although the USPTA began in 1927, membership was limited almost entirely to the eastern U.S. until the 1960's, and there was no certification process for membership until 1969. Today, the USPTA lists over 4000 members and offers a rigorous two-day test of playing and teaching qualifications for certification. The ATP and USPTA participated in exploring the possibility of a merger in the 1970's, similar to the alignment of the Professional Golf Association (PGA), but elected to remain sep-

arate organizations. The ATP serves the playing professional, while the USPTA serves the teaching professional; but both organizations exist to protect the interests of their members, and those interests are integrally combined with the health and growth of tennis.

Why were the ATP and USPTA practically non-existent prior to 1968? Why did tennis remain almost wholly an amateur game until 1968? And why has tennis, along with the ATP and USPTA, grown since then in such spectacular fashion? A review of the history of tennis, with particular emphasis on the cultural and economic forces that have helped shape its history, may offer at least partial answers to these and other questions.

Although the origins of tennis are shrouded in myth and speculation, most historians are in agreement that the earliest recognizable form of tennis was a game called *Le Jeu du Paume*, which appeared in thirteenth-century France and which was restricted to the nobility. *Le Jeu du Paume*—"the game of the palm"—was played with a spherical ball on an elaborate indoor court. Originally, the ball was struck with the hand, but rackets were soon added. The game grew in popularity until the beginning of the seventeenth century, when several hundred courts existed in Paris. But the growth of the game brought an upsurge in gambling, which led to the banning of *Le Jeu du Paume*

Major Wingfield's patented court layout for lawn tennis

Court nobles playing *Le Jeu du Paume,* "game of the palm," which is the earliest recognizable form of the game of tennis.

in public in the seventeenth century. Restricted once again to the nobility, *Le Jeu du Paume* evolved into the game known today as court tennis. As was the case with its progenitor, *Le Jeu du Paume*, court tennis is played on an elaborate indoor court with extremely complicated rules. Only seven courts exist in the U.S., so the game has remained in the hands of a few.

Near the end of the sixteenth century, the game spread to England. Since the royal families of England and France often intermarried, and because the French royal family represented the height of elegant culture during the thirteenth, fourteenth, and fifteenth centuries, it was almost inevitable that England should adopt the game as well. Edward III (1327–1377) built a court inside Windsor Castle, and in 1414 Prince Dauphin of France sent balls for the game to Henry V, a gift recorded by Shakespeare in his play *Henry V*, Act I, Scene 2, lines 261–62:

> When we have match'd our rackets to these balls,
> We will in France (by God's grace) play a set. . . .

After the French Revolution, *Le Jeu du Paume* was eliminated in France, along with the nobility, but continued to exist in England with the assistance of *Paume* experts from France who came to England to contribute to the evolution of the game. In England at this time there also existed two other racket and ball games, badminton and rackets. Badminton originated in the village of Badminton, located in Gloucestershire, England, in 1873 and soon became a popular lawn game for men and women. A shuttlecock, or feathered bird, was hit back and forth over a net with long-handled rackets. Rackets, which soon evolved into squash, was an indoor game in which a small, hard ball was knocked against a wall, in turn, by players utilizing long-handled, small-headed rackets. Each game consisted of fifteen points. In addition to the "racket" sports of badminton, rackets, and court tennis, other popular English sports of the day included croquet, an elegantly-paced game of mallets and rock-like balls played on manicured lawns, and cricket, a faster-paced game similar to baseball, also played on special lawns.

Each of these games lent one feature or another to a game patented by Major Walter Clopton Wingfield in 1874. He called the new game Sphairistike, which means "play" in Greek. From croquet and cricket, the major borrowed the close-cropped lawns which lent an air of elegance to those sports. From rackets came the scoring system, based on fifteen-point games, and from badminton and court tennis came the net and the long-handled rackets. The balls were a compromise between the fluffiness of the badminton shuttlecock and the hardness of the court tennis and rackets balls.

What compelled the major to invent and patent this new game? Upon returning to England in the 1860's from a China military command to find the family coffers depleted, Major Wingfield needed to find a means of supporting himself without giving the appearance of working. Sphairistike, or lawn tennis, was Major Wingfield's attempt to capitalize on the craze for sports then sweeping England. Shrewdly attributing the wide popularity of croquet and badminton among the leisured classes to the outdoor element of each and the possibility of feminine participation, the major devised a lawn game which combined the attractive features of both games while eliminating the slow pace of croquet and the erratic flight of the badminton shuttlecock. As soon as his patent was granted in 1874, Major Wingfield went out on the road extolling the virtues of his game and selling the necessary equipment to interested parties.

Unfortunately for the major's financial well-being, potential buyers easily recognized the similarities with other racket sports and, instead of buying his expensive equipment, they improvised with nets, rackets, and balls from other sports. As a result, many variations arose in the rules and regulations of the game, variations that became increasingly troublesome as the game grew and flourished. The popularity of tennis soon proved a problem for England's most revered sport, cricket; for tennis players found that cricket lawns served as perfect courts for lawn tennis. Not only did tennis players intrude on cricket's pitch, but also they appropriated the traditional cricket costume of white shirt and white flannels.

Alarmed by the increasing popularity of the new game, the Marylebone Cricket Club, governing body of England's national game, attempted to take control of lawn tennis in 1875 before it could threaten cricket's preeminence. Major Wingfield resisted the advance of Marylebone, insisting upon his status of founding father and arbiter of the new game, until the Marylebone faction was supported by the All England Croquet Club. Founded in 1868 in a suburb of London known as Wimbledon, the All England Croquet Club had pressing financial reasons (just as Major Wingfield had when he invented the game) for ensuring the game's success. Herbert Warren Wind, in *The New Yorker*, October 8, 1973, wrote:

> Commercially, croquet had fallen far short of the club's hopes for it, so in the mid-seventies the All

An early ladies' tennis costume

England Croquet Club had, as an experiment, laid out a tennis court in one corner of the club property. As it turned out, the court was filled with players from morning to night. Obviously the way to make money was to plunge into lawn tennis in a big way. Very much in the manner of the Marylebone Cricket Club, the All England Croquet Club was soon challenging Wingfield's right, patent or no patent, to run lawn tennis singlehandedly, particularly since the game had already developed an alarming number of variations and seemed to be developing more.

Wingfield might have been able to retain his identification with lawn tennis had he been a bit more flexible, but he insisted upon maintaining his unique hourglass court configuration and fifteen-point scoring system as parts of the game, and his adherence to these impractical traits allowed Marylebone and the All England Croquet Club to "steal" tennis from him.

Not content with the numerous rule changes established under the aegis of the Marylebone Cricket Club in 1876 and eager to capitalize financially on the success of the new game, the All England Croquet Club decided to hold a tournament on its grounds in 1877. Wind continues in *The New Yorker* article:

> . . . in 1877 control of the game was captured by the All England Croquet Club and Lawn Tennis Club —note the change in name—which, under the lead-

ership of three members who were both veteran administrators and ambitious ballgame intellectuals, announced not only that it would be holding a national lawn tennis championship in July but that the event would be played on a rectangular court, under a new set of rules worked out by the club's high-powered troika.

The new rules changed the scoring system to the "15–30–40" method utilized by court tennis, lowered the height of the net, and changed the configuration of the court surface from Wingfield's hourglass to today's rectangle.

The first "Wimbledon" began on July 19, 1877, with 22 men vying for the championship. Spencer W. Gore, a rackets player, captured the gold prize before 200 spectators. The lure of a national tournament allowed the All England Club (AEC)—note the omission of both croquet and lawn tennis—to gain jurisdiction over the game of tennis throughout England and the world for almost 100 years. Once the AEC gained control of tennis via its tournament, the rules of the game and the size of the court changed hardly at all. Ever since 1877, the AEC has referred to its tournament simply as "The Championships," leaving no doubt as to the tournament's status. And players and spectators alike have supported Wimbledon's status as the premier tennis tournament in the world. England's national tennis federation receives a gener-

The All England Lawn Tennis and Croquet Club

Dwight Davis and the Davis Cup

ous share of Wimbledon's profits each year, profits which influence the federation to protect Wimbledon's status and which are employed to further the growth of amateur tennis in England. In much the same fashion, national federations emerged in every tennis-playing country. All these federations were amateur, and almost always the officials performed their tasks voluntarily. However as tennis grew, amateur tennis officials came to relish the power they wielded and the perquisites they were granted as a result of that power. So the ILTF and all its national federations worked very hard to maintain tennis as an amateur game.

Only in the U.S. did the amateur federation, the United States Lawn Tennis Association (USLTA), agitate for some accommodation of professional tennis in the twentieth century. Dr. James Dwight, often referred to as the "father of American tennis," helped to organize the first national tournament in 1881 at the Newport Casino, in Rhode Island; so America was not far behind England in recognizing the virtues of the new game and promoting a national tournament. Unlike England and Wimbledon, however, the U.S. National Championships have moved several times (to Forest Hills, New York in 1915, and from there with a brief interlude at Germantown Cricket Club, 1921–1923, to Flushing Meadows, New York in 1978). The championship changed surfaces as well (from grass to Har-Tru in 1976, to Deco-Turf in 1978).

And even though tennis developed rapidly in both the U.S. and England, it was in the U.S. that the entrepreneurial spirit first shown by Major Wingfield flourished and eventually led to the open tennis decision of 1968, which launched tennis as a modern professional sport. Prior to 1968, however, quite a bit of groundwork needed to be done before the revolution could succeed. As a first step, Dwight Davis donated the Davis Cup in 1900 for team competition, which began between the U.S. and England and grew to include every nation that enjoyed tennis. Ironically, it was the Davis Cup success of France's "Four Muskateers" (Henri Cochet, René Lacoste, Jacques Brugnon, and Jean Borotra) from 1927–1932 that helped influence the dominant figure in tennis at that time (and perhaps all time), William Tatem Tilden II, to turn professional in late 1930. A promoter named C.C. ("Cash and Carry") Pyle also played a part.

Pyle had signed Red Grange, one of the greatest college football players ever, to a professional contract, organized a team around him, and challenged all the professional football teams of the era to games. Trading upon Grange's enormous suc-

Suzanne Lenglen

Various examples in the evolution
of the tennis racket

"Big Bill" Tilden

cess as a collegian, Pyle filled football stadiums across the land in the space of two weeks playing a game almost every day on a whirlwind tour. Grange emerged battered and rich; Pyle emerged rich.

Following his success with Grange and football, Pyle signed the brightest star in tennis, Suzanne Lenglen, an aristocratic Frenchwoman who had not lost an amateur match in eight years, added Mary K. Browne of the U.S. as an opponent (plus Howard Kinsey versus Vinnie Richards for male interest), and set up a whirlwind tour from 1926–1927. Despite numerous commercial tie-ins (i.e., perfume, dresses) enhanced by the theatrical appeal of Lenglen, the professional tennis tour failed to match the success of Grange's football tour, and weary Lenglen returned to France.

Unlike football, which boasted teams and stadiums all across the U.S., with supportive fans, tennis had always been concentrated in the private, aristocratic clubs of the Northeast. There were no tennis stadiums anyplace else in the U.S., nor was there an eager tennis public anywhere but along the East Coast. Pyle, however, was unable to penetrate the bastions of amateur tennis because the club officials and the USLTA realized that the success of professional tennis would mean loss of their power, so they excluded professionals from their grounds. In doing this they were only following the precedent set by the AEC, which traditionally extended membership privileges to the men's singles champion, and just as traditionally revoked those privileges should a champion turn professional.

Nevertheless, despite the efforts of amateur tennis to retain control over the players, amateur champions one after the other began to turn professional. In rapid succession "Big Bill" Tilden, Ellsworth Vines, Fred Perry, Don Budge, Bobby Riggs, Jack Kramer, and "Pancho" Gonzales traded their silver trophies for a shot at the professional dollar. All were more or less stymied by the lack of proper facilities and the general public's lack of familiarity with tennis. Professional tennis existed primarily in the U.S. as a barnstorming operation, transporting one portable court from town to town in search of high school gymnasiums with open dates. These tennis pioneers, barnstorming through Middle America, laid the foundation for the eventual success of professional tennis in the 1970's by gradually educating and preparing a tennis public outside the East Coast.

Tilden was the first male amateur champion to turn professional. He had swept all before him in the 1920's, until the "Muskateers" of France arrived in 1927 to capture the Davis Cup from the Tilden-led U.S. team. Soon the Frenchmen began winning the Wimbledon and Forest Hills titles, which had become almost exclusively Tilden possessions. Possessed by a desire for the spotlight, and never one to underestimate himself, Tilden had made many enemies among amateur officials while he was winning championships. When he began to lose, these enemies were all too ready to help him continue down that path. Unwilling to allow others to control his destiny and inspired by Pyle's example with Lenglen, Tilden turned professional in 1930 and promoted his own professional tour in 1932 against a Czechoslovakian player, Karel Koseluth.

Shortly after Tilden's departure from the amateur ranks, Ellsworth Vines of California shot like a meteor to the top of the game and almost immediately turned pro, in 1933, to challenge Tilden. Worried by Tilden's lack of success with the Kozeluh-Tilden tour, Vines persuaded Tilden to leave the promotional aspects of the following tours in the 1930's to Jack Harris.

When Vines defeated Tilden in 1934 to become professional champion, Harris signed Fred Perry, who had just won Wimbledon three times running, to challenge Vines in 1937 and 1938. After Veins disposed of Perry, Don Budge was ready to challenge.

Budge had just completed the first Grand Slam ever, winning the national championships of Australia, France, England, and the U.S. (the four nations to have won the Davis Cup) all in 1938, and he led the U.S. to the Davis Cup. He continued his success on the professional level, but the onset of World War II played havoc with the overseas components of the 1939 tour. In late 1941, Lex Thompson of the Philadelphia Eagles (professional football, again!) organized a round-robin tour in-

"Pancho" Gonzales

volving Budge, Perry, Frank Kovacs, and the latest amateur champion Bobby Riggs, but World War II stopped that tour almost before it began.

During the war, tennis continued to exist for charity purposes. Forecasting the eventual success of open tennis, Don Budge played Jack Kramer, still an amateur, in Madison Square Garden and the Seventh Regiment Armory, drawing huge crowds for War Bonds and the Red Cross.

After the war, the promotional responsibilities passed briefly from Harris to Bobby Riggs, and soon to Jack Kramer. Although Kramer is regarded by many historians as a player equal to "Big Bill" Tilden, Kramer's greatest service to tennis has been as a promoter and administrator. Under Kramer's guidance, the professional tour began to evolve from the head-to-head duels of the 1930's and 1940's to a more traditional tournament format.

In the first postwar tour in 1946, Bobby Riggs defeated Don Budge. Riggs, in turn, was defeated by Jack Kramer in 1947, and when "Pancho" Gonzales challenged Kramer in 1949, Riggs was the promoter. Riggs continued to promote the 1950 tour, featuring Pancho Segura and Kramer, but then the reins passed to Kramer, who promoted his own tour against Frank Sedgman in 1951. Sedgman's professional debut marked the beginning of the Australian era, a period of nearly two decades when the Australian Davis Cup team, led by captain Harry Hopman, included a succession of players who dominated amateur play and then signed on with Kramer and the professional tour. Sedgman began the dynasty, and was soon followed by the "Whiz Kids," Lew Hoad and Ken Rosewall, who in turn were succeeded by Neale Fraser, Roy Emerson, Fred Stolle, and Rod Laver, with John Newcombe and Tony Roche adding the final punch.

Great as the Australians were in the amateur ranks, they soon fell before the expertise of Kramer's successor "Pancho" Gonzales when they turned professional. With Kramer promoting, Gonzales dispatched Tony Trabert (1956), Ken Rosewall (1957), and Lew Hoad (1958) in succession. From this point on, Kramer continued to sign Australians and Americans to professional contracts after they had won Wimbledon, Forest Hills, or the Davis Cup. There were now enough top professionals available to justify small tournaments, or round robins, in place of the head-to-head tours that ushered professional tennis into the 1960's. The handwriting on the wall appeared in 1967, two months after John Newcombe of Australia had defeated Wilhelm Bungert of West Germany in a lackluster Wimbledon final. Kramer promoted an

Jack Kramer

Ken Rosewall

eight-man professional tournament at Wimbledon that sold out every day. Shortly after Forest Hills that year, Dave Dixon signed the "Handsome Eight" to professional contracts.

After 40 years in the back room, professional tennis was about to take center stage! But why did professional tennis have to wait until 1968? Why was professional tennis not popular and accepted in 1926?

Perhaps the intervening years were necessary to give promoters Harris, Riggs, and Kramer time to educate the American and international public to the excitement of professional tennis, or maybe it was the flowering of a number of extraordinary talents in the late 1950's and 1960's that gave Kramer's professional troupe the leverage they needed to force amateur tennis to accommodate them. Three factors were present in the 1960's, moreover, that had not been present in 1926 when C.C. Pyle signed Lenglen to a professional contract. The three new factors were television, stadiums, and the tie breaker.

When television began exploiting sport for commercial profit, tennis had another opportunity to explode in popularity, as football had back in the 1920's. C.C. Pyle was no longer around, but Texan millionaire Lamar Hunt followed Pyle's program precisely. Hunt first used his oil millions to promote the American Football League (AFL) as a rival to the established National Football League (NFL). Despite huge initial losses, Hunt's league eventually achieved parity with the NFL, merged with it, and shared in the financial success of pro football. Like Pyle before him, Hunt saw no reason why the same plan would not work in tennis. Hunt also had an ulterior motive, which, coincidentally, was similar to Major Wingfield's original plan for the game of tennis! The first executive director of Lamar Hunt's World Championship Tennis (WCT), Bob Briner (later executive director of the ATP), recounts how Hunt became involved in tennis:

> I was a public relations assistant for the Miami Dolphins of the AFL when I got an opportunity to go with the domed-stadium project in New Orleans. There I was working with Dave Dixon (who started the "Handsome Eight" and sold out to Hunt) and the Governor of Louisiana, mostly as a liaison between the project and various sport groups around the country. While we were trying to consider potential tenants and teams for the stadium, we got to talking about the potential of tennis for the stadium. We spoke to Lamar Hunt about it, and he was immediately interested in the professional tennis side. This led us to consider the formation of the WCT.

Just as Major Wingfield had invented tennis in order to capitalize on current trends in English sport, so Lamar Hunt envisioned tennis as a way of utilizing, to his financial benefit, the large indoor arenas recently built for professional football and other professional sports. C.C. Pyle's dream had failed because tennis was not yet popular all over America and because there were no appropriate sites for tennis other than private clubs in the Northeast.

In the interim between Pyle in the 1920's and Hunt in the 1970's, modern technology had produced artifical court surfaces for tennis that could easily be utilized in the large multipurpose indoor sport arenas being built all over the U.S. And television would provide the exposure that would draw crowds of fans to see the new professional sport of tennis. However, one large problem remained before Hunt and the WCT would successfully utilize television and indoor arenas to exploit professional tennis. The game of tennis, as it existed, had no time limits. A tennis match could conceivably go on forever. This element of tennis, built into the scoring system of the game, ensured fairness to the participants. But the open-ended scoring format was unacceptable to television and Madison Avenue. A scoring system needed to be devised which would allow television networks at least a sporting chance of determining when a match would be over. The result was the tie breaker, a special game played when a set reached six games apiece.

Although the concept of the tie breaker had been around for a number of years, and had been tirelessly pushed by a maverick member of the eastern tennis establishment named Jimmy Van Alen, the USLTA and ILTF strongly resisted it. As amateur bodies, their only thought was to preserve the game as they knew it. It took Hunt's recognition of the promotional force of television and the necessity to change the game to fit that medium to bring the tie breaker into tennis. Ironically, the ILTF and USLTA, by insisting on maintaining the integrity of the game as they knew it, lost their control of tennis, just as the AEC, predecessors to the ILTF, had gained control of tennis from Major Wingfield, the game's inventor. Wingfield had insisted upon maintaining his hourglass court and fifteen-point scoring system while the AEC recognized that promotion of the game was more important than the shape of the court and the scoring system. In similar fashion, the ILTF insisted upon maintaining traditional scoring while Hunt and the WCT recognized that the promotion of the game via television was more important than the scoring system.

Lew Hoad

Rod Laver

Beginning in the late 1960's, Hunt signed more and more of the top amateur players to professional contracts, and for a while a rival professional organization, the National Tennis League, competed with WCT for both amateur players and the professional dollar. Before 1960, only a few players at a time had ever turned professional—the money did not exist for more. But Hunt's entry into tennis prompted a wholesale departure of the top players from the amateur ranks. Fearful that too many top players were turning professional and that Wimbledon would cease to be the premier tennis tournament in the world, the AEC joined its prestige with the English and the U.S. federations to force open tennis on the ILTF in 1968, thus allowing amateurs and professionals to compete together. Since all the major federations depended upon the financial success of major tournaments, they really had very little choice. Without the best players their national tournaments would never raise the amounts of money they had come to expect. Unfortunately for the amateur associations, when amateurs and professionals began competing together the professional polish of the WCT compared to the bumbling efforts of voluntary amateur officials soon became obvious to the players, who began gravitating en masse to WCT events. Rex Bellamy, in his *The Tennis Set* (London, 1972), tells it this way:

> Their (ILTF tournaments) traditional preeminence is being shaken by the energetic challenge of the slick WCT circuit and by the fact that the U.S., rather than Europe, threatens to dominate the professional game.

> In 1971 they (WCT) promoted their own circuit of twenty-one tournaments carrying a million dollars in prize money. The exclusively professional game had the strength, coherence, and sense of purpose it had previously lacked. Competition and incentive had been intensified. Joining WCT became a privilege and a commitment: a privilege because it marked a graduation in terms of proficiency, and a commitment to a consistently high playing standard, to a way of life, and to a new personal and corporate responsibility.

When the national federations found that even their national players, developed with their aid, were choosing WCT events over their national tournaments, the ILTF attempted to exert sanctioning power over the players. Although one national federation alone could not compete with WCT, all of them together, as the ILTF, could affect a player's potential welfare considerably by suspending him or her from ILTF tournaments. However, while the national federations were

fighting with WCT and reaffirming their commitment to ILTF, the players themselves saw an opportunity, for the first time in tennis history, to have a voice in the running of the game. They formed a player's union, the Association of Tennis Professionals (ATP), in the early 1970's.

The ATP grew out of the dreams and frustrations of many tennis players over the years. For example, the amateurs of the early 1960's had worked together to provide meals for all the competitors at the Orange Lawn Tennis Club in New Jersey, site of a grass court tournament preceding Forest Hills. At the same approximate time, the touring professionals were advocating changing the tour from a head-to-head challenge format to a tournament format. And when open tennis finally happened in 1968, giving brief birth to "independent" and "contract" professionals, the players attempted to unite. All the players had one thing in common: a desire to be heard and recognized within the sport of tennis. Since the inception of "The Championships" in 1877, control over tennis had been vested in the hands of the national associations and federations around the world, the ILTF, which was confronted from time to time by players looking after their individual interest.

Despite the opportunities of open tennis, the players were unable to organize effectively until September 1–3, 1972, when Cliff Drysdale, Arthur Ashe, Ismail E. Shafei, Stan Smith, Mark Cox, Nikki Pilic, Jim McManus, Ray Ruffels, and Andres Gimeno met in the clubhouse at Forest Hills and, guided by Donald Dell, Frank Craighill, and Bob Briner, laid the foundation for the ATP. On September 3, 1972 a general meeting of the players was held under the famous old Forest Hills Stadium and the voices of the 43 players in attendance were overwhelmingly in favor of the establishment of the ATP. Bylaws were written and adopted, 13 directors were elected, and Cliff Drysdale emerged as the first president of the ATP. The bylaws of the new organization were:

a. to promote and protect the mutual interests of all tennis professionals;

b. to unite all tennis professionals (including teaching professionals) in a single association for the purpose of maintaining a representative and unified organization to consider, agree, and act upon all matters affecting the activities of its members;

c. to promote and encourage the promulgation of just and reasonable rules and regulations to govern the sport of professional tennis;

d. to strive for the improvement of playing and working conditions generally, to regulate and correct abuses relative thereto, and to secure and maintain freedom from unjust and unlawful rules and regulations affecting each member's career as a tennis professional in the sport of professional tennis;

e. to encourage the maintenance of minimum levels and continued growth of prize money and to insure the just and equitable distribution thereof;

f. to formulate and maintain ethical standards to govern the conduct of its members in their relations with each other and the public;

g. to encourage mutual understanding and cooperation among members of the Association and other individuals and the organizations directly or indirectly involved in the promotion of the sport of tennis;

h. to develop programs through which the Association and its members will derive further benefits and/or revenues;

i. to furnish reliable information to its members with respect to matters of mutual concern;

j. to assist its members in securing employment;

k. to voluntarily aid and assist members or families, relatives, or dependents of such members as the Board of Directors may deem worthy or in need of relief or assistance;

l. to cooperate with and assist other organizations having purposes or objectives in whole or in part similar to those of the Association's; and

m. to provide all tennis professionals with an organization dedicated to the promotion and the advancement of the sport of tennis.

Recognizing his many years of service to professional tennis and his influence throughout the sport, the directors asked Jack Kramer to be their first executive director. Kramer immediately established offices in Los Angeles and Paris. Finally, after nearly 100 years, the players had a meaningful voice in the game.

Less than one year after the formation of the ATP, however, the newly established unity of the players was challenged by the ILTF. In early 1973 a top Yugoslavian player, Nikki Pilic, was suspended by his national association for refusing to play Davis Cup, after he had supposedly promised to do so. Although the facts of the case were never clear-cut, the ILTF supported the Yugoslav Association and cleverly arranged the suspension to begin with Wimbledon. Pilic's absence from Wimbledon would have no noticeable affect on the tournament, and the ILTF and Wimbledon were willing to gamble that the top players of the ATP would be unwilling to sacrifice their participation in the most prestigious of all tournaments in exchange for winning a point of principle involving a player of lesser stature. However, the ATP vigor-

ously opposed the suspension, both through legal action and concerted activity, and when the ILTF and Wimbledon refused to accept Pilic's entry, 79 of the 81 ATP members accepted into Wimbledon withdrew. The ATP was boycotting Wimbledon!

The issue at stake went far beyond the immediate factor of the Pilic case, which the members of the ATP recognized. What was at stake was whether the national associations and the tournament directors had the authority to issue edicts barring players from tournaments when such edicts were based upon rules and other terms and conditions of employment to which the players had no input and to which they had never agreed. The ATP's withdrawal from Wimbledon represented a great personal sacrifice for the players, but also a great victory, for they had remained united under the fiercest pressures possible and made their point.

After the Wimbledon boycott, which forced the ILTF and the tournament directors to recognize the unity and the strength of the players, the ATP, ILTF, and tournament directors set about correcting and improving the administrative structure of professional tennis. The result was the Men's International Professional Tennis Council (MIPTC, or the Council), a board of nine (originally seven) representatives with equal membership from each of the three major factions involved (players, tournaments, and federations) which would have complete scheduling and sanctioning power for all tournaments world-wide, and the power to suspend the ILTF rules of tennis as necessary.

The ATP's three representatives are elected directly by the players. Each player ranked in the top 150 has the opportunity to nominate anyone in the world to represent him or her on the Council. The current ATP representatives on the Council are Mike Davies, Ray Moore, and Stan Smith. Through their representation on the MIPTC, the ATP has injected itself into the rule-making process, and in so doing, the ATP has followed the lead of other labor unions in helping to establish most of the rules that affect their own working hours, wages, and conditions. Through their ATP representation on the Council, the players have achieved direct input into the body that administers the prestigious Grand Prix circuit. The Council facilitates communication, interchange, and bargaining among the representative parties and provides a forum for negotiation. The players' participation on the Council has actually served to increase the essential labor identity and effectiveness of the player group.

The MIPTC administers and continually modifies the Grand Prix, a system devised by Jack

Kooyong Tennis Club, Melbourne, Australia

Center Court, Wimbledon, England

Yoyogi Stadium, Tokyo.

Seiko Super Tennis, Yoyogi Stadium, Tokyo.

French Open, Stade Roland Garros, Paris.

Kramer to solve the uncertainties created by open tennis. Currently in its sixteenth year, the Grand Prix is a series of 87 tournaments in some 30 countries throughout the world, presently under the overall sponsorship of Volvo. The series includes the U.S. Open, Wimbledon, and every other major championship in the world. Because of this system, whereby the newest and/or remotest tournaments are linked to even the oldest and most famous events, the Grand Prix has grown and prospered over the years. In addition to nearly $20 million in prize money, the players compete for points throughout the season. At the end of the season a bonus pool is divided among the top players and the top 12 players in the standings play in the Volvo Masters playoff at Madison Square Garden in New York City.

The most important issues to the players are determining player qualifications for entry into Grand Prix tournaments and supplying objective criteria to ensure that the top players are seeded fairly. The ATP computer was created and is administered by the players, for the players, and ensures that the entries and seedings in tournaments are based on one objective criterion: merit. Since the computer ranking system was just implemented in 1974, the players have developed a complex, but totally impartial method for determining tournament entries and seedings through objective records maintained on a computer. Separate singles and doubles rankings are calculated approximately 40 times per year in the ATP operations headquarters, and every player who has competed in a professional tournament that meets ATP ranking criteria (and offers at least $25 thousand in prize money) during the preceding 12 months is included in the ranking. A special committee composed of ATP members determines the ATP ranking policies subject to the approval of the ATP Board of Directors. Thus, the players now decide the rules which most affect their livelihood, not the promoters or the tournament directors.

Shortly after the implementation of the ATP computer ranking system, Bob Briner succeeded Jack Kramer as executive director of the ATP. Kramer left Briner an infant organization that had gained immediate respectability, prominence, and prestige in the world of tennis. During Briner's tenure as executive director, from 1975 to 1980, the ATP added its own new paper, the *International Tennis Weekly (ITW)*, and hired "road representatives" for every Grand Prix tournament, ensuring that each tournament follows proper entry acceptance and seeding procedures, and assisting the players should any off-court dispute arise.

Far more important than the *ITW* and the "road reps," however, was the ATP's role in formulating and promulgating a code of conduct to govern player behavior, along with six Grand Prix supervisors to enforce the code and a continuing series of Grand Prix schools to raise standards of officiating on the world circuit. Under the leadership of Briner and ATP's second president, Arthur Ashe, the ATP persuaded the Council to accept player input into the rules governing player conduct on the world circuit. Prior to the acceptance of the Code of Conduct and implementation of it by Grand Prix supervisors working for MIPTC, the ILTF and its member federations were responsible for player disciplinary processes. But while tournament directors and promoters were in favor of good behavior in principle, in fact, they were loathe to invite box office disaster by taking disciplinary action against a top star. Therefore, it took action by ATP members, to whom fair and uniform enforcement of the code was paramount, to bring the Code of Conduct into existence.

With the ATP's aid and encouragement the Council hired Dick Roberson to find and train full-time Grand Prix supervisors (there are now six), whose roles are to attend every Grand Prix tournament as the Council's representatives and to ensure that the rules of tennis are interpreted correctly and the Code of Conduct enforced fairly and consistently. In addition to the supervisors themselves, the ATP initiated, and the Council has continued, Grand Prix certification schools for international tennis officials. These schools are presided over by the Grand Prix supervisors. Their purpose is to raise the quality and consistency of tennis officiating world-wide. Even though the entire officiating and enforcement program has been taken over by the Council, the ATP continues to lend its enthusiastic support.

Following Bob Briner's five years in office, Butch Buchholz became executive director of the ATP in 1980, to be succeeded in 1982 by the current executive director, Mike Davies. Of the four executive directors in ATP history, only Briner had never been a top player himself. This may help to explain why benefits to ATP members have grown so quickly. Every ATP member is covered by life insurance and personal property insurance, trainers/physiotherapists are provided free of charge at every Grand Prix tournament, Adidas clothing and shoe contracts are available, with performance bonuses yearly, and the Jaime Fillol Pension Plan has just begun for retiring players. And of course there are many smaller benefits, such as tollfree phone calls, cash management accounts, *ITW* subscriptions, and many other services.

ATP Executive Directors

Jack Kramer	1972–1975
Bob Briner	1975–1980
Butch Buchholz	1981–1982
Mike Davies	1982–

ATP Presidents

Cliff Drysdale— *South Africa*	1972–1973 / 1973–1974
Arthur Ashe— *United States*	1974–1975 / 1975–1976
John Newcombe— *Australia*	1976–1977 / 1977–1978
Jaime Fillol— *Chile*	1978–1979 / 1979–1980
Harold Solomon— *United States*	1980–1981 / 1981–1982 / 1982–1983
Ray Moore— *South Africa*	1983–

ATP Officers

Ray Moore	—	President
Mike Estep	—	Vice President
Jim McCanus	—	Secretary
Mike Estep	—	Treasurer
Mike Davies	—	Executive Secretary

Board of Directors

Ray Moore	—	*South Africa*
Mike Estep	—	*United States*
Stan Smith	—	*United States*
Ferdi Taygan	—	*United States*
Mark Edmondson	—	*Australia*
Paul MacNamee	—	*Australia*
Carlos Kirmayr	—	*Brazil*
Rolf Gehring	—	*Germany*
José Higueras	—	*Spain*
Balazs Taroczy	—	*Hungary*

Beginning with an initial membership of 43 players in 1972, the ATP has grown to an organization of over 360 members. Players ranked among the top 200 in the world are eligible for Division I membership upon payment of $750 annual dues, while players ranked from 201 to 500 are eligible for Division II membership upon paying $250 per year.

Current ATP members enjoy the lucrative fruits of a world-wide tournament circuit, and actively participate in the management and well-being of that same circuit, primarily due to the cumulative efforts of the touring professionals and promoters who kept professional tennis alive from 1926 to 1968, and who educated the international audiences who today support the Grand Prix circuit. But first among all those to whom today's

Martina Navratilova with Women's Singles trophy at Wimbledon

Federation Cup (left). Consolation Cup (right)

Bjorn Borg, winner at Wimbledon

1982 Seiko Super Tennis singles winner, J. McEnroe

professional is indebted must be Jack Kramer. As one of the best players in tennis history, with a long tenure as a successful professional promoter, as the architect of the Grand Prix design that serves all tennis today, and finally as the first executive director of the ATP, Jack Kramer more than anyone else has raised the status of professional tennis players to its current eminence in the world of sport.

However, tennis professionals live and work these days in two guises, as playing professionals or teaching professionals. Just as the playing professionals worked to keep professional tennis alive until 1968, so the teaching professionals labored in those same years to keep the game of tennis moving forward. Today there is a clear dividing line between playing and teaching professionals, despite the ATP bylaws (b. to unite all tennis professionals [including teaching professionals] in a single association . . .). Prior to the 1960's, almost all the top professional players held club teaching jobs at one time or another in order to supplement their playing income, and many of these same playing professionals, including Jack Kramer, joined the association of teaching professionals at one time or another. Even top players of the more recent past, such as Rod Laver, Roy Emerson, and Fred Stolle, who are still active as playing professionals on the "Legends" and "Grand Masters" circuits, have joined the teaching professional association as well.

There are other associations of teaching professionals existing today, particularly Dennis Van Der Meer's Registry of Tennis Professionals. But the largest association, the oldest association, and the only association that requires completion of a two-day certification test to be eligible for membership, is the USPTA. Just as the ATP grew out of the professional players' desires to have some impact on their working conditions, so the USPTA developed from the teaching professionals' desires to improve their working conditions (primarily at indoor and outdoor tennis clubs) and to enhance their tennis teaching skills. ATP members are classified as Division I or II members according to their success on the tour, whereas USPTA members are classified as Professional I, II, or III according to their performance on the certification test. A professional player who has not attained a ranking above 500 is not eligible for ATP membership, and similarly a professional teacher who fails the certification test (about five percent) is not eligible for USPTA membership.

As the following brief history of the USPTA demonstrates, the open tennis explosion of 1968 affected the size and scope of the USPTA even more positively than it did the ATP. Although tennis was introduced to the U.S. in 1874, it was not until the years following World War I that tennis became popular enough to warrant professional instructors, and the great majority of them were located on the East Coast.

Following the conclusion of C.C. Pyle's first professional tour, Vinnie Richards and Howard Kinsey, the male contestants on that tour, met with a number of other noted tennis professionals in an upstairs room at Spalding's building in New York City in order to organize a national body that would work to further the best interests of the game of tennis, its instructors, and its participants. In addition to Richards and Kinsey, others in attendance at that meeting on September 23, 1927 were Van Richards, Spalding representative and well-known tennis official; George Agutter, first head professional at the West Side Tennis Club (Forest Hills); William J. Croker, head professional at the Longwood Country Club, Boston, Massachusetts; James Burns, Sr.; Ed Faulkner; Henry A. Geidel; Paul Heston; Walter Kinsella; Frank Lafforgue; Harry A. McNeal; Harvey Snodgrass; James Reid; and Charles M. Wood.

As a result of that initial meeting and a few more planning meetings that followed, the group elected Agutter as chairman and McNeal as secretary-treasurer and sent out the following notice to all recognized tennis professionals under the name of the Professional Lawn Tennis Association of the U.S. (PLTA):

> For some time past there has been a very strong feeling among lawn tennis professionals that there is a need for some organization to protect and promote their interests, and to assist them in obtaining a proper and recognized status in the tennis world. A meeting was accordingly held September 23, and it was decided to form an Association. This meeting was followed by others, at which the following regulations were agreed upon. An initiation fee of ten dollars will be charged to all new members. Dues are to be five dollars annually.
>
> An executive committee has been elected and a constitution adopted. It is the desire of this executive committee to have all tennis professionals of accepted standards become members of this Association. As one of these, you are cordially invited to fill out the enclosed application blank for membership.

Response to the notice was encouraging, and the USLTA recognized the new group at its annual meeting in Chicago on February 11, 1928 and passed a resolution stating that its membership should foster and encourage the growth and continuance of the PLTA along sound and conservative lines.

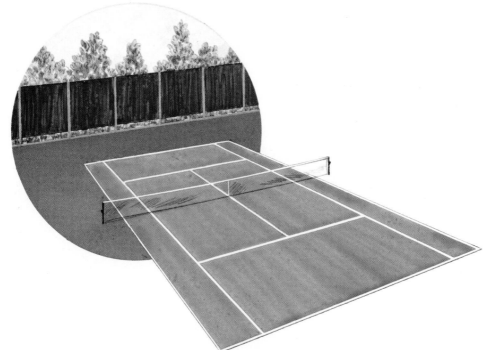

George Agutter was elected the first president. He was succeeded by Ed Faulkner, Henry Geidel, James Pressley, and Charles Wood, who served until 1946. During these first years of its existence, the PLTA held annual meetings and promoted a national tournament, for professionals only, from 1927 to 1943. Winners of the PLTA tournament included Vinnie Richards, Bill Tilden, Ellsworth Vines, Fred Perry, Don Budge, Jack Kramer, Bobby Riggs, and Pancho Segura.

Although the PLTA remained almost exclusively an eastern organization until the end of World War II, the election of Frank J. Rericha to the presidency in 1946, and the appointment of Roy Miller as executive secretary led to legal incorporation of the PLTA, adoption of *American Lawn Tennis* magazine as the official voice of the association, a job placement service for members, two meetings a year, and the establishment of sectional organizations throughout the U.S. Within two years membership had increased to more than 200 of the nation's top professionals, including Pauline Betz, Sarah Palfrey Cooke, Bobby Riggs, and Jack Kramer. In ensuing years membership fluctuated, but progress continued. A model professional contract was drawn up for use between members and their clubs, three movies were made (*Topflite Tennis, Great Moments of Great Matches with the World's Greatest Pros; Tennis by Contrast, Compara-*

tive Games of Riggs, Budge, Perry, Stoefen, and Tilden; and *Mixed Troubles,* a tennis comedy starring Mickey Rooney, Walter Pidgeon, Pauline Betz, and Sarah Palfrey Cooke), and the association acquired an official song, "I'm in the PLTA now!"

The official song was dropped when the association changed its name to the USPLTA in 1957. Under the direction of president William C. Lufler in the early 1960's, stricter standards for admission of prospective members were established. Lufler, who was concerned with communications among professionals, toured the country urging tennis professionals to join and, despite the stricter standards, membership increased to over 550 professionals in eight geographical divisions.

Working in conjunction with the USLTA, Lufler established the U.S. Professional Tennis Registry, a listing of all organized tennis groups and recognized tennis professionals (whether USPLTA members or not), and arranged to publish the registry in the USLTA's 1965 Yearbook. Despite Lufler's altruistic intentions, the registry failed to continue. Instead, the USPLTA took up the banner of certification during Jack Barnaby's years as president (1969 and 1970) and instituted the first comprehensive written/playing certification test in professional tennis. Even though he was simultaneously serving as tennis and squash coach at Harvard, Barnaby also managed to fulfill Lufler's

Arthur Ashe

Jack Kramer

goal of a truly national organization. With the assistance of Jack Campbell, who brought in the San Diego area and thereby opened up the far West, Barnaby's administration was able to add California, Texas, Intermountain, Missouri valley, and Southwest. Shortly thereafter northern California, Pacific Northwest, and Hawaii joined. Today the USPTA includes 18 geographical divisions throughout the U.S.

During Dave Muir's presidency, from 1971 to 1972, the USPLTA dropped the *L* and became the USPTA, anticipating the same action on the part of the US*L*TA by three full years.

As membership grew to more than 1000, the USPTA hired its first full-time executive director, Ray Bovett, in 1974, and established a national office in Houston, Texas. Within a year Bovett died from a heart attack but his successors, Bill Tym, Michael Fryer, and Tim Heckler, have continued to build upon the foundation he left.

In the ten years since Bovett took office as executive director, the USPTA has increased from 1000 to 4000 members. A national home for the USPTA was established at the Colony Beach and Tennis Resort, Longboat Key, Florida for five years. The USPTA has just moved to beautiful new quarters at Saddlebrook, the golf and tennis resort, near Tampa, Florida. USPTA members have their own exclusive ball, the Pro-Penn, auto-

matic one-million-dollar liability coverage, group medical, disability, and life insurance plans, a teaching professional's magazine *(ADDvantage)*, and official magazine *(Tennis)*, a yearly directory, and access to a full-time executive director and staff for assistance at any time.

But the USPTA does not serve only its members, it also serves the entire tennis community, actively supporting such causes as National Tennis Week, the National Junior Tennis League, and the National Tennis Rating Program. Additionally, under the guidance of former president and testing committee chairman George Basco, the USPTA continues to improve its certification process and offers weekend and week-long tennis academies to tennis professionals seeking to improve themselves (open to members and non-members), and cooperates with the USTA sectionally with coaches academies and nationally with the USTA Annual Tennis Teachers Conference in New York.

Early in 1982, at the invitation of the Japanese Professional Tennis Association (JPTA), the USPTA board of officers and Fred Stolle conducted a tennis academy in Tokyo, Japan, and negotiations began that concluded with the JPTA becoming the first member of the International Division of the USPTA.

Continued growth and expansion of both the ATP and USPTA are inextricably linked to the popularity of tennis. As tennis attracts more participants, demand will rise for more teachers and more tournaments. Both organizations recognize the importance of nurturing tennis at all levels and are working to guarantee a bigger, better, and brighter future for the game.

JACK KRAMER
SEAN SLOANE
JACK CAMPBELL
JIM MCMANUS

Sources Consulted

BOOKS

Bellamy, Rex. *The Tennis Set*. London: E.J. Burrow and Co., Ltd., 1972.

Blau, Peter. *Exchange and Power in Social Life*. New York: John Wiley & Sons, Inc., 1964.

Buchanan, Lamont. *The Story of Tennis*. New York: The Vanguard Press, Inc., 1951.

Cole, Arthur H. *Business Enterprise in Its Social Setting*. Cambridge, Mass.: Harvard University Press, 1959.

Cummings, Parke. *American Tennis*. Boston: Little, Brown and Company, Inc., 1957.

Kenyon, Gerald S., and Loy, John W., Jr., eds. *Sport, Culture, and Society*. New York: The MacMillan Company, Inc., 1971.

Potter, E.C., Jr. *Kings of the Court*. New York: Charles Scribner's Sons, 1936.

Powel, Colonel Nick. *The Code*. Princeton, New Jersey: USTA, 1978.

Revie, Alastair. *Wonderful Wimbledon*. London: Seeley, Service and Co., Ltd., 1972.

Schickel, Richard. *The World of Tennis*. New York: Random House, Inc., 1975.

Sears, R.D. *50 Years of Lawn Tennis in the United States*. New York: USLTA, 1931.

MAGAZINES *(Articles)*

Amdur, Neil. "An Interview with Bob Briner." *World Tennis Magazine*, May 1969, pp. 58–60.

Heldman, Gladys. "Sudden Death." *World Tennis Magazine*, June 1970, p. 5.

Wind, Herbert Warren. "The First One Hundred Years." *The New Yorker*, 8 October 1973, pp. 114–127.

YEARBOOKS

Men's International Professional Tennis Council (MIPTC). *1982 Volvo Grand Prix*. United States of America: Tennis New, Inc., 1981.

United States Tennis Association (USTA). *The Official Yearbook, 1981*. Lynn, Mass.: H.O. Zimman, Inc., 1981.

2

The Basic Tennis Skills

There are many ways to stroke the tennis ball, and the more advanced player will use most or all of these during a match, i.e., topspin, backspin, slice, chip, chop, drop, lob, and smash. However, there are four basic strokes that form the foundation of your game. These are the GROUNDSTROKES—FOREHAND and BACKHAND—the SERVE, and the VOLLEY. Spinshots, dropshots, lobs, and smashes are variations of the basic strokes and are covered later as specialty shots.

The following pages present a complete description of each of the basic strokes, fully illustrated with checkpoints for each, along with helpful practice suggestions. The descriptions are written for right-handed players. Left-handers will need to reverse the instructions involving parts of the body.

The stroke patterns presented here are often referred to as *classical,* and are used by many teachers when introducing the game to beginners. But stroke patterns merely form the foundation for the game. Once a solid foundation has been built, the individuality of the player takes over and a style begins to emerge.

Build a strong base and your game will bring a smile to your face and consternation to your opponent's. Build a weak foundation and the smile will be on your opponent's face, the consternation

on yours. Learn the basic strokes and you will be well on your way to a lifetime of happy, healthful tennis.

The Groundstrokes

With few exceptions, when two players first step on the court, they begin to hit balls on a bounce from one baseline to the other. They are hitting GROUNDSTROKES, and these are the strokes we describe first.

Both groundstrokes, the FOREHAND and the BACKHAND, are presented by describing the parts in a definite sequence, i.e., GRIP, STANCE (ready position), BACKSWING (turn), STEP, FORWARD SWING TO CONTACT POINT, FOLLOW-THROUGH, and FINISH. Each part is analyzed and the description supplemented by one or more illustrations to make it easier for you to follow. Checkpoints remind you of what you should look for at the completion of each move. Finally, practice patterns (drills) are offered.

The strokes have been reduced to a very simple form. An example is the flat backswing. Once you learn it, you may find yourself building in a loop. Both forms are used by top players. You will eventually adopt the one that fits your style of play. But first, learn the simple movement. When you learn the basic skills, then you can begin to take liberties with the strokes and add the flourishes.

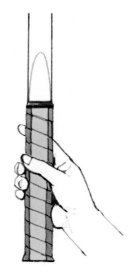

Continental grip

Finally, we proceed by describing the forehand and backhand simultaneously. This way, when you move on to the tennis court to "hit a few balls," you will be able to stroke and return balls hit to both sides of your body, using the forehand or backhand.

The Grips

Several GRIPS are used, and it is a fact that tournament players constantly make slight grip adjustments during the course of play. Grips may vary because of differences in court surfaces, causing the ball to bounce higher, lower, slower, or faster. They also may vary because of the stroke pattern being used, i.e., topspin or flat.

It is acknowledged that the grip of the racket is the foundation of all tennis shots. How you hold the racket influences the angle of the racket face, where you meet the ball in relationship to your body, and especially, what happens when the impact between ball and racket occurs.

The three basic grips—Eastern, Western, and Continental—all have advantages and disadvantages, and a professional teacher knows the advantages and disadvantages of the various grips. This knowledge aids in analysis of a student's form and results. A student may be frustrated at a certain level of play or on a particular shot because the nuances of racket work required are unavailable or awkward with the grip used.

It is, therefore, imperative that both teacher and student recognize that grip selection is flexible, depending upon the factors of height, bounce, court surface, height of contact point, and the intention of the student's placement and spin. Although a grip selection may be awkward or uncomfortable initially, the student must be encouraged by the teacher and persuaded that with practice and work, the desired result of the shot will occur and the grip will feel more natural.

THE CONTINENTAL GRIP

Originating on the soft clay courts of Europe where the ball stayed low, and perfected by grass court players, this grip is the same for both forehand and backhand. This is often an advantage, and for this reason some tennis teachers recommend the grip for net shots where there is little time for grip changes. Generally, however, because of the improved bounces on today's courts, this grip has lost favor when hitting any ball above waist height, since it is extremely difficult to gain good racket face control using it. Except for low balls, which call for an open racket face, all shots hit with the Continental grip require an exceptionally strong wrist and excellent timing, which take players a long time to develop. The open racket face on the

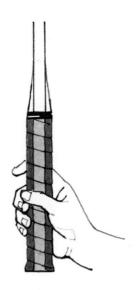

Western grip

Continental grip means that all shots generally have a backspin or side slice generated by a downward chopping motion. Players who use a Continental grip are not known for their powerful groundstrokes, but rather for consistent control and placement.

Point of contact with a Continental grip is usually closer to the line of the body than with the other grips. This can facilitate a change of direction by players who wish to disguise their intentions. When used on the serve, this grip makes it easier to hit a slice.

THE WESTERN GRIP

The opposite extreme of the Continental grip, the Western grip originated on the high bouncing cement courts of California and is suited to balls hit above waist height. This grip closes the face of the racket and is used for exaggerated topspin and groundstrokes where contact is made in front rather than alongside the body.

Since the hand is basically under the racket to close the face, it is extremely awkward to rotate the wrist sufficiently to open the racket face for low balls, and this is the main problem with the grip.

Some players who use the Western grip for forehands keep the same grip for backhands, hitting the ball with the same face of the racket. This technique puts extreme tension on the elbow and

arm and can cause tennis elbow. An alternative Western backhand is to lay the thumb directly up the handle. The player must choose to go "under" or "over" for a grip change, which still necessitates a high elbow on the stroke and causes difficulty with low balls.

On serving, the Western forehand presents an extremely flat racket face, making the chance of hitting with spin and power negligible.

THE EASTERN GRIP

This grip calls for a definite change between forehand and backhand positions. It originated in the eastern U.S. on courts that provided a waist-high bounce. The Eastern grip is the one most popularly taught by professionals and is often referred to as the "shake hands" grip. As the line of the wrist and the palm of the hand are behind the line of the racket, this grip has some disadvantages when players are hitting low balls or want to generate a slice without wrist movement, but its versatility on all surfaces, the ease of generating power, the feeling of strength because of hand support, the vertical racket face for good topspin development, and its overall comfort for beginning students qualify the Eastern as the most commonly used grip. And the Eastern grip offers flexibility for individual stroke production styles.

The grip change for backhand strokes usually

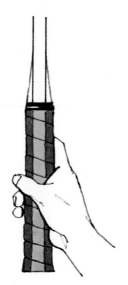

Semi-Western grip

requires a quarter turn in a counterclockwise direction. Generally, the contact point with a vertical racket face allows the feel of prolonged contact, emphasizing the "stroking" effect.

NOTE: It is recommended that students have racket across the body rather than pointing in front to find the Eastern backhand grip. It is further recommended that students wait for ball in ready position of racket across the body in Eastern backhand grip to facilitate the grip change. Most students will develop the change more quickly if they go from backhand to forehand grips rather than the reverse. When pressed for time, the student can comfortably hit a ball late on the forehand side. On the backhand, contact must be made in line with or in advance of the leg closer to the net (right leg). By holding the racket at the throat with the left hand, the player can rotate the racket with that hand, holding the right hand still. This is preferable to moving the right (playing) hand around the handle.

Two-Handed Grips

Two-handed grips have gained in popularity since the 1970's, due to the success of Jimmy Connors, Chris Evert Lloyd, Bjorn Borg, Tracy Austin, et al. It should be recognized that two-handed shots are not "new," but the people mentioned have attained success by overcoming the disadvantages of two-handed strokes and capitalizing on the advantages. It is recognized that two-handed players have shorter reach and follow-through, difficulty on balls close to the body, and need quicker, more precise footwork. Compensating for these factors are the increased power generated, the disguise advantages of hitting a ball later, and the more acute spins and angles that can be generated by the wristiness of a well-hit two-handed shot.

For young players, the extra hand provides support to manipulate the racket better. And the extra hand can exert a restraining effect upon excess rotation and strain that can contribute to tennis elbow.

Variations of Two-Handed Grips

Using two hands, there are many combinations of the standard one-handed grips that can be utilized.

If both hands are in Eastern forehand positions, the left hand is usually dominant and control may suffer for inexperienced players.

If right hand (dominant hand) is in Eastern backhand position and left hand in Eastern forehand, either hand may control the racket. This grip allows for letting go with left hand after shot. The left hand is used more for power than support.

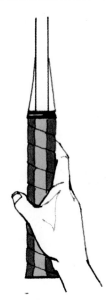

Eastern grip

If right hand is in Eastern forehand and left hand in Western forehand grip, then the left hand is usually dominant.

If right hand is in Eastern backhand and left hand in Western forehand grip, either or neither hand may be dominant.

WRIST ACTION

If wrists are locked in a laid back position through the stroke, a controlled shot lacking power is produced. When the wrists are used to generate racket head velocity through the stroke, a "coupling" effect is produced, which accentuates power. When these forces work laterally, tremendous pace can be developed. If worked in an up and down direction, excessive spin results, either topspin or backspin.

Two-handed strokes have restricted backswing and follow-through and require more body action than one-handed shots. This accentuates the pace of a two-handed shot.

A professional should emphasize the need to develop extremely good, quick footwork with two-handed strokes as this is the only way to balance the advantages against the disadvantages of the technique.

VARIATION OF ONE-HANDED GRIPS

The Australian grip is a modification of the Eastern grip. The placements of heel of hand, V of thumb, and index finger are moved slightly towards the Continental grip. This slight opening of the face of the racket accommodates the low bounce and volleys typical of grass court play in Australia.

In the Semi-Western grip, the inclination of the hand is toward the Western. This grip is very common with untutored players because of the comfortable feeling of the hand behind the racket. It can be utilized on low balls, serves, and volleys —all of which are too difficult to handle with a full Western grip.

PRESSURE OF HAND

It is important to remember that the contact of ball and racket is the driving and guiding point of all shots and that the tension with which a player grips the racket directly affects the feel and speed of a shot. Pressure points for "squeezing" the rackets vary with grip variations. Students may feel that the racket is part of the body or they may conceptualize the racket as an instrument to be used. This can determine whether a player accentuates the grip with pressure at the palm, or with finger strength. Should loose, indecisive impact between racket and ball occur, no matter what grip is being used, check whether the tension of grip is suffi-

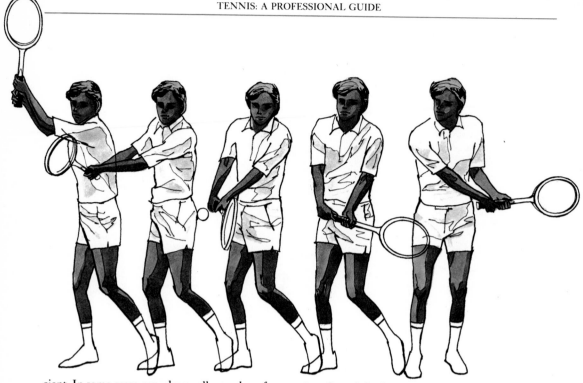

cient. In some cases, e.g., drop volleys, where force of the ball is more than required, lack of pace can be achieved by *relaxing* the grip at time of contact between racket and ball.

The Eastern forehand grip is generally taught as the initial grip because it is probably the best grip for the beginner who has yet to develop a strong hand and wrist.

There are several ways of taking the Eastern grip on the racket, such as placing the palm of the hand on the strings and sliding the hand down to the handle and closing the hand, or placing the base knuckle of the index finger on the right panel of the handle and closing the hand, or more simply, holding the racket in front of you in a vertical position with the left hand, then placing the palm against the right panel and "shaking hands" with it. In every case the palm of the hand will be on the same plane as the face of the racket and any turn of the hand and wrist will result in a similar movement of the racket face.

Once the grip has been established, the following adjustments are made:

1. Move the hand so that the grip feels comfortable for you. All hands and racket handles are not the same.
2. Move the thumb to contact the outside of the middle finger of the hand. (Contacting the index finger results in an unwanted "hammergrip.")

3. Spread the fingers with the index finger, forming what is sometimes referred to as a "modified trigger finger."

You will note that the pads of the last three fingers are pressed against the front plate, and the tips are looking up at you. Check the strength of the grip by placing the racket face against a post (or your left hand) and pressing your racket against it. You will find little or no give.

A common fault of beginners is placing the thumb on the top plate. This causes a weakness in the grip and the racket will spin out of the hand if the ball is not hit squarely.

Practice gripping and regripping your racket until you can do so correctly and automatically.

The grip change is made at the beginning of the backswing on the backhand side. With practice and repetition the change becomes automatic and quite simple. The hand, instead of being vertical on the handle (forehand), is moved a quarter turn to the left of the top of the handle so that the palm is facing down. The hand then closes to complete the grip. Using the base knuckle of the index finger as your guide, place it on the top plate of the handle and close your hand. The thumb is placed either diagonally or down the handle and the fingers are spread. The thumb and index finger attempt to meet each other through the handle. You may test

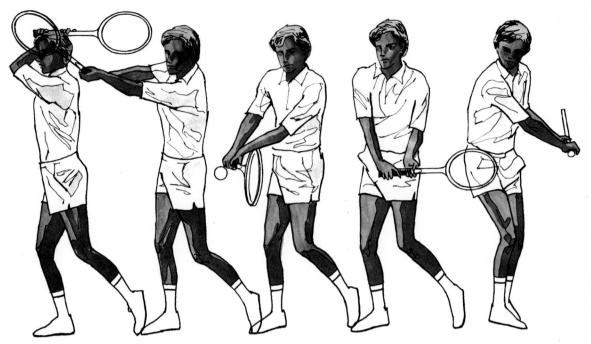

the strength of the thumb and index finger by holding the racket with those two and swinging the racket in the backhand motion. You will quickly realize the importance of the thumb for the backhand grip.

You may wish to place the fleshy part of your palm against the handle of the racket. This may give you a little additional support, and serve as a guide in taking the backhand grip.

Observing the backhand grip you will note that the back of your hand is now toward your face. The pads of the last three fingers have moved to the beveled edge. Practice the grip changes by starting with the forehand grip, moving your racket a few inches to the backhand side, and changing to the backhand grip. Observe the checkpoints and then return to the forehand grip. REPEAT! REPEAT! REPEAT!

The Stance or Ready Position

It is important that the STANCE taken by players be comfortable, balanced, and active so that movements forward, backward, and side-to-side are easily made, putting them into position to return the ball most efficiently.

Observe the following checkpoints and incorporate them into your own READY POSITION.

1. The feet are spread comfortably, a little more than shoulder-width apart, the legs bent at the knees, and the back straight.
2. The weight is slightly forward—on the balls of the feet—with the heels almost starting off the ground.
3. The racket is cradled in the fingers of the left hand, pointing either straight ahead or toward the left net post.
4. The racket is held with an Eastern grip. It should be firm—not tight enough to turn the knuckles white.
5. The head and eyes are focussed on the opponent and the oncoming ball.
6. Above all, be loose, be relaxed!

From this position practice transferring your weight from side-to-side, picking up your feet an inch or so off the ground. Try pushing off either foot and sliding a step or two to the left and right. Be active! Be smooth! Be relaxed! Stay balanced!

Assume the ready position whenever you have returned a groundstroke and are waiting for your opponent's return. It is an essential part of your total groundstroke pattern.

The Backswing or Turn

The key to a well executed groundstroke is *early preparation*. To begin, you must move the racket back in preparation for the forward movement to

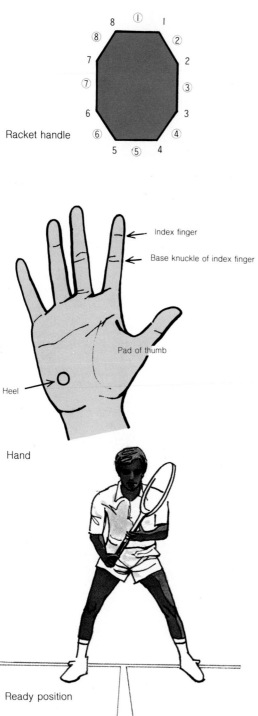

Racket handle

Index finger

Base knuckle of index finger

Pad of thumb

Heel

Hand

Ready position

meet the ball. This is the BACKSWING.

There are several methods of executing the backswing, i.e., circular or loop, straight-back, semi-circular, hairpin, and tear-drop. All are appropriate. The straight-back, accompanied by a lowering of the racket head prior to the upward movement into the ball, is perhaps the simplest and may be the best for the beginner. A variation is to take the racket back at shoulder level and then drop the head below the line of flight of the oncoming ball before moving into the impact area. Either of the two is recommended for the beginner.

Regardless of the method employed to take the racket back, it is important that the movement begin the moment the ball leaves the opponent's racket. The backswing is initiated by the shoulders. Picture a giant rod projecting from the oncoming ball to your shoulder, pushing as it comes toward you. This will give you an idea of the speed required in making your turn. A hard-hit, flat ball that moves fast will necessitate a quick shoulder turn and backswing; a slow-spinning ball, a slower turn and backswing. By the time the ball hits the ground on your side of the net, your racket should be near the end of the backswing and ready to move into the impact area.

From the forehand side, the backswing is started by a TURN or PIVOT. A slight push

Straight-back backswing

against the throat of the racket with the left hand may help you to initiate the movement as well as to start the shoulders turning. As the shoulders turn and the racket moves back, the weight is transferred to the right foot. At the same time, the left heel comes off the ground and the left knee moves in toward the right. The action of the knee and the racket moving back occurs almost simultaneously. Practice turning to your right until your racket is pointing toward the side fence, then recover to the ready position. Repeat this move several times. You will find that the turn of the hips and shoulders alone will result in almost half the path the racket will travel. TURN—RETURN; PIVOT—RETURN.

Repeat the same movement, but instead of pivoting on the right foot, pick it up about an inch off the ground and put it down pointing slightly to the right. You are now ready to complete the backswing.

Repeat the instructions in the previous paragraph. However, instead of stopping your racket, allow it to continue until it points to the back fence. TURN—RETURN; PIVOT—RETURN; WEIGHT RIGHT—RETURN; PIVOT—RETURN, etc.

During the backswing you have a choice of keeping the elbow down or moving it up and away from the body. Keeping the elbow down will help

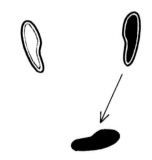

Loop backswing

set the face of the racket and keep the racket on edge or in a vertical position. Lifting the elbow will result in a closed face. The vertical racket face is recommended for most beginners. Later, you may wish to experiment with the closed face at the end of the backswing. Many players use it today as an aid for imparting topspin on the ball.

It is also recommended that you avoid *locking* your elbow during the backswing. Starting with a bent elbow and then straightening it as you move into the impact area will not only provide you with a little more power but will also be a little easier on your elbow.

Begin your practice with a straight-back backswing for simplicity, and then build a slight loop into the swing later. The change from the straight-back to a loop is very simple. Move your racket up and back, then down and around in a semi-circular pattern, and you are ready for the forward swing.

On the backhand side, as on the forehand, the shoulder begins the turn, this time accompanied by a lifting of the right heel. The left hand, cradling the racket, *pulls* the racket to the rear. Continue the motion until the racket points to the side fence to your left. Make certain, at this point, that you have switched from the forehand to the backhand grip. The right knee moves toward the left and the weight transfers to the left side. Practice the start

of the backswing until it becomes smooth and easy. TURN—RETURN; PIVOT—RETURN; WEIGHT LEFT—RETURN; PIVOT—RETURN, etc.

Complete the backswing by continuing the turn until the right thumb is next to the left hip. Keep the right elbow bent slightly. Keeping the left arm fairly straight will result in a straight-back backswing. Bending the elbow will provide you with a loop or circular backswing. As for the forehand, it is recommended you begin with the straight-back and build in the loop as soon as possible.

Now that you have practiced and learned the forehand and backhand backswings, begin alternating them. Start with the half-swing and then move on to the full backswing, FOREHAND TURN—RETURN; BACKHAND TURN—RETURN; FOREHAND TURN—RETURN. Work in a short step or slide. Work on good balance as well as correctness of execution and you will be ready to make the next move.

The Step and Forward Swing to Contact Point

Although the FORWARD SWING of the racket is actually a continuation of the backswing, the movement of the racket into the impact area is important enough that it is discussed separately.

For the beginner, and for the sake of simplicity, we present the movement as a single motion.

The forward movement of the racket is preceded by a STEP in the direction of the oncoming ball, accompanied by a transfer of weight to the forward foot. The weight transfer facilitates an uncoiling of the hips. The racket begins its movement forward just prior to the moment when the front foot hits the ground. Moving the hips out of the way will allow the racket head to change from a circular path to a straighter line toward the target area. You will see later that this will provide you with more accuracy in stroking the ball toward your intended target area.

In addition to providing direction to the ball, the path of the racket face as it moves into the hitting area also determines the amount and type of spin imparted, i.e., topspin, backspin, or sidespin. Movement of the racket from low-to-high, brushing upward on the back of the ball with a vertical racket face, will cause a forward rotation of the ball (topspin or forward spin). Movement of the racket from high-to-low, brushing downward on the back of the ball will cause the ball to spin backward on its horizontal axis (backspin or underspin). Brushing the ball from left-to-right or right-to-left will cause the ball to spin on its vertical axis (sidespin or slice). In each case, the ball will swerve in the

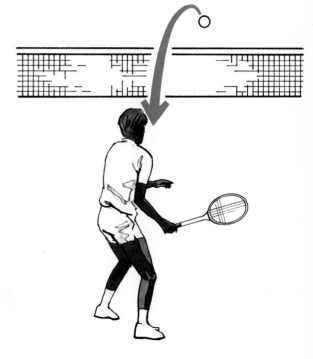

Timing the backswing: imaginary rod from ball pushes shoulder back to initiate backswing

61

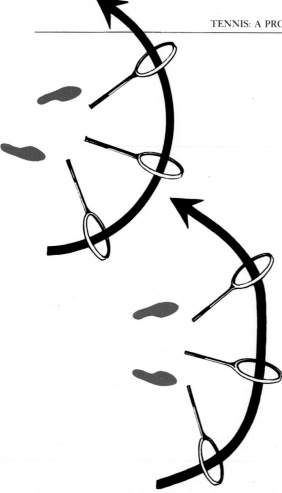

Closed stance: hips locked, square stance: unlocked hips allow greater contact area

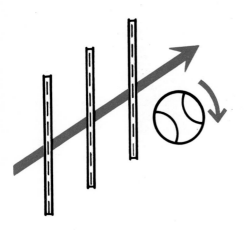

Imparting spin

direction of the rotation. The amount of spin and the trajectory of the return will be determined by the plane of the swing. A level (or flat) swing will result in a flat drive which has little or no spin. Increasing the upward or downward plane will result in a number of trajectories. With practice, you can control both the depth and the direction with which the ball approaches the ground.

It is equally important that you know the reaction of the ball after it bounces. Keep in mind the rule that "the angle of incidence equals the angle of reflection (almost)" and you will be prepared for most returns. Topspin makes the ball bounce lower, farther, and somewhat faster. The higher the angle at which the ball approaches the ground, the higher the bounce; the lower, the lower the bounce, etc.

Backspin (underspin) acts in the opposite manner of topspin and is achieved by striking the ball from high to low, a glancing blow that will cause the ball to rotate backward in its flight. The plane of the swing, as well as the slant of the racket face on impact, will determine the degree of backspin. A sharp downward blow on the bottom half of the ball, accompanied by a sharp slant of the racket face, will cause the ball to spin very fast and rise almost vertically. A slight downward blow with a vertical racket face will cause the ball to rise only slightly and travel farther when hit with some degree of force. The former will provide a higher bounce—the latter a lower one. Like the topsin, the backspin can be controlled and used to advantage during the course of play. It is interesting to observe that a ball coming to you with topspin is hit back more easily with backspin. This is because the direction of rotation does not change. In the event you wish to hit a topspin drive back with topspin, you must first equalize the oncoming spin and provide additional power to start the ball rotating forward again.

Returning to the mechanics of the forward swing, a few suggestions are offered to assist you in moving your racket into the impact area.

1. Transfer your weight toward the ball by pushing off your back foot and at the same time bending your front leg at the knee. Place the front foot on the ground at a 45° angle to the net.

2. Allow your hips to turn (uncoil) by raising the heel (right for the forehand and left for the backhand) and allow the knee to move in.

3. As your weight transfers, move your racket forward and upward into the impact area, firming the wrist and grip on the racket. Squeezing your fingers will help you accomplish this.

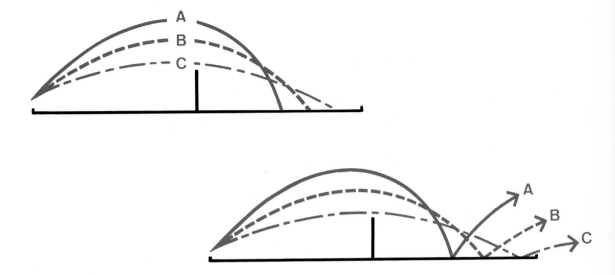

A Heavy topspin B Medium topspin C Little or no topspin

A High angle—high bounce B Medium angle—medium bounce C Low angle—low bounce

4. The racket face is vertical as it approaches and contacts the ball.
5. Contact is made alongside the body and opposite the forward foot for the forehand. For the backhand, the impact point is slightly ahead of the lead foot.

To determine the point of impact for the backhand make your TURN and STEP. Transfer your weight over your right foot and allow your racket to hang down. The spot indicated by the racket is approximately the impact point for the backhand drive.

NOTE: To visualize the relationship of the ball and the face of the racket at impact, assume the face of the racket has eyes.

The ball will go where the face of the racket is looking at impact (approximately). Place a pair of glasses on the strings, and turn your racket forward, backward, sideways, up, and down. If the racket is looking straight ahead and moving straight ahead, the ball will rebound straight ahead. If the racket moves straight ahead and the face looks to the left on impact, the ball will rebound somewhere between where the racket is moving and where the face is looking.

To practice the movement of the racket into the ball, begin with either the forehand or backhand. Take the side-to-net position, the feet fairly close together, the racket at the end of the backswing. Step forward with the front foot, uncoil, and move the racket to the point of impact. Stop and check the racket face for direction. Repeat this movement until it becomes smooth and comfortable on both forehand and backhand. Take the READY POSITION. Make your TURN, STEP, and FORWARD SWING to the point of impact. Check the face of the racket. Alternate forehand and backhand until both motions are smooth.

Follow-Through and Finish

The FOLLOW-THROUGH is a continuation of the forward swing of the racket through the ball and toward the target area. Although our research tells us that the ball is on the strings only .004 to .005 seconds and the follow-through serves little purpose in placing the ball (the ball is already gone), the combination of the forward swing and follow-through does have a purpose. The forward swing and follow-through move the racket toward the target and set the racket face to provide direction. Attempting to stop the racket at impact will slow the racket, resulting in a loss of power. Moving the racket on a straight line through the impact area will also permit you to mistime the ball and still send it to the intended target. A good follow-through will add continuity and fluidity to the stroke pattern.

4. Grip the racket just firmly enough to avoid a droopy wrist.
5. To avoid leading with the wrist, start the tip of the racket back first on your backswing.
6. Transfer your weight onto the forward foot as you start your forward swing.
7. Adjust the plane and direction of your forward swing to achieve the result you desire.
8. Swing the racket face through the ball and toward your intended target.
9. Finish your stroke with your weight forward, racket high and in front of your body.
10. Keep your head still throughout the stroke.
11. PRACTICE! PRACTICE! PRACTICE!

Footwork

Once you have learned the mechanics of the groundstrokes, you are ready to proceed. Since tennis is a game of movement, the FOOTWORK becomes a very important and necessary part of your training. The ball seldom comes to you in perfect position to be hit with the stroke patterns you have been practicing. It comes high, low, long, short, toward you, away from you, and with a variety of spin.

Footwork is one of the most important fundamentals of tennis and must be practiced as diligently as the strokes themselves. Good footwork moves you into a position of good balance, under control and ready to make the return from any spot on the court. Poor footwork may cause you to hit late, off-balance, and out of control, making easy shots difficult and hard shots almost impossible. Watch good players as they move on the court. Much of the ease of execution, the smoothness of the stroke may be attributed to proper movement on the court.

The following tips will assist you as you perfect your movement on the court. Practice moving side-to-side, up-and-back, and diagonally. You will be pleased with the results.

1. Start from a position of balance; alert, active, and ready to move for the ball.
2. Your first step is accompanied by an appropriate turn of the shoulders. This will start the racket moving.
3. When moving only a short distance to your right, left, or on the diagonal, slide, turn, and step to the ball. This may be described as step-together-step-turn. At the completion of the turn you have completed the backswing and are ready to make your forward swing. For the short slide, move the foot nearest the ball first. Push off the opposite foot.

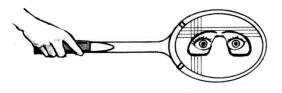

The "face" of the racket—where the "eyes" look is where the ball goes

Practice the follow-through by repeating the swing from the side-to-net position. This time, instead of stopping at the point of impact, follow through toward your target and FINISH the stroke with your racket high and in front of your body (topspin). Complete the uncoiling action by lifting the heel and pivoting on the ball of the foot. At the completion of the forehand swing, your hips will be almost parallel with the net. The turn is not quite so pronounced on the backhand. At the completion of each stroke return quickly to the ready position. Continue your practice by starting from the ready position. Remember, READY; TURN; STEP—SWING; RECOVER. Practice the forehand, then the backhand, then alternate forehands and backhands.

The following reminders will assist you in perfecting your forehand and backhand drives. Concentrate on one at a time each time you grip your racket or work on your strokes.

1. Check and re-check your grip. Make certain you are changing the grip when you begin your backhand drive.
2. Wait for the ball in a position of balance. Relax, but be alert.
3. Start your backswing early, transferring your weight as you do so. Time your backswing to coincide with the speed of the oncoming ball.

Forehand swing

Backhand swing (slight topspin, to correspond with forehand)

Forehand (Jimmy Connors)

Backhand (Ivan Lendl)

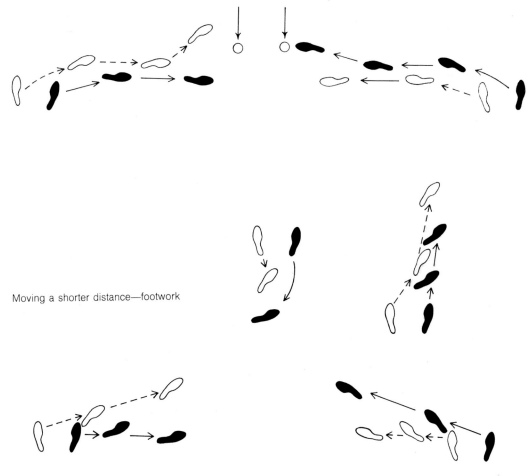

Moving a shorter distance—footwork

Moving a greater distance—footwork

Prior to stepping to the ball, the weight has transferred to the back foot. You may now step wide, straight ahead, or away from the oncoming ball.

4. For a ball going deep, turn and step back with your right foot. For a ball landing short, turn and step forward with the left foot. Follow the turn with slides or "adjustment steps" to place you in position to stroke the ball. Use these movements only when you have to move a few feet.

5. When moving greater distances it is more efficient to cross over with the foot farthest from the ball and begin with short running steps, gradually lengthening them. As you approach the ball, slow down, adjusting the length of the steps to move you into a well-balanced position behind and alongside the flight of the

oncoming ball. Your final steps will be similar to those described in 3 and 4. Keep your racket in front of you until you begin the turn part of your backswing.

6. To move away from a ball coming directly at you on the forehand side, move your right foot back and to your left, making your backswing as you do so. Then, step in the direction of the ball and begin your forward swing. If you feel more confident on your backhand side, move your left foot back and to the right.

Following each stroke, return quickly to a position of readiness. Practice each of the movements described separately, and then put them together into a series of movements. You will soon find that you, too, will move quickly, easily, and more efficiently on the court.

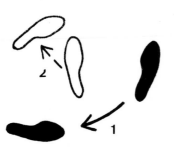

For ball coming directly at you on forehand side

REMEMBER:

1. Make your move quickly.
2. Turn your shoulders as soon as you make your first step.
3. As you approach the ball, slow down and make your adjustment steps.
4. Use your arms to maintain balance.

The Serve

The SERVE is often referred to as the most important stroke in the game of tennis. It is the stroke that puts the ball in play. Picture two players serving double-faults, unable to get the ball in the service court. This may be an extreme example but sometimes it happens. In addition to starting the point, the serve is an important offensive weapon. A well-placed, wide serve to the forehand or backhand will draw the opponent off the court and open it for an easy volley winner. A strong serve may force a weak return or be a direct winner. Unfortunately, many players spend little time in developing this stroke that is such an important part of the total game.

The serve, to a point, may be likened to the overhand throw in baseball. However, the service toss, the placement of the ball in the air prior to being served, adds a dimension not present in the baseball throw. Add to this the fact that the front foot remains planted during the serve and you have a distinct difference between the two. The coordination of the ball toss (left hand) and the striking motion (right hand) adds an element that requires a great deal of practice to master. You might get the feeling for the serve by tossing a ball into the air in front of you with the left hand and attempting to hit it with a ball held in your right. Gripping your racket by the handle and throwing it over the net may also give you the feel, but it may be an expensive lesson.

The Grips

The grip for the serve taught to many beginners is the Eastern forehand grip described earlier. However, it is advisable to proceed to the conventional serving grip, the Continental, as soon as possible. Some tennis teachers are successful with the Continental from the beginning and bypass the Eastern except for the student experiencing difficulty. The Continental gives the player more flexibility in hitting slice and topspin serves.

In the Continental grip, the base knuckle of the index finger is placed on the top right bevel of the handle (halfway between the Eastern forehand and backhand). The fingers are spread and the thumb is wrapped around the grip. If this feels uncomfortable, slight adjustments may be necessary. The grip is firm, not tight, and is basically a finger grip. As a beginner, you may wish to hold the racket more with the palm of the hand. As you get stronger and more proficient, slide the hand down until the butt of the racket is in the palm of the hand. Use slight variations in the wrist and fingers for power and control.

The Stance

The sideways stance is the one most often used, although there are possible variations. Take your position at the baseline, three or four feet from the center mark, an imaginary line through your toes pointing to your target area. The left foot is two or three inches behind the baseline, pointing toward the right net post. The back foot is almost parallel to the baseline and both feet are spread comfortably. For the time being, start with your weight on the back foot.

Cradle the racket at the throat, in the fingers of your left hand, the elbows fairly close to the body. The racket head is tilted upward and points in the direction of your target. The fingers cradling the racket hold either one or two balls. The hips and shoulders are closed, in a line with the toes. Your entire body is poised, relaxed, and ready to begin the service motion.

Ball throwing

Once you have taken the stance and have decided on the direction, spin, and speed of your serve, fix your attention on the toss and hit. Remember, the lines and the court are not going to move!

The Ball Toss

The ball toss (or placement) is the key to a well-executed serve. A consistent toss places the ball in position to be struck properly. A poor toss spells trouble and is often the cause of a poor serve.

The balls are held by the thumb and fingers of the left hand, the palm up. The ball to be tossed is held by the thumb, and the middle and the index fingers. The second ball is pressed against the heel of the hand by the remaining fingers. If a single ball is held, it is placed near the end of the extended fingers and held in place by the thumb.

The ball is tossed by dropping the hand and arm to the left thigh and then continuing the motion in the direction of the right net post (the direction the left foot is pointing). The arm continues upward and releases the ball by opening the fingers, allowing it to rise to a spot slightly higher than you can reach with your arm and racket extended. Bending the elbow will provide a more consistent toss by allowing the hand to move upward in a straight line rather than in an arc. This way the ball may be released a little early or late and still move straight up. If the ball were allowed to drop from this spot, it would land in the court and in front of the right shoulder.

Control of the toss is of prime importance. Practice the toss until you can make it with your eyes closed. You are now ready to coordinate it with the downward-upward or drawing action of the arm and racket.

The Backswing (Downward-Upward)

Take the basic serving stance, the weight favored on the back foot. Begin the backswing by dropping both hands simultaneously, the left hand to the left thigh and the right hand moving to serve the ball. The right arm and racket move down past the knee, the edge of the racket leading, and continue toward the back fence. As the racket moves toward the fence, the face turns out, the racket again moving to a vertical position. The arm and racket continue upward until the elbow is slightly higher than the shoulder. At this point, the elbow bends, allowing the racket to drop behind the back. The wrist bends on the thumb side. Avoid bending the wrist at the back of the hand. This will cause the racket face to "look" up at the sky and will result in a slap serve. Practice the downward-upward motion of the arm and racket then combine it with the ball release. Work on the weight transfer and the knee bend as the racket falls behind the back.

The whole motion of the backswing is slow and deliberate and may be likened to the archer pulling the bow string, the coiling of a steel spring —the power buildup. What follows is the explosive action of the racket head, moving through the ball —the upward-forward swing and contact.

The Upward-Forward Swing and Contact

As the ball descends the legs straighten, the hips, trunk, and shoulders rotate forward, and the wrist and elbow straighten forcibly to propel the racket head upward and forward, contacting the ball with the body, arm, and racket extended. The edge of racket, rather than the face, moves to the ball. As it approaches the ball, the hand and wrist pronate outward. Brushing outward causes the ball to spin counterclockwise on its vertical axis. This will cause the ball to spin from right to left (slice). Practice this motion with your racket behind your back. Vary the angle at which the edge of the racket approaches the ball and makes contact.

The movement of the left hand varies with the player. Some players thrust it past their left side, while some tuck it into the chest. Those that thrust it past the left side feel it helps them speed the rotation of the body. Those that use the "tuck" feel that it stops the rotation, allowing the arm, wrist, and racket to snap like a bull whip. Try both and use the one that works best for you.

Service stance: rear foot parallel to baseline, front foot pointing to right net post; line drawn across toes leading to aim point in service box

Beginning the serve

Ball toss

Serve sequence

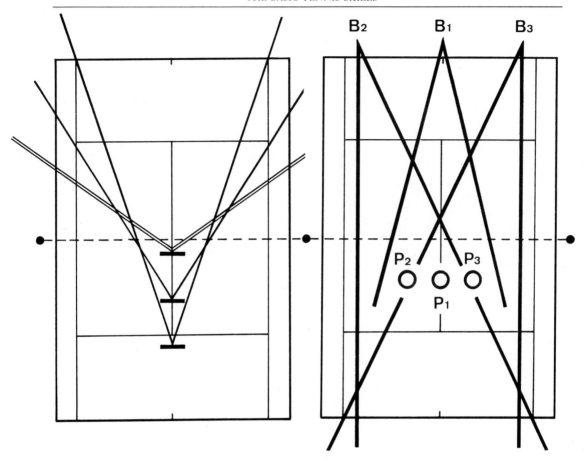

Volley angles—possibilities for kills increase as one
gets closer to the net

Volley sequence

As you do for the groundstrokes, try to watch the racket make contact with the ball. Once you have decided on the serve you intend to use, concentrate on the toss and hit. Remember, the court is not going to move.

The Follow-Through and Finish

The follow-through, as stated earlier, is forward, not down. Hitting down on the ball will send it into the net. Think upward-forward or upward-out and you will find few balls on your side of the net.

The follow-through is a natural continuation of the stroke, the racket moving toward the target area before starting its downward descent past the left side of the body. The right foot swings across the baseline and continues toward the target. It also helps you maintain your balance. Later on, this step becomes the start of your approach to the net.

The serve is important, so spend as much time as you can perfecting it. Learn to serve to both service courts and get into the habit of deciding where and how you want the ball to go each time you serve. And remember, work first for CONSISTENCY, then for CONTROL, and finally for POWER.

Note the following checkpoints and keep them in mind during your practice.

1. Check your grip. Check your feet. Toss the ball and swing.
2. Toss the ball in the direction of the right net post.
3. Let go of the ball by opening your fingers.
4. Keep your head up and watch the ball.
5. Think—"down together, up together."
6. Hit up and out—not down.
7. Relax—work for consistency and control, then power.
8. Follow through and finish.

The Volley

The VOLLEY is a stroke that hits the ball in the air before it falls to the ground and is usually hit in the vicinity of the net. Although it is possible to play tennis without volleying, the lack of volleying skill limits the offensive potential and can give the opponent an edge. Doubles play is built around the ability to serve and volley, and volleying is a part of the "big game," a trademark of many modern champions.

The volley is an abbreviated stroke, in some ways similar to the groundstroke. To be effective, it is made above the net where it can be hit downward for a winner. The closer to the net the ball is

Forehand volley

Backhand volley

Volley stance

volleyed, the more court is open for the shot, and the higher percentage of winners. Care must be taken, however, because moving too close to the net leaves you vulnerable to the lob. Allowing the ball to fall below the net makes it necessary to open the face of the racket to lift the ball over the net. This may be what your opponent is waiting for, a high ball he or she can put away for a winner.

Learning to volley is quite easy, but using the volley in competition may be quite difficult. To become a proficient volleyer requires many hours of dedicated practice. Nevertheless, the end result, the ability to execute the volley from either side of the body, is well worth the time spent.

The Grips

The grips for the volley may be the same as those used for the groundstrokes, the Eastern forehand and backhand. They are preferred for most beginners because of the support offered. The Continental grip is used by most advanced players, although a few use the Eastern.

The Stance

The basic volleying position is approximately halfway between the net and the service line. The ready position is similar to that described for the groundstrokes except that the head of the racket is raised to approximately eye level. The position is an active one, the feet in motion and ready to move quickly to the oncoming ball.

The Backswing

The basic backswing is initiated by a slight shoulder turn and transfer of weight to the back foot. As the shoulders turn, the rear knee moves in slightly to release the hip. It is often necessary to take a short step to adjust to the oncoming ball. Sometimes this is the only step necessary prior to the forward swing and contact with the ball. The step is made with either foot to the left or right, or slightly forward or back with the left or right foot. The length and direction of this movement will vary according to the flight of the ball.

On the forehand side, the backswing is very short and in many instances is limited to the shoulder turn and the placement of the racket face in the path of the oncoming ball. For balls traveling at high speed this may be all you have time for. The move to the backhand side is also short. The racket is drawn back by the left hand, which helps to position the racket head in preparation for the forward move to impact. Practice both moves, limiting the length of the backswing to the range of your peripheral vision, i.e., the point where you lose sight of the racket head while looking straight ahead. Another way to practice the abbreviated

Forehand volley

backswing is to back up against the fence or a wall and practice taking the racket back. For a ball approaching softly, it is sometimes necessary to turn the shoulders more and increases the length of the backswing to provide additional power.

The shoulder turn is often accompanied by a step in the direction of the oncoming ball. When you have time, as you do when the ball is being returned from the opposite baseline, step toward the ball and make contact early. This will allow you to volley the ball out in front of your body. For wide balls, step diagonally and meet the ball before it moves away from you. As with groundstrokes, the forward knee bends to provide for the weight transfer.

The Forward Swing to Impact

The forward swing is basically very brief, very compact. The motion is similar to a short punch or a block. The movement forward is accompanied by the positioning of the face of the racket to give the ball direction. Keep in mind the "eyes" of the racket face described in the section on groundstrokes. Squeeze your fingers around the grip just prior to impact to firm the wrist. Later you will learn to change the speed of the volley by adjusting the pressure exerted by the fingers.

On the forehand side, placement of the ball may be made with the wrist, as well as by timing the ball early or late. A laid back wrist and a forward motion of the racket will result in a down-the-line volley. Straightening the wrist will result in a crosscourt placement. On the backhand side, raising the elbow away from the body will drop the racket face and position it for a down-the-line shot. Lowering the elbow on the backhand side will result in a crosscourt return.

For balls hit below the net, bend the knees and open the face of the racket to make the ball move upward and over the net. Moving the racket forward with an open face will provide some degree of backspin, which will also cause the ball to rise.

There will be times when the ball is hit directly at the center of your body. On these occasions step to the right or left and pull the right elbow away from the body. This will position the racket face to make a backhand volley. Care must be taken to keep the racket head in a vertical plane, not tilted back, or the ball will slide off the strings and hit you in the face. A slight forward motion will send the ball on its way.

For a ball coming directly at your face, step to your left and use a forehand volley.

The Follow-Through and Finish

In the description of the groundstrokes, the follow-through is described as a continuation of the forward swing through the ball. This also applies to the volley. The follow-through is usually short and compact and in the direction of the intended target area. A slight high-to-low movement will provide some degree of backspin which is sometimes desirable. Avoid making the "chopping" motion that can result in a mishit or ineffective shot.

When you have completed the volley return immediatley to the ready position. Pull the elbows and racket back and you will be ready for the next ball.

REMEMBER:

1. Watch the ball closely at all times.
2. Get ready by being in an active ready position at the net, on your toes, racket head up and in good balance.
3. Turn your shoulders early in preparation for the volley. Keep the backswing short.
4. Step toward the ball and make early contact.
5. Firm the wrist by squeezing your fingers.
6. Use a short punching or blocking stroke.
7. Use your left hand to guide the racket on the backhand side.
8. Bend your knees for low balls.

Now that you know how to hit the ball it is important you PRACTICE as much as possible in order to perfect each stroke. NO PRACTICE, NO PROGRESS. You don't need a tennis court or racket to execute the basic moves and footwork. Use your hand, simulating the forehand, backhand, or service grip, and practice the stroke in your living room. Turn on music and practice your footwork to the rhythm of the two-step. Use your full-length mirror to observe the checkpoints listed.

The backboard, the wall of your house, or the garage are excellent aids for learning the groundstrokes and volley, even the serve. Drop and hit balls to the wall or to a target. Stroke the ball against the wall, hitting it on the second bounce. Move in close and volley against the wall.

Move to the court and practice hitting balls over the net to a target. Have a friend toss balls to you and practice stroking the ball over the net. Then, rally, rally, rally. Work first for CONSISTENCY, then CONTROL. POWER will come later.

Finally, if you do get serious, take a lesson—a lesson from a *licensed* tennis professional. If you do not know where to find one, call the USPTA for references.

PAUL J. XANTHOS
IAN CROOKENDEN

3

Specialty Shots

In the preceding chapter the basic shots of the game—the serve, the forehand and backhand drives, and the conventional block volleys are described and illustrated. As valuable and as necessary as these strokes are, they won't suffice to enable you to respond properly to all of your opponents' shots and to hit effectively in all of the play situations you're likely to encounter during a match. You will need additional strokes and shots, more weapons, so to speak, to play effectively at higher levels of competition. Several of these "specialty shots," are described in this chapter. Work on them as much as you do on the basic strokes. Practice to make these parts of your arsenal too. You will be a better player when you learn them.

The Groundstroke Slice

The GROUNDSTROKE SLICE can be a valuable addition to your game, an adjunct to the conventional drives described earlier. You can use it to return serves and to sustain a rally, as an approach shot, and to thwart a net player. You can lob with it, dropshot with it, and use it to break up the rhythm of a smooth-stroking backcourt player. Plainly, it is one of the most useful shots in the game, one well worth the time it takes to learn.

The grip and stance for a slice resemble those for your drives, on both the forehand and backhand. The swings differ, however, especially in the plane your racket travels. For a slice your racket should move from high to low even though sometimes this downward plane is so slight as to be barely noticeable.

Another difference is in the setting of your racket. When slicing a ball that is below net level you will have to "open" your racket face slightly to give the ball lift enough to clear the net. The more you open your racket face and the more pronounced your downward swing plane, the more backspin you will apply to the ball. You can learn to adjust those two variables at will to vary the trajectory and the spin of your shots. Of course you will also have to adjust the third ever-present variable, the force of your swing, to the play the situation of the moment.

When using the slice as a rally shot, you apply backspin with a downward glancing blow. The spin may be merely a by-product of your attempt to take the speed off a rapidly approaching ball. You hit the ball obliquely rather than directly, and the result is less rebound off your racket. Consequently, errors in timing, judgment, and racket setting are likely to be minimized.

But you may purposely spin the ball to cause it to bounce differently from your drives. This change of pace can be troublesome for your opponents and may cause weak returns on baseline rally shots and on approach shots.

Slice (forehand)

On return of serve, the slice can be invaluable, but its use is generally restricted to the backhand, and against high-bouncing balls. (On serves to the forehand, players have little trouble raising the racket during the backswing to swing properly at high balls.)

On the backhand, not many players can draw the racket back far enough to drive while also raising it in line with high balls. Since their backswings are restricted, they are more inclined to slice. Serves to the backhand are often played on the rise. The ball is "pulled" down by their racket on its way down and forward through the contact point.

To slice when returning serve, raise your racket during your backswing so you can start your forward swing higher than the intended point of contact. Let the rising ball come up higher than your waist so it will be higher than the net at impact. Then swing diagonally downward at it, with your racket face set to meet the back of the ball, not the bottom of it. These two variables, your racket's path and your racket's setting (its slant), together with the amount of force in your swing, must be adjusted carefully on each return to provide the proper amount of spin and speed.

Since when you slice you are not intending to hit very hard (spin and speed are mutually exclusive; a great deal of one results in less of the other), you need not turn your shoulders much as you

swing. To hit short, as is usually your intention—from baseline to service line, for example—you can get enough force from elbow and arm action (at the shoulder) and from weight transfer. Consequently, you will not need a forceful swing with a long follow-through. In fact, you may have to purposely shorten your follow-through to recover quickly and to prepare for your next shot.

As you practice the slice, avoid two common faults. Do not raise your elbow. This will cause you to hit under the ball, to make contact on its underside. As a result you will almost always hit a "pop-up," a high, floating shot. Secondly, do not relax your grip and wrist, letting your racket drop lower than your hand. This will cause excessive spin and lack of control. Move your racket in a downward plane with total arm action at the shoulder, not by wrist action.

Used against a serve, the backhand slice can become an effective defensive shot. Though it may not be as spectacular or as lethal as a drive, it may be the best way for you to get a good percentage of your service returns in and to reduce the server's advantage by forcing him or her to volley a low ball. For these reasons it is frequently used as a variation to the drive even in world-class competition, where one service break often affects the outcome of a set. At a lower level of play, where you must often break your opponent's serve more than

Slice (backhand)

Variations of the Volley

In the preceding chapter you were told to use a simple kind of volley in which you placed your racket at the intended point of contact and merely held it there to intercept the ball. You were told to block the ball and to punch it, with only a slight backswing and a short forward swing.

All this is good advice, but the block volley and the punch volley are only two of several kinds of volleys possible for effective net play. From certain locations and in certain play situations you will often have to do more than punch or block the ball to make an effective shot. Other kinds of volleys to use are the drag volley, the snap volley, the drive volley (or swing volley), and the drop volley. They can be considered specialty shots, supplemental shots, to be used along with the basic volley described in Chapter 2.

The Drop Volley

The DROP VOLLEY is a soft, "touch" shot meant to drop vertically (or nearly so) close to the net, and to bounce with very little forward motion. Use it as an adjunct to your crisp, deep volleys and you will often be able to surprise opponents who are in the backcourt. Expecting a deep shot, they will not be ready to run forward. As a result, they will not be able to reach the ball before it takes its second bounce.

To hit a drop volley, loosen your wrist and grip at impact. Let your racket recoil slightly as the ball hits it. At the same time, turn your wrist and forearm quickly in a clockwise direction (on a forehand) to put backspin on the ball. The loose wrist will let you take the speed off the oncoming ball, and the backspin will slow the bounce of the ball and reduce its forward motion.

The Drag Volley

Use the DRAG VOLLEY (so named because the racket is dragged down and across the ball) when you want to impart a moderate amount of speed to the ball with a minimum of risk. Hit the ball a downward glancing blow, with your racket face open a great deal for a low ball and less so for a high one. The combination of your downward swing and your open racket face will let you hit the ball obliquely, not squarely, and as a result you will have taken the speed off the approaching ball. You will probably be able to control this shot better than when you make a more direct solid hit, particularly on low balls, where your problem is to hit the ball softly enough to keep it from sailing beyond the baseline.

once to compensate for having lost your own service game, it can be even more useful.

Drop volley

The Snap Volley

When you are making a play on a high ball and you want more speed in your shot than the drag, punch, or block volleys provide, use a SNAP VOLLEY. As the name implies, snap your wrist to move your racket face into the ball. Lay your wrist back during your backswing then make it straighter as you hit. The quicker your wrist action, the more speed you will add to your shot. Tighten your grip and make your wrist firm at impact. And since ball speed is your objective, hit the ball flat; make a square, solid hit rather than a glancing hit of a drag volley.

The Drive Volley (or Swing Volley)

The DRIVE VOLLEY is especially suitable when you want to hit very aggressively at a high ball. As the name implies, you can swing on this volley, much as you swing when you drive a ground-stroke. You can generate racket speed either by arm action alone (at the shoulder) or by combining arm action with shoulder rotation. Because of the longer swing and your intention to hit hard, there is a greater element of risk in this shot than in other volleys. To reduce the risk, hold your racket firmly. This will eliminate wrist action, and the result will be a kind of one-piece swing with no "slack" at your wrist or elbow. Make your racket function as an extension of your arm.

Drive volley or swing volley: to make the shot aggressive this volleyer makes a longer backswing and a longer follow-through than he does for a conventional block volley. Firmness in the hand, wrist, and forearm muscles prevents "slack" from developing in the swing. As a result, he is able to hit hard with control.

Drag volley: the wrist is cocked and laid back to raise the racket above and behind the ball. The wrist then leads during the forward swing so that the racket is dragged down and across the ball, hitting the ball a glancing blow. As a result, the volleyer is able to take some of the speed off the approaching ball. This shot is often safer than when the volleyer swings directly into the ball to hit it squarely head-on.

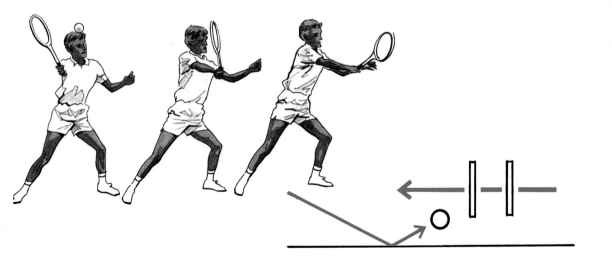

Half volley: racket is placed very low and perpendicular to ground. Ball is contacted just after bounce with a follow-through that is firm and controlled, having just enough lift to carry ball over net and deep into back court.

The Half-Volley

The term "HALF-VOLLEY," which is applied to the pick-up stroke when the ball is played on the short hop, is a misnomer: the shot is not a volley at all but a groundstroke (the ball first hits the ground before the player strokes it). For this reason you ought to play this shot similarly to the way you hit a regular groundstroke. But since this shot is usually played from a volley location, you will probably have to use your volley grips.

Because you are at least part way up to the net as you play this shot, your swing will be shorter than on full-length backcourt drives. You will have to adjust the length of the stroke, depending on your distance from the net and from your aim point. And you will have to adjust the setting of your racket too, closing it more when hitting from close to the net and opening it when hitting from farther back.

Keep your wrist firm and allow little or no "slack" at your shoulder and elbow joints. Bend your knees to lower your racket; do not change the angle between your wrist, forearm, and racket handle from that which gives you maximum control of the racket.

Adjust the plane of each swing according to the strategic situation. When you are hitting from your service line and your intention is to hit deep, you may close your racket face slightly and swing in a flat plane, parallel to the ground. When you want to lift the ball more than that swing allows, open your racket face and swing in an upward plane. Make these adjustments with your wrist and forearm. To do so accurately you will have to consider the possible angles of deflection of the ball off your racket on each swing.

Many good net players believe this shot is easier made when they hit the ball quickly after the bounce, when it has risen only three or four inches from the ground, rather than when the ball is allowed to bounce up to shin height. Try this method. It may work best for you too.

The Lob

The LOB is a high shot, usually played as a groundstroke. It is used most often against an opposing net player as a defensive shot when the lobber's intention is to draw either an error or a weak shot (after which the lobber hopes either to win with aggressive shots or simply to prolong the rally). In this latter case we can say the player lobs to get out of trouble.

Occasionally a lob is intended to fly completely over the net player and thus to bounce deep in the court for a winner. When it is used this way

it is called an offensive lob. Defensive lobs are hit with either no spin (flat) or with backspin. Offensive lobs are usually hit with topspin.

For either kind of lob, you can use a stroke similar to your normal groundstroke drive. You can use the same grip, stance, preparatory swing, and point of contact. But since your intention is to hit the ball high—higher than a regular groundstroke—you will have to swing in more of an upward plane than you normally do. You will probably also have to slant the racket face back (open it) more than you do for drives. This combination of upward plane and open racket face will provide the lift, the upward trajectory to cause the net player to retreat in a hurry.

One major difference between your drives and your lobs will be the amount of force you apply as you swing. The swing for a lob should be less forceful and more controlled; it may even be simply a steady push at the ball rather than a swing.

To get the soft upward flight you want on your lobs, you may have to use some subtle wrist and forearm motions just before your racket meets the ball. On the forehand you may have to turn your forearm clockwise; on the backhand, counterclockwise. As a result of these turning actions the ball may have backspin. The spin is simply a by-product of the mechanics of the stroke; do not apply it deliberately to affect the flight of the ball or its bounce.

These techniques for lobbing apply only when you have time to move properly into position for your normal drive motion. But you will not always have that much time. You will often have to use a much shorter motion to make a play on a fast-approaching ball. This short, compact motion may resemble your volley stroke; it is a short punch, a block, or a push, with little or no wrist action. To loft the ball you will have to either move your racket up into the ball or turn your wrist and forearm to open the racket face at impact. With this latter action you will almost certainly put backspin on the ball.

To distinguish between these two kinds of lobs you may think of the first one as a "drive lob." The motion resembles your drive. The second can be called a "volley job" because you hit it much as you do a volley at the net. In each case, drive lob or volley lob, the critical factor in the stroke is the "touch," or the "feel" necessary to hit softly and accurately. This is not easy to learn or to teach, but you will improve at it with practice.

The offensive topspin lob mentioned earlier resembles a heavily spinning, high-looping drive. The stroke, too, is similar to your drive stroke. But

Overhead smash

again, to get the high trajectory you want, you will have to swing in a markedly upward plane while opening the racket face more than you do for a drive. It is the proper combination of swing plane and racket setting that produces both the upward flight and the topspin that causes the ball to curve sharply downward after sailing over the net player.

The Overhead Smash

The OVERHEAD SMASH is used to return a lob, either before or after the lob bounces. It can best be compared to the flat serve: your grips, stance, and hitting motions are similar. As you move into position to smash, however, you must prepare to swing differently.

When smashing, do not swing the racket down past your knees before you raise it behind you. Instead, take the racket back at waist height, or perhaps even higher. These shorter, more direct backswings will give you more racket control than do the free-flowing backswings of your serves.

As you see your opponent lob, turn sideways and raise the racket behind you. Carry it in this "cocked" position, with your elbow raised to shoulder height and with your grip firm enough to keep your racket up behind you, not dangling loosely down behind your back.

Move your racket into the cocked position as you move into position to hit. If the lob is short and

you have to move forward to hit, run or skip in that direction. Skipping may be adequate if you have to move only a step or two. But if you have to cover more ground to get properly under the lob, run forward. Here, time your steps and adjust the number of them and the size of them so your left foot will be in front as you swing. In this sense, your stance will resemble your service stance.

To get under a very deep lob you may have to turn to your right and run sideways. Here, too, you will have to adjust the number and size of your steps so that you can be properly sideways and ready to swing when the ball is within reach.

Start your hitting motion from the cocked position. Quickly dip the racket behind your back, then bring it up forcefully into the ball. For best control permit no "slack" between the movement of your arm at the shoulder and your elbow and wrist. Instead hold your racket firmly and tense your arms and shoulder muscles slightly to control your swing.

But you may not always have time to move back and to set yourself nicely under the ball to smash it. Instead, you may have to jump toward the baseline to reach a ball that would otherwise be beyond reach. This jump-smash requires slight adjustments in weight distribution and timing.

As you move back to reach the deep lob you can either run sideways or skip that way. In either

Overhead smash with scissors kick

case, time your movements so that you are setting your right foot down in time to jump as the ball comes within reach.

Jump up and slightly backward, taking off from your right foot while swinging your left foot back so you can land on it. Time your moves, your jump, and your swing so that you make contact while you are in the air, before you land on your left foot.

Very high lobs are difficult to judge and to time. They are usually easier to play after they bounce. And since a very high lob is dropping nearly vertically it will bounce nearly vertically. You will not, then, have to back up much farther than the point at which you could have played it "on the fly." For these reasons you should let high lobs bounce.

The Dropshot

The DROPSHOT is a delicate "touch" shot requiring precise timing and deft racket work. It is used by a baseliner against a baseliner who is out of position, off balance, or notably slow-footed. The intention is to make the ball descend nearly vertically close to the net, and to hit with so little force that the ball will have very little forward movement after it bounces. As a consequence, the opponent will not be able to reach and make a play on the ball before it bounces twice in his or her court.

This shot, too, can be built on your ground-stroke patterns. Use the same grip, stance, and backswing you do on your drives. Start your forward swing the same too. But here you will have to slow your swing just before contact to hit the ball softly. You may also have to open your racket face quickly as you hit, to apply backspin to the ball. The spin will cause the ball to bounce more toward the vertical axis than normally. As a result your opponent will have to run farther to reach the ball before its second bounce. Because of your slower forward swing you will not need to follow through much, if at all. You will need to extend your arm and racket along the line of your shot (your target line) only far enough to steer the ball delicately toward your aim point.

You may best use this shot when you are close to one of what can be called the "net corners" (those sections of your opponent's court close to the net and the sidelines) and when your opponent is not close to it. Aim at that particular corner, hitting as softly as you can while dropping the ball as close to the net as you can. And disguise your stroke as best you can so as not to give away your intention. The dropshot has to take your opponent by surprise to be effective.

Return of Service

RETURN OF SERVICE is your first shot on half

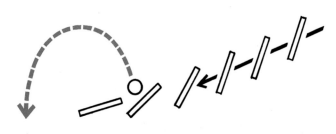

Dropshot sequence: preparation and backswing are same as regular groundstroke. Just before contact, racket face opens and wrist relaxes so ball is caressed upwards softly, to die over the net. The open racket face imparts backspin to keep the ball close to the net.

Poorly executed dropshot: ball is hit to skim the top of the net, which means its trajectory will be too flat, carrying the ball too far into the opponent's court.

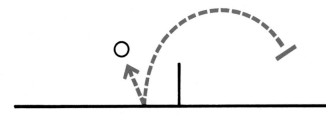

Well-executed dropshot: ball is hit up, so it is *dropping* down as it clears the net, allowing the backspin to hold the ball close to the net.

the points you play in singles, and one quarter of the points in doubles. Could anything be more important unless it is service itself? But when serving you have the initiative, you can make the decision on how play starts. On return of service, you must be prepared to meet any option the server selects. Much more technical versatility is demanded, and more ability to adapt and find a way to counter whatever is served to you. There are hard, flat serves, there are high bounders to your backhand, and there are sliced angles to your forehand. You cannot handle them all the same way.

First of all, let us be realistic. There is much talk about how a return should be deep, hard, and forceful, with all your weight in it. That is lovely for someone writing a book. He or she has lots of time. In actual play there is very little time indeed. A ball going 60 miles per hour goes 88 feet per second. The server is less than 80 feet from you, and many hard serves go well over 60 miles per hour. Also, some of your time is taken up in spotting that it is coming to your forehand or backhand. So at the most you have a half second in which to react. How much can you do, how much can you move your feet, how much can you swing —in a half second or less? If you are very quick, like Jimmy Connors, you can do more than most—and doesn't he have a *great* return of serve? But most of us are less endowed and must make do with more limited physical assets. So let us analyze the problem with a clear realization of the importance of tempo (how fast things happen) and the defensive situation you are in.

First Principle. Stand in, do not back way up. Many singles players and all good doubles players follow their serves to net. In both cases the most important consideration for the receivers is to get the ball back before the servers can get in where they can put their volley away. Standing far back means the ball travels farther to you and farther going back, giving the servers that extra step or two that puts them in a commanding position from which to volley. In doubles, if you stand far back, your return will not get past the server's partner at net. This player will cut it off, because it takes too long to get past him or her. So you *must* stand in, whether it hurries you or not. In singles, the only exception is when your opponent does not follow in. Then you can take your time and play for good depth from farther back.

What does "stand in" mean? A good general rule is, stand with your toes touching the baseline, and try to step forward into the court to play the ball. This can vary with different serves, but should seldom vary backwards.

Second Principle. Always move into the ball. Serving and receiving can be likened to a shoving contest. When I serve, I hope to push you back on your heels so none of your weight gets into your shot, your ball flutters back weakly, and I proceed to take advantage. Your job as receiver is to push back, give as good as you get, and return the ball as firmly as possible. Getting your weight into it is essential. Therefore, you always step into the ball if you humanly can. If you cannot, your return will float, and the only floater that is any good is a lob.

To put this policy into practice, you must develop certain habits of footwork, particularly on balls that come close to you. For a forehand, always step *in* with the left foot, never step back with the right foot. For a backhand, always step in with the right foot. When the ball is more to the side, try to move sideways and diagonally forward, never sideways at a right angle or a little backwards. If you do this, your shot will occur when your weight is moving forward and will average out to be much firmer. It also means you will play the ball inside your baseline, achieving the early hit stressed in the first principle. Watch Jimmy Connors—he shoves his weight into just about every return.

This again brings up the question of tempo. How can you be quick enough to take sharp serves briskly and aggressively?

Third Principle. Learn to play with almost zero backswing. Pretty backswings (particularly circular ones that go up, back, down, then forward) take time. You do not have time. Any kind of a big swing is impossible. On the other hand, you *do* have time to get your racket to the side and turn your shoulders a little. It is a good bit like volleying the ball after it bounces instead of before it bounces. If you do this and also move into the ball, it will go back hard, just like a firm volley. Perhaps it is best described by the phrase "block and follow through." A good follow-through (more than on a volley) is desirable and gets even more weight into the ball. But the big point is that this is something you CAN do in the infinitesimal span of time permitted by a serve that has pace. It is realistic.

This third principle should be stressed, because without it, you cannot be quick enough. If you stand back too far, or step back to give yourself more time, you will fail to achieve a quick, firm return. In coaching a college team for 44 years, I found the greatest shortcoming in most freshmen was too much swing. With a big swing they were competent up to a certain level of play. When the calibre of the opposition went above a certain tempo, they were in trouble, particularly in good doubles, but also against a net rusher in singles.

Jimmy Connors, with perhaps the best return of serve in tennis today, attacking a backhand return of serve by moving *in*

Bjorn Borg, hitting his patented open-stance forehand return of serve (Note the extreme upper-body rotation.)

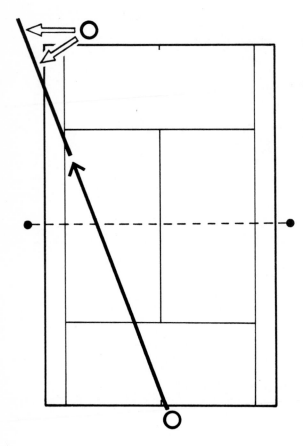

Receiver has less distance to cover to reach ball if he or she steps *in*.

Many had been taught a full and generous backswing for baseline drives, and naturally used it for return of service. Perhaps teachers should think about this and judge what they teach not by whether it will work for beginners and intermediates, but whether it will work in advanced play. The big swing will not. Moreover, if players are taught short backswings, with the idea that you don't "swing back," you merely get your racket ready to play, then swing *forward*, it is easy to tell them later, "When you have time, at the baseline, why don't you haul off a bit more?" It is very easy to expand a small swing. It is very difficult to "unlearn" or cut down a big swing after it has been practiced over time. (I know from bitter experience as a coach!)

Try working on the following specific tips to improve your return of serve.

(1) Be ready to move. Your ability to move quickly depends in part on how well you prepare to move. If in the ready position you habitually stand flat-footed with your knees straight and your weight back on your heels, work to correct these faults. Bend your knees and shift your weight forward slightly. Make yourself feel light and bouncy. Be ready to spring into motion the moment you determine the direction of your opponent's serve.

One good way to get the feel of the proper ready stance is to hop into it as most good players do. As your opponent tosses to serve, make a little hop. From your hop, land in the ready posture—that's why this is called a "ready hop"—just as your opponent's racket meets the ball. From the ready posture, move to intercept the oncoming ball.

(2) Look at the ball. But you cannot move properly until you determine where the served ball is going. And the sooner you see where it is going, the sooner you can move. It is to your advantage, therefore, to learn to see the ball quickly.

As you make your ready hop, focus your attention on the ball. Look up to see it as your opponent tosses and as he or she swings at it. Check to see that you are not looking at the total figure of the server and then waiting for the ball to come out of that background, as many inexperienced players mistakenly do. Focus on the ball. Let the mechanism of starting quickly be incidental, automatic in a sense, and uncontrolled by your subconscious.

(3) Adjust your grip. Besides seeing the ball quickly, standing properly, and making a quick start, you will often want to move your racket as quickly as possible. To do this you may have to adjust your grip.

If you can manage a no-change grip, one that

you can use for both forehands and backhands, well and good; you will not have to worry about having time to adjust your grip during a backswing. But if you feel you must hold the racket differently for forehands and backhands, experiment to see which change you make faster: from forehand to backhand or from backhand to forehand. In your ready stance, use the grip that permits you to make the faster change. Whatever your decision, place your left hand at the racket's throat and use it to move the racket during the backswing.

(4) Shorten your swing. While in the ready stance, hold your elbows in at your sides and bend your arms at the elbows to bring your hands and racket closer to your body. With these adjustments you will be able to make a short-radius swing. You will then have less inertia of your arms and racket to overcome and as a result you will probably be able to swing the racket faster than when your arms are extended and the racket is farther from your body.

After only a little practice at watching the ball, making a ready hop, and using a short-radius swing, you will probably be able to react and to move faster. Your service returns are likely to be more effective as a result.

Fourth Principle. Return serve crosscourt. You are under pressure. You are rushed. You will very probably be a bit inaccurate. Therefore, give yourself the biggest target over the lowest part of the net. The chances of error playing crosscourt are far less than playing straight. You can also keep the ball lower to a net rusher. Furthermore, whether the server comes to net or stays back, a crosscourt gives him or her less chance to play the ball away from you. By contrast, if you play straight, your opponent can angle his or her second shot (volley or groundstroke) sharply away from you. The straight return should only be used if the serve is so ordinary that you think you can make a forcing shot or a winner. The crosscourt is the shot that makes it most difficult for your opponent to capitalize on the advantage of being the server, and it is the shot that puts the least pressure on you when you are on the defensive and hurried.

Fifth Principle. Be versatile. Dan Magill (Georgia's fine coach) once made a telling remark about return of serve. He said, "You have three choices: stand back and whale away, move in to block and chip, or lob." Some serves, such as flat serves, can be blocked and poked right back at the feet of the net rusher. Others, such as high arching twists that are calculated to bounce high to your backhand, are best handled by closing in to take them early, before they get uncomfortably high

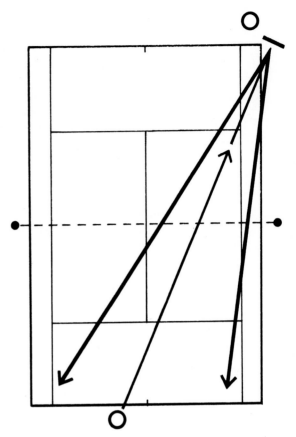

Crosscourt return of serve is more effective because it crosses the net at the lowest part (center) and utilizes the long diagonal of the court, adding almost five feet of court to hit into.

and before the net rusher is way in. Some serves that are in between and bounce reasonably low but are not cannonballs can be handled with devastating results by taking them on the rise and playing a hard topspin drive.

Such versatility is not easy. To take a serve on the rise and hit with topspin requires a somewhat special technique: the racket face must be more than ordinarily closed, because the rising ball will try to ride high off your racket. You must cover it a little. Taking the ball early enough so it is not uncomfortably high for such a drive means you must have the zero backswing trick pretty well perfected. On the other hand, if you become very quick at this skill, you can make aggressive topspin returns off almost all serves. Don Budge used to do this, forehand and backhand, with extraordinarily intimidating results. Connors does it today, and, like Budge, seems always to be the aggressor no matter who is serving.

Chipping the ball is a very effective way to return twist serves that tend to hop high to your backhand. Here again the absence of a backswing is essential. You do not take your racket back so much as lift it to the side, above the ball, so you can chop down as you move your weight into the shot.

Lobbing the net player in doubles is important. If you do not do this now and then with your return of serve, the server's partner is free to crowd in close, poach, and generally make trouble. You must keep him or her honest. The trick is to prepare as though you intend to chip, then at the last instant curl your racket under the ball so as to pop it up in a controlled way with no advance warning to the opponent. It is important also to close in as much as possible to take the ball early, so it pops over the net player's head before he or she has time to back up for a smash.

A truly versatile player should also aim to become adept at using the open stance for the forehand. Since your available time is very short, there is one absolute must: get the head of the racket to the ball. If you do not do this all else is academic. Your hitting arm is hung over your right leg. If, when the ball comes to your forehand, you step over with your left foot, you do not get your racket any closer to the ball. If the ball is coming fast you have time for only one step: this step *must* be with the right foot to get you within reach. This is why practically all leading players use the open stance: it is because they have to.

If tennis were like golf, a game in which the ball sits still, allowing you all the time you wish to address the ball and make your swing, then no doubt everyone would use the closed stance and a much fuller swing than is advised here. But in golf, there is no tempo at all, while in tennis tempo governs or modifies many of our decisions. There have been bitter arguments about the open and closed stance, but on a forehand return of serve tempo decides the issue beyond any dispute. That is why all good players use the open stances: they do what they have to do to get their racket onto the ball before it gets by them.

Using the open stance is an advanced technique. Certainly one would not teach beginners to play with an open stance. It should be added to a person's bag of tricks after he or she becomes advanced enough to be in higher tempo situations. From an open stance, you can step sideways with the right foot, twisting a bit at the waist to get some body turn into the shot, and lean forward into the ball. Thus we can get an early, firm return with reasonable weight behind it. Often it requires a somewhat laid back wrist to prevent the ball from going too much crosscourt.

The open stance is not used much on the backhand because in moving the right leg to get the hitting arm within reach, we automatically create a closed stance. Again, tempo governs technique.

Above all, *be resourceful,* the most successful players are usually the most open-minded. They will try *anything* just to see if it will work against this opponent on this court under today's conditions (hot, cold, windy, hard or soft court, regular or heavy-duty balls). A couple of examples will illustrate. Rafael Osuna once retreated almost to the backstop and returned towering lobs as his return of service. Doing this he succeeded in getting a couple of breaks against Frank Froehling III, a player who was serving everybody off the court. Osuna won Forest Hills.

John Newcombe defeated Stan Smith by practically dropshotting his return of serve. "Big Stan" was roaring in to net and making devastating first volleys. Newcombe changed tactics and began to poke his returns softly, so they landed well inside the service line. Smith had to half volley, making weak shots. Newcombe passed him time after time. Smith should have checked his rush, let the ball bounce and made an approach shot, but he did not. He kept right on storming in, and Newcombe kept right on making his soft, fading chips. Newcombe won handily.

Now what teaching pro would advise pupils to retreat far (ten to fifteen feet) behind the baseline to lob their return? What coach would say, "When they serve and rush, dropshot 'em"? Yet these apparently bizarre tactics worked, and won matches against top-flight opposition. The winners are to be congratulated not on their great shots so much as on their ingenuity: they found a way.

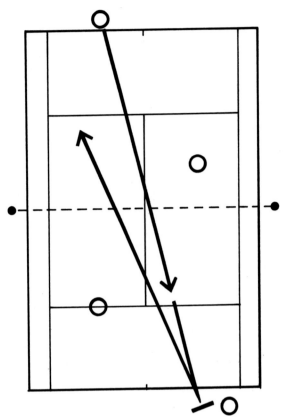

Inside-out backhand return: a very difficult return because receiver naturally wants to hit through the ball, but the net player blocks that shot, so receiver must angle his or her racket face *inside* the flight of the ball and return it *out and away* from his or her body to avoid the net player.

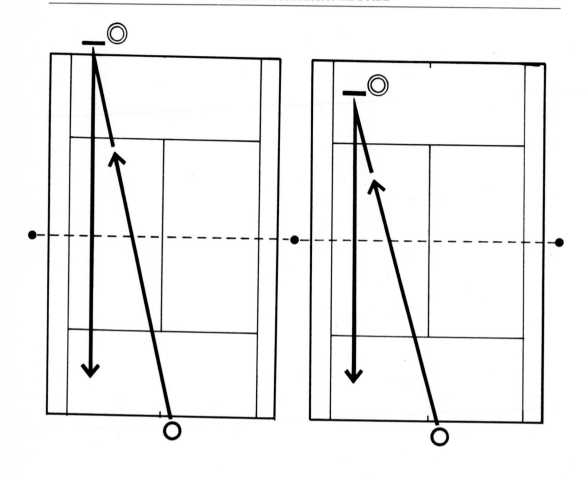

Deep first serve: receiver plays behind baseline in
order to have time for a good return. Shallow second
serve: receiver moves well inside baseline and still
has the same amount of time to hit a good return.

It is easy to advise everyone to be resourceful and to try everything until something works. But you cannot try everything unless you can do everything. An intelligent idea is useless unless you can execute it with your racket. Advanced players should drill on specific skills. Have someone serve high bounces to the backhand: close in and chip crosscourt. Have someone serve hard: try to be so quick that you move into it, forward, on every return. Practice topspinning your backhand return, using a full Eastern grip to close the face (even if your regular grip is a bit Continental as many are). Above all, use different partners, because after you get very good at returning one style of service, another may frustrate you entirely. Never get the feeling you know it all. Maybe your mind knows a lot. How much does your racket know?

To be good at return of serve demands that we master certain athletic techniques. Always crouch just as your opponent is about to strike, so your legs are bent, ready to shove back against the force of his or her shot, or to spring to either side if the ball is placed at the edges of the service court. Learn to play your backhand with a laid back wrist: when opponents serve to you in the forehand court and place it down the center, you need to play a trifle inside the ball to slide it off to the left. This is desirable in singles, and an absolute must in doubles —if you do not do this, you play it right to the net player! Vic Braden, the California top pro, has made much of the difficulty of returning the ball crosscourt in doubles from this position. He asserts it is the most difficult return of serve, because most people come around the ball a bit with their regular stroke, and find this adjustment difficult. The trick is to lead through with the butt of your racket, so the face plays the inside of the ball. Here again, drilling on it brings mastery much faster than merely playing. It is not difficult *if* you have the knack.

Mental attitude is very important in return of serve. Most players have a tendency to be so defensive in their attitude that even if a service is very short, they will stay back and let it bounce all the way to them and then play a defensive shot. Actually a short serve, unless it has terrific "stuff" on it, is an invitation to attack. If, during a rally, I played a ball to you that landed eight feet inside the service line, would you not move in and try to hurt me? Then, why not attack if I hit a short serve? Only the top players serve their second ball deep almost every time. Are you playing McEnroe? Be ready to jump on short balls and do things with them. You can sock it if it is a backhand. In more elderly tennis

(the kind I play) it can even be devastating to close in on a short serve and dropshot. (Older people are slow moving in.) But at any level it is important to realize that any shortcoming in your opponent's serving is an opportunity for you—provided you are watching for chances and seize them. Be ready!

Some may object that to do this hurries them into error. Not so. You stand roughly at the baseline so that if a serve lands close to the service line you will have time to judge it and meet it. If a serve lands ten feet inside the service line, and you move in ten feet, you have the same amount of time in which to judge the bounce, address it, and play it. If you are rushed, it is probably because you did not think of it until too late. If you are more aggressive minded, you will react sooner and be in there playing your shot from a commanding position. Practice it!

Above all, players should practice aggressive returns of second services. Even great servers do not always get the first big one in. They must sacrifice some speed for spin and safety on the second ball. This is your chance to do better than just try to block it back, which is all you can usually do with the big one. Even if a player gets a hot streak and serves you off the court for a while, do not become totally defensive. Somewhere along the line he or she will have a spell of hitting that first one just out or in the net. You must be mentally ready to go after your opponent whenever this happens. If you have allowed yourself to become intimidated by the first ball, you will not have the confidence or initiative to do much with the second ball.

A great deal of tennis is played on hard, fast courts these days. I have heard it said, "Hard court tennis is all serve, volley, and overhead." So everyone works on these. Little is said about return of serve. And yet: if you can win your serve and I can win my serve, what makes a winner? The answer of course is whichever of us can now and then break serve.

Taking this attitude—that in hard court tennis breaking serve makes the difference—brought Harvard a big win on one occasion. Another Ivy team was ranked between eight and twelve in the country. We were not even considered for a national ranking. We worked all winter on return of serve, played our rival on hard courts where they, being big hitters, were supposedly invincible, and won four of six singles and a doubles for a 5–4 upset. They had big serves, and at times blew us off the court. But not all the time. When they missed the first one, we were ready to attack that second ball, and we got a few more service breaks than

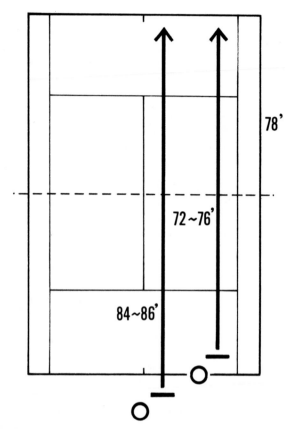

Difference in feet between shot hit behind baseline and shot hit inside baseline: when a player moves inside the baseline, he or she loses anywhere from 8 to 14 feet of court space to hit into.

they did. Working by systematic drilling on return of serve can really pay off. Try it.

The Approach Shot

The importance of the APPROACH SHOT can scarcely be exaggerated. Players often rally until one makes a mistake: a short ball that invites an attack. This· is the opportunity the attacker has been hoping for. He or she can now move to the net for the kill. What happens at net is determined by the quality of the approach shot. If it is good, the chances are high that he or she will get a reasonable chance to volley or smash for a winner. If it is poor, he or she merely gives the opponent an opportunity to display whatever skills he or she possesses at passing shots and lobs. Your net game is only as good as your approach.

An attacking approach calls for a variety of techniques, all designed to get you to the net ready to put away any return. In the past, most teachers assumed that if their pupils acquired satisfactory baseline skills these would also serve for shots in the halfcourt area to be followed to net. This turned out to be a vast oversimplification. Why is it advisable to treat halfcourt shots as separate skills needing specific emphasis and drill?

In general, if good players can advance a step and a half or two steps inside the baseline to play a groundstroke, they have the option of following the ball to the net. When they make this shot they are usually six to twelve (or more) feet nearer the net than they are when rallying from the baseline with no intent to follow their shot. Therefore their ball has much less depth to go into before it goes out. A beautiful deep baseline forehand or back- hand may well be a yard out if used as an approach without alteration. Second, a player is usually sta- tionary (leaving out weight transfer) when playing from the baseline. In playing an approach, moving in behind the shot is actually part of and a continua- tion of the follow-through. This forward move- ment tends to carry the ball farther than at first expected. Again it is easy to hit out. Third, all teachers (no exceptions, I believe) teach to play well above the net from the baseline to get good depth and avoid the most common error (hitting the net). But now we wish to limit the length of our shot for the reasons already detailed. We must aim closer to the net. Fourth, we wish to be a bit decep- tive and have a quick release stroke that is held until the last second, thus threatening options such as playing to the unexpected side or dropping the ball. This means we use a shorter backswing and a more sudden strike as contrasted with a sweeping base- line swing. Fifth, in order to aim lower and restrict

Forehand slice approach: note how the player continues moving forward *through* his shot to gain an attacking volley position, and how his racket moves from high to low.

Backhand slice approach: again the swing is from high to low, and the forward movement is continuous. Note how the player's left (rear) foot slides *behind* the right (front) foot at impact to keep the body and racket correctly aligned for an approach shot down the line.

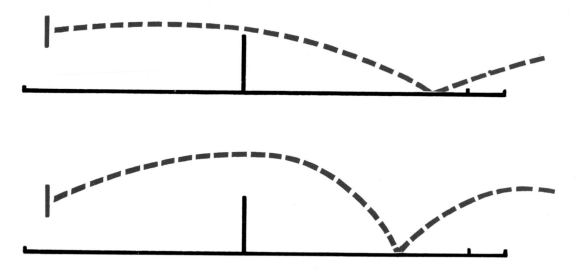

Slice approach stays low on bounce; opponent must hit *up* to player at net. Topspin approach hops up and allows opponent to hit harder. Also, topspin shot has more pace, and therefore, volleyer cannot reach optimum net position before ball is returned.

the length of our shot we prepare a little higher so as to play level rather than up and get more of a net skimmer rather than a ball that goes high over the net. If our opportunity is a high bouncing ball (above the height of the net) we shall probably close the face of the racket a little, again to keep our shot only a foot or so over the net as contrasted with the "three feet at least" clearance wisely taught as desirable in a baseline exchange.

Think of all these differences! A shorter stroke, a more closed face, a higher preparation on high setups, a shorter aim, an aim that only clears the net by a foot or so, and a deceptive, sudden, quick release. Does this sound anything like your baseline drive?

Perhaps it may be asserted that I have grossly exaggerated the differences. That of course can be argued, *but* at Harvard, I had freshmen come to me year after year from all over the country, often boys who had junior rankings and some tournament experience. Most had practiced their baseline drives until they were reasonably solid. If I rallied deep, they stayed right with me. All I had to do to beat them was to hit short. Most frequently, they hit it out because of too much length. Then they hit the net trying to keep their big shot in. They seldom fooled me at all. I was right there if they did get it in. I could make all kinds of mistakes and still pull out most of the points. In other words, they were

talented players but when they got a good chance, they could not hurt me. Why? Because they had no concept at all concerning halfcourt techniques: approach shots, dropshots (on clay), deceptive angles. Not realizing it involved different techniques, they had devoted no time to the problem, so they were comparatively incompetent.

By contrast, when Gar Mulloy brought his Miami team north and played Harvard, he would play me a fun set or two. Every time I made a mediocre shot, I got hurt. He was a complete player who effectively exploited every opportunity. (NOTE: Mulloy won the sets. He ranked in the U.S. first ten for 20 consecutive years.)

There are two types of approach shots. (1) Rock 'em and sock 'em—hit hard and rely on the speed and pace to rush and press your opponent enough so his or her attempts to pass or lob will be hampered enough to give you the edge. (2) Slice, the idea of which is to create a low bounce that obliges your opponent to hit up. A mean slice also "kicks," that is, it jumps or skids a bit unpredictably so an opponent is bothered and the quality of his or her return is impaired. Above all, the low bounce is important. Few learners realize how much more difficult it is to pass off a low ball than a ball that bounces to a more comfortable height. Anyone in doubt might try this: stand a competent player at net, stand at either corner, drop the ball

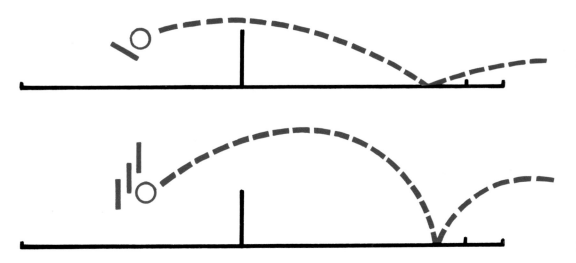

Slice is best approach technique for a short, low ball. Slice stays low and is easier to keep within boundaries of court. Topspin is harder to control, and the bounce to opponent is higher.

out of your hand so it bounces quite low, and try to pass him or her. Then toss the ball for yourself so it bounces more where you like it, and try to pass again. The difference is quite marked. That is why most successful net rushers have developed a mean slice. Billie Jean King is a prime example: a beautiful backhand slice approach which she even uses as a return of service if the serve is not pretty strong. After all, a weak serve is a short ball that invites attack. Some players even slice high forehand chances, though most prefer sheer power: sock it!

Lowness can work the other way. Many short balls are short because they barely cleared the net. They do not bounce high. When you play them, they are at or below the middle of the height of the net. Such a ball invites an attacking move but cannot be hit hard. The angle of elevation to clear the net is so great that our shot will go out if we hit for speed. But if we hit any clean shot gently, it is a setup for the defender. The only effective answer is a mean cross slice: hit from the outside in, and of course a trifle under it to clear the net. This has to be learned, because it means you get your racket out to the side (not back as usual) and cut in sharply across (not through) the ball. It takes practice. When players first try this, they draw back too much, therefore, swing forward too much, therefore, get too much length and the ball goes out. The point is to spin the ball (rather than hit it) so

it takes a low skid bounce and kicks out also. This is a valuable skill few players develop. Even a player of the calibre of Connors may be weak on short balls to his forehand if they are low, because he knows only one policy: hit hard. This hole in his technique has on occasion been his undoing. He should plug it. If someone suggests, "Jimmy does pretty well!" the answer is, "He does well in spite of this shortcoming, not because of it."

Where should one aim an approach shot? There seems to be almost universal agreement that it should be aimed deep. This writer disagrees with this consensus, and bases his logic on experience teaching approaches to hundreds of advanced but unfinished players. It is better to aim approach shots to strike a little (five feet) behind the service line. Why?

First, if you aim deep, you rule out all angles. You cannot place the ball very far from your opponent. You are hitting it back to where he or she is: behind the baseline. Unless your shot is very powerful, indeed, your opponent may do quite well defensively. Second, unless we use the center theory, the idea of placing the approach is to put it to one side, thus opening the other side for a winner. We are thus aiming as close to the sideline as we dare. If we aim deep, we are also aiming close to the baseline. This is a double risk, and it can be argued that risking two lines simultaneously is one too

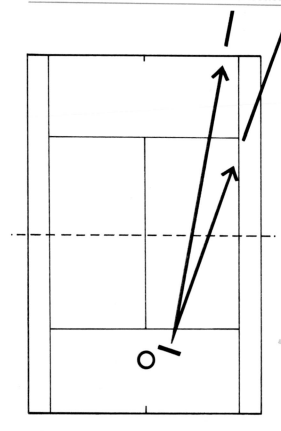

Effectiveness of short angle approach: by aiming short and close to sideline, opponent is pulled further out of court and up toward the net, making his or her passing shot more difficult and giving the volleyer more room to exploit.

many, and is not percentage tennis. Limiting one's risks is a cardinal ingredient in consistency.

What if we aim short—that is, five or six feet behind the service line? Several advantages result. We reduce our risk to one line, not two. If our setup were near the center of the court, we would get more angle and place it farther from our opponent. He or she has to move an extra step or so and is more hurried and is that much farther out of position when he or she plays. It is a fact that if your approach bounces across the side line before crossing the baseline, it is usually successful: you get your chance for a winner off the return. A third advantage is that if your approach is a low slice and if aimed rather short it will not bounce to your opponent. By the time he or she gets to it, the ball is very low. The difficulty of passing off a very low ball has been discussed. A fourth gain is that aiming short allows something for the tendency everyone has to overhit in terms of length. A ball aimed deep goes out. A ball aimed shorter goes farther than planned but is still in the court.

When an opponent hits you a setup to one side of the court, it is usually wise to play straight down the line so you can go straight forward to the net and be in position. Jack Kramer, a great tactician and net player, once wrote that he believes this so strongly that he would play his approach straight and follow straight up behind it, and then he used italics for emphasis to add, "even if my opponent is standing there." By doing this, he covered every return that used the full length of the court, forcing his opponent to lob or attempt a sharply angled crosscourt. The latter is a tough shot when one is pressed because the target is so small. Kramer was above all a percentage player. Oh yes, people passed him, but very seldom enough to win the match.

Why not play crosscourt? Because you then must run across the court as well as forward, or your alley is wide open. If you rush to cover the alley, a crosscourt return catches you moving the wrong way. Moreover, you probably move across so much that you fail to get well forward, so you do not achieve a winning position at net and may get the ball at your feet. Certainly if an opponent is overanticipating your straight shot, you may choose to play crosscourt on rare selected occasions, but you should go for a winner rather than a preparatory shot because if he or she gets to it at all, well, he or she has the devastating options previously outlined. So, play straight and use the crosscourt only to play a pronounced weakness or to keep an opponent honest.

Perhaps it should be noted that crosscourt means across the court, not across yourself. If you run around a serve to the left court so as to take it on your forehand, and then play to the other left court, this is a crosscourt.

How about the center theory? Play straight down the middle, thus reducing the defender's possible angles, and move right in onto the center of the net. This has been used successfully on occasion but is wise only in rare circumstances. Bill Tilden of legendary fame had brilliant running passing shots off both wings. After he had repeatedly pulled off winners on the dead run, one realized he was not lucky: he was that good. So players used the center theory as the only alternative in going to net against him. But how often does one encounter a player so lethal at passing with both strokes that you feel it is poor percentage to attack either side? Moreover, if you espouse the center theory, you had better be a super net player. Your approach goes right to your opponent and puts him or her in perfect position for defense on subsequent shots. The entire burden is on your volley and smash. Is your net game that good? So, for most players and most match situations, the center theory is not as good as the more orthodox concept: force one side thus opening the other, and cover the alley so as to leave your opponent nothing but a tough angle.

A little more can be added about aiming short. In teaching scores of reasonably good athletes who came to me with poor court skills, I found aiming shorter made an immediate improvement. The ball still often went farther than they aimed it, but was still in the court. I told them I did not mind if their ball went deep, I disapproved only if they aimed deep.

Teaching a restricted backswing is of great importance. Smaller swing for smaller shot—and an approach is a good bit smaller than a baseline drive. It is lower and carries a shorter distance—or it is out. Also a very quick preparation, made possible by a smaller swing, enables one to hold the shot a bit, and we all know this is basic to deception.

Often there is argument about this. "So and so (famous player) takes a big swing and he has good approaches." This is good observation but poor analysis. It is quite possible to take a considerable flourish which looks like a big swing but only actually releases the real hit when the racket is rather close to the ball. This is not a big swing. It is a camouflaged small swing. Many players will flourish threateningly when making a drop shot—the smallest shot in the game. Deception is fine, but should only be added after the fundamentals are

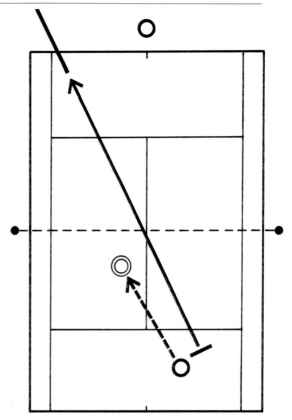

Ineffectiveness of crosscourt approach: offensive player must cover much more court to reach effective volley position. Defending player has two good options: the down-the-line passing shot before volleyer reaches good position, or the crosscourt passing shot to take advantage of offensive player's momentum to reach good volley position.

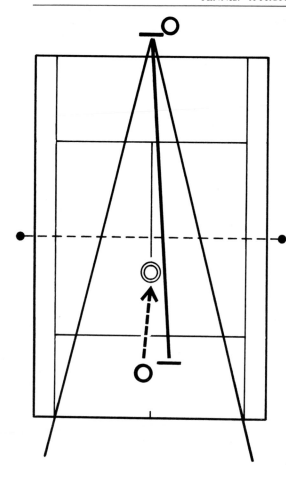

mastered. The fundamental in the halfcourt is to have a smaller, sharper swing. Deceptive mannerisms can be added later.

To sum up: approach shots involve an entire group of skills that differ from baseline skills. Shorter swing; a quick release hit that is, we hope, a bit vicious and deceptive; cross slicing for low chances; aiming more level rather than up; sweeping in as part of the follow-through, so when you finish the shot you do not have to go up—you ARE up there almost as part of the shot; aiming shorter to control length and to get some angle if the location of the setup permits—all these need to be drilled by aspiring players.

How do we learn to do all this? There is only one answer: drill. It is unfortunate that most players take the court, hit drives, volleys, overheads, serves, and say, "I'm ready." When they practice they do the same. Everyone seems to recognize that the overhead occurs only intermittently in play, so to get good at it, you must practice it separately as a special project. But the approach shot and the dropshot (another halfcourt shot) are also shots that occur less frequently in actual play. They, too, need to be drilled, and the approach is of key significance: here is your chance to take the initiative, to attack and win. Question: Will you blow it, or are you ready?

Perhaps some think this emphasis is overdone. If so, it is because this is an area generally neglected by most aspiring players and, alas, by most coaches and teachers. It is actually ignored by some. Perhaps a small anecdote is in order. Harvard was preparing for an Ivy rival. The teams were rated quite even. All the first sets were very close, most going to extra games. Harvard won the singles 6–0. Surely it was not merely coincidence that we had spent over half our singles practice time in the week preceding the match on one thing: approach shots. The percentage results were quite visible: when we got a short ball, we made good on it a little more often, and made a few less errors, than our opponents. Working on approaches really pays off.

CHET MURPHY
JACK BARNABY

Center theory: volleyer can easily cover possible passing angles. However, volleyer's attacking angles disappear also.

4

Evaluating Yourself
as a Player

Whether a casual weekend player, a serious intermediate, or an established teaching pro, it is important for a tennis player to be familiar with the National Tennis Rating Program (NTRP). In searching for compatible matchups, participating in a league, or planning a path to continued improvement, the NTRP can be a very helpful tool.

In 1979 the USTA, USPTA, and the NTA (National Tennis Association) collaborated to create the NTRP. Their hope was to establish a universally acceptable rating program that would be free, easy to understand, and available to everyone. With the number of tennis players growing rapidly, it was felt that a consistent, nationally used rating system was necessary to insure continued growth and satisfaction in the sport.

The NTRP rates all players' abilities based upon performance in open adult categories. There is no age discrimination, but the two sexes are rated separately. A sixty-year-old man rated a 4.2 should be competitive with a sixteen-year-old boy with the same rating. The same holds true for females.

Rating categories are generalizations about skill levels. There is no substitute for on-court performance as a measure of playing ability for an accurate rating. A player's competitive record against others rated at similar levels is the best test of his or her rating. People may find that they actually play above or below a category that describes their skill level, depending on their competitive ability. It is common for a player with a stroke deficiency in one area to be rated at the same level or higher than a player without such a deficiency if he or she can play competitively at that level.

A "competitive" match is one in which the outcome is unpredictable. The ability levels of the players are so close that either player is capable of winning. Properly rated players within .2 of each other should be very competitive in playing ability. When one person consistently beats another they are not really considered competitive. Players with a .5 to 1.0 difference are usually compatible in ability. Although they are capable of having close matches, the outcome is predictable: the player with the higher rating usually wins.

When men and women compete with each other the women should normally carry higher ratings. A general guide is a difference of .5 at the 3.5 level and 1.0 at the higher levels.

Self Rating

Since the NTRP is so well organized it is easy for players to rate themselves. Players who can be objective can rate themselves accurately. Although a pro can be helpful in determining or verifying a rating, it is not necessary to depend on one.

The ideal rating is one which has been self set

and then adjusted based on match results. The category chosen is not meant to be static, but should be revised when skills change or match play demonstrates the need for reclassification. Players winning more than one tournament at their skill level should automatically move up to the next level.

Self ratings can be fun as well as informative. To place yourself, read through the NTRP instructions and rating categories that follow. It is easy to see which one best describes your present level.

To Place Yourself

1. Begin with 1.0. Read all categories carefully and then decide which one best describes your present ability level.

2. Be certain that you qualify on all points of all preceding categories as well as those in the classification you choose.

3. When rating yourself assume you are playing against a player of the same sex and the same ability.

4. Your self rating may be verified by a teaching professional, coach, league coordinator, or other qualified expert.

5. The person in charge of your tennis program has the right to reclassify you if your self placement is thought to be inappropriate.

NTRP Rating Categories

1.0 This player is just starting to play tennis.

1.5 This player has limited playing experience and is still working primarily on getting the ball over the net; has some knowledge of scoring, but is not familiar with basic positions and procedures for singles and doubles play.

2.0 This player may have had some lessons but needs on-court experience; has obvious stroke weaknesses but is beginning to feel comfortable with singles and doubles play.

2.5 This player has more dependable strokes and is learning to judge where the ball is going; has weak court coverage, or is often caught out of position, but is starting to keep the ball in play with other players of the same ability.

3.0 This player can place shots with moderate success; can sustain a rally of slow pace, but is not comfortable with all strokes; lacks control when trying for power.

3.5 This player has achieved stroke dependability and direction on shots within reach, including forehand and backhand volleys, but still lacks depth and variety; seldom double-faults and occasionally forces errors on the serve.

4.0 This player has dependable strokes on both forehand and backhand strokes; has the ability to use a variety of shots including lobs, overheads, approach shots, and volleys; can place the first serve and force some errors; is seldom out of position in a doubles game.

4.5 This player has begun to master the use of power and spins; has sound footwork; can control depth of shots and is able to move opponent up and back; can hit first serves with power and accuracy, and place the second serve; is able to rush net with some success on serve in singles as well as doubles.

5.0 This player has good shot anticipation; frequently has an outstanding shot or exceptional consistency around which a game may be structured; can regularly hit winners or force errors off of short balls; can successfully execute lobs, dropshots, half-volleys, and overhead smashes; has good depth and spin on most second serves.

5.5 This player can execute all strokes offensively and defensively; can hit dependable shots under pressure; is able to analyze opponents' styles, and can employ patterns of play to assure the greatest possibility of winning points; can hit winners or force errors with both first and second serves, return of serves can be an offensive weapon.

6.0 This player has mastered all the above skills; has developed power and/or consistency as a major weapon; can vary strategies and styles of play in a competitive situation; typically has had intensive training for national competition at junior or collegiate levels.

6.5 This player has mastered all of the preceding skills and is an experienced tournament competitor who regularly travels for competition, and whose income may be partially derived from prize winnings.

7.0 This is a world-class player.

Although it is possible to be rated in increments of .1, most organized tournaments, leagues, and ladders are set up on increments of .5. A player rated 2.7, for example, would be required to play in the 3.0 category in a league situation.

Some may prefer to be rated by a pro or an objective observer familiar with the system. Since

there is no set test to establish a rating, classifications are subject to change when competitive play results are analyzed. Verification may sometimes be required by a pro or a committee in league or similar situations.

The Professional Verification Guidelines are much more descriptive and can be very useful in rating, verifying, and planning improvement programs. These guidelines break each level down, stroke by stroke, and can give a more accurate reading of where a player stands and how to improve from there.

(Most teaching pros rate between 4.0 and 6.5, with the majority somewhere around 5.0.)

NTRP—A Guideline for Improvement

The NTRP can be extremely useful in pinpointing areas of weakness that need improvement. Because the levels are so well described, it is not too hard to figure out what it will take for a player to advance to the next level. Pros can use the NTRP as a guideline for their own improvement as well as that of their students.

One of the best examples of a program for improvement using the NTRP is Clarence Mabry's chart on "Effective Programing for the Adult Player."

Players rated at 5.0 or above are usually serious tennis players. They consist of talented juniors,

PRO VERIFICATION GUIDELINES

Rating	Forehand	Backhand	Serve
1.0	No concept of waist-level stroke. Most often swings from elbow at eye-level.	Most likely avoids backhands or misses completely.	No knowledge of service motion or procedure.
1.5	Late preparation; No follow through; Erratic contact; No direction.	Avoids backhands when possible. No change of grip.	Inconsistent toss and motion: Infrequent contact on center of strings; No follow through; No backscratch or full swing; Frequent double faults.
2.0	No directional intent. Infrequently in position. Can keep a rally of up to 3 hits when set up.	Grip problems; No follow through; Erratic contact; No direction; Faces net.	Mostly ½ swing; Frequently a back-forth motion; Can frequently get the ball into play; Double faults still common.
2.5	Form developing. Well prepared for moderate shots. Follows through on most shots. Fairly consistent on set-ups.	Still has grip and preparation problems. Lack of confidence; No follow through; Can compensate frequently for a ball coming to the BH side.	Starting a full motion; Can be consistent on the second serve; No directional intent; Frequently no backscratch.
3.0	Fairly consistent with some directional intent; Lacks depth control.	Little directional intent. Frequently prepared; Usually lacks follow through; Can be consistent on set-ups.	Developing rhythm; Little consistency when trying for power.
3.5	Good consistency on set-ups. Still lacks depth on difficult shots; Has directional intent on moderate balls; May have good preparation, but still weak on deep shots.	Preparation problems; Starting to hit with directional intent on easy shots; Starting to follow through instead of punch.	Starting to serve with some power and control. Tries to direct serves; Usually flat serves; May be trying to learn to use spin.
4.0	Dependable most of the time with consistent depth and control; Can control running FH; Starting to develop topspin; Frequently may try to hit too good a shot off the FH.	Player can direct the ball with consistency on each shot; Returns difficult shots defensively; Little control on running BHs; Still lacks depth.	Places both first and second serves; Frequent power on first serve with some control; Starting to use spin; Tends to overhit first serve.
4.5	Very dependable; Uses speed and spin effectively. Tends to overhit on difficult shots; Offensive on easy shots.	Can hit with depth. Usually not offensive; Can control direction and depth, but not under pressure.	Aggressive serving, with limited double faults; Uses power and spin; Still developing spin and offense on second serve; Frequently hits with good depth.
5.0	Strong shot with control, depth and spin; Uses FH to set up offensive situations; Has developed good touch; Consistent on passing shots.	Can use BH as an aggressive shot with good consistency; Has good direction and depth on most shots. Difficult shots are returned without intent of direction or depth, but can frequently hit winners off of set-ups.	Serve is placed effectively with the intent of hitting to a weakness or of developing an offensive situation; Can mix topspin, slice, and flat serves; Good depth and spin on most second serves, and few double faults.
		The 5.0 player frequently has an outstanding shot around which he can mold his game or protect weaknesses. Has sound strategy in singles and doubles and can vary game plan according to opponent. This player has become "match wise", and "beats himself" less than the 4.5 player. Covers court well,	

5.5 This player can hit dependable shots in stress situations; Has developed good anticipation, and can pick up cues from such things as opponent's toss, body position, backswing, preparation, etc. First and second serves can be depended on in stress situations and can be hit offensively at any time. Can analyze and exploit opponents' weaknesses.

6.0 These players will generally not need NTRP ratings, as their rankings or past rankings speak for themselves. The
to 6.0 player frequently has a teaching knowledge of the game and often travels from city to city for competition. The
7.0 6.5 player frequently makes travel-for-competition a part of his life-style, and sometimes earns a portion of his

(General Characteristics of Various Playing Levels)

Volley	Special Shots	Other
Makes little contact with the ball at net or doesn't go to net at all.		Little knowledge of scorekeeping and basic positioning.
Only FH volley; Infrequent success.		Little knowledge of - Difficulty with scorekeeping.
Frequently swings; Reluctant to play net; Avoids BH; No footwork; Successful on set-up FH's; No depth.		Can keep play moving in singles and doubles.
Can angle FH volley when set up. Does not bend for low volleys (usually drops racket head). Still uncomfortable at the net, especially on the BH side. Grip problems.	Can lob intentionally.	Weak court coverage; Cannot return lobs; Can return serve on FH consistently; Cannot adjust to variance in serves; Usually remains in the initial doubles position.
Consistent FH volleys; Frequently uses FH racket face on BH volleys; Can be offensive on set-ups. Inconsistent BH volley when using BH racket face; Has trouble with low and wide balls.	Can occasionally handle balls hit at the feet (but not with a good half-volley form). Can make contact on overheads; Can lob consistently.	Can frequently cover lobs in doubles; Recognizes offensive doubles play, but weak in its execution; Can return serve on the BH, but with little directional intent. Developing match play sense.
More aggressive net play. Some ability to cover side shots. Using proper footwork; Can direct FH volleys; Consistent contact, but little offense on BH volleys.	Can use full overhead swing on shots within reach. Recognizes approach shots and half volleys; Can place the return of serve.	Moves up and back well. Covering court fairly well. With doubles partner, can effectively cover the net.
Depth and control on FH volley; Can direct BH volleys, but usually lacks depth; Developing wide and low volleys on both sides of the body.	Can direct easy overheads; Can poach in doubles; Can hit both offensive and defensive lobs; Follows aggressive shots to the net; Hits to opponents' weaknesses.	Has more confidence, but rallies are still commonly lost due to impatience. Not yet playing good percentage tennis; Has developed teamwork in doubles.
Can handle a mixed sequence of volleys; Good footwork; Has depth and and directional control on BH; Developing touch; Most common error is still overhitting.	Approach shots with good depth and control; Can consistently hit overheads as far back as the service line; Starting to hit drop volleys; Can change pace on groundstrokes.	More intentional variety in game; Covers up weaknesses well; Plans tactics more than one shot ahead.
Can hit most volleys with depth, pace and direction; Can hit either flat or underspin volleys. Plays difficult volleys with depth; Given opportunity, volley is hit automatically for a winner.	Has added drop shot and lob volley to repertoire; Approach shots and passing shots are hit with a high degree of effectiveness.	

plays percentage tennis, and has good anticipation. Hits mid-court volley with consistency, but may lack depth. Serve return is consistent, and can gain offense against a weak second serve. Overhead can be hit from most any position on the court.

income from prize-winnings. The 7.0 player is generally committed to tournament competition as a life-style and frequently depends on tournament winnings as a portion of his income.

EFFECTIVE PROGRAMMING FOR THE ADULT CLUB PLAYER

Clarence Mabry

I. 2.5 Player—National Tennis Rating Program

A. Player Qualifications
1. Can keep ball in play—"Friendly Shots"
2. Usually gets serve in play, no power—"Powder Puff"
3. Can judge where balls will hit, difficult to move to it
4. Usually out of position

B. Activity Schedule
1. Leagues—clubs, city
2. Tournaments—clubs, city
3. Practice
   a. Bucket of balls
   b. Wall
   c. Practice partners
   d. Ball machine
   e. Pro workout
4. Instruction—sets and matches

C. Instruction Series
1. Forehand moving—backhand consistency
2. Forehand moving, lob—backhand consistency
3. Service placement and singles points from backcourt
4. Basic volley and overhead
5. Basic doubles—court position

D. Objective
1. Improve movement and court position
2. Learn basic volley and overhead
3. Improve placement of serve

II. 3.0 Player—National Tennis Rating Program

I'm frustrated!!

I still have trouble beating a 2.5 player and I've done everything that you recommend to become a 3.5 player.

I practice the forehand for power and worked on my placement of the serve. It's better but it just does not have the power that my 3.5 friends have.

I know I should play with the 3.5 players but I'm just not good enough.

What's my problem?

Answer

You answered your own problem—you are frustrated because you *know* more tennis than you can *execute*.

You are about a 3.0 player and are pressing to get to the 3.5 level.

The 3.0 level is somewhat of a transition level and progress becomes easy if you will be patient and evaluate your priorities.

First, gain confidence in placement of the ball before you worry about power. Power comes gradually with time and timing. Work now on placement and control. You know placement can be from side to side and short and deep.

Your groundstroke should land in the deep or maneuvering zone of the court, but you must learn to hit that zone from all positions on your court.

Your serve should be placed to the forehand, backhand or into the body of your opponent. Remember after you can place the balls, you must vary the placement.

Let's take a look at your program for the next few weeks.

Activities

Play as many different players as possible. Play 2.5 and 3.0 and occasionally 3.5 players just to practice your technique against different styles of play.

Practice without a partner—(wall, ball machine or bucket of balls) to improve form and confidence.

Instructions and Practice

Play forehands cross-court and down the line building intensity by repetition at a slow or moderate pace.

Work on playing balls from all three zones of the court, manuevering (deep), approach (mid-court) and at the net. Hit most of the balls back deep into your opponent's maneuvering zone.

Serve for placement to your opponent's forehand, backhand and into the body. Learn to vary these placements to keep your opponent off-balance.

Play points, games and sets with your pro and as many different players as possible.

Objective

Refine placement and control of the ball from all parts of the court.

Learn to play against different players.

O.K.—Now back to the basics and I'll see you at 3.5!

III. 3.5 Player—National Tennis Rating Program

A. Player Qualifications
1. Can move better, hits most balls from baseline
2. Placement of forehand both crosscourt and down the line, but the backhand still struggles for crosscourt consistency
3. Can volley easy balls and can return most lobs
4. Hits a few winners off of serve—better placement
5. Capable of playing balls in all zones of court with fewer easy errors

B. Activity Schedule
1. Leagues—really into the team tennis concept
2. Tournaments—need as many as possible for individual improvement
3. Practice—team practice and individual practice should become more frequent and better structured
4. Pro workouts or team workouts popular and recommended
5. Instruction—personal and team workouts needed

C. Instruction Series
1. Shot combinations
2. Doubles refinement—Serving team (1st & 2nd shot)
3. Doubles refinement—Receiving team
4. Doubles variations
5. Movement drills

D. Objective
1. Improve doubles and shot combinations

IV. 4.0 Player—National Tennis Rating Program

A. Player Qualifications
1. Effective doubles player
2. Ability to produce a variety of shots
3. Good placement of first serve
4. Dependable forehand and backhand

B. Activity Schedule
1. League and team play from varied areas
2. Plenty of doubles matches and tournaments
3. Practice on two week schedule to include basic groundstrokes, volleys, serves & overheads, plus shot combinations
4. Instruction—team workouts on a regular schedule most important
5. Good physical condition important

C. Instruction Series
1. Serve—targets and spin—return
2. Volley refinement
3. Play situations—singles
4. Play situations—doubles
5. Moving and winning shot drills

D. Objective
1. Refine shots, touch shots and singles styles

V. 4.5 Player—National Tennis Rating Program

A. Player Qualifications
1. Control of pace and spins (good racket control)
2. Able to move ball from all zones and hit into all zones
3. Solid serves, both first and second

B. Activity Schedule
1. Same as 4.0 with more singles play and competition

C. Instruction Series
1. Shot execution—serve/return
2. Shot execution—drop shot, passing shots & approach
3. Advanced volley, 1st volley, angle volley, drop volley, overhead, open court volley
4. Moving in baseline and ¾ court drill

D. Objective
1. Improve execution of serve and return
2. Learn to apply pressure on opponent with sound fundamentals and court position
3. Add new shots to basic abilities

college players, ranked seniors, competitive tournament players, and teaching pros.

These players have all the shots and can hit offensively from anywhere on the court. Tournaments, team competition, and plenty of practice are their major activities. Good physical and mental conditions are very important. Players at this level are primarily striving for more consistency, better execution, and good shot selection. They spend a lot of time playing matches and working on tactics and different styles of play.

The NTRP has come a long way since 1979. The establishment of new leagues, tournaments, and club and park programs has helped pave the way for increased activity and nation-wide acceptance of the most complete rating system in the world today.

JIM REFFKIN
CLARENCE MABRY

5

Eating for
Peak Performance

Nothing is more frustrating to me as a sports nutrition consultant than to watch weekend and world-class tennis players practice hour after hour, day after day, only to cripple their sports performance because of poor nutritional habits. Quite often, it's a player's extraordinary skill with knife and fork, not lack of skill with a tennis racquet, that determines the outcome of a tennis match.

Peak performance on the tennis court—those all too rare games or matches when everything seems to go right—can be *nutritionally engineered.* Even world champions such as Jimmy Connors and Martina Navratilova do not consistently enjoy the thrill of peak performance during every game, set, or match, but I maintain that they can—and just as importantly—so can *you.*

My research and work with amateur and professional tennis players has demonstrated that anyone, regardless of age or level of ability, can improve their endurance, stamina, energy, strength, and health through the science of sports nutrition. I work individually with athletes such as Gene Mayer, Sandy Mayer, Stan Smith, Harold Solomon, and Fred Stolle, and I can show *you* how to eat to win, before, during, and after you play.

Fueling Up before You Play

Imagine the perfect body fuel. It would supply pure energy, vitamins, minerals, and other nutri-

ents, and would be clean burning. Does such a perfect fuel exist? It certainly does, and it's no further away than your pantry shelf or local supermarket.

Unrefined complex carbohydrates—found in foods such as oatmeal, shredded wheat, and other whole grain cereals, brown rice, whole grain breads, buckwheat pancakes, fresh fruits, pasta, and potatoes—provide the perfect nutrition-packed fuel to energize even the most sluggish bodies before a tennis match or workout. But aren't these the very foods that most athletes avoid in order to stay trim and fit? And where is the protein? Steak and eggs, the time-honored "high protein" training table fare that well-meaning coaches and trainers recommend to help build stronger muscles and better athletes, is conspicuously absent from this ideal body fuel list.

My research has shown that the breakfast, lunch, and dinner of champions should contain plenty of complex carbohydrates, but only *moderate* amounts of protein. A high protein meal can actually deprive exercising muscles of vital water just when they need it most. Proteins require many times more water for digestion than carbohydrates, and excess protein (above 15 percent of the total kilocalories in a pre-match meal) can cause the loss of important vitamins and minerals in urine. Pro-

tein-induced dehydration and vitamin-mineral losses are two things that anyone who wants to eat to win can and should avoid.

Jimmy Connors, who regularly feasted on red meat prior to each tennis match, was surprised to learn that his pre-match high protein meal actually hampered rather than helped his on-court endurance and stamina. When I first discussed nutrition with Jimmy in 1981, he was sure of two things: (1) his opponents were getting younger and younger each year, and (2) he wasn't. Jimmy was looking for a winning edge, and I told him that the science of sports nutrition could provide the competitive advantages of increased endurance, energy, and stamina.

Jimmy followed my advice on a part-time basis at the Caesar's Palace-Alan King Tennis Classic, Wimbledon, and the U.S. Open. I would like to think that Jimmy's pre-match high carbohydrate/moderate protein meals fueled his enormous tennis talent and competitive drive to help him win these and subsequent tournaments at an age when most professional athletes consider retirement.

On-Court Nutrition

Anyone who has observed a professional tennis match already knows that players rarely eat solid food during match play. Liquids—soft drinks, fruit juices, fluid and electrolyte replacement beverages —seem to be the pick of the pros. Drinking, not eating, prevails as the most popular form of nutrient replacement during the change of sides.

In this case, the pros rightly choose liquids over solids, but the *type* of liquids they drink actually may hamper rather than help their performance. The American College of Sports Medicine (ACSM) has given popular commercial sports drinks, fruit drinks, and even natural fruit juices low marks for fluid replacement *during* physical activity. An ACSM research panel has determined that these beverages contain too much sugar and-/or salt for optimal sports performance. Consumption of sugar-saturated and salt-laden beverages can lead to stomach cramps, nausea, and can delay the absorption of water (the most important ingredient in all of these beverages) from the stomach to water-starved parts of the exercising body that need water most.

While research on the use of these and similar beverages is still inconclusive, the drink I recommend for weekend and professional athletes is water, water, and more water. Since thirst does not keep abreast of need, you will probably not be able to immediately replenish your total water loss during a tennis match: Harold Solomon, for example, can lose eight pounds of water in a single match.

That's why I advise all athletes to drink one pint of water prior to physical activity, and then consume *at least* one pint of water for every half hour of continuous exercise or competition. Actually, Australian tennis players have had it right for years. Champions such as Lew Hoad, Ken Rosewall, and Rod Laver replenished their body fluid losses with a drink made from water and orange juice—a mixture that comes very close to the fluid replacement recommendations of the ACSM.

Post-Match Nutrition

What you eat after your match or workout is just as important as what you eat before and, once again, complex carbohydrates assume a vital role in refueling your nutrient-depleted and match-weary body. Post-play nutrition, however, requires that you also eat a low fat protein source (usually from the animal kingdom) along with those all-important complex carbohydrates.

Martina Navratilova knows the value of a scientifically sound post-match meal and she diligently adheres to my nutritional recommendations to replenish her energy stores and to feed her nutrient-depleted body after each match. Martina enjoys animal protein sources such as poultry, chicken or turkey; seafood such as cod, scrod, lobster, halibut, sole; and an occasional but well-deserved "cheat"—Peking duck. She also chooses skim or low fat dairy products such as cottage cheese, yogurt, and milk to obtain additional protein as well as calcium, magnesium, and B vitamins. (Vegetarians can choose tofu [soybean cheese] and/or beans, peas, and lentils as good post-match protein sources.) In order to scientifically refuel *your* body and properly prepare for the next day's match or workout, choose complex carbohydrate foods such as pasta, potatoes, whole grain breads, fruits, and vegetables, and *supplement* these peak performance staples with four ounces of a low fat protein source such as seafood or poultry. (Vegetarians should consume approximately two cups of beans, peas, or lentils, or about eight ounces of tofu.)

A Final Word about Fat

With one exception, fat is a non-essential nutrient for human life. Linoleic acid, an oil abundantly found in whole grains, cereals, vegetables, and certain fish, is the only "fat" the body requires. While other fats and oils perform important biological functions, linoleic acid is the single fat that we must eat to live.

Peak performance eating requires that you consume no more than 20 percent of your daily kilocalories from total fats and oils. Since fats and oils supply nine kilocalories per gram, an athlete who consumes 2000 kilocalories per day should eat no more than 44 grams of total fats and oils. I counsel athletes in all sports to limit their total fat to between five and 20 percent of their total daily kilocalories for two reasons: (1) excess dietary fat can reduce the maximum oxygen carrying capacity of blood and, thus, can decrease aerobic power and peak performance and (2) high fat diets can increase the risk of cardiovascular disease and diet-related cancers.

The nutritional recommendations of the past are unsound and inappropriate for today's athletes. If you consistently want to play your personal best, then forget the traditional high protein, high fat sports diet, and adopt my high carbohydrate, low fat dietary recommendations. You really *can* nutritionally engineer peak performances—just ask Jimmy, Martina, or any of the other professional athletes I've counseled. These champions don't play to lose; they eat to win.

Slow Down Aging with Anti-Oxidants

Anti-oxidants help protect us from premature aging and damaging chemicals in our food, air, and water supply. None of us can escape the ubiquitous environmental pollution, rancid fats, and oils in our diet, and free radicals (harmful atomic and molecular structures that damage the body's cells) with anti-oxidants such as vitamins E, C, and beta-carotene (pro-vitamin A).

I strongly recommend that you get these and other important anti-oxidants first from the foods you eat and then, if required, from pure supplements. Since the foundation of a proper anti-oxidant regimen begins with diet, here is a list of foods you can enjoy while deriving the anti-aging and health promoting benefits of anti-oxidants.

Beta-carotene. Beta-carotene is a non-toxic form of vitamin A that can protect your lungs against air pollution, cigarette smoke, and other damaging substances. It promotes healthy lung function and may protect us against several forms of environmentally induced cancer. It is an excellent scavenger of free radicals and can be found in abundance in your local supermarket. Sweet potatoes, yams, hard yellow squash, and carrots are just a few of the vegetables that provide ample amounts of beta-carotene.

Vitamin C. Vitamin C, the anti-scurvy vitamin, is another powerful scavenger of free radicals. While scientists continue to debate its effectiveness in preventing and ameliorating the common cold, vitamin C's anti-oxidant protection is well-known for inactivating cancer-causing chemicals in our foods such as nitrates and pesticides. Vitamin C is a water soluble vitamin that is easily destroyed or lost in cooking and storage of foods. A fat soluble form of vitamin C, ascorbyl palmitate, can also help protect cells from free radical attack and is available in some non-prescription vitamin preparations. Mother Nature has added Vitamin C to tomatoes, citrus fruits, broccoli, and many other fruits and vegetables.

Vitamin E. Vitamin E occurs in unrefined grains and cereals and vegetables and is a potent free radical deactivator. A high fat diet, such as the ordinary American diet, not only contains sub-optimal amounts of vitamin E, but also destroys large amounts of this important anti-oxidant as well. Brown rice, oatmeal, whole wheat, and soy-beans provide a rich supply of this all-purpose anti-oxidant.

Selenium. Recent research has shown that cancer frequency increases in areas of the U.S. where the selenium content of the soil is poor. While the evidence is inconclusive, scientists have shown that a highly refined diet of white flour, sugar, and red meat contains sub-optimal amounts of this potent anti-oxidant that works with vitamin E to protect our bodies from free radical damage. Since selenium can be toxic even in small amounts, try to get the selenium you need from whole grains, fresh fruits, and vegetables. If you must take a selenium supplement, take no more than 50–100 micrograms daily.

The New Peak Performance Supplements

Tennis players, indeed all active people, seem to be searching for that special substance that will give them increased energy, endurance, and stamina. The search for the "right stuff" has created an area of nutrition known as ergogenics, or the science of energy enhancing foods and food concentrates.

Health faddists and opportunistic vitamin manufacturers offer all sorts of ergogenic nostrums —bee pollen, spirulina, super-oxide dismutase, and a host of other substances—to trusting athletes in search of a magic pill to boost their performance. Responsible research has shown, however, that several widely available, legal, and non-prescription compounds really do seem to provide a competitive edge for weekend to world-class athletes. While the research with these substances is far from con-clusive, there is *suggestive* evidence that one or more of the following substances may prove to be a true ergogenic aid.

Octacosanol. Octacosanol is a 28-carbon, straight-chain fatty acid found in wheat germ oil and other vegetable oils. Scientists have tested oc-tacosanol in laboratory animals with some success, and the U.S. Navy has tested it in divers. Oc-tacosanol appears to enhance the delivery and utili-zation of oxygen by active muscles (including heart muscle) and, thus, provides the potential for in-creased endurance and stamina.

L-Carnitine. L-carnitine is a molecular car-rier of fatty acids from the cytoplasm of a cell into its energy-producing plant called the mitochond-rion. L-carnitine, thus, promotes the efficient burn-ing of fat with the release of over twice the energy derived from protein or carbohydrate. Even though the human body can synthesize L-carnitine from other chemicals, additional intake of L-carni-tine may prove to further enhance energy produc-tion. More research is needed, however, before we can be certain of the efficacy of L-carnitine.

Coenzyme Q-10. This is an electron-tran-sporting molecule that helps our body replenish its supply of ATP (adenosine triphosphate), an essen-tial high energy compound required for muscle contraction. Like L-carnitine, co-enzyme Q-10 is present in almost every cell in our body, but ath-letes may benefit from additional amounts, espe-cially during strenuous competition or training. Research with co-enzyme Q-10 will require careful testing for several more years before scientists can rightly claim that it is a true ergogenic substance.

The Unique Nutritional Needs of Female Tennis Players

The National Academy of Science's (NAS) Food and Nutrition Board suggests that women eat 1800–2200 kilocalories per day to maintain their ideal weight. My research and clinical experience has convinced me that for most women, this recommendation may be excessive. Most women, even those who enjoy regular physical activity, tend to gain weight on 1800 plus kilocalories a day. In fact, many active women I've counseled have had trouble reaching their ideal weight until they reduced their intakes to less than 1000 kilocalories daily.

Unfortunately, many nutritionists still believe that if you eat 3500 kilocalories less than you nor-mally do each week (or if you burn off that same number of kilocalories through exercise), then you'll lose a pound of fat. If that kind of reasoning were correct, then most of the 30–50 million markedly overweight Americans would all be thin

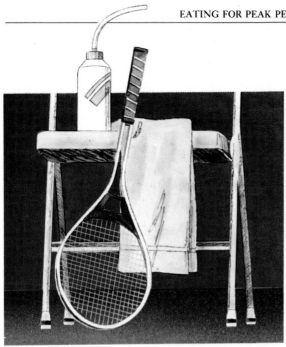

by now. The nutritional truth is that your body, in all its wisdom, hasn't yet learned the 3500 kilocalorie rule. When you reduce your food intake or increase exercise, or both, your body eventually slows down its rate of burning fat and eventually you reach the bane of every weight-conscious dieter—the dreaded plateau! Active women who count calories may actually require *less energy* to maintain their body weight than their fatter, lazier friends need.

Blame Mother Nature. Even in all her wisdom, she still hasn't learned that this is 1984; that you microwave your evening meal instead of hunting and killing it; that you drive to the grocery store for food instead of planting, sowing, and harvesting it. You see, dear Mother Nature still thinks that you're a cavewoman. Well, why not? You still live in the same primitive body, with the same genetics, as your prehistoric ancestors. Yes, Mother Nature, like the Food and Nutrition Board, still lingers in the past.

Active women require more exercise and less kilocalories than they've been led to believe. A moderately active woman who exercises 3–5 days a week and weighs about 125 pounds (and stands about 5′5″ tall) probably requires no more than 1400–1600 kilocalories per day of a high complex carbohydrate, low fat diet—the kind I've recommended and described in *Eat to Win: The Sports Nutrition Bible* (Rawson Associates, New York,

1983). My "Peak Performance Program," which takes into account the special nutritional needs of active women, provides the optimal amount of proteins, fats, carbohydrates, vitamins, and minerals for your individual needs, based on your gender, blood chemistry, and specific sport requirements.

Ironing Out Iron Needs

Active women need iron, but not from a bottle or tablet. Long ago, an advertising genius invented the phrase "tired blood" for a well-known iron-rich liquid vitamin supplement, and since then generations of American women have mistakenly assumed that (1) there's such a thing as tired blood, and (2) they need to take iron supplements for good health. The name of one popular iron supplement even implies that it's formulated especially for women. Move over Geritol and FemIron—make way for beans, peas, lentils, vegetables, and fruits!

The NAS's Food and Nutrition Board recommends that women consume 18 milligrams of iron each day, especially iron from animal sources such as red meat, poultry, and seafood (milk and cheese are poor sources of iron). Women who eat an ordinary American diet would have to consume at least 3000 kilocalories as well as excessive amounts of animal products (with their associated saturated fat and cholesterol content) each day in order to meet this arbitrarily high RDA (recommended daily allowance) for iron. Even more confusing, *pregnant and lactating women cannot meet the RDA for iron at all through food intake!*

Iron supplements have been reported to cause constipation and gastrointestinal irritation, and have also been associated with liver, kidney, and bone damage.

From 1400 to 1600 kilocalories per day for weight maintenance, 3000 or more kilocalories per day to meet the U.S. RDA for iron—is this modern woman's "Catch-22"?

Large iron intakes pose a nutritional risk and a caloric disaster. You can safely meet your body's need for iron if you consume unrefined cereals and grains, along with legumes, dark leafy vegetables, and fresh fruits. On this kind of nutrient-dense diet, you'll even achieve the RDA of 1.8 milligrams of daily iron without the health risks associated with excess calories, saturated fat, cholesterol, and protein—something you can't do if you eat the ordinary over-processed American diet.

Protein Problems

Even though research scientists long ago established that high protein diets foster osteoporosis (a progressive disease affecting mainly women that results in calcium and mineral loss from bone, resulting in bone fractures and spinal column degeneration), toxemia of pregnancy, kidney damage, and increased risk of heart disease and cancer, the U.S. RDAs for protein have remained too high. The Food and Nutrition Board is getting the message—s-l-o-w-l-y. Since 1941, the board has lowered the protein RDA by a full 20 percent. The current protein RDA for women is still too high, but if the Food and Nutrition Board stays on schedule, they'll publish the optimal protein RDA for women by the year 2027!

Please don't wait until then to eat the correct amount of protein. Even if you take calcium and other mineral supplements, studies have shown that a high protein diet will still cause more calcium and minerals to be lost than you ingest.

You don't have to rely on milk or other dairy products to get calcium. Since dairy products provide active women with little iron and no fiber, I recommend that you choose dark green vegetables such as broccoli (don't rely too heavily on spinach to get your calcium because it contains oxalates, which prevent the body from absorbing the calcium that it contains), beans, peas, or lentils as excellent sources of calcium, fiber, vitamins, and minerals. If you're trying to reduce your cholesterol intake, remember that there's not a speck of it in the vegetable kingdom (spirulina—a blue-green algae—is the only exception to this rule I have found). Broccoli provides the most calcium for the least amount of fat (and calories) of any of the foods listed.

A high complex carbohydrate intake (lots of brown rice, whole grain cereals and breads, potatoes, a variety of vegetables including legumes, fresh fruits), skim milk dairy products (up to 1½ cups per day if desired), and several ounces of poultry and seafood will provide more than enough protein and calcium for any active woman, including those who are pregnant or lactating. Most nutritionists and physicians I've talked to forget that the six to seven percent protein content of human breast milk is more than adequate for babies who will *double* their birth weight in the first six months of life. There is no other growth period during life that requires so much protein, yet dietitians today still recommend that pregnant women consume 74 grams of protein each day (that's 30 grams *more* than they recommend for non-pregnant women) despite the fact that a fetus requires less than six grams of protein per day during its entire nine-month growth period!

A high complex carbohydrate intake and active lifestyle can help reduce a woman's protein and calcium requirements; a high protein diet raises them and, along with inactivity, promotes osteoporosis and other degenerative diseases. I think the message is clear. Optimal health requires that active women reduce their currently high protein intake and increase their consumption of legumes, whole grains, and dark green vegetables.

ROBERT HAAS, PH.D.

6

Fitness, Conditioning, Injury Prevention and Treatment

Tennis players of all levels, from beginners to professionals, generally have a strong interest in fitness. At the higher levels, players worry about being fit enough to play well, while at the lower levels, players try to play enough to keep fit. But no player can achieve fitness with tennis alone. And unfortunately for beginners, it's the more highly skilled players who derive the greatest benefits from playing tennis.

The reason for this is that advanced players and professionals can hit the ball harder and faster and keep it in play longer than recreational players. They are much more likely to engage in specific practice drills and they are highly motivated to improve their fitness. They also play harder and longer than recreational players. As a result, they are more apt to improve the areas of fitness appropriate to tennis.

There is no denying that beginners and players at lower levels gain some fitness benefits from playing tennis. But the player's level of expertise clearly affects the extent of those benefits. As it happens, even professional tournament players fall short in some aspects of physical fitness. So tennis players at all levels need to assess their strengths and deficiencies and set goals for improvement.

Remember—no one should play tennis to get into shape, rather everyone should get into shape to play tennis.

Conditioning

No one sport can offer a total conditioning program for the human body. However, playing tennis automatically provides elements of conditioning, so all players can improve their general fitness to some degree while they develop their tennis skills. For total conditioning supplemental exercise is essential. A program of exercise must give serious attention to the following: strength, flexibility, aerobics, and anaerobics.

Strength

In all sport-specific exercises, including tennis, the more you play the more likely you are to create muscle imbalances, thereby risking injury. Later, we will discuss how to avoid problems in these areas. The following are the body's potential trouble spots for tennis players.

Forearm. The muscles that bend (flexors) and straighten (extensors) the forearm and the muscles that turn the palm up (supinators) tend to be quite strong. The pronators, which turn the palm down, are also relatively strong. But the muscles that move the forearm laterally (the radial and ulnar deviators) and those that straighten (extensors) are characteristically weak and susceptible to injury.

1, *Faulty Backhand:* Lack of lower body and shoulder action invites forearm injury

Arm. Biceps and triceps as a whole are weak, amazingly so in comparison to the forearm musculature—even in world-class players.

Shoulder. External rotators and shoulder blade muscles generally are weaker than other muscle groups.

Neck and Upper Trunk. Musculature in the neck and upper trunk is generally weak.

Abdomen. The opposite abdominal muscles (e.g., left abdominal muscles in right-handed players) are usually stronger than muscles on the same side.

Thigh and Groin. The groin muscles are generally weak compared to the leg, hamstring, and hip-thigh muscles.

Leg. Calf muscles are generally strong, but there is a weakness in the front shin muscles.

Flexibility

Tennis playing does very little to improve flexibility, with the possible exception of shoulder rotation. In fact, playing often inhibits flexibility in the racket-wielding arm and in the legs. As in other sports involving running, constant tennis playing tightens the back, groin, hamstrings, and calves. Since almost everyone plays tennis primarily with one arm, the forearm extensors will be much tighter at the elbow of that arm. It is clear, then, that activity to improve flexibility must come from another source.

Aerobics

Tennis is not aerobic to the extent that biking, swimming, and running are, but tournament players do develop reasonably good aerobic capacity.

Anaerobics

Since tennis is by nature a stop and start sport, anaerobic conditioning of selected muscles (forearm, shoulder, calf, abdominals) is inevitable.

What this discussion comes down to is this: you can't get into peak condition and stay there by simply playing tennis. And you can't play your bet tennis until you get into condition. The answer is conditioning exercise. Recreational and tournament players alike should structure an exercise program to strengthen inadequate muscles and to promote flexibility to counteract the tightening effects of tennis playing. Ask your doctor for a specific fitness evaluation and fashion an exercise program tailored to your condition and level of play.

Injury Prevention

A very important first step in preventing injury is to establish your goals. Do your tennis ambitions include world-class performance, or are you content with a social mixed-doubles game once a week? Understanding your goals will help you to design a conditioning program that will forestall injury.

It is especially important for adults learning the game or picking it up after many years to review their medical histories so that a proper conditioning program can be designed to strengthen any body areas that might break down under stress. Consider an ex-football player who suffered a knee injury at 18 and wishes to begin playing tennis at 45. Taking up tennis without a rehabilitative knee program beforehand would surely invite trouble.

Once you have set your goals, reviewed your medical history, and designed an appropriate conditioning program, it becomes important to develop correct tennis technique. Poor stroke technique can quickly lead to wrist sprain, tennis elbow, or shoulder tendinitis, so beginners are advised to seek instructional help from a certified pro. The following injuries are often related to errors in technique.

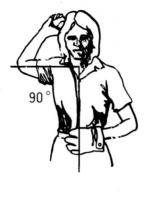

2, *Shoulder Technique:* 90° angle invites injury to rotator tendon cuff. Higher angle is more protective

*SOURCE "Arm Care," by Robert P. Nirschl, M.D. Courtesy of Medical Sports, Inc. Publishing, Arlington, Virginia.

Wrist Sprain

The exaggerated laid back wrist position is a common factor in causing sprain of the ligaments of the small finger (ulnar) side of the wrist as well as the back of the wrist. Tennis students often overdo the tennis instructor's admonition to lay the wrist back. Unfortunately, in this position, shock absorption is nil, inviting sprain of the wrist ligaments.

Tennis Elbow (Lateral)

The faulty technique causing lateral tennis elbow is exaggerated use of the forearm wrist extensor muscle, for example, leading with your elbow or punching backhands. Power source and control source are concentrated in relatively weak muscles that quickly "overload," resulting in lateral tennis elbow tendinitis. The correct stroke pattern of course uses the more powerful shoulder muscles, proper weight transfer, and knee action.

Tennis Elbow (Medial)

This condition often results from an overload caused by rolling the forearm over in an attempt at topspin. Consistently late forehand strokes requiring excessive wrist snap are also a common cause. This stroke pattern is usually accompanied by poor weight transfer and knee action. Even tournament-class performers become victims of medial tennis

elbow. In their case, the problem is caused by the overhead and serve. The difficulty stems from the acceleration of the racket head out of the back-scratch position. Unfortunately, the technique is perfectly proper, which makes the malady more difficult to remedy.

Shoulder Tendinitis

For recreational players, excessive serving or overhead practice are often the cause. Pain is felt in the front of the shoulder. Any tennis technique that places the arm at 90° to the trunk—for instance, the serve, overhead, and any high follow-through—invites irritation of the rotator cuff.

Selecting Equipment

In addition to poor technique, poor equipment can also lead to tennis injuries, and correct use of proper equipment can help any player to avoid and/or overcome many tennis-related problems.

Although wrist sprain and shoulder tendinitis are troublesome to a few, tennis elbow is easily the most common problem for tennis players. The following suggestions on equipment can help prevent tennis elbow problems for the average adult tennis player:

1. Light mid-sized racket (12½ ounce range)— Hitting from a proper position is the best way

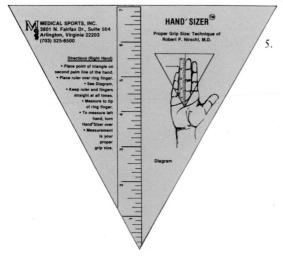

MEDICAL SPORTS, INC.
3801 N. Fairfax Dr., Suite 504
Arlington, Virginia 22203
(703) 525-8500

HAND'SIZER ™

Proper Grip Size: Technique of
Robert P. Nirschl, M.D.

Directions (Right Hand)
• Place point of triangle on
second palm line of the hand.
• Place ruler over ring finger.
• See Diagram.
• Keep ruler and fingers
straight at all times.
• Measure to tip
of ring finger.
• To measure left
hand, turn
Hand'Sizer over
• Measurement
is your
proper
grip size.

Diagram

3, *Hand Sizer:* Nirschl's technique of hand measurement to determine proper grip size. Measure from 2nd palm crease to tip of ring finger.

to avoid tennis elbow. A lighter racket makes it easier to attain the correct position. So find one that suits your game. In particular, graphite, graphite composite, and metal frames with OPS design offer a combination of power, light weight, and maneuverability. Mid-sized frames seem preferable to standard or oversized frames for most players.

2. Proper grip size—To be sure the grip of your racket is the correct size, check with the measuring scale illustrated here. The measurement is made between the long and ring fingers since this line bisects the palm of the hand from the thumb to the small finger.

3. String—Although gut strings may be easier on the elbow at first, the benefits disappear as the gut ages. So a good nylon is probably best for most tennis players.

4. String tension—It is my clinical observation that medium string tension is best for sensitive arms and, therefore, probably wise to use as a preventive measure. Tennis elbow sufferers should string their rackets three pounds less than the manufacturer's specifications. Of course, there is a wide range of personal preferences which should be considered in choosing a racket. In fact, you should test a variety of rackets for playability as well as comfort.

But be sure to select a weight light enough to discourage tennis elbow.

5. Counter-force bracing—Counter-force braces are non-elastic supports that decrease force overloads and pain. Characteristics of the true counter-force brace are a curved design to fit the conical shapes of arms and legs, non-elastic materials to enhance muscle control and eliminate the potential for nerve pinch and blood vessel blockage, and multiple tension straps to allow adjustment by the patient. Recent biomechanical studies done in the laboratory at the University of Illinois have indicated that counter-force braces change the sequential firing of the muscles as well as the angular velocities in and about the areas braced. Statistical evaluation reveals that the use of counter-force braces minimized the intensity of the symptoms in the overwhelming majority of patients. In view of the evidence, we can conclude that the use of counter-force braces can act as a deterrent to injury and pain symptoms, provided the patient also performs strength training exercises.

6. Intensity and duration of activity—An awareness of skill level, equipment used, and overall conditioning is critical in establishing an exercise program. Under-conditioned individuals who participate in sudden, aggressive activities or are active for too long a period invite injury (the weekend warrior syndrome). So, exercise, but don't overdo it.

Emergency Care

Emergency care procedure is similar for all body injuries. To remember the steps to be taken for the treatment of emergency injury, think of PRICE:

P—Protection.

R—Rest.

I —Ice.

C—Compression.

E—Elevation.

Protection can be undertaken in a variety of ways. It is best to allow the injured individual to test the injured area. If there is obvious distortion of the injured part, splinting is called for (even wrapping the part with a pillow or with rolled magazines if more sophisticated equipment is not available). In injuries to the lower body the athlete should not attempt to put full weight on the lower extremities.

Rest is the companion of protection. Moving

the injured part should be avoided. On the other hand, movement of uninjured parts that do not cause pain to the injured part are to be encouraged, as this minimizes atrophy and speeds healing. Rest helps prevent further injury and allows the healing process to proceed unimpeded. Rest must be interpreted not as absence from activity, but as absence from *abusive* activity.

Ice is most effectively used for cold applications. Cold applications are beneficial in blocking pain, relieving spasm, and decreasing the risk of swelling and inflammation. Applying ice cubes in a plastic bag to the injured areas, 30 minutes on and 30 minutes off, has proved effective. Ice application is helpful for as long as potential for inflammation/swelling is present. This determination is made by examination of the injured area for inflammatory signs (i.e., local tenderness, swelling, presence of heat or fever in the injured area, and pain in the injured part at rest). If any of these signs are present, the application of ice should be continued. (NOTE: On occasion, this situation may persist for a matter of days or weeks.)

Compression is helpful to control swelling. It should be understood that excessive elastic compression applied in the mid-part of a limb, for instance, the knee, may cause swelling distally (i.e., in the ankle and foot). Compressive bandages should, therefore, be applied starting from the end of an extremity. An air sleeve which intermittently milks fluid out of an extremity has proved an excellent advance in the control and elimination of swelling.

Elevation helps greatly to control swelling by encouraging the flow of fluid from the injured member to the heart. To be effective, the elevation must be above the level of the heart. An injured lower extremity whether it be knee, leg, ankle, or foot must be elevated above shoulder level for best results. Upper extremity parts likewise must be elevated above the shoulder. For example, an injured hand should be carried on top of the head if possible, rather than carried in a sling.

Definitive diagnosis is extremely important. Once the preceding five emergency steps have been carried out, the injured person should be taken promptly to a physician for diagnosis and treatment. This is especially true in major ligament injuries to the lower extremities, especially the knee, where early surgical repair often offers the best long-term solution. (Fortunately, this injury is rare in tennis.)

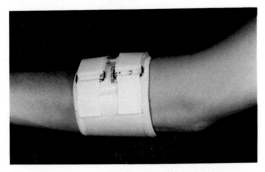

4, *Lateral Elb'-aid:* Counter-force brace for lateral tennis elbow.
True Counter-force braces are non-elastic, wide, curved to fit conical extremity shapes and have multiple tension straps for full controlled support.

Definitive Care of Common Tennis Injuries

The basic ingredients for definitive care of all sports injuries, including tennis ones, are as follows:

Inflammation and pain control.
Healing promotion.
Exercise.
Force overload control.
Surgery (when indicated).

Inflamation and pain can be effectively controlled with the steps described for emergency care. Of course, a much wider range of anti-inflammatory medications is available to physicians. A physician, skilled in sports diagnoses and the use of medications for swelling, can approach each injury as a unique case. Also, physicians have access to physical therapies, which have proved helpful in the control of pain and inflammation.

Healing is indirectly related to the control of inflammation and pain. However, anti-inflammatory medications as well as rest do *not* actually promote the healing process, but are instrumental in eliminating further aggravation. At present, two basic options are helpful in the promotion of healing. Rehabilitative exercise and high voltage galvanic stimulation.

Rehabilitative exercise is very specific and precise, highly supervised, graduated, and best performed under the directions of a physician, physical therapist, or certified athletic trainer. Lay books and magazines offer a wide variety of exercises, but performing them is left to the discretion of the injured patient and could possibly result in injury.

5, *Iso'-flex Exercise:* Convenient, effective exercise for rehabilitation and conditioning, utilizing tension cord resistance.
*SOURCE ''Arm Care,'' by Robert P. Nirschl, M.D.

High voltage galvanic stimulation is prescribed by a physician and supervised by a physical therapist or athletic trainer.

Exercise may be divided into two main categories: rehabilitative and sport. The goals of the first are to encourage healing and maintenance of healed tissue. In sport exercise the goals are to win and to improve skill. Since the goals are divergent, we must be careful not to confuse our exercise needs.

Exercise programs include strength, endurance, and flexibility exercises. In the early stages, strength exercises are generally most productive. Strength exercises include isometrics, calisthenics, isoflex exercises, isotonics, and isokinetics.

All of these five have a place in fitness and rehabilitation programs. Often, all five are prescribed at various stages. Each system can also be used in different ways—by varying arcs of motion, amounts of resistance, number of repetitions, speed technique (i.e., pushing versus pulling).

Endurance programs utilize the same general systems as strengthening exercises, but usually the amount of resistance diminishes as the speed of exercise and quantity of repetitions increases.

For most injured body areas, exercises to increase flexibility are not very important. Indeed, it has been my observation that early flexibility exercise for the hamstring muscles and groin invites further aggravation of the injury rather than aiding in healing, as is commonly thought. In general, flexibility is tackled last—with the possible exception of exercises for the shoulder.

Rehabilitation requires that we neutralize the forces that were instrumental in causing injury. The methods available to control abusive force loads have already been described. They include counter-force bracing, selection of proper equipment, use of correct technique, and care in monitoring the intensity and duration of physical activity.

I have been prescribing counter-force bracing since 1970 and have had ample opportunity to observe its helpful effect in a variety of areas, including tennis elbow, wrist sprain, back and abdominal problems, groin and thigh injuries, runner's knee, shin splints, and heel spurs. But, to repeat, each counter-force brace must be designed to conform to the anatomy of the injured part and must support the injured area.

Correct technique is vital to control harmful force overloads. In tennis, we are fortunate that good technique is good medicine. All patients suffering from tennis elbow, shoulder tendinitis, or wrist sprain should check their tennis strokes and overall technique to uncover any deficiencies. It would be wise as well to seek professional tennis instruction to correct any problems in tennis mechanics.

Finally, if players are sporadic and inconsistent in their activity, they invite injury. Even with steady play, stress and fatigue can result in injuries.

Surgery is indicated only when all other options have been exhausted. It has been my observation that, after some types of surgery for tendinitis about the shoulder and elbow, a player may have trouble returning to tennis. It is vital that a patient discuss thoroughly with his or her surgeon exactly what is proposed and how the surgeon proposes to do it. In general, it is better to avoid muscle-slide operations about the elbow and to avoid any major dissection of the shoulder acromion bone or the deltoid muscle about the shoulder. Overall, surgical success at elbow and shoulder is 85 percent cure and 12 percent improvement, using modern techniques.

The common tennis injuries treated over a period of years at Virginia Sports Medicine Institute include, naturally, tennis elbow, shoulder tendinitis, wrist sprain, and knee, leg, and back problems. A description of our treatment of lateral tennis elbow at Virginia Sports Medicine Institute will serve to illustrate the comprehensive attention given all victims of sports injuries. Tennis elbow is treated with anti-inflammatory medications, and tennis activity is halted for approximately three weeks. Treatment continues with high voltage galvanic stimulation, whirlpools followed by massage, a graduated exercise program, a full review of equipment, and a lateral elbow counter-force brace.

This procedure is followed by a gradual return to tennis activities, concentrating on stroke mechanics, with the aid of a certified tennis professional.

The usual time required for this treatment is from two to three months. If proper exercise programs and rehabilitation procedures have been followed and the patient makes no progress during this period, surgery to repair the damaged tissue should be considered.

But keep in mind that surgery is a last resort, to be called upon when all other options have been tried and failed.

ROBERT P. NIRSCHL., M.D.

7

Effective Planning and Drills for Improvement

In tennis, match play itself does not provide sufficient practice for you to improve your abilities at many of the strokes and shots you need to play well. For example, in a particular match you may have to hit only four or five overhead smashes. If your smash is weak, you are not likely to improve it with that meager number of hits. Instead, you need the opportunity to repeat the shot time and time again. The same goes for other strokes and shots in the game. Skill comes through repetition. It is only through repetitive practice, during which you consciously work on specific points of form on specific strokes, that you can learn to use strokes effectively in serious play.

You can arrange this repetitive practice for yourself with the aid of a partner. Ask among your playing friends to find one who wants to practice with you. You should have little trouble finding someone whose deficiencies in the game are similar to yours. Plan some drills designed specifically to help you both to overcome those deficiencies.

In the remainder of this chapter I describe several drills used by experienced teachers and coaches. Study them briefly and then use as many of them as fit your needs.

As you select drills, start by carefully analyzing your game. Break your game down so you can best determine your strong points and weak ones. What do you do best and where are you weakest?

Which shots are you confident with and on which shots are you uncertain? What tactics and strategies usually work for you and what tactics do you seldom use or perhaps never use? And what about your opponents? What tactics and strategies of theirs bother you? How can you play better against those opponents? Do you have the strokes and shots to use effectively against them?

One good way to analyze and understand your own game is to prepare a "Personal Form Analysis Sheet." An example of one is shown.

Analyze each stroke in your repertoire; forehands and backhands for groundstrokes and volleys, serves and returns of serve, lobs and smashes, and other special shots such as dropshots, topspin lobs, sliced approach shots, etc. Then describe your strength or weakness on each stroke and/or shot. As you do so, judge your stroke for form and your shots for tactical use. In writing, rate each stroke and shot for quality, either in narrative form or with terse comments.

On the back of the analysis sheet prepare a graphic picture of your game, as shown in the example. Rate your strokes and shots on a scale from one to ten and draw in the zigzag line to show how they rate. This kind of graphic picture will reinforce your comments made on the analysis sheet. But more importantly, it will vividly point out the need for certain kinds of practice.

MY PERSONAL FORM ANALYSIS CHART

GROUNDSTROKES Forehand Footwork Backhand Application—steadiness, speed, accuracy, control of depth, control rally	
VOLLEYS Forehand Footwork Backhand Application—consistency, placement, crispness, take speed off	

SERVE Application—consistency, variety, placement, depth, effectiveness
RETURN OF SERVE Application—consistency, defense, attack, variety (control speed and direction)
OVERHEAD SMASH—consistency, speed, placement, movement

LOBS—variety, control of depth, height; Tactical use of Tactical use of	DROPSHOTS—control of depth and direction

READINESS, QUICKNESS, AGILITY, MOVEMENT

APPLICATION OF FORM

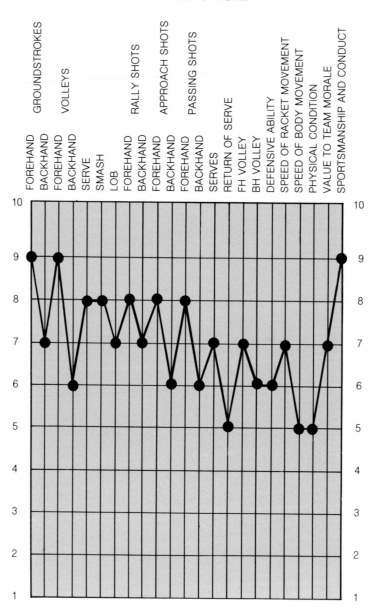

A graphic picture of your game, based on a scale of
1 to 10, with 10 representing an excellent score (an
excellent stroke or shot) at your level of competition

As you plan your practice sessions allow time for regular work at the several shots, strokes, and tactics that occur regularly in match play, primarily serving and returning serve—skills required on every point. Also, the ability to sustain a rally from the backcourt is necessary. And sooner or later, skill at volleying and at passing a net player is required. These are basic skills, and practicing them will provide the groundwork for effective play.

As you plan your practice you must weigh various limits. For example, you must decide how much time you can spend on stroke practice and how much time on tactics, and how much time for "play for practice" as contrasted to time spent on serious competitive play. Here you must be selective. You may have to choose only drills that you need most and that give maximum return for the time you spend on them.

A master practice chart can help you keep track of the kind and amount of practice you are getting. Prepare one for yourself, one like the example shown.

On the left-hand margin of a blank sheet of paper, list all the practice items you feel you need. For example, you will want to practice at least the following: backcourt rallying for steadiness, approach shots, passing shots, serves, and first volleys.

In addition to these basic items you will probably also want to practice other skills. For instance, you will want to return some serves early and short, others, late and deep. You will want to stay back after some service returns and to move in to volley after others. You will want to practice volleying from the ideal volley location and from the "T," and possibly even from "no-man's" land. You will want to practice passing a net player and passing a net rusher coming in on an approach shot. List all of these in a column.

As you practice these special items and the basic ones, indicate so by making a checkmark opposite the appropriate one. Review this chart at intervals so you can compare what you are doing in practice to your needs as shown in your "Personal Form Analysis Sheet." In this way you will be prompted to change your practice routines if necessary to make them conform to your needs.

Methods of Practice

You may practice methodically, working carefully on one item at a time and attending to each point of form carefully. Or you may practice casually, attending to whatever comes up at the moment. A drive or a slice, an aggressive shot or a defensive one—these are some of the varieties you can work on in this kind of practice.

Perhaps you may choose to vary your practice methods to suit your temperament and mood of the day. If you feel that you want to be especially active you may want active drills. If you feel competitive you may want to play. Or if you are lazier than usual, more tired than you would like to be, you may want only some easy stand-around practice, perhaps on strokes against balls fed conveniently to you by your practice partner. Whichever method you choose, work on some part of your game rather than simply hitting carelessly.

Stroke Practice

For stroke practice you and your partner should take turns feeding shots to one another. If, for example, you want backhand practice ask him or her to hit shots to your backhand. If you are working on some special, specific point of form here, do not always be concerned about the result of your strokes. You may need time to catch the feeling of a movement or a posture even while missing your shots. Later, as you do get familiar with that point of form you will try to apply it to good shots, to connect it to the other parts of your stroke.

You might even ask your partner to coach you as you practice this way. Tell him or her what it is you are trying to do—to start the swing close to your rear hip, to maintain your wrist angle, to swing properly along your target line, or whatever. Show that point of form in slow motion, then ask your partner to check to see if you are doing it properly at regular speed.

The point I am making is that you first practice strokes in situations where there is no consequence to hitting or missing, to winning or losing. Of course, you will have instant feedback on every shot—you see whether it is in or not. Nevertheless, it may often be best for you to ignore the result and to concentrate instead on the feel of each shot and on the particular point of form you are working on.

Practice this way on all your strokes—your groundstrokes, volleys, serves, lobs, and smashes. Practice to strengthen your weak strokes and to solidify your strong ones. It is only through confidence gained in practice that you will have confidence to use your strokes and shots in a competitive play.

Strategy Practice

Though in some drills your emphasis may be on stroking form, in other you and your partner can combine stroke practice with practice on various tactics. For this, devise drills in which you duplicate specific play situations. For example, follow-

DRILLS FOR SKILL

SERVING	Going to the net	
	Staying in the backcourt	
	With opposing net player	
RETURN OF SERVE	Deep to backhand	
	On the rise	
	Going in after it	
GROUND-STROKES	Rallying from the backcourt	
	The deep game	
	Crosscourt-liners	
PASS SHOTS	Against a stationary volleyer	
	Against the approach shot	
	Against two volleyers	
VOLLEYS	Volleying for quickness	
	Volleying through midcourt	
	Volleying from the "T"	
	Against two baseliners	
LOBS	Defensive lobs	
	Mixed lobs and drives	
SMASHES	Smash for consistency	
	Mixed smash and volleys	
	Smash with doubles partner	
DOUBLES	Poach on return of service	
	Signals	
	Odd formations	
	Protecting your partner	
	Returns against a poacher	
	Return and move in	
	1st volley to feet or deep	
HALF-VOLLEYS		
DROPSHOTS		

Your master practice chart

Place a checkmark opposite each item each time you practice it. Note the checkmarks at intervals to see that you are not neglecting some important part of your game.

ing stroke practice for form you may ask your partner to start rushing to the net behind approach shots. You can then practice passing him or her. Or you may attempt to hit all your shots deep to your partner's weak stroke to prevent him or her from advancing to the net.

As an alternative, you may use your "new" point of form as you try to make aggressive approach shots. Your partner would try to pass you, using whatever points of form he or she has been working on.

A few drills like these are described in sections that follow. Use them as they are presented here or modify them to make them more suitable for your level of play.

Play for Practice

Though drills are useful and often necessary to develop habitual responses, they are not substitutes for competition. You will learn to play better by playing more. Practice alone, without a great deal of competition, will not guarantee that you will perform as well in competition as you do in drills. But neither will endless competitive play without special practice make a finished player of you.

Continuous play without practice often leads to bad habits. For example, you may avoid your weak stroke in play and thus not improve that stroke. But eventually a skilled opponent may exploit that weakness. When that occurs you will be sorry you neglected special practice on that weakness.

Now, since play may be more appealing to you but practice more beneficial, you may solve the dilemma by combining the two in what may be called "play for practice."

As the name implies, you and your partner serve and return and continue to play points out to their finish, but will not keep score. And since there is no consequence to winning or losing, each of you should be willing to use uncertain strokes and to try uncertain shots that you hope to eventually learn.

To gain maximum benefit from this kind of practice agree with your partner to stop play after an easy miss and to repeat that play situation, that stroke and that shot, so the misser can correct the mistake. For example, if you miss an easy high volley, stop right there so your partner can feed you several similar balls to hit so you can repeat the stroke. You, of course, will do the same for your partner after he or she misses. This kind of play moves along slowly but it can be extremely beneficial. And if you are serious about improving, you should be willing to spend considerable time at this kind of practice.

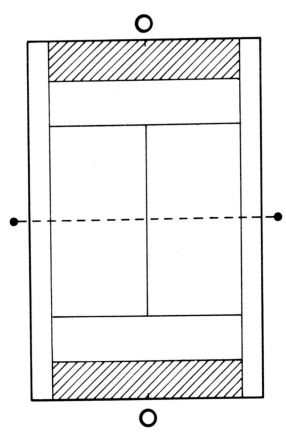

Depth drill: both players must hit to shaded areas in back of court.

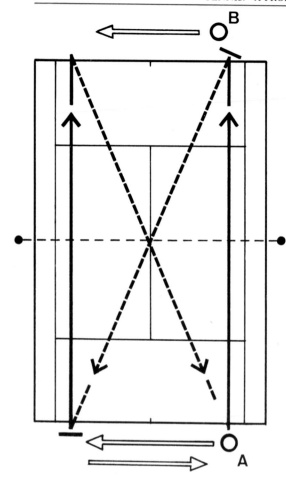

Figure eight drill: A hits only down the line, B hits only crosscourt. The ball and the players describe a "figure eight."

Drills

In the remainder of this chapter I list several drills used by experienced teachers and coaches. The first group I call "basic drills" because you are likely to find yourself in one or another of these situations at any time in a match.

Backcourt Rallies for Steadiness

You and your practice partner take your places in your respective backcourt areas. Either of you starts a rally with a bounce-and-hit. The object is to keep the ball in play, to develop steadiness. You may both hit a mixture of forehands and backhands or you may designate that one of you is to hit only backhands or forehands while the other player places all shots to the designated stroke.

Try to hit at a realistic speed, the speed at which you usually play. Count the number of good shots made successively in each rally and try always to prolong the rallies. In this way you will be creating some pressure for yourself which makes this practice even more beneficial. You can learn to play well under pressure by practicing under pressure.

Backcourt Rallies for Depth

As a variation of the preceding drill, rally with your partner while each of you tries to hit the ball into a "deep area" marked on both sides of the net. Use chalk to mark a line, or stretch a cord across the court midway between the service line and baseline. The deep area is that court space between the marked line and the baseline, extending from sideline to sideline.

Start each rally with a bounce-and-hit and stop each rally when a ball lands outside of the deep area, whether it be too short or too long. Agree with your partner not to go to the net; this is exclusively for backcourt practice.

Rallies for Crosscourts and Liners

This drill is for the purpose of developing accuracy in placing the ball crosscourt and down the line.

Again, begin a rally while each of you is at the center mark in your respective courts. One of you is to hit all shots down the line; the other is to hit crosscourt. With this sequence, and if your shots are placed reasonably accurately, both of you will hit forehands and backhands alternately. To explain, you may hit a forehand crosscourt and next a backhand down the line.

Start by hitting as softly as necessary to sustain the rally. Play "out" balls if they are reasonably close but try always to hit inside the singles lines. As you gain skill, increase the pace of your shots.

After a reasonable time, reverse roles with your partner; you hit down the line while he or she hits crosscourt.

Though tennis is not generally considered an aerobic sport because of the frequent pauses after points are played, this drill can become an aerobic activity. If you stayed at it long enough and if you start a new rally quickly after each miss you are likely to be able to get your heart rate up to its training level. Then, if you continue the drill actively for fifteen minutes or so, you will be gaining cardiovascular fitness for tennis.

This drill offers a second advantage, namely, the chance to practice footwork. For this purpose run carefully for each shot, making certain that you stop to hit or at least slow down as much as you can for each shot. Practice running "softly" to make your head steady as you swing. Do not deliberately hit while in the middle of a step with a foot in the air. And do not start running slowly for the purpose of speeding up as you approach the ball. Instead, set the leading foot down as you start each swing and move fast, then slower, to reduce sideward movement as you swing.

Rallies for Winners

In another version of rallying drills, you and your partner can hit for the purpose of ending the rallies with hard, aggressive backcourt shots.

Decide that one of you will be the offensive layer, the harder hitter. The other will play defensively. The offensive player tries to mix up his or her placements to move the other player and to create an opening through which he or she can hit a winner or draw an error. When you are the offensive player, use whatever mixture of shots you think will be effective. Hit crosscourt and down the line, short or deep, topspin or flat or sliced; use whatever in your repetoire will win for you.

When you are the defensive player, do whatever you can to get out of trouble. Hit time-saving deep shots or play everything to your partner's weaker stroke. Mix your shots, using changes in spin and speed. But do not go to the net. In this practice stay in the backcourt to improve your skills there.

Serving and Returning the Serve

Here, one of you serves in the regular manner and tries to serve effectively enough to draw a weak return. Meanwhile, the other player tries to return the serve in such a way as to be in good position to continue the rally *if* one were to ensue. In this practice, however, *do not rally;* merely serve and return. Each of you is to note the quality of your

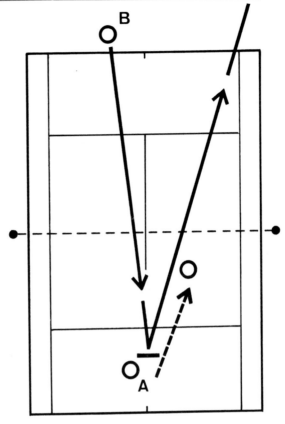

Approach drill: B begins drill by hitting a soft drive near A's service line. A moves in, hits the approach down the line and takes the net. B tries to lob or pass.

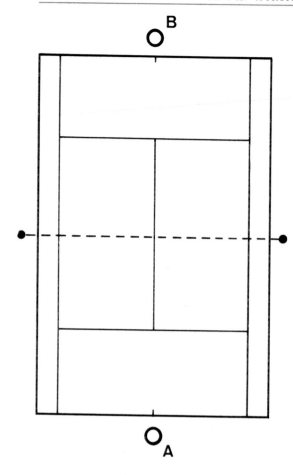

Head-to-head drill: B puts ball in play to A and moves in 2–3 steps. A returns B's drive and moves in 2–3 steps. Players continue to hit at each other and move in until one can volley the ball for a winner.

If you or your partner's match tactics include rushing to the net after a serve, practice that here. The receiver then will try to pass the net-rushing server or to merely hit low to draw a weak volley (or a half-volley). But here, stop the rally after the first volley to emphasize the importance of the serve, the return, and the first volley.

If the server stays back because he or she plays that way in competition, the receiver will try to return deeply enough to prevent the server from using aggressive shots against the return. Here, too, stop play after only one groundstroke; emphasis is still on the quality of the serve, the return, and the first shot afterward.

Going to the Net and Defending Against a Net Rusher

This drill provides practice at making approach shots and at passing a net player.

Again, rally with your partner while each of you is in the backcourt. Agree that one or the other of you is to run forward to a volley whenever that player is hitting from inside the baseline. You are both to try to keep the other behind the baseline, and to try to pass him or her after a short shot permits a net attack.

If one of you needs extra practice on approach shots, agree that only he or she will be a net rusher in this drill. Conversely, if one needs extra passing shot practice this same agreement would allow for it.

For even more attentive practice at approach shots and passing shots you may modify this drill slightly. Let one of you make a feeder shot, hit short purposely to *allow* the other to move forward for an aggressive approach shot and volley. The feeder then would either pass, hit low to the feet, or lob over the net rusher.

Special Drills

You and/or your partner may need practice on various special shots or special qualities. Footwork, quickness, stamina—these are some of the attributes that may be improved in practice and that help you play more effectively.

Volleying through Midcourt

This drill provides practice at volleying after moving in, volleying from several locations, and varying and controlling the depth of volleys.

With both you and your partner standing at your baselines, either of you starts a rally and then moves forward two or three steps to await the return. The other player returns the shot and also moves forward two or three steps. The rally continues with both of you moving forward two or three steps *after each shot.* The objective is to draw a weak shot or an error by forcing your partner to hit up to you from a ball you have placed low to his or her feet.

You are both to choose whichever shots will be most effective—crisp hard volleys angled sharply downward, or soft "touch" volleys dipping in an arched trajectory to the other player's feet.

Volleying from the "T"

You may practice specifically to gain skill at making the first volley, that which occurs after your approach shot in actual play.

Stand at the intersection of the service lines, at the so-called "T," to return balls hit to you from your partner at the baseline. As your partner hits either directly at you or tries to make you reach for wide shots (whichever tactic you agree on) you try to hit deeply enough so you can move forward— as you would in actual play—for a more aggressive net volley. In this drill, however, stay at the "T" to get continual practice at volleying from that location. In a match, the first volley usually has to be played from there; do not overlook the importance of practice from there.

Half-Volley Practice

Take a position at your service line across the net from your partner who should be at his or her service line. Let either of you start a rally and each of you is to try to sustain a rally of half-volleys. Move forward or backward whenever you must to play your partner's shot on the short hop, as a half-volley.

After suitable practice let one of you back up to the baseline and hit drives and slices to the other's feet, which are at the opposite service line. That player at the service line will attempt to make returns while hitting low volleys or half-volleys. Reverse your roles.

Lobs and Smashes

One of you at the baseline lobs to the net player. Lobs are to be purposely short at first to let the smasher gain confidence and to have the chance to apply specific points of form. Later, lobs are to be deeper, some deep enough to force the smasher to jump to reach the ball.

After suitable time, let the lobber hit very high lobs so the smasher can practice hitting them after they bounce. This practice is often neglected, probably because the lobber has very little chance of

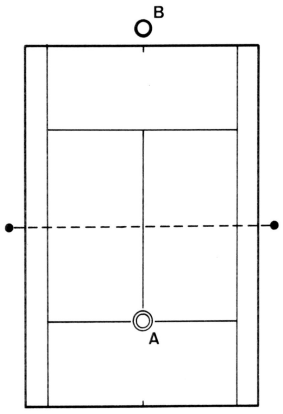

Volley from "T": B keeps ball in play from baseline. A stays on the "T" and volleys, trying for depth.

returning smashes of bounced lobs. And so this is not pleasant to practice. Yet it is extremely beneficial.

Another helpful variation is to have the lobber mix lobs with low shots placed to the feet of the net player. Here the smasher will have to recover to good volley location after each smash, just as he or she would hope to do in match play.

Having stressed the value of practice and having described several drills to use in practice, let me now suggest that you evaluate your practice program and that you measure the effectiveness of the various drills you use. If you have a regular practice partner he or she can help determine whether time spent on a particular drill is paying off. He or she may know better than you whether your shots are becoming more effective.

But only you know the degree of confidence you have in the various shots you attempt in match play. Needless to say, you should plan to practice even more on those shots that feel shaky. Meanwhile, you should continue to work on other shots to maintain a high level of confidence there.

Lastly, I suggest that you bear in mind that learning takes time, and not just the passage of time, but time spent in thoughtful, meaningful practice. Work on your game, so you can make your game work for you in competitive play.

CHET MURPHY

8

Singles Tactics and Strategy

The ultimate tactic in the game of tennis is *consistency.* Whether you are a beginner, intermediate, or advanced tournament player, consistency is your most devastating weapon. It does not really matter whether you hit one-handed or two-handed, or whether you are a topspin, underspin, or power player, your ability to win at any time will be based on your level of consistency—your ability to return every ball so that it goes over the net and inside the lines.

Good shot selection is the cornerstone of a tactically sound game. Once players reach a certain level with basically sound shots, their chances of winning will depend on their ability to hit the right shot, to the right spot, at the right time. Success is more dependent on *where* and *when* you hit a shot —rather than *how* you hit it. If you were to hit the greatest shot you have ever hit, but to the wrong spot at the wrong time you would probably lose the point. However, if you were to hit the worst shot in the world, but to the right place at the right time, you would likely win the point with a clean winner.

There are literally thousands of players in the world today who hit the ball as well, if not better, than the ranked pros who are winning big money on the tours. But we will never see nor hear of 99 percent of these players because they cannot win at a high level. Their inability to win is not a result of physical inadequacies, because in many instances they have faster feet and superior conditioning. Their inability to win is directly related to their inadequate mental or tactical habits.

Sound tactics are based on two vitally important concepts. To be capable of playing tactically sound tennis, a player must know what his or her limits and capacities are. Good shot selection is based on a player's understanding of his or her capabilities on any shot at any time. How hard you hit the ball before your consistency and accuracy deteriorate or fail? How close to the lines are you able to aim your shots before you begin spraying the ball wide? In other words, what is your optimum level of play—under what conditions or circumstances do you play your best? Does pressure, power, or spin affect your consistency and accuracy, and if so, how much?

The foundation of sound tactical play is the individual's knowledge of his or her limits at any point under any and all circumstances. If a player fails to have this self-knowledge or self-realization, then it is impossible to play consistent tennis and win at the higher levels of competition.

But understanding one's limits is only half the foundation. The other half, which is equally important, is this: players must be willing to play within their limits—once they have established and measured them. All players have some sense of their

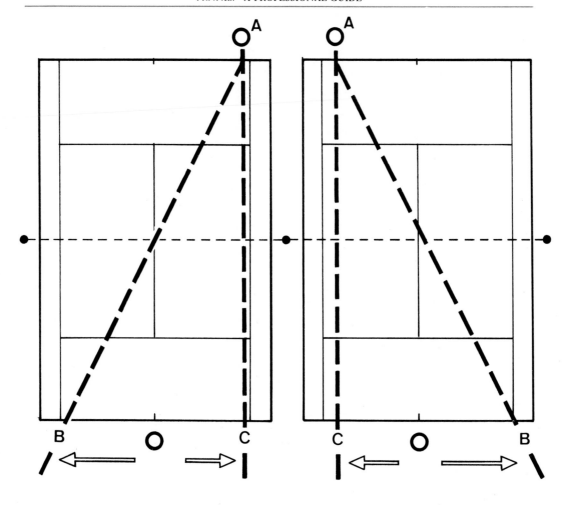

Crosscourt pulls opponent wide

limitations on certain shots, either consciously or unconsciously, but only a small percentage are willing to recognize their limits and play within them. The elite players who are willing to discipline themselves to play within their limits are known throughout the world of tennis as winners.

The limits on your shots can and will be affected by various factors. One of the primary factors that directly affects tactics is the physical layout of the court. If we disregard other factors and consider only the dimensions of the court, the tactics are basically simple. I refer to this tactical plan as the geometric theory. Thus, the deep crosscourt (AB) automatically becomes a higher percentage shot than the down-the-line (AC)—providing all other things are equal.

This is true because the crosscourt groundstroke can travel approximately 82½ feet, almost four and one-half feet longer than the down-the-line distance, which measures 78 feet. The crosscourt will also pass over the vicinity of the center of the net which measures three feet in height, while the down-the-line shot will pass over the net where it measures three and one-half feet in height. So the crosscourt carries over the longest part of the court and the lowest part of the net, which makes it a safer, higher percentage shot.

The crosscourt (AB) will also pull your opponent wide of the sidelines and, consequently, establish a greater opening—something that the down-the-line (AC) is not able to accomplish. So if we consider the geometric theory only, the crosscourt is your best shot.

However, there are other factors that must necessarily be considered if you wish to be successful. Three considerations that will cause you to make necessary modifications to the geometric theory are: (1) position of the ball in relation to you, (2) position of the net in relation to you, and (3) position of the opponent in relation to you. If we expand on each of these considerations you can see how they will affect your tactics.

(1) Position of the Ball and (2) Position of the Net in Relation to You.

When the ball is low (below net level) and you are stretching forward (toward the net) your highest percentage shot will still be the crosscourt. The lower the ball bounces and the wider you are pulled toward and beyond the sidelines, or the closer you are pulled to the net, the more the crosscourt becomes a sounder shot tactically.

As the ball bounces higher (above the level of the net) and closer to the net, the risk of hitting down the line is reduced—although geometrically

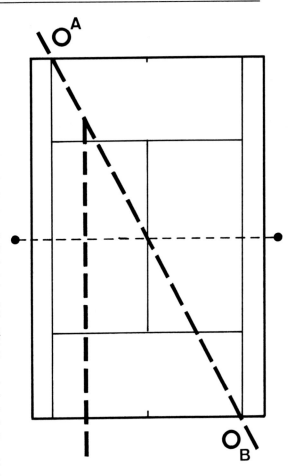

A forces B wide with the crosscourt, and hits down the line for a winner when B fails to recover position.

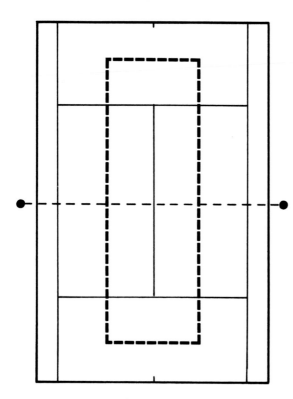

Eighty percent of all shots land within the dotted lines.

the crosscourt still remains the better choice. Remember that we are still basing this theory on the assumption that all other factors are even, i.e., your opponent has no outstanding weaknesses.

(3) Position of the Opponent in Relation to You. This consideration will have a very significant affect on your tactics and any modifications you might make. If your opponent is pulled wide to the forehand side and maintains that court position rather than returning to optimum tactical position near the middle of the baseline, then the down-the-line groundstroke becomes an appealing and effective option to the crosscourt since your opponent is now on the full run to his or her backhand. The higher your opponent's return bounces and the closer to the net you can execute your down-the-line shot, the more effective the shot will be. Example: A hits to B, B stays wide after returning crosscourt to A, A then drives ball down the line. However, if B returns with power and depth to A, then A should stay with the crosscourt. The optimum time to go down the line is when B fails to regain position in the middle of the backcourt and hits a weak, short ball back to A.

Shot selection should also vary according to your opponent's strengths and weaknesses in relation to your strengths and weaknesses. For instance, you might find after several games that your opponent has a stronger backhand than you do and is winning a high percentage of the points when you have assumed a backhand crosscourt pattern. Under these circumstances the risk of going for a lower percentage shot (breaking the angle and hitting down the line) may be worth the advantage that you gain. You should make every attempt to establish patterns that you are confident with and that allow you to match your strengths against your opponent's weaknesses whenever and wherever possible.

Many of the top players in men's and women's competition use a basic crosscourt game plan and incorporate modifications when necessary. It is important to note where most of their crosscourts land to interpret their tactics correctly. In analyzing the performance of the world-class players we find that approximately 80 percent of their shots, whether they be groundstrokes or volleys or overheads, land within the dotted lines of the diagram as shown.

Unfortunately most spectators only recall the 20 percent that land closer to the line. As a result, many observers fail to interpret the play of the world's best players correctly. They believe that the top players are literally aiming at the lines when they hit the ball in the 20-percent zone. Bjorn Borg, in his book, says that he aims a yard or two beyond the service line and that when the ball strikes close to the line it is an "accident."

I believe this is an important piece of information. If you are going to play tactically sound tennis, you must realize that you lack "perfect" timing and coordination and, consequently, need to establish a conservative aim point well inside the lines if you want to be consistent and successful.

A fundamentally sound game plan might very well include the following tactics: when you opponent has hit a deep or forcing shot to your backcourt area, then automatically respond with the basic crosscourt—which gives you the greatest margin of safety. It is the highest percentage shot, particularly when you are under pressure and it will help open up your opponent's court. I would do this 80 percent of the time under these conditions.

When your opponent hits a short ball with less pace you can break the angle or respond by hitting the ball to your opponent's weakness or more limited shot. If your opponent's shot is short and weak, then take the "short" ball on the rise (or as early as possible) and hit your approach shot to your opponent's more limited shot. I would not do this always, perhaps 80 percent of the time.

When you are at the net and you find yourself in a "defensive" volley position, volley deep to your opponent's weaker shot—particularly if it is down the line—80 percent of the time. When you are in an "offensive" volley position, attack the volley and hit it as high and as close to the net as possible to the "obvious" opening 80 percent of the time.

Your primary consideration in shot selection is to attempt only those shots you know you can make. The secondary consideration is where your opponent is. Many players make a dangerous tactical mistake by reversing these considerations. They attempt to hit to an opening, but fail to consider whether they can make the shot.

If your opponent has taken the net and you are relegated to the backcourt, do not be intimidated. Players often miss passing shots because they are so worried about the volleyer at the net that they try to make their passing shots too good and, consequently, make unforced errors. Give yourself sufficient margin and hit for the target area—within your limits. If the volleyer has hit a forcing approach shot and he or she is in good tactical position, then your best passing shot is directly at him or her:

1. At your opponent's midsection if you want to hit a power drive.

2. At your opponent's feet (chip or topspin) if your opponent is anticipating a lob and is not close to the net.

3. Over your opponent's head (lob) if your opponent is crowding the net.

On passing shots remember that there is nothing wrong with hitting the ball hard, or with aiming close to the lines. The problems arise when you try to do both of these things simultaneously. One effective tactic is to break the angle (hit down the line off a crosscourt hit to you) when hitting to an opening. You can prevent an error by increasing your margins over the net and inside the lines when breaking the angle or when increasing power. There is nothing wrong with going down the line off a crosscourt, providing you give yourself sufficient room to compensate for mistiming or mishitting the shot. There is also nothing wrong with increasing the power of your shots, providing you also increase your margin by moving your imaginary target to a more conservative spot. Most players do not make errors because they aim the ball too close to the line or because they hit the ball too hard. The errors are made because the player tries to hit the ball too close to the line and hit it harder at the same time.

Keep in mind that the lob is one of the greatest all-around tactical shots. When you are pulled out of court, it allows you additional time to return to a good tactical position. If you disguise your lob and use it frequently against aggressive volleyers, the lob will enhance your passing shots and help tire your opponent. If you are having difficulty with your lob, hit it over your opponent's backhand side; even a poor lob can be very effective over the backhand.

Good tactics do not necessarily dictate playing conservatively all the time or playing timidly. You should learn to play *up to* your limits as well as within your limits. When you have an opportunity to play aggressively and hit with authority, by all means do not hesitate to do so. Just as it is tactically sound to play consistently, it is also sound to play forcefully when the opportunity presents itself.

I also suggest that you take some risks at specific times throughout the match, particularly when the risk is worth the potential advantage gained. The intelligent time to take a risk is when the score favors you. Remember that every point is important, but some points are definitely more important than others and are referred to as critical

points. Although all players make unforced errors throughout their matches, the ultimate winners do not make mistakes on these critical points. The first and fourth points of each game are critical points. But probably the most critical is game point. You should relax before each of these critical points and program yourself to be consistent. The critical games are the first game, the seventh game, and the game for set.

By reducing your errors you will increase your chances of being successful. A maximum effort on the critical points and games will insure the success you are seeking. Recognize your limits and be willing to play within your limits. Restrain yourself from doing what you would like to do and make yourself do the things you have to do in order to win.

If you have employed a specific tactic and you are not being successful with it—then change it. The old cliché that says, "change a losing game, but stay with a winning game," is very sound advice and good strategy.

No matter what tactic or pattern you are using you can systematically improve your chances of winning if you will deal with the immediate problem in the following manner. If your opponent comes to the net and you lob, but your lob is not very good and your opponent puts the overhead away for a winner, you can correct the problem several ways. First, ask yourself if you could hit a

better shot and still maintain your consistency and accuracy. Chances are you could not or you would have done it in the first place. If that is the case, you should ask yourself if you can hit a different shot and be more successful. Instead of lobbing, perhaps you could chip it at your opponent's feet or pass him or her down the line or crosscourt. If these options do not work, then you might try hitting the same shot—but then anticipate where your opponent will hit the overhead. A fourth tactical option would be to avoid a similar situation by getting to the net yourself so that your opponent would have to hit the passing shot. By dealing with the immediate problem in this way you will eventually find the pattern that works for you against the opponent you are playing on that day. Rather than getting more frustrated and aggravated as the match progresses, you will be more positive and confident, and eventually find the right combination to win.

Sometimes the simplest tactics are the best. If your opponent is beating you by repeating a set pattern you might be successful by fighting fire with fire. If he or she is coming to net and winning, perhaps you should come to net. Even though you may not be as confident at the net, you are preventing your opponent from winning where he or she would like to be.

Many times players fail to win because they try to dominate their opponent physically and are unable to do so. Remember that power is only one form of pressure that you can apply. Some players actually thrive on a ball hit with power so it is important to utilize alternate styles of play. If you are losing, keep your opponent on the court as long as possible. The longer you sustain the match the better the chance you have of tiring your opponent, either physically or mentally.

Some players have difficulty with shots hit with an exaggerated change of pace. You can change the pace by hitting with either topspin or underspin, by looping or floating your shots deep, or chipping and keeping them short and low. Take extra time before starting your points so that you are able to program yourself for the task at hand.

It is not poor sportsmanship to use the elements to your advantage, rather, it is an excellent tactical ploy. If the sun is bright or the wind is blowing so that it is difficult to hit overheads, draw your opponent to the net—make the elements work for you. If the wind is blowing toward your opponent, come to the net since it will be more difficult to pass you when hitting into a strong wind. If the wind is against you, utilize the drop-shot/lob combination; both shots may well be more effective with assistance from the wind.

Most importantly, you must keep your poise and a positive outlook. With a positive outlook and an open mind you have a better chance of finding the tactic that will work. Keep an open mind, be flexible in your thinking, and do not hesitate to experiment when losing.

To summarize, the main points to keep in mind are:

1. Consistency is your ultimate weapon.

2. Play within your limits—but do not hesitate to play up to your limits.

3. When under pressure or exerting pressure, the crosscourt is the soundest tactical shot.

4. Do not use too much imagination on passing shots "at your opponent."

5. Always change a losing game.

6. Maintain a positive attitude.

Bill Tym

9

Doubles Tactics and Strategy

Australians have always been good doubles players. Frank Sedgman and John Bromwich were a world-class team as far back as 1950. They were succeeded by Sedgman and McGregor, Hoad and Rosewall, Fraser and Cooper, and Laver and Emerson. These five teams accounted for exactly half of the Wimbledon and U.S. Open titles won from 1950 to 1960. As recently as the 1981 U.S. Open over 20 years later, John Newcombe and Fred Stolle were in the semifinals, losing in five close sets to the number one team in the world, McEnroe and Fleming. What accounts for this record of success in doubles?

First and foremost, as we shall see, doubles is an attacking game which rewards offensive tactics. Since the most popular surface in Australia in our day was grass, all Australians were well versed in serve and volley techniques and the aggressive receiving tactics necessary for success at the international level. Additionally, we were all fortunate to be trained by and play for Australian Davis Cup captain Harry Hopman. Because "Hop" was the Davis Cup captain for so many years, we all developed a strong team feeling, so any two Aussies from our era were likely to be a threat in doubles when they joined up. Both would automatically have the aggressive grass court games and teamwork tendencies which lead to success in doubles.

But you do not have to be Australian to be a good doubles player. Just learn the doubles principles we describe in the following pages, determine your team's best serving and receiving formations according to your skills, and start thinking strategically on the court and you will be a team to be reckoned with.

The basic principles underlying successful doubles play are really quite simple. They are, in order:

1. Keep the ball in play.

2. Play together as a team.

3. Attack!

The first principle is quite obvious, but many doubles players fail to follow it when they are playing poorly, or losing. Many doubles players try to emulate the tactics and techniques they have observed at professional tournaments, even though they do not have the necessary skills. Doubles should be played at the net, but if your volley is terrible and your backcourt game is strong, stay at the baseline during matches while you work on your volley in practice. Gradually you will develop the skill and confidence to take the net. Should anyone criticize your backcourt position, remind them that teams on the top professional level often

receive with both players behind the baseline, and "Peaches" Bartkowicz and Nancy Richey of the U.S. formed a very successful partnership in the late 1960's while *never* taking the net, even when serving.

Nancy and "Peaches" were great groundstrokers and lobbers. By playing back, they increased their chances of keeping the ball in play. And they were observing the second principle of doubles: teamwork. Because each recognized the other's reluctance to take a volleying position at net, they threw traditional doubles positioning out the window. Their strengths as baseline players and their willingness to play together there were more than enough to defeat many of the serve-and-volley teams they faced. Teamwork is important in doubles for two reasons. First, a team that plays parallel is stronger than a team that plays up and back. So teams should stick together in the physical sense. If your partner goes to net, you should too, and if your partner retreats to cover a lob, so should you. Second, two players on court together must support each other in order for the team to play well. Communication between partners is vital in order to keep spirits and enthusiasm up; it is almost impossible to play good doubles in silence. Good teams consist of partners who respect each other's opinions, plan strategies together, compliment each other for shots that lead to putaways, and are generally positive about playing together.

As an example of good teamwork, Server's Partner, observing that Server is struggling with his or her service in a particular game, may offer to poach more often in order to take some pressure off Server. Or Server's Partner may advise that most of Server's faults are in the net, information that can help Server to regain proper form. Either way, Server's Partner is not silently stewing at net over Server's difficulties, but actively helping to overcome those difficulties.

The third principle of doubles, attack, breaks down to three subheadings. Attack territorially by taking the net. Attack physically by taking the ball as early as possible at every opportunity. And attack mentally by maintaining concentration as a team throughout the match.

Taking the net is vital in doubles, and you should make every effort to improve your volleying so that you can be an attacking doubles player. Two players at the net together have only nine feet more than the width of a singles court to defend, and we all know how difficult it can be to pass a singles player at net. So two doubles players at net offer a tremendous challenge. By taking the net, good doubles players are giving themselves wider

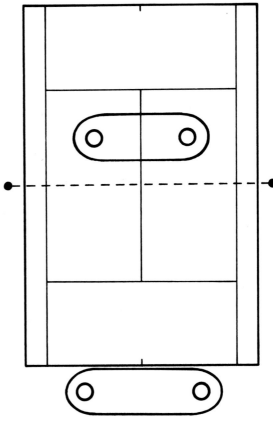

This doubles formation allows nearly complete coverage. "One up, one back" leaves a vulnerable area through middle that neither player can cover.

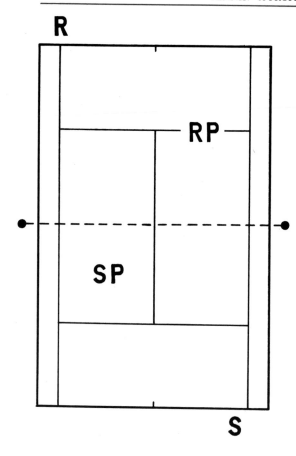

Standard doubles position

angles to play and more chances to hit down into the court for winners. They are closer to the net, so they should have less difficulty hitting over it. Clearly, attacking doubles players are giving themselves better chances to keep the ball in play, and simultaneously they are exerting tremendous offensive pressure on the other team. So, attack!

You can improve your territorial aggression by learning to play the ball early. The more aggressive you are at the net, the more angles and clearance over the net you will have. The closer you stand in to receive serve, the sooner you will be at net behind your return, and the less time the serving team will have to reach their position at net. Learn to cut down your stroke. A very short return stroke, almost like a volley, will allow you to stand in closer and will encourage you to play the ball out in front, with all your weight moving in behind the shot. When serving, learn to serve at ¾ speed so you can get in close to the net for your first volley. Speed and pace on the serve are far less valuable in doubles than location and consistency. Get your first serve in deep to the backhand and get in close for your first volley and even great players will have difficulty breaking your serve.

Finally, attack mentally by maintaining your concentration. So many doubles matches go three sets because the team that wins the first set relaxes momentarily just as the other team digs in, and in minutes they are starting the decisive third set. Good doubles players encourage each other constantly to be aggressive. One service break is not enough, and one set is not enough. The doubles team that eases off because they are ahead is asking for trouble. Easing off mentally leads immediately to a lack of aggression and decisiveness at net, and shortly thereafter the losing team finds that they can win by aggressive play, and now you have a dog fight again, instead of an easy victory.

Keeping these doubles principles in mind will give you fresh insights into the positions you should take on the court in your various roles of Server, Server's Partner, Receiver, and Receiver's Partner.

Most doubles players never stop to think about why they take certain positions on the court. Beginning doubles players watch doubles being played and they soon discover, by observation, that the four players (Server, Server's Partner, Receiver, and Receiver's Partner) usually take the same positions prior to the serve, so they follow suit. But there are reasons why these positions are taken, and if you use your head in doubles you will find that there are often reasons why these positions should *not* be taken automatically.

Let us just look at the standard doubles positions, and the reasons why they are standard. Then we will discuss some alternative positions and reasons for them. In the diagram, all four players are in the normal (or standard) positions for doubles prior to the first point. Server (S) stands wide in order to cover Receiver's (R) return of serve, which will be angled crosscourt away from Server's Partner (SP) at net. Receiver's partner (RP) straddles the service line on his or her half of the court, ready to move forward, or retreat, as the point develops. If Receiver returns wide and low, Receiver's Partner will move to the net; however, if Receiver returns high and soft, Receiver's Partner will hastily retreat. At the highest levels of expertise, all four players will be advancing towards the net most of the time, as soon as the ball is in play. That is because they all know that good doubles is won at the net, so that is where they are going. However, at the other end of the spectrum, it would be pointless to require a beginning player, who has not yet learned to volley, to rush the net just because he or she was playing doubles. And there are many gray areas in between. So let us look more closely at our four basic doubles positions, and then at some alternative positions.

Server generally stands fairly wide to serve in order to be able to cover the angle of the return as he or she comes to net for the first volley, following serve in. However, many club players do not really know how to serve and volley, and so they stand back after serving. This leads to "One Up One Back," a common formation for club doubles. The advantages of this formation are that the backcourt player can cover lobs over partner's head, while the net player is free to roam across the net, confident that partner will cover behind him or her. A team that consists of one player who likes the net and one who hates it will discover this formation very quickly. The disadvantage, however, is that the "One Up One Back" formation leaves a gaping hole in the diagonal between them, and an offensive-minded team will surely exploit that weakness. (See illustration.)

For those players who are willing and able to follow their serve to net, a serving position closer to the center mark will often be rewarding at most levels of play. By moving in towards the center, server can far more easily serve down the center to a right-handed receiver's backhand, which allows Server's Partner at net more freedom to lean into the center, and to poach. Furthermore, a right-hander in the deuce court is usually going to have a strong forehand and a weaker backhand. And

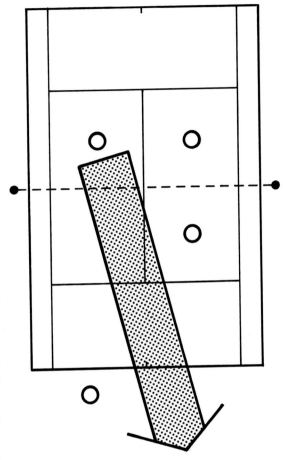

Weakness of "One Up, One Back"

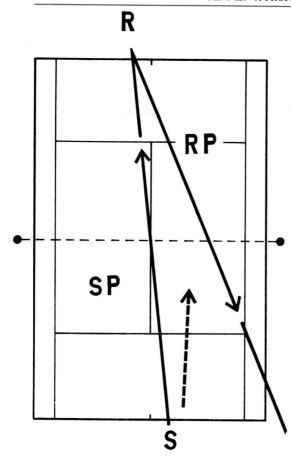

Standing near center mark when serving to deuce court

finally, by serving down the center Server forces Receiver to hit an inside-out, or reverse crosscourt, backhand return of serve. This is an extremely difficult shot, one of the toughest in tennis. Not only is it a tough return to make, but the Server who has forced it (by his or her position close to the center line) will often be able to volley it on his or her forehand, which is preferable to playing a backhand volley for most players. The disadvantage, of course, is that the short, wide-angled return is almost surely a winner. Then again, if your opposition can hit that short angle off the backhand return of serve consistently, you may be in way over your head. For all these reasons, it pays to experiment with your serving stance for the deuce court.

By contrast, serving to the ad court offers far less choice. The only variation here might involve standing very wide, so as to get a more severe angle into Receiver's backhand. Your partner will still be able to cover returns up the middle because a backhand return down the line will be very difficult. At the club level, where most players favor their forehands, good strategy might involve a serving stance in the doubles alley, so Server can then play forehands from the backcourt against the expected angled return.

Server's Partner will invariably take a position at the net where he or she can follow up partner's good serves with easy volleys for winners. Most intermediate players tend to stand toward the alley, but world-class players always take a position almost exactly in the center of their service box. At their level they know that the explosiveness of the serve, either first or second, dictates against any returns down the alley, so they are constantly looking to the middle. At the intermediate level though, especially on second serve, Receiver can often bring a big forehand into play, so Server's Partner must be more conscious of the alley in the deuce court. Location of the serve is important. If Server's Partner knows that Server can control both serves to the center of the court, he or she can relax about the alley and concentrate on the center; the angles for a return of serve from the center of the court to the alley are just not very good. If Server's Partner is tall and has a good overhead, he or she might experiment with playing in closer to the net for more effective volleys. Many players refuse to lob on return of serve, and if this is the case, why stand back to protect against them? If they do lob, adjust your position.

When Server serves to the backhand court, there is even less reason to cover the alley, for a backhand down the line return is a very difficult shot. But if Server has a weak second serve, and

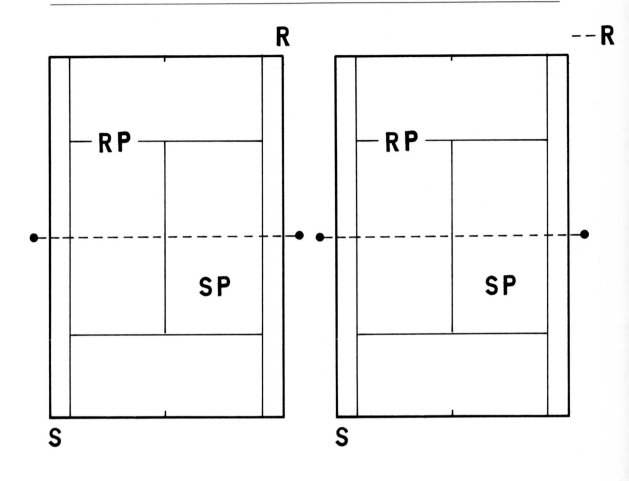

Standing wide when serving to ad court, to protect a weak backhand

Receiver moves wide when server moves wide

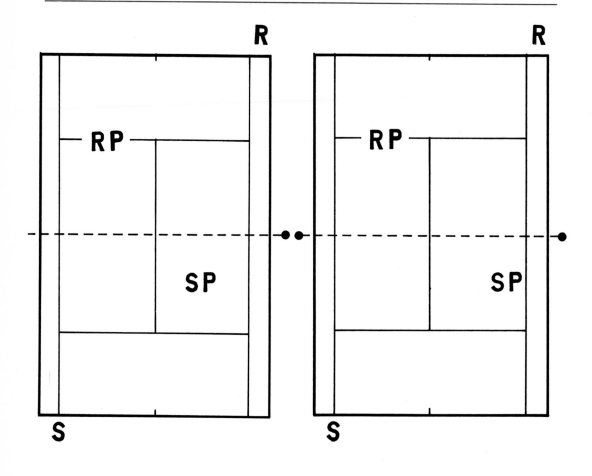

Server's partner stands in center of service box to begin point.

Server's partner adjusts stance at net to protect alley on second serve.

Receiver runs around it to play a forehand, you had better be there to protect that alley!

Receiver's position is dictated by Server's positioning and strength of serve. Many players make the mistake of standing a step behind the baseline for every type of serve—they are clearly not using their heads! Receiver must take a position laterally which almost directly bisects the Server's possible angles, while slightly protecting against the wide serve which will take him or her out of court. The wide serve has to be returned severely across the body in order to avoid the net player, so this side must be protected somewhat. That is why world-class doubles players usually stand near the sideline to receiver serve. Even though they look vulnerable to a serve down the middle, they know their movement to that side will enable them to play the return relatively safely while stretched, something that is not true when the serve is wide.

If you are a player with a strong forehand and a weak backhand, you will probably want to adjust your receiving position so that you can take as many returns on your forehand as possible. You may give up a few aces by moving over to protect your backhand, but that may be better than a stream of errors from that vulnerable side. Over the long run, of course, you must play backhand returns in order to improve on that side. Here you must make a decision based on your short- and long-term priorities as a player: exploit the stronger forehand for gains now, at the risk of never developing your backhand for success later. The choice is yours, but you must realize that there is a choice to be made!

Where most players err is in not adjusting their receiving position forward to take advantage of weak servers. Why stand behind (or on) the baseline to receive a weak serve when you can move in six or seven feet? By playing the return earlier you rob the server of time to prepare for the return, you move yourself closer to the advantageous net position, and you give Server's Partner less time to poach your return. Clearly, it is to your advantage to move in as far as you can, whenever you can.

In addition to moving in for weak serves, if you favor one stroke over another, make sure that you return weak serves with your stronger shot. John Newcombe was famous for this "run-around forehand" in both singles and doubles. Miss a first serve against "Newk" on a big point and you knew you were staring down the barrel of a gun—his forehand. If it worked for Newcombe, it can work for you.

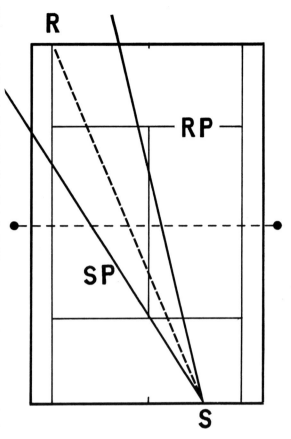

Receiver's position bisects angles of the serve, but slightly favors forehand side.

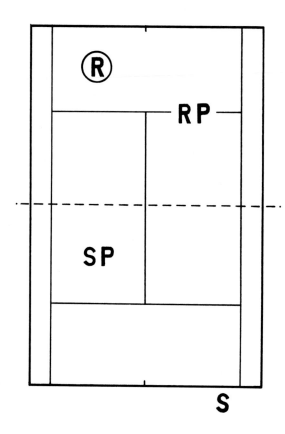

Receiver moves in to return a second serve.

Strong players will always try to follow their returns of serve in and take the net, but if you are not that confident of your volley, you can stay back. This often means that you will be in the "One Up One Back" formation discussed earlier under Server's position. The same advantages and disadvantages are true here as they were for Server and Partner. In general, you will be better off taking some volleying lessons and learning to come in—net is where the fun is—and that is where you win more often.

Receiver's Partner's position is the most misunderstood position in doubles. We have seen players annihilated point after point in the "halfway" position, and they never adjust, simply because someone told them once that they should stand on the service line. Receiver's Partner's stance on the service line is only a beginning position! Once the point is underway, Receiver's Partner should retreat or advance, depending upon the strength of Receiver's return. If Receiver mishits a weak floater to the net person, Receiver's Partner must retreat quickly and try to defend the volley or smash which will be coming his or her way. But if Receiver crushes a return hard and low, Receiver's Partner should move in quickly and look for an opportunity to intercept with a volley.

By the way of contrast, the same Server who fires cannonballs on the first serve may offer up a puffball for a second serve. Now Receiver's Partner should move up from the baseline to a net position, just as though partner were serving instead of receiving! Any reason why not? The serve is no threat, and Receiver is sure to return aggressively, so take advantage of the situation and go right to the net for the winning volley. A weak second serve is an opportunity for the receiving team to turn the tables on the Serving team. If Receiver moves well forward for the second serve, and Receiver's Partner takes a position at net, the Receiving team will beat the Serving team to the net and should win the majority of the points!

To summarize, there is no one *right* place to position yourself in doubles, whether you are Server, Receiver, Server's Partner, or Receiver's Partner. Everyone's position depends upon the variables we have mentioned. Good doubles positioning means using your head!

Among today's top player's only John McEnroe consistently plays doubles. His relationship with partner Peter Fleming is a perfect example of good doubles teamwork. John is a superb doubles player who rarely plays less than brilliantly. Peter Fleming, by contrast, is a streak

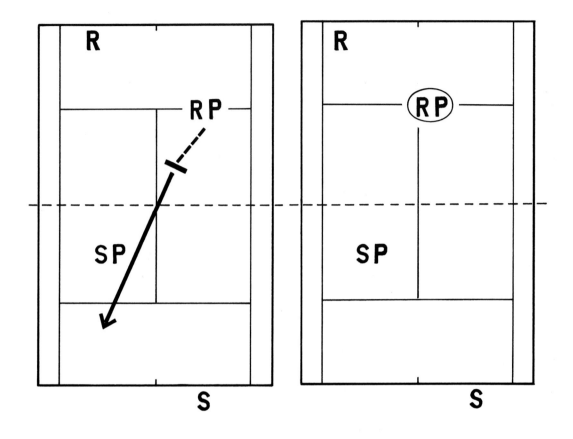

Receiver's partner intercepts return.

McEnroe and Fleming take aggressive positions for returning a second serve.

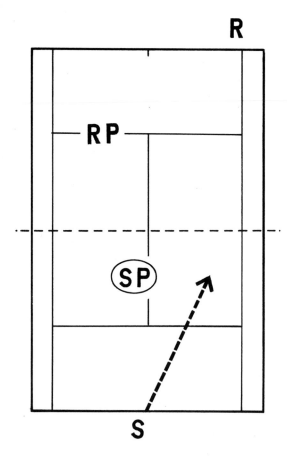

"Australian" formation

player, a big hitter who can be "on" and "off" in the same match. (Fleming's singles ranking on the ATP computer has fluctuated between 100 and 400.) But John never criticizes Peter during a match; he is always supportive. John has confidence that he can hold their team in the match until Peter returns to form and bashes a few winners. And Peter, knowing that John is behind him 100 percent, continues to serve hard and to use his 6' 5" size to blanket the net after John's serves and returns until his own strokes begin to find the mark again. Even when he is playing poorly Peter rarely shows his distress—to do so would be to let John down and could only encourage the opposition. McEnroe and Fleming's number one world ranking is testimony to the effectiveness of their teamwork.

At the advanced level of McEnroe and Fleming one shot rarely wins a point. McEnroe has a great serve, as everyone knows, but he needs an aggressive partner at the net to capitalize on the weak, returns forced by his serves. So teamwork is necessary to hold serve.

Teamwork is even more important when receiving serve, for both players must work together to overcome the serving team's advantages. McEnroe and Fleming often use a receiving formation that allows them to employ a tactic called the "drift," or "intercept." Since they want to win points at the net (the most important strategy in advanced doubles), even when the other team is serving, they put tremendous pressure on second serves by placing Receiver's Partner almost on the "T" where he can volley away a poor first volley by Server. In this formation they are gambling that Receiver will be able to return serve low, forcing the Server to volley up, and Receiver's Partner is now in perfect position to intercept the weak first volley with an aggressive volley winner. Receiver must set up the play with a good return and Receiver's Partner finishes the point with a winning volley. The volleyer (Receiver's Partner) does not always come across because if he or she did, Server would begin to volley down the line for a winner. Australians call this tactic the "Drift" or "Intercept." McEnroe and Fleming have utilized it extremely effectively, and their aggressive positioning forces many errors by intimidated volleyers.

Similar teamwork was used effectively by Tony Trabert and Vic Seixas in the decisive doubles match of the 1954 Davis Cup in Brisbane, Australia. Although Lew Hoad and Ken Rosewall were favored to win the doubles, Trabert and Seixas developed a system of poaching signals which gave them an edge. Before the Americans

The Australian and Spanish Davis Cup Team, 1965.

served, Server's Partner would turn his back to the net (and the opposition) and use a hand signal to tell Server whether or not he was going to poach. Hoad and Rosewall were put off their game by that aggressive teamwork play and the Davis Cup went to America.

Another advanced doubles formation is often called "Australian," after some Australian teams used it successfully in the 1920's, but in Australia we call it "Tandem." Whatever you call it, the purpose of the formation is to force Receiver to change the direction of his or her return. Usually we used the formation when one player was returning extremely well. By placing Server's Partner on the same side of the court as Server, the Receiver is forced to change his or her return of serve from crosscourt to down the line, and sometimes this change is enough to reduce the effectiveness of the returns. Ham Richardson and Alex Olmedo turned the tables on us in the 1958 Davis Cup playing "Australian" against the effective cross-court returns of Neale Fraser in the left court (with Mal Anderson as partner), effectively nullifying Fraser's returns.

Slightly less advanced players might want to try the "Australian" formation to the backhand court in order to give Server a forehand volley coming in, instead of the backhand first volley which usually answers a crosscourt return of serve in the normal formation. Also, by playing "Tandem" Server has the advantage of making his or her first volley without the threat of the opposing net player right in front of him or her, which can be psychologically important.

Notice that all of the formations we have suggested, entail aggressive play at the net. That is because advanced doubles is played, and won, at the net. So get up there yourself!

ROD LAVER
ROY EMERSON

10

Preparing
for Matches

If you are serious about your tennis, sooner or later you will wind up in a tournament match. Competition is the crucible that shapes your game. Weaknesses and strengths both tend to be magnified by the pressures that accompany any competition, so look at every match as a chance to find out a little more about yourself and your game. For players just getting involved in competition, and even for some advanced players, a tension-reducing idea that always leads to improvement is to go into a match with one or two single goals. For example, maybe you know that you have had trouble in the past hitting out on your backhand under pressure, so your goal for the upcoming match may be to really "pop" that backhand in situations where you have always previously tended to hit a weak slice or a lob. By concentrating on that smaller, specific goal, you may find that your concentration overall improves during the match because you are not so likely to be distracted by thoughts of winning and/or losing, thoughts which can often inhibit your performance by increasing tension. In addition to reducing tension on court, setting specific goals for your matches can help you improve faster as a player, by focussing on particulars, and can decrease the negative impact of losing a match. Even if you lose a match you may be able to achieve some positive results by reaching a goal or two you set in advance for your-self, which will help you to look forward to another day, and another match.

Tension is a serious problem that affects every tournament participant. The best competitors are those who learn to use the tension generated by competition to bring out their best tennis. However, for most of us, tension brings out the worst. Our elbows lock, our knees freeze, and the ball dribbles into the net or sails into the backstop.

Probably the best way to turn the tension of competition into a positive attribute for you is to make sure that you are thoroughly prepared in every possible way for your match. After all, hitting a tennis ball is pretty difficult even when you are just rallying across the net. It gets even more difficult when the other person is trying to keep you from hitting the ball successfully. And when you add such hazards as spectators, friends, sun, wind, and countless other elements, even making contact can seem like a triumph. So the more successful player learns to eliminate as many elements of uncertainty as possible. By doing so, he or she is free to concentrate on the task at hand, and eliminates all excuses for poor performance. Many club players, on the other hand, seem to invite distractions, probably so they will have a convenient excuse for failing. But if you are serious about the competition you have entered you will want to be at your best, and the only way to ensure that is to

Vitas Gerulaitis, re-wrapping handle on changeover

prepare in three different ways: procedurally, physically, and mentally.

Procedural preparation refers to all the details that need to be taken care of prior to the beginning of your match. Most players know enough to check their equipment beforehand, but countless players hurt their chances by being careless about one detail or another affecting their match. How many times have you seen a tournament participant arguing with the tournament director about his or her USTA number, which he or she forgot to bring? Or how many times have you arrived at a site just in time for your match, without giving yourself a chance to relax? I see these things happen at every tournament I attend. And I can guarantee that the added stress from these incidents never helped a single one of the players I watched. So you should be no different.

Send your entry in well before the deadline and call or write just after the deadline to confirm that your entry was, indeed, received. As you are confirming your entry acceptance, you may also be able to get the date, site, and time of your first match. Be sure to ask the name of the person you are talking to, and write it down along with your information. If a mistake is made, your record will be important. And be sure to be specific with your questions. An Australian Davis Cup player once called in to a $100,000 Grand Prix tournament Tuesday afternoon after his singles and asked if he was scheduled for doubles on Wednesday. The answer was "no." At 10:00 p.m. that night he was defaulted from his doubles, scheduled Tuesday night! He was upset, but he had only himself to blame. He did not ask about Tuesday night. Once you know when and where you play, plan how you will get to the site and back. If you have not been there before, get specific directions and allow extra time for confusion. You should always allow extra time for driving anyway, because most people I know usually underestimate the time needed and end up speeding the last 15 miles to the site and rushing on to the court—not a great way to begin.

As long as you obtain good directions and allow plenty of time, you will be able to check in at the site with the tournament director, find out where your match has been assigned, and still have time to walk around the site for a while, or relax. Of course, you will have remembered to bring some extra money, your checkbook, the records of your confirmed entry, your USTA membership, and your phone record of your match date and time, so there will be no problems at check-in.

Knowing that you have considered every possible problem in advance allows you the freedom to concentrate on the match you are about to play, and you might want to use a few minutes beforehand to review your equipment. You have at least two rackets, preferably three—all the same balance, all strung recently—so that you can change rackets without loss of efficiency if a string breaks. If you are like Vitas Gerulaitis, you have plenty of gauze on hand, to rewrap your handle at every change-over. In your bag you also have towels, extra clothing for changes, extra sneakers and laces, and whatever you like to use on your grip—resin, sawdust, whatever. I have always favored sawdust as a natural way to keep my hands dry, but not every tennis court comes equipped with a saw and old wood nearby, so if I want sawdust I make sure to bring my own. Most major tournaments also supply drinks at courtside, but if you favor a particular beverage when you play, bring it along rather than risk being disappointed.

Having all your equipment ready and in place is important, but your most important equipment is your body. Now is a good time to review your physical preparations. You knew well in advance you were entering this tournament, so you spent your practice time on the same surface as the tournament courts, using the tournament ball. Since the surface often indicates how much of your play will be offensive and how much defensive, you have geared your practices appropriately. If you are playing on fast cement, you have worked especially hard on serve and volley, and on return of serve. If the tournament is on slow clay, you have emphasized groundstroke consistency and depth. If you have had to fly to the tournament you may well be facing different climactic conditions and you have tried to anticipate them during practice. For instance, if you are flying to a warmer climate, you should wear extra clothing during a few workouts in order to simulate the extra heat you will be facing. Of course, the best solution to climatic problems is to arrive early enough to become acclimatized naturally, but this is not always feasible, so use your imagination.

Imagination is also necessary when it comes to choosing your practice partners. Try to find a mix of stronger and weaker players. Against the weaker players you can work on your weaknesses, holding your strengths in reserve, while against stronger players, who are sure to exploit your weaknesses, you must employ your strengths from the beginning in order to be competitive. In both cases, be sure to work on some drills before playing. The appropriate mix of play and drills is up to each player and coach, but remember that in tournaments all you do is play, so your practices should probably include plenty of drill, with a few practice sets as tournament time draws nearer.

When you find yourself actually on site, awaiting your match, do the same warm-up exercises and calisthenics you use before your practices and, if possible, get a practice hit for 15 to 20 minutes, just enough to tune your strokes, break a sweat, and relieve a little of your nervous tension.

Most players have individual preferences regarding intensity and duration of practices as a tournament nears. Some, such as Martina Navratilova, continue to practice hard not only up to, but right through a tournament. But then not everybody dominates their opponents as thoroughly as Martina has in the past year, so most players taper their sessions to some degree in order to be fresh, rested, and eager for the tournament matches. Practice can make perfect, but too much practice can make you stale, too. Each player needs to find the optimum amount for himself or herself.

Finally, in the last few minutes before your match is called, you may wish to review your mental preparations for the tournament. During your practice sessions you have made the proper mental adjustments for the surface you will be playing on. For faster surfaces, you have concentrated on aggressiveness, whereas slower surfaces call for patience and consistency. Leading up to and during the tournament you will be employing positive thinking and visualization techniques. Tennis is an easy game to approach negatively, so you have made special efforts in practice to accentuate your positive skills and results, especially as the tournament draws near. In conjunction with your positive thinking you have devoted 10 to 15 minutes each night visualizing yourself playing well in the tournament, winning point after point, playing according to the techniques, tactics, and strategies you have been working on in practice. Now, just prior to your actual match, take a few private moments to visualize again, and do some deep breathing to keep yourself relaxed and ready.

When you feel tense on court, utilizing deep breathing can calm your fears and remind you of your training, your practices, and your visualization, and free you to play better. Whenever possible, scout your upcoming opponent in a tournament so you will have an idea of his or her strengths and weaknesses. Then you can formulate a strategy beforehand, rather than having to think it out on court. Also, during your match utilize the changeovers to relax and review your strategy.

Well, the tournament director just called for your match. The other player may be good, but you know he or she cannot be better prepared than you. Good Luck!

Fred Stolle

11

Mental Training
for Tennis

Players at all levels have experienced great variations in ability caused by changes in mental attitude. Some people play very well all the way up to the point of winning an important match, but then just fall apart. Others compete effectively against players they know they can beat, but poorly against superior competitors. Most tennis players have "choked" in tense situations, lost their temper when provoked, or had their minds wander when playing poor opponents in unimportant matches. The importance of mental attitude in tennis performance is widely recognized. Many have concluded that tennis, more than most sports, is a "mental game."

Since the mental dimension of tennis is so important, a mental training program is clearly necessary for achieving maximum performance. It should be integrated with the other crucial programs that bear on a player's skill level. Strokes, strategy, agility and quickness, strength, endurance, flexibility, and nutrition all require individual attention. Training programs in each of these areas contribute to improved play. While some coaches and players may leave one or more of these areas to chance, a specific training regimen is clearly more efficient. The following mental training program has emerged in a pragmatic way for me through many years of college coaching, tennis camp directing, and tournament playing.

Goals and Benefits

The goal of mental training for tennis is to achieve a state of mind that will maximize the likelihood of high performance. Skilled mental competitors are able to create an ideal mental state whenever it is needed. This state can best be described by identifying important emotions and attitudes that characterize the mentally trained players. They are relaxed and calm inside, yet move at a high energy level. Extremely confident of their playing ability, they feel no compelling drive to prove themselves to others. Skilled mental competitors remain focussed on the present moment, avoiding the pitfalls of rehashing the past or worrying about the future. Knowing that they are in complete control of their actions and emotions, they remain actors rather than reactors in every new situation. Playing tennis is fun, tennis opponents are appreciated, and losing does not dampen their enthusiasm. Each setback becomes the prod for renewed effort. Finally, skilled mental players, like themselves and what they have accomplished, but never belittle others to achieve the feeling of self-worth. Instead, they know that through elevating others, both they and the others are uplifted.

Embarking on a complete mental training program will lead you to a number of important *anticipated* benefits. You will experience a more consistent level of play in all situations. Your ability to handle pressure, aggravating situations, and boring predicaments will improve. Practicing will become more fun and the incidence of burnout will decrease. You will feel better about yourself and, in turn, will relate better to others. Since losses and poor play will not bother you as much, your way will be cleared for higher levels of sportsmanship and general court behavior. You will feel like expending maximum effort to accomplish your goals even when things are not going your way. In general, your appreciation of both tennis and other phases of life will be enhanced.

Program Summary

A complete mental training program for tennis goes beyond the tennis court. Your conditioning began at your birth and has been influenced by a variety of relationships. Although it is difficult to separate the components completely, the program is divided into eight areas. They include: (1) self-confidence, (2) competitive attitude development, (3) role modeling, (4) concentration-relaxation techniques, (5) self-talk, (6) visualization, (7) goal setting, and (8) a daily mental training routine.

The program would be simpler if the first three components were eliminated. When self-confidence, competitive attitude development, and role modeling are included, every phase of the player's and coach's life becomes involved. On the other hand, a more limited approach is not as effective because general life forces can easily work against the mental training program without the coach or player being aware of it. When this happens, disillusionment with the potential of mental training grows. Indeed, some coaches and players have insecurities, attitudes, and habits that destine any training program to failure. Therefore, a total approach involving all eight areas of mental training is clearly best.

Self-Confidence

Genuine self-confidence is the fundamental building block on which the rest of the mental training program depends. The key to self-confidence is the inner knowledge of being accepted unconditionally—knowing that you are loved, that you are important in the eyes of people who are important to you. This love and importance do not depend on anything you are expected to do or accomplish. In Christian theology, God's acceptance of you is called grace. God loves you regardless of whatever evil you might commit, just because you are you. Alcoholics Anonymous teaches that alcoholics must first be loved with all of their shortcomings as a prerequisite for rehabilitation. Parent effective-

Breathe deeply,

ness counselors stress that children must be loved because they are the parents' son or daughter, not because they have lived up to the parents' hopes or expectations. In a similar fashion, coaches make it clear that each player is equally admired and respected, regardless of bad losses or failures. The bottom line, of course, is that you feel good about yourself, even when your poor play is inexcusable and the cause of a lost championship that should have been yours.

Self-confidence is built upon the acceptance of the person, but not the person's shortcomings. Although many of us have trouble distinguishing between who we are and what we do, the distinction is crucial. God accepts sinners, but not sin. Families accept alcoholics, but not their inconsiderate actions. Parents love their children, but not their selfish acts. Coaches admire their players, but not their unsportsmanlike deeds. And we love ourselves, but not our lack of openness. Genuine acceptance will never make sense, nor excellence be achieved without full appreciation of the difference between a person and his or her actions.

The absence of genuine self-confidence can be observed in many ways in the tennis environment. It can be seen when the need to impress others becomes too strong. Some players need to play number one on the team or not at all. Others want newspaper publicity, spectators, the coach's undivided attention, or who knows what else in order to feel good about their tennis playing. Often there is talk about "proving" themselves. Bragging is another sign of insecurity. All of these people find themselves wondering, "What will they think if I lose?" Confident persons do not care what "they" will think.

Lack of self-confidence can also be seen in self-abuse. Players who shout profanities at themselves or who abuse their equipment obviously do not feel good about themselves. This leads them to treat others the same way. By putting others down, they hope in the process to make themselves look better. They suspect the worst in others, and thereby discover that many of their opponents often make mistakes or cheat. The connection between themselves and others is strong, but the insecure often do not realize this.

When self-confidence is lacking, coaches and fellow players need to say and do things that will build confidence. The following statements, said at the right time and in the right way, will have that effect. "Gee, I'm fortunate to have you on our team." "I enjoy working with you guys." "You really gave it everything you had today." "Your serve (backhand, overhead, volley, etc.) is really improving." "Your example is really an inspiration to the rest of the team." "Thanks for helping me— I really appreciated that." "You are a nice person." These statements and many others like them need to be combined with a smile and perhaps a hug or a handshake. Use people's names, share important thoughts with them, initiate contacts with them, spend time with them, look them directly in the eye as you speak with them, and listen carefully to what they say. Appreciate people at all times, even when they fall short of your expectations. Believe honestly that you are working with some of the most beautiful jewels in God's creation. If you do not feel this way about them, you are not contributing to their self-confidence in an optimum manner. The same is true of yourself. Unless you know that you are most precious in God's eyes, you will never be as confident as you can be.

Confidence in your ability to perform various tasks can be built only through doing them successfully. It is counterproductive to repeat unsuccessful attempts with only a steadfast resolve to keep trying. Tennis practices, lessons, and drills need to be planned to build confidence. It is critical to play at the correct degree of difficulty. If success cannot be achieved after several tries, the task should be simplified. This can be done in many ways, depending on the situation. The person can be moved closer to the net, the speed of the ball can be reduced, the

length of the swing can be shortened, the targets can be brought further inside the lines, the ball can be hit higher over the net, the spin on the ball can be increased, or only one part of a stroke can be focussed upon. As successes are achieved, the degree of difficulty can again be increased.

Coaches skilled in helping their charges to build competence and confidence will pick the right beginning level. As immediate successes are achieved, they will give honest, specific praise frequently. If the new task at hand is preparing the shoulders earlier for the forehand stroke, the phrases "Beautiful shoulder preparation!" or "That's the way to prepare early!" will be heard often. Once in a while we should hear, "You were a little late on that one." A good rule of thumb is three words of praise for every word of constructive criticism. Players need continual feedback. As they master a specific skill, verbal praise for that facet of their game will no longer be necessary; the focus will move on to something else. That too will pass, but the instructor should never stop showing appreciation and approval.

Competitive Attitude Development

Ideally, you need to find attitudes that help you perform well when the competition is intense, the stakes high, and the pressure great. You should look forward to the excitement of being down match point in a third-set tie breaker. You should be able to see yourself giving the point everything you have with no fear of the consequences. You may end up playing the point badly and losing to an inferior player, but this should not worry you at all. The competition is what you love.

As a competitor you also will need an attitude that carries you through slumps in your game. As the losses pile up and tennis is no longer as much fun as it used to be, you will need to keep going. When opponents cheat and deprive you of a championship that was rightfully yours, you need to take it in stride. When you are insulted and your integrity challenged, you need to remain undaunted. When you work your hardest and your goals still are not reached, you must cope with the situation. Finally, when you treat others with respect and they seem to have no regard for your feelings, you need an attitude that will give you support. If you have been mentally well trained, you will be prepared for all of these developments.

There are three primary expectations that cause problems for competitors. One stems from the extraordinary emphasis on winning. There is no question that prize money and championships are determined by wins. Even making the school team depends on one's record. Every important match is followed by the inevitable question, "Did you win?" In single elimination tournaments, even the right to continue participating depends on wins.

However, too strong an emphasis on winning keeps many from playing confidently at crucial moments. On the last point of a third-set tie breaker can you be certain of winning? Consider all the things that could go awry on any one point: a bad bounce, a lucky shot off the tape, a mistaken line call, a sudden gust of wind, or a superhuman effort by your opponent. If you judge your success by wins but cannot control the outcome of the match, fear of losing will undermine your performance. Therefore, success needs to be based on something besides winning if "big points" are to be played with genuine confidence.

A second expectation that causes problems for competitors is that they play well. I have heard players say that it does not matter if they win or lose as long as they play well. At first glance this attitude seems to offer more potential than the focus on winning. You have only yourself to worry about. Your success is not thwarted by bad line calls, acts of nature, or heroic efforts of the opponent. Factors outside your control are not threatening. Confidence is built even in losing efforts. What matters is playing well, not winning.

But this demand of yourself that you play well can undermine your confidence even more than an emphasis on winning. If you need wins you can usually find a tournament with lower calibre players. But what can be done when you expect to play well but do not, no matter how hard you practice and try to improve? I have watched players lose their composure, throw their rackets after poor shots, or yell at the top of their lungs, "How could anyone miss such an easy shot? Even a two-year-old could play better!" All they expected was to play well, yet that goal was eluding them.

That is not surprising. Expecting to play well when it counts most is like assuming you are Superman. John McEnroe, when playing Arthur Ashe for $100,000 and the biggest title of his career, double-faulted three times in a row at set point and went on to lose the set. If McEnroe can do this, how do you expect to avoid untimely disasters in important matches? Be honest with yourself; you know how poorly you are capable of playing. Sometimes poor playing comes and goes, and other times it lasts for a whole tournament. Whom are you kidding if you change from the expectation focussing on winning to one that stresses playing well.

Visualize sequence of shots,

A third detrimental expectation that undermines a strong competitive attitude is that you should always be treated fairly. Like the expectations centering on winning and playing well, it leaves you vulnerable. You do not control how other people are going to act. If their actions and attitudes determine your direction, you are severely limited.

A strong competitor must remain an actor rather than a reactor. Therefore do not be shocked when your coach puts you at number five singles and you know that you deserve to play number one. Do not be frustrated when you have been calling your lines fairly while your opponent has been cheating. When you have worked hard on your game and seem to realize no improvement, be patient. When you start to feel incensed about how unfair your situation may be, stop and think. How fair is it that you enjoy good health while others do not? How fair is it that you can even play tennis while many people in the world must devote all their energy to the task of finding enough food to stay alive? Many things in life are not fair. If you let this fact impair your attitude while competing, you will never be as mentally tough as you could be.

While expectations centering on winning, playing well, and fairness can handicap you in many difficult situations, there is an alternative attitude that can liberate you to do your best. The key concept is maximum effort. It is clear why Avis adopted the motto "We try harder." You can feel good about giving a challenge "the old college try." In any tense, competitive situation you have the power to try. If success is based on effort, you will have it within your grasp to succeed.

Now picture yourself in a tense, third-set tie breaker. Since the match has gone that far you cannot be certain of winning. However, strength and confidence for facing this situation can be based on knowing you will try. Your opponent may hit an ace that leaves you flat-footed, but you can feel satisfaction if you were trying to return the ball. You may end up "blowing" an easy ball near the net, but that will not destroy you because you know you tried. You may win or lose, but that is immaterial as long as you gave maximum effort. You may play well or not, it makes no difference. Giving it your best effort is the important thing. Who could ask for more?

Confidence grows out of certainty. Confident "all-out" efforts often cause you to play well—but not always. When you play well you may win, but not necessarily. When effort is the only criterion, success lies within your control.

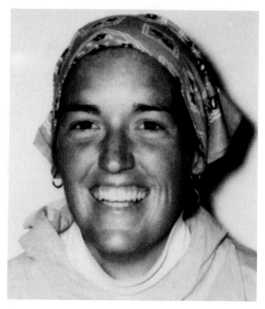

Good Role Model Karen Gibbs

Role Modeling

Conceptualizing the proper attitude toward competition is an important step forward. It sounds so simple: starting tomorrow you will go out there on the court and give the match your full effort. Nothing else will matter and many of your former worries will be gone. However, opposing attitudes are deeply embedded in most of us. Many of the things that we do and say reveal conflicting loyalties. Body languages—our gestures and expressions—may communicate a message that differs from the one being spoken. Most of us realize that actions speak louder than words. We do not want to be hypocrites; we want to live the philosophies we profess.

So many factors in American culture point to winning as the bottom line, the final measure of success. Opponents of this view are regarded with suspicion—as naive idealists who are out of touch with reality. Competitors achieve recognition by winning. Coaches keep their jobs if they win. Countries control their own destinies if they win wars. Trying is not enough according to conventional American wisdom, you need to win. Is it any wonder that this attitude is communicated through our actions, even at the moment that we may be affirming the importance of effort? If we refuse to let go of the need to win, we carry the inhibiting pressures with us.

People will claim that the emphasis on winning is necessary. If the tennis game is not played to win, then it is not even tennis. All tennis strategy is based on trying to win points, not lose them. All team seasons are based on trying to win championships, not lose them. This is obviously true, but these points do nothing to negate the proper emphasis on effort. Trying is directed toward winning, but the important rewards need to be found in effort itself. A win or loss is not an accurate measure of success.

With these points in mind, consider how confusing parents can be as role models. On the one hand, they may tell their child that only effort is important. On the other hand, after a match they first want to know if their son or daughter won. They wonder why he or she should lose to someone who had been defeated so easily before. The parents talk proudly to friends and relatives about wins, not good efforts. The newspapers are sent detailed information after big wins or championships. Much time is devoted to rankings, and discussing whether someone should be above or below someone else. College is discussed, and the parents make it clear how nice it would be for their child to earn a scholarship. With so much money invested in lessons, traveling, equipment, etc., a scholarship would represent a nice return on their investment.

Coaches can also be transmitting conflicting signals. While proclaiming that effort is most important, they may be ignoring the player with poor skills who may be trying harder than anyone else on the team. Instead they may be spending most of their time with the top players. When they talk about their past teams, they may dwell on the championships won. Display cases featuring the team may emphasize the players' rankings. Being a member of the top six or winning championships may be stressed. Criticizing players when they lose and being elated only after wins can also be unsettling.

Players too can be poor role models. While affirming that it is effort that counts, they become visibly upset when they lose or play poorly. They label themselves and their teammates "chokers" when their performance level has dropped in critical, tension-filled situations. They become excited when a championship is at stake, but find it hard to concentrate or even care about playing while practicing.

Upon reflection you may realize that winning, not effort, is often the goal, even for coaches who are seeking to emphasize trying. Consider the current significance of Bjorn Borg in Sweden, where

Focus on ball off opponent's racket, bouncing on court, and making contact,

a whole generation of younger players seem to have copied his two-handed backhand, extreme topspin, and cool court temperament. On the other hand, note the influence in the U.S. of John McEnroe, whose fiery temper, poor sportsmanship, and unique service stance have gained much notoriety.

There are other American tennis celebrities who offer better examples. Consider, for example, Chris Evert Lloyd, Arthur Ashe, and Stan Smith. Each of us has probably known a friend who was particularly inspiring. I had the good fortune of knowing Karen Gibbs, a lovely young lady whose story I will share with anyone who will listen. She is a wonderful model for both tennis and life.

Karen Gibbs, known affectionately as "Gibber," entered Gustavus Adolphus College in the fall of 1974. During her freshman year she was one of the top tennis players in the upper Midwest . . . until cancer ended her season. Part of her right arm was amputated and her struggle for life began. Immediately Gibber decided that she was going to play tennis left-handed. Surprisingly she again made the team during her sophomore year and even won her match against the University of Minnesota.

As the cancer spread, radiation and chemotherapy treatments caused Karen to lose her hair and almost 50 pounds. In her weakened condition Gibber had a shoulder separation which ended her tennis competition. Even so she was there at most practices, leading the women through conditioning drills and assisting in every way possible. She died on August 18, 1977 at the age of 21.

Karen's legacy has not been forgotten. She is still remembered for her ability to find the bright side, no matter what happened to her. Losing the use of her right arm brought the challenge of playing left-handed. Frequent stays in the hospital were fun because of all the visitors, losing weight fit into her diet plans, and being bald made Halloween disguises easier. She felt comfortable sharing her feelings and ideas on cancer, handicaps, and the prospect of early death. However, if anybody started feeling sorry for her, she quickly changed the conversation.

Also Karen demonstrated good sportsmanship. She genuinely cared about her opponents as well as her teammates. She seldom made excuses or lost her temper. "Excuses," she claimed, "detract from the accomplishments of my opponents. So does losing my temper. In effect, I am blaming a loss or poor performance on my own mistakes rather than giving credit to my opponent. I do not want to do that."

Gibber is a model of the mature approach to tennis competition and life. She strove for excellence through daily discipline and an undaunted spirit that saw each new setback as a creative opportunity to accomplish more. She wanted to win, but was not afraid to lose. She wanted to improve, but starting over again left-handed did not discourage her. She wanted to live, and the threat of death did not deter her. Gibber continued to try, in spite of everything, thereby revealing a key to both tennis and life.

This story of Karen Gibbs is displayed on the college tennis courts that are named in her honor. A lounge in a dormitory near the courts features her pictures and excerpts from her journal. Scholarships to the college and summer tennis camps bear her name and the standards that she exemplified. It is hard for me to imagine how anyone could model the standard of full effort any better than Karen. It is so easy to abandon your resolve to keep trying when everything is going against you. Not even the threat of death seemed to deter Karen. Just a few months before her death she wrote in her journal:

> "I must be thankful for the rough spots, too, because that is when I seem to really grow and discover not only new things about myself, but also others around me as well. I must remember to always be thankful for what I have because there are so many people who are worse off than me, and I really have no reason *not* to be thankful . . . LOOK AT MY ABUNDANCE!!!"

Concentration-Relaxation Techniques

Thus far, this mental training program describes a general approach, which will decrease your tendency to become nervous, angry, or bored. No matter how well you have followed the program, you will find yourself doubting your own ability at times. In especially critical situations, you may become tense and play poorly. Your mind will wander at times while playing lesser opponents. When this happens you will benefit from concentration-relaxation techniques which can assist you to control your emotions.

The following techniques need to be practiced if you are going to use them effectively. You would never consider using a new serve that you had never tried before if you were encountering difficulties with your regular serve during an important tournament. Do not expect wonders from concentration-relaxation techniques you have never tried before. Effectiveness comes through practice.

Remember that techniques need to be varied according to what you need at the moment. One technique may work well for several minutes. Then it may be necessary to switch to another technique in order to deal with the problem at hand. For this reason it is important to know a variety of concentration-relaxation techniques. Five effective ones for use during competition are:

(1) *Between points breathe deeply and follow the movement of your breath.* Feel the air as it comes through the nose, passes down the throat, and fills the lungs. The stomach should expand as the lungs fill. Then as you breathe out, feel the stomach contract while air passes up the throat and out of the body. As long as you breathe deeply and concentrate on the breath, you will automatically relax and maintain concentration. When the break between points is over, then focus switches back to the ball.

(2) *Visualize what you wish to do before each point.* See the sequence of shots emerging according to an overall plan that you have established. You are the person in control; you have the ability to execute the shots and strategy that are necessary. Just before serving or returning serve, you need a few moments of positive visualization. You can do this while you bounce the ball a few times before serving or while you look at the ground for a few moments before returning serve.

(3) *Focus on three important spots as each point is being played: the ball coming off your opponent's racket, the ball bouncing on the court, and the ball making contact with your racket.* The first spot lets you know immediately where the ball is headed. The second spot tells you how the ball has come off the court. And the third spot forces you to watch the ball until your racket has made contact. Concentration on these spots is aided if you say to yourself "hit" at spot one, "bounce" at spot two, and "hit" at spot three. Using the "hit-bounce-hit" works much better than trying to follow the entire flight of the ball. When the latter is attempted your mind often fatigues and you end up not concentrating at all.

(4) *Focus on the point of contact between your racket and the ball until the ball crosses the net.* Avoid the temptation to look for your opponent's position, your target, or where the ball is going. Unfortunately, most people look up before they hit the ball when it is still five or six feet away. Looking up ruins concentration on the ball, changes the position of the head and body, and often causes the shoulders to rotate prematurely. All of these actions make solid contact with the ball less predictable.

Hold focus on contact until ball crosses net.

Because the temptation to look up is so strong for most people, additional techniques are often necessary to keep the eyes on the point of contact. For example, you may wish to say to yourself "concentrate" or "focus" *after* contact has been made. You permit yourself to look up only after one of the words has been repeated.

(5) *Repeat a phrase or sing a song to yourself quietly between points.* The phrase can be "watch the ball" or "the Lord is my shepherd" or "Nan Myo Horen Geikyo." It can be *anything*, as long as it is repeated over and over until the next point is ready to begin. Also, any song may be sung, as long as you keep singing it. Remember, in respect to your opponent, to do all of this *very* quietly.

Self-Talk

Competitors generally talk to themselves before, during, and after competition. These self-directed conversations have the potential to either assist you in meeting the pressures of competition or to help you self-destruct. It is important that you be able to distinguish positive from negative self-talk. Competitors skilled in mental training will say only those things to themselves that build self-confidence. They will speak to themselves in the same encouraging way that they would speak to a respected doubles partner. The words could be re-

peated in front of any audience and the competitor would not be embarrassed. Unfortunately, many of us would never wish to see our thoughts, silent words, or words muttered under our breath revealed to those whose opinions we cherish. But who could be a more special person for you than yourself?

There are three main types of self-defeating talk that need to be identified and then corrected. One type includes such classic statements as: "You have got to be the *worst* player (volleyer, server, groundstroker, etc.) I've ever seen!" Or "I can't believe anyone would miss that shot!" Or "You deserve a prize for your absolute stupidity!" Notice the addition of sarcasm to the last statement. All of these statements put you down in a manner that you would never consider appropriate for others.

Another type of self-defeating talk occurs when you load yourself with unrealistic demands: "I've got to win!" Or "Nobody loses to a team as weak as they." Or "Everybody who has ever amounted to anything can perform this skill." With each of these statements you have left yourself vulnerable, unable to guarantee your own success. These "must" situations are bound to raise

your anxiety level and most likely to decrease your performance level.

The third type of self-defeating talk occurs when you fret about the past or the future. If you look back, second-guessing yourself can be very destructive. Typical statements are: "Why didn't I play more aggressively in the first set?" Or "I never should have called that one shot good." Or "Why did I let his (or her) antics upset me?" If you look forward, worrying about the future could include such thoughts as: "Gee, I hope we don't blow this match." Or "What will all my friends think when they see the results of this match?" On the other hand, positive self-talk directs your attention to the present, to the creative opportunities that are possible *now.*

When negative thoughts surface, it is best for you to say, "Stop!" Then begin to repeat over and over the positive messages that you want to dominate your mind. It helps to act out the attitude that you want, even though you may not feel that way at all. A confident stride and a smile on your face can help change your negative emotions. So can tapes that combine your favorite music with important thoughts. Also, posters and signs placed in frequently-viewed locations can have a positive im-

Pre-Match Self-Talk

NEGATIVE	POSITIVE
1. I lost to Joe three times. I do not have a chance.	I love to play people who have defeated me before. The challenge will bring out the best in me.
2. I am not ready to play. I have been hitting my forehand terribly all week. I know it is going to let me down.	I can hardly wait to play. I am a versatile and resourceful player. If one part of my game should temporarily let me down, I will depend on my other strengths.
3. Let us not blow this next match. I could not believe how poorly we played last year when we reached this round.	This is the match toward which we have been practicing all year. We are ready to play well.
4. We played so poorly last round. We do not have a prayer against this team if we play like that.	Anybody can have a bad match. We have played so well during the last week. We did not prepare ourselves mentally for the last match, but we sure are ready now.
5. I get so nervous when I play in front of crowds. I hope there are not many people there to watch.	It makes no difference to me if there is a crowd or not. I play equally well in both situations. I concentrate so completely on the match that I hardly even notice the crowd.
6. We have *got* to win this match. Our whole season depends on it.	It would be nice to win, but we do not *have* to win any match. It will be fun giving this match our best effort.
7. I really want to play well in front of my parents (or girlfriend, professional scout, coach, etc.). It sure would be disappointing if they came this far to watch me play and then I had a bad day.	I do not worry about the impression I will make on others. I play to please myself. I know I will be satisfied, since success for me is based on maximum effort. You can be sure I will be giving the match everything I have.

Match Self-Talk

NEGATIVE	POSITIVE
1. What a dumb shot that was! I must be an idiot to go crosscourt in that situation.	That time I chose the wrong shot. Next time I will go down the line.
2. I cannot believe I missed that easy shot!	No big deal, I will get the next one.
3. Every time the score goes to 3–3 in a game, I lose the final point.	The 3–3 point is no different from the rest. I play it with the same concentration and energy that I give to the other points.
4. I am so far behind. What is the use in trying?	No need to worry. Just one point at a time. I have been down worse than this and still won.
5. I must look like a fool!	Keep concentrating. Breathe out when hitting the next shot.
6. Players who stall irritate me.	Extra time can work to my advantage. My superior powers of concentration will really work for me now.
7. I cannot believe he (or she) would question my call. Does he (or she) think I am a cheater?	I feel good about my calls. I always give my opponent the benefit of the doubt.
8. My serve is terrible today! There is no way that I can expect to play well when my serve is not working.	My serve is not going in as well as I had hoped, but there is no reason for concern. All I need to do is put a little more spin on my first serve, and rely more on my volleys and quickness. I am a well-rounded player who can use a variety of strategies.
9. He (or she) cheated me! I cannot believe he (or she) would do that! I have worked so hard for this match, and now it is going to be taken away by his (or her) cheating.	He (or she) made a mistake. That is bound to happen. After all, he (or she) is human. I am out here to give this match my best effort, win or lose. Bad line calls by my opponent will not prevent me from reaching my primary goal.

Post-Match Self-Talk

NEGATIVE	POSITIVE
1. Why did I ever serve and stay back on match point? I am such a choker in critical situations!	I made a mistake when I stayed back at match point. Next time I will be more aggressive.
2. I let the team down when I lost. Because of me we lost the championship. I feel so bad. They worked so hard for this, and then I ruined it all.	Even though I lost, I gave the match my total effort. I feel proud of my contributions to the team. They are far more important than winning or losing.
3. How could I ever play so poorly? I feel so embarassed having lost to him (or her).	There is no shame in having played poorly. It happens to the best players. I could lose to *anyone* and it would not bother me.
4. What a choker I am! Every time I have an opportunity to win a big match, I find some way to lose.	I missed a golden opportunity to win a big match, but I am not going to spend any time worrying about it. I will get it next time.
5. I am never going to improve.	Today I will continue to work on weaknesses. Through practice I will improve.
6. I hate to practice during a slump.	When the going gets tough, the tough get going.
7. I never get the breaks.	Losers wait for the breaks to happen. Winners create their own breaks through disciplined practice. I am a winner.
8. I hate competition! I play so much worse in matches than in practice.	I love competition. It brings out the best in me.

Repeat a phrase or sing a song to yourself.

pact on you. With all of these strategies you need to keep in mind that you are in control of your own thoughts and emotions. You can change them to serve your own purposes.

Self-talk can be placed in three time frames: before, during, and after matches. By juxtaposing negative and positive comments that relate to typical situations I hope you will see clearly your freedom of choice. What you say to yourself makes such a great difference in your ability to perform. So often what you expect is what you get.

Visualization

You need to see yourself performing successfully. In your mind's eye your goal is already an accomplished fact. Before each match is played you see yourself executing the skills and strategy that will produce victory. Before each point you perceive the sequence of shots that will win the point. As you stroke you see each ball dropping in the target area. This vision is implanted firmly in your mind before your eyes leave the point of contact to follow the flight of your ball. When this occurs you are visualizing.

Visualized action is not a pipe dream, a faint hope of how you will play someday. Therefore, you should not picture yourself as Bjorn Borg, hitting shots that you could not expect to hit now. Visualization will not cause you to do things be-

yond your present skill level. Picture yourself hitting consistent, high percentage shots. Pick targets that are consistent with good strategy and your skill level. Visualization is a way of seeing in advance the way you will play today—not two years from now. Do not dream about unbelievable shots. Be an objective, pragmatic realist as you visualize. You are freeing yourself to do what you can do, not what you hope to do someday.

Your visions need to be repeated over and over—the oftener the better. All of your senses should be used—touch, smell, hearing, taste, and sight. The total experience comes alive in your mind—just the way you want it to happen. You see your opponent, hear the racket striking the ball, feel the pressure of your hand against the grip, smell the fragrance of the nearby pine trees, and taste the salt on your lips after a series of long and strenuous points.

Visualization occurs at both the subconscious and conscious levels. At the subconscious level alpha waves (7 to 14 cycles per second) are emitted by the brain. In this state the mind is uncluttered and most receptive to suggestions. The ideas implanted at this time continue to influence you long afterwards, even as your conscious thoughts move on to other topics. On the other hand, the brain emits beta waves (14 to 21 cycles per second) at the conscious level. When this mode is used, the visualization effects are lost as soon as your thoughts switch to another topic. However, both levels of visualization are important to a mental training program. Alpha programing is used to influence the subconscious level while beta programing is important at the conscious level.

Alpha programing at the subconscious level usually requires a quiet, subdued environment. An isolated, semi-darkened room is best. You can naturally achieve an alpha brain wave state just before dozing off to sleep or just after awakening. Therefore, you should consider repeating outstanding visions of yourself playing at these times.

However, an organized, alpha-level visualization session could not be conducted by a coach at those times. Therefore, group subconscious programing requires meditative techniques that can induce an alpha brain wave state. You need to practice deep, relaxed breathing with your mind focussed on some object of concentration. Perhaps the most effective object is the movement of the breath itself. You can focus on your stomach, slowly contracting as you exhale, and then expanding more quickly as you inhale. After a few minutes of deep breathing in this fashion, the alpha state is achieved.

Alpha programing in a group setting can be part of an official practice session or a preliminary to match competition. No talking except by the group leader is permitted. You can relax and concentrate best if you close your eyes and lie quietly on the floor. The leader needs a firm, soothing voice. Once the alpha state is reached, you will be asked to focus your attention on areas that need reinforcement.

During pre-match meditation you should visualize the strokes, strategy, footwork, and mental attitude that you will need to win that day. On practice days other important topics can be covered. You need to be reminded to try when you are down, to respond unemotionally when provoked, and to remain cool under pressure. Some of your past failures can be recalled. Then you visualize positive outcomes to these events. You are encouraged to realize that your emotions, thoughts, and actions stem from your own free choices. Visualization exercises in an alpha state influence the subconscious and increase the likelihood that future actions will be in keeping with your wishes.

Equally important is beta programing. In contrast to alpha programing, which requires a quiet environment accompanied by meditation, beta programing is possible in any setting. You can be riding in a car or train, listening to a coach explain your tennis program, or rehearsing your next point during a match. If you see yourself performing the task successfully, you are proceeding properly.

Whenever you do beta programing there are resulting benefits in your tennis game. However, three times are particularly important for the tournament player. One is immediately before the match begins—even as late as the pre-match warm-up. Picture yourself hitting well and following an effective strategy. Likely trouble areas can be anticipated and solutions visualized. You see yourself in control of your own actions and emotions, not controlled by your surroundings.

A second important time for beta-level visualization comes between points. During this time you first follow your breath and the corresponding movement of your stomach. As you begin to feel relaxed you picture clearly the target for your serve or service return. You have an idea of the following shot sequence and how you will win the point. You see the point as an accomplished reality to be acted out, not as a hope of the way things might be.

The third time for visualization comes during points as each stroke is hit. You should see in your mind's eye the exact target for which you are aiming. Your eyes should remain glued to the point of contact for at least a second after you have hit the ball. During this time you continue to visualize the target while resisting the temptation to follow the flight of the ball. Since most people start looking toward their target before the ball has made contact with their own racket, they are changing the position of their head and body as they hit the ball. Understandably this movement increases the difficulty of the shot and decreases consistency. Visualization (instead of looking) therefore improves consistency while providing the brain a clear destination for the ball. So often players simply hit the ball. When asked where they were aiming they say, "I was just trying to get the ball back." That imprecise goal clouds the adjustments that should be made on ensuing shots if, for example, most of their groundstrokes are dropping short in the opponent's court. Visualization clearly improves stroke mechanics, target adjustments, and consistency.

Visualization at both the alpha and beta levels is an important key to a higher level of play. Its impact is greatest when your visions are combined with proper self-talk, concentration-relaxation techniques, and all the other area of mental training. Together they reinforce the wisdom of the following words:

It's All in the State of Mind

If you think you are beaten you are;
  If you think you dare not, you don't;
If you think you'd like to win, but you can't;
  It's almost a "cinch" you won't;
If you think you'll lose, you've lost;
  For out in the world you'll find
Success begins with a fellow's will;
  It's all in the state of mind.
For many a race is lost
  Ere even a race is run.
And many a coward fails
  Ere even his work's begun.
Think big and your deeds will grow
  Think small and you fall behind.
Think that you can, and you will;
  It's all in the state of mind.
If you think you are outclassed, you are;
  You've got to think high to rise;
You've got to be sure of yourself before
  You can ever win a prize.
Life's battle doesn't always go
  To the stronger or faster man.
But sooner or later, the man who wins
  Is the fellow who thinks he can.

Goal Setting

A strong mental training program is tied together by well-defined, measurable goals. They are written down and then reviewed periodically. Written goals remind you what you should be doing. They encourage you to use your practice time efficiently and provide a summary of your progress. All important elements of the mental training program can be incorporated in your goal setting process.

When setting goals, address three different time periods. First, decide on immediate, short-term goals. Decide what you wish to accomplish in the next few weeks of practice. These goals can be clearly in focus as you go out to play. A number of them can be attempted simultaneously. For example, you can work on getting 70 percent of your first serves in the service court, keeping the groundstrokes within ten feet of the baseline, never showing *any* signs of anger on the court, and never questioning an opponent's line call. You reach a point, however, when you are not able to keep all you goals in focus as you practice. When this occurs they need to be cut back to a manageable level.

Place short-range goals on a card and take it to practice. Reread your goals a couple times during breaks in play. After each goal make spaces for self ratings. Rate yourself from one to a perfect score of ten after each practice session. If you score a ten for three consecutive practices, then consider that goal temporarily accomplished. Now add another goal to replace the accomplished one. In this manner your goals continue to change with accomplishments and new priorities.

However, sometimes goals can be frustrating and counterproductive. When this occurs, you also should feel free to drop a goal. For example, I once worked on developing a better topspin, backhand passing shot. The more I worked, the more frustrated I became. Finally I ended up developing tennis elbow because of my efforts. I had to quit playing for several months. When I was able to play again, I did not resume my practice on the topspin backhand. This goal had not generated in me a feeling of progress toward a higher level of play, a necessary prerequisite for meaningful goals.

A separate short-term goal card for an individual match can be useful, particularly when the practice goals have centered on your strokes. Refer to the card as you switch sides. Your match goals need to focus on strategies that maximize your strengths and exploit your opponent's weaknesses. Also keep your mind relaxed and alert. Keep your concentration on the present moment and avoid rehashing the past ("Why didn't I do this or that?") or worrying about the future ("I hope I do not blow my final set lead").

Besides short-range goals, intermediate-term goals are important as well. These vary in length from the end of the season to a year from now. Separate cards have a space for a self-evaluation after approximately five practices. Daily players evaluate themselves weekly, while twice a week players assess their play every two or three weeks. If for some reason you were unable to work on one of your goals, then simply draw a line through the appropriate space. Except for the frequency, procedures for short and intermediate goals are the same. Give additional reinforcement to your goals by placing them on bulletin boards, corners of mirrors, or other frequently viewed spots. Continual reminders keep you moving on the course that you have charted.

The third set of goals is long-term. A twelve-year-old may want to play on a good college team. A collegiate player may dream of making it to the top of the pro ranks. An adult beginner may wish to be an "A" player some day. A recreational player seeking enjoyment and good physical activity may commit himself or herself to playing so many hours a week. Whatever the long-term goal might be, there can be a realistic plan to get you from the present to where you want to be. This plan and the time commitment it requires are balanced with other priorities. Basic values, purposes, and relationships are considered. Your activity on the tennis court is put into perspective. Potential conflicts are anticipated and you hope minimized. Your goals become more realistic, appropriate, and fulfilling.

While pursuing all objectives, realize that effort toward a goal is more important than reaching the goal itself. This attitude reflects the fact that life is a journey rather than a destination, a process instead of a static state. An accomplished goal can be savored for a short while, but then your attention is directed forward. A failure is treated similarly. Make your disappointment time brief, and then formulate a new goal to capture your interest, enthusiasm, and dedication.

No matter which goal you select, emphasize trying. In this way you can "hang loose" as to the final outcome. There are no "must" goals, nothing which has to be accomplished. Give a goal your best effort, but in the final analysis "let it happen." You are not perfect or omnipotent. Some goals will not be reached no matter how hard you try, for reasons outside your control. So do not force the issue, do not struggle against yourself and others when the tension produced moves you further away from your goal. At times trying too hard can create a serious problem.

Normally trying plays an important role in competitive events. Michelob Light commercials

depict the fun of trying, of "going for it" win or lose, of giving full effort to the goal of winning. Although the competition is intense, play seems to exist within the bounds of good sportsmanship. When the contest is over, the same mood prevails. Winners and losers are still having a great time, enjoying the camraderie, sharing a pleasurable drink together, and complimenting each other for their accomplishments. You get the feeling that both sides can hardly wait for another day when they will be able to go at it again. Everyone was successful because they tried and gave to the game their all.

Contrast with the Michelob vision another typical postgame scene. Imagine a locker room filled with dejected losers. Their heads are bent low while they offer one excuse after another. They believe they were cheated out of a well-deserved victory. The coaches are frustrated. They "chew out" their players for "stupid," unnecessary mistakes. They feel no pride in their improvements because it is impossible to be pleased with anything after a loss. In this situation success is based on winning, not trying.

Effort also is vital in practice sessions. You may be working on a new slice backhand, more agility and quickness, or improved strength on the serve. Normally you would anticipate progress, but sometimes there is a step backwards before forward progress is realized. As you pass your peak physical age your proficiency may drop instead of rise. If your practice time decreases while other priorities become more important, your skill level may drop. If you compare yourself to people with better athletic backgrounds, you may be substandard. The disappointment of not meeting certain levels of excellence can be more damaging than the discouragement associated with losing. Remember that many important goals may not be achieved. New ones may need to be formulated. However, through all adversities and failures you can continue to try.

Daily Mental Training Routine

Many elements of this mental training program for tennis players are incorporated in the following written exercises, recommendations for daily action, and concentration-relaxation-visualization routines. Begin by reviewing carefully the preceding seven sections. Then fill out the questionnaire. This information about yourself is used in completing short-, intermediate-, and long-term goal cards, as well as a 14-minute routine for practice and a 10-minute routine before matches.

Begin by filling out the following questionnaire in detail. Do not attempt other mental training activities without this important first step.

Mental Training Questionnaire

I.   What things do you like most . . . (1) about yourself as a person? . . . (2) about your tennis game? . . . (3) about your coach or pro as a person? . . . (4) about the way he or she teaches? . . . (5) about your tennis partners as people? . . . (6) about the way they play tennis? Practice saying these things to yourself and each other every day.

II. (1) How positive is your self-talk? Rate yourself on a scale from 1 to 10 for pre-match, during match, and post-match comments. Give yourself a 10 if you would not mind having your comments repeated in front of a church audience. (2) Which negative statements do you repeat most frequently? (3) What positive statements should you substitute for these negative statements? (4) Which positive statements do you use most frequently? (5) What other positive statements could be most helpful to you? Practice saying the positive statements to yourself every day.

III. (1) What is the most significant lesson you have learned from the story of Karen Gibbs? (2) Who is the person you most admire? Why? (3) Which top tennis pro do you admire the most? Why? (4) What characteristics are most important for you to model? Practice those characteristics every day.

IV. (1) Visualize yourself in slow motion, hitting each of your strokes perfectly. What characteristics do you observe now which are not present when you are hitting poorly? Write individually about each stroke. (2) Visualize yourself concentrating completely. See yourself being aware of the moment when the ball leaves your opponent's racket, when the ball bounces and when it makes contact with your racket. See yourself having your target in your mind's eye and resisting the temptation to look up too soon. When are you most likely to concentrate completely? When do you have the most difficulty? What is the key to get you to concentrate more frequently? (3) Visualize yourself playing the best match of your career. When and where was it? Who were you playing? Describe the playing conditions. Who was watching? What was at stake? How did you feel inside? Did anything happen just before the match that caused you to play well? Were there any key points? What were you thinking when you played those points? What were you saying to yourself? Do you member the clothing you wore and the racket you used? How did you feel just after the match was over? What did you say to your opponent? What did others say to you?

V. (1) Visualize a match in which you became very nervous and played poorly. Use the questions in IV-3 to describe the situation. (2) Visualize a match in which you overcame your nervousness and did well. Again use the questions in IV-3. (3) Visualize a match in which you became very angry and played poorly. Use IV-3. Also identify what contributed most to your anger. Were there reasons unrelated to the match, frustrations associated with your poor play, or things which the opponent did? (4) Visualize a match in which you overcame your anger and did well. Use IV-3. (5) Visualize a match in which you became bored and indifferent and played poorly. Use IV-3. Identify the circumstances or style of play that contributed most to your boredom. (6) Visualize a match in which you overcame your boredom and did well. Use IV-3. What were the keys to your success?

VI. (1) Excluding family members or a person in whom you have romantic interests, who are your most important people? (2) For what would you like to be remembered by them? (3) Besides family responsibilities, what are your most important purpose(s) in life? (4) What relationship does your involvement in tennis have to your most important purpose(s) in life? (5) What are your long-term (2 or more years) goals for tennis? Be as specific as possible. (6) What are your intermediate (end of season or year) goals for tennis? Are they realistic? How will you measure your progress toward your goals? How do these goals relate to your long-term goals? (7) What are your immediate short-term goals? Will they lead you to your intermediate goals?

After writing your responses to the mental training questionnaire, prepare your short- and intermediate-term goal cards. Transfer your goals from the questionnaire onto two separate cards, creating spaces for evaluation marks on the appropriate dates. On the short-term card there should be a space for every practice date after each goal, while on the intermediate-term card there are spaces for approximately every five practices. Ratings from one to ten are used except in situations where you were not able to work on your goal. Then draw a line through the appropriate space. Goals are added or dropped according to criteria outlined earlier.

With your questionnaire and goal cards completed, you are ready to start the 14-minute mental training routine for tennis practices. Find a quiet, uninterrupted spot where you can lie on your back and follow the movement of your breath. The first six and a half minutes are spent relaxing yourself completely and starting your alpha brain wave activity. Begin by stretching your arms behind your head and pointing your toes downward. Continue to stretch every muscle in your body (½ minute). Then completely relax, placing both hands on your stomach. Pretend that your stomach is a balloon. As you breathe out, imagine that your hands are pressing all the air out of the balloon while you count slowly to four. As you breathe in, allow the air to rush back into the balloon as you count to two. Your breathing is quiet and slow (1½ minutes). Next proceed through a progressive relaxation technique, starting with your toes. Tense them tightly for about ten seconds. Then relax completely while you breathe deeply, follow the movement of your stomach, and observe the relaxed feeling of your toes and feet. After 30 seconds do the same with your legs, stomach, hands, chest and shoulders, mouth and jaw, and eyes and forehead (4 minutes). Follow this deep breathing (½ minute).

After you are completely relaxed, move into the heart of the mental training routine. Visualize a situation that has made you nervous. (On other days you will choose ones that have made you angry or bored.) Bring to mind all the details that you summarized on your questionnaire in part V-1. The incident comes alive. You feel that you are there, experiencing it again (2 minutes). Then let the incident go as you relax completely and follow your breath (½ minute). Next visualize yourself overcoming your nervousness in the same or a similar situation as you summarized it in part V-2. You have the freedom of choice to be calm when you know the principles of mental training (2 minutes). Breathe deeply again (½ minute). Then visualize yourself playing well. Keep in mind the observations you recorded on your questionnaire in part IV-3 (2 minutes). End the session with deep breathing (½ minute).

Besides the 14-minute routine for practices, use a 10-minute routine for pre-match preparation. Begin with stretching (½ minute), deep breathing (1 minute), progressive relaxation (3 minutes), and deep breathing (½ minute). Then move on to visualizing yourself hitting the ball well (2 minutes), deep breathing (½ minute), visualizing yourself using proper tactics that maximize your strengths and exploit your opponent's weaknesses (2 minutes), and deep breathing (½ minute). The ability to cope with nervousness, anger, and boredom has been instilled through the practice routine, but it is not repeated now. Only positive thoughts relating to the upcoming match are contemplated.

Mental training procedures for use during both practices and matches were outlined earlier. When you think negative thoughts or feel disruptive emotions, you should first yell silently to yourself, "Stop!" Then follow the movement of your breath for several seconds. This can shock you out of a negative spiral downward and leave you prepared to try a positive course of action. Remember the positive self-talk for any situation and the various concentration-relaxation techniques. Use the recommended visualization techniques between points and while the point is in progress. As you hit you know in your mind's eye where the ball is headed.

The preceding mental training routine for tennis players makes it clear that an ideal mental state can be learned and practiced. You can be a skilled mental competitor, moving at a high energy level while relaxed and calm inside. The impact of aggravating situations can be diminished. You can proceed with the knowledge that you are in control, that you are the actor rather than the reactor. You have within you the power to make tennis fun, to build the confidence of others as you build your own, and to play with more consistency. You can give your full effort, even when nothing seems to be going your way. The result is a higher quality of both tennis and life.

STEVE WILKINSON

12

How to Teach Yourself
to Play Tennis

Teach *yourself* to play tennis. It may not be the best way to learn the game, but it is an alternative if your local club's teaching professional is booked up, or you do not have the money for lessons. This chapter tells you how.

You will not need much to start: an inexpensive racket, a description of tennis fundamentals (which you can find in earlier chapters of this book), and a good deal of patience. Do not expect to start learning on the tennis court. You will be more relaxed and better able to concentrate if you first practice at home in front of a mirror without a ball.

Look in this book and learn the fundamentals of each groundstroke, one at a time (leave the serve until later). First notice the grip, then the stance and ready position, the backswing and pivot, the step, the start of the swing, the point of contact with the ball, and finally the follow-through. You will find it easiest to learn the conventional strokes using the Eastern grip for the forehand and backhand and the Continental grip for the serve.

Now practice the stroke you have learned in front of the mirror before learning the next stroke. Practice the stroke step by step, stopping at each of the checkpoints previously mentioned and comparing your image in the mirror with the illustrations in this book. When satisfied that you are copying the illustrations, try the complete swing.

Do not snap your wrist when swinging. Hold your follow-through for a three-second count. Check your balance at the end of the stroke, return to the ready position and repeat. If the complete swing gives you trouble, return to the step by step method briefly. Practice the complete stroke until you are comfortable with it; then learn the next stroke step by step.

After a few practice sessions at home, you will be ready to try hitting balls. Before heading out to the court, review your strokes in front of the mirror. Then get a bucket of balls—old ones will do fine. Place a target on the other side of the court to aim at. Use the bounce-hit technique, beginning with your forehand and progressing to your backhand. Start with your racket back. Drop the ball with your free hand and say "bounce" aloud; when you make contact with the ball say "hit." Try to hit the ball at the highest point of its bounce and follow through for a count of three to check your balance. If you are standing in the center of the court, your follow-through should point at the left net post if you are right-handed, the right post if you are left-handed. If you never hit the ball near your target, go through the swing, stopping the racket at the contact point. Keep your racket in this position and grasp it with your free hand. Now let go with your gripping hand and get behind your racket to look through the racket face—this is where your ball

Forehand, backhand, and serve

will usually go. If the balls you hit are not landing far enough in the direction of your follow-through, the racket face is probably not pointed far enough in that direction—you will need to contact the ball a little farther in front of your stepping foot. If the balls are going too far in the direction of your follow-through, and in fact past it, you need to hit the ball more behind your front foot. If getting the ball over the net is difficult, check to be sure your racket drops below the ball and that you are swinging from low to high. If your shots land behind the baseline on the opposite side of the court, you are swinging too much from low to high.

You should practice the bounce-hit technique until you gain a little control over your forehand and backhand. Then progress to having someone toss balls to you. Have a friend stand at the net on your side of the court and toss balls so that they bounce once, about two-thirds of the way between the two of you. He or she should toss the balls slowly so that you have time to adjust to each toss and execute your stroke. Continue to say "bounce" and "hit," and hold your follow-through. As you improve, have your friend move around to the other side of the net.

Now that you can hit balls coming to you, you can practice on a backboard, rebound net, or against a wall. The ball will come back at you fast, so stand far enough away for it to bounce twice

before you hit it. Try to hit five consecutive forehands. You will need to hit the ball as straight in front of you as you can in order for it to come back to the side on which you are swinging. To do this your contact point should be such that the plane of the strings is parallel to the backboard. When you can hit five consecutive forehands, set a goal of ten. If after some time this is still difficult, stop your racket at the various checkpoints to be sure your swing is correct. When you can reach this goal, place a target on the backboard and try to hit it. Repeat this process for the backhand. Concentrate on the stroke and do not try to hit the ball hard.

When you can hit ten consecutive forehands and backhands on the backboard with some frequency, you are ready to hit balls with a partner on the court. Begin by hitting forehands, trying to keep the ball in play. Once you can return the ball over the net five times in a row, try hitting backhands; when you can hit five consecutive backhands over the net, rally using both forehand and backhand. And hit with both strokes when you use the backboard.

After some practice you will be able to keep the ball in play using both groundstrokes, so arrange a game situation with a friend and play out points. Begin with a forehand setup and then rally the point out. Alternate setting each other up to begin rallies. At first the practice of playing out points is what is important. But you can make a game out of it by keeping score, say, to twenty-one points. You will find that hitting groundstrokes under game conditions is more difficult. If hitting groundstrokes seems beyond you, go back to the previous step and practice some more. Coping with the additional pressure of winning points is an important part of the learning process if you want to play competitive tennis.

Once you have gained some confidence in your groundstrokes, take on the serve. Study the motion of the serve as illustrated in this book. The service motion may seem more difficult, but lends itself to the step-by-step method of analysis which you have seen work. The motion is the same as in throwing a baseball. You can feel your arm performing this motion by throwing a few balls over the net into the service box the next time you practice groundstrokes.

Practice the service motion step by step in front of a mirror. Check your grip and stance first. Then drop both arms together and bring them up together until they are at a "V." Now your racket arm goes through the pitching motion: dropping behind your back as if to scratch it, then bringing the racket up, out and away. Your follow-through comes across your body. Check it with the illustrations in this book and be sure you can keep your balance for a count of three. Practice the swing until you feel somewhat comfortable with it—then you can add the toss to it.

Do not underestimate the toss; it is just as important as the service motion. Even top playing professionals understand that their serving problems are caused by their toss. There is a simple drill to learn the toss however. Go through the service motion and stop when your wrist starts to roll at the point of contact. Bring your racket straight down to the ground and place a ball on the ground where the center of the racket face is. This is where a good toss would bounce if you did not swing at the ball. It should be just in front of your front foot and slightly to the right for the right-handed player, slightly to the left for the left-handed player. Now move both arms, but concentrate on the toss and only swing your racket until it is behind your back. Form the "V" and try to hold onto the ball until your left shoulder approaches your left cheek before you release the ball. Let it bounce and see how close it comes to the ball you placed on the ground.

Practice this drill, trying to keep the ball from spinning as much as possible. Hold the ball with your fingertips, not in your palm. Keep the label towards you and try to have the ball go up and come down with the label still facing you. Think of lifting the ball rather than tossing it.

When you have developed consistency with your toss, go out on the court with a bucket of balls. Start from the service line, one step away from the centerline, and serve ten balls. When you can hit five out of ten balls into the diagonally opposite service box, take a step backwards. You may have to stay at one or two positions for a while, but if you keep at this drill you will reach the baseline. Then you should alternate trying to get five out of ten serves into the left and right service boxes. When you can do this you have learned the fundamentals of the serve.

It is most important to get your serve in. To develop a better game you should improve your serve a step at a time. Although you get two chances to get a serve in per point, to win matches it is important to get your *first* serve in. So start improving on a fundamentally sound serve by raising your efficiency to six out of ten serves. Then try to serve the ball deep in the box while maintaining your accuracy. Next try for more by attempting to place the ball deep and in one of the corners. When you become good at this you can try adding spin to your serve: instead of hitting the ball flat, your racket brushes up the back and over the top of the ball, staying in contact with it longer. Finally, you will want to try to add power and speed to your serve, but only if you can keep your accuracy.

When you can get your serve in the service box regularly you should start deciding where in the service box you want it; likewise, you will want to start thinking about location on every shot. Now that you know what to do you should start adding a why to it.

An overall court strategy should emphasize the fundamentals you have learned. Become more efficient at getting the ball in the service box. Work on strengthening the consistency you are starting to develop. Try and keep the ball in play one more time than your opponent. Points will be won on the basis of an opponent's not being able to keep the ball in play as much as they are won by your hitting a particularly good shot.

Along with the serve, you want to keep the majority of your groundstrokes deep and to the corners. It is easier to hit the ball crosscourt; the net is lower in the middle where the ball will cross it, you have more court to aim at, and you have more time and are in better position to get ready for your next shot. If you make the mistake of hitting the ball down the line and short, you open up the court to your opponent. He or she can either hit cross-

Topspin (forehand)

Topspin (backhand)

Topspin (serve)

court or down the line and have you out of position. However, there are times you can hit the ball down the line and put your opponent on the defensive. But you need to be in good position to make the shot while moving into the ball.

Professional players have a reason for making every shot, and think two to four shots ahead. These players also have a larger selection of shots because they can hit several variations of the groundstrokes you have learned. Topspin forehands and backhands are akin to the spin serve previously mentioned. Get your racket lower than the ball and brush up the back of it; bend your knees and move them from low to high. Topspin adds some power to your game but still enables you to play percentage tennis. You can hit the ball a *little* harder and the spin will keep it in play and send it bouncing back far behind the baseline.

A slice will cause the ball to spin in the opposite direction and not bounce very high, giving your opponent less time to get to the ball. Hit a slice with the racket face open (tilt it back a little) and move down the back of the ball. The stroke takes the shape of a smile. Look for illustrations of these spinshots along with the volley and the overhead in this book.

Top players mix their shots and the pace of the ball by using topspin, slice, and hitting at different speeds. Once you have gained some consistency you will be tempted to hit the ball harder, but, as

with the serve, you should add power to groundstrokes last. Power may seem important, but it is not *the* key to winning matches. The harder you hit the ball, the smaller the margin of error, the faster the ball will come back to you, and the less time you will have to get ready for the next shot. When you do think you can add a little power to your game, move into the ball, shifting your weight. Accelerate the racket head and take the ball on the rise rather than at its peak. You should hit the ball flatter and aim lower over the net.

If you teach yourself tennis and take it patiently step by step, you will improve, and the learning will become more enjoyable. You will eventually play some competitive matches. You will gain more from the experience if you find a friend to chart the match. Your friend should list your forehand, backhand, and volley errors in one column, and your winners in another column and should also keep track of how many first and second serves you get in. From this record, you can see what areas you need to improve. Charting for someone else can help you notice more in a match. Try charting tournament matches in person or on television. This will get you involved in the match, and you will be surprised to discover how few errors are made.

GEORGE BACSO

13

Junior Tennis

At the Nick Bollettieri Tennis Academy we are pleased that we are able to help top players of all styles reach peak efficiency. Current academy players include such diverse stylists as Jimmy Arias, Eric Korita, and Aaron Krickstein. Their games matured at the academy, yet they are completely different in almost every way. Arias is small, quick, and bases his game on a thunderous forehand; Korita is huge and relies on an overpowering serve; and Krickstein has punishing groundstrokes off of both sides.

Our philosophy for success calls for an understanding of and adherence to the latest principles of nutrition and conditioning, nurtured by sound practice goals and planning, and toughened by tournament competition. We are convinced that any junior who duplicates the following academy program will improve. Remember, the key to success is "Ability, Dedication, and Discipline."

Nutrition

No one becomes a successful player today without paying the price in practice. But, if your body is not prepared correctly, how can you pay that price? Therefore, the foundation of a successful junior player depends upon a knowledge of correct nutritional habits and the discipline to avoid temptation. *First* and most important, be sure that your diet is well-balanced and includes the basic food groups. A deficiency in any of these can mean trouble on the court.

Milk and Milk Products (twice daily)—calcium, vitamins B2, B12, and A, minerals, and protein

Breads and Cereals (twice daily)—carbohydrates, protein, B vitamins, iron

Meat, Poultry, Fish, and Nuts (twice daily)—protein, vitamins, and minerals

Green, Yellow, and Leafy Vegetables (once daily)—vitamins A, E, B, and minerals

Potatoes and Other Fruits and Vegetables (once daily)—vitamin C, minerals, and protein

Second, and almost as important for young players, avoid "junk food." Candy, potato chips, and other junk foods that contain sugar and fats, are high in calories, yet, offer very few essential vitamins and minerals.

Third, monitor the amount of food you eat and alter your intake relative to the amount of exercise you are getting. If you are training and playing hard, you need plenty of calories. However, if you are resting for a week or more, you must curtail your appetite or your game will suffer when you return to active practice and play.

Jimmy Arias

Aaron Krickstein

The Three-Hour Law.   Between the end of a meal and the start of physical exertion, at least three hours must elapse. The stomach, it is true, usually digests a meal in one and one-half to two hours, but before a competition a player is always more tense, which slows down the digestive process. Players should not go into competition with a full stomach, but an empty stomach is of no advantage either. Instead, players should supply themselves with a moderate amount of carbohydrates every hour up to the hour of competition.

By combining exercise with two simple behavior modifications, you can lose weight easily and consistently without affecting your energy levels. First, cut out snacks. Rely on meals for your food, and you will have less opportunity to be tempted by empty junk food calories. Second, slowly reduce the amount of each portion of food that you eat.

Dieting

Observing tennis players on the circuit, one can see that many are indeed overweight. At the academy, we have our own "Weight Watcher's Club." This is completely voluntary, as dieting must come from within. We, as coaches, can only help and advise players. It ultimately must be you yourself who controls your diet.

Everyone in the club aims to lose two pounds per week, which is equivalent to 7000 calories. We lose these two pounds by two methods: (1) a decrease in food intake, and (2) an increase in physical activity. It is very important to stress here that three meals a day must be eaten. It is foods such as donuts, pastries, cookies, all the goodies from the snack machines, desserts, soft drinks, and so forth which are cut out altogether. Also, no second helpings.

The physical activity program takes the form of aerobics, endurance runs, skipping, interval training, circuit training, and so forth. Apart from our regular intense fitness program, these students must also attend these extra classes a minimum of two times per week.

Also, calorie intake and output are monitored, thus ensuring that all calories taken in are burned, plus an extra 1000 per day to ensure two pounds per week loss. This may seem only a small amount to lose, but it is our aim to make it a gradual process. Players cannot afford to suddenly change their diets completely and cut down on their meals as they spend up to seven hours per day on the court. This requires much energy indeed. Also, most of the athletes are still growing and, therefore, need energy to develop physically. Dieting, therefore, must be a gradual process and something the athlete can live with. By way of contrast, the crash diet, which many overweight people resort to, impairs your physical capabilities and often leads to a cycle of dieting to lose weight followed by overeating to regain strength.

A final factor connected with proper nutrition involves your drinking habits before, during, and after practice and match play. Every well-conditioned athlete needs to replenish water lost through sweating during heavy exercise and juniors are no exception. Your normal diet should supply you with all the necessary vitamins and minerals. But liquid replenishment is vital. Before a match or a heavy practice session, you should periodically stop for water (at *every* changeover during a match); and after a match or practice session, you should continue taking water. Water replaces what you lose faster than anything else. Soft drinks and energy drinks (such as Gatorade) contain extras that inhibit your body from absorbing the water quickly.

General Principles to Apply after Competition

1. In the first hour, low food consumption. Calming down comes first.

2. Replenish carbohydrate reserves through massive intake of carbohydrates.

3. Replace lost fluids, but not hastily.

4. No great intake of fats.

5. Salt intake through bouillon, vegetables, fruits.

Conditioning

If you understand and follow correct nutritional practices, you have established a foundation for success. Now, in order to increase your chances for success, you must build upon that foundation.

It is obvious that players in good condition have many advantages over their less well-conditioned opponents. They recover faster between rallies, have a better chance of getting to the ball and hitting a good return, are less fatigued and, therefore, less likely to become injured, and know they will not fade in a tough match. They can also hit harder, move faster, and think quicker than their opponents. Clearly this conditioning will make the difference between winning and losing. Merely playing the game of tennis will not get you into top condition. Match play needs to be supplemented with an off-court conditioning program.

Our tennis players follow a training routine that improves all the components of physical fitness for tennis; namely, agility, balance, cardiovascular endurance, muscular endurance, flexibility, strength, power, speed, and reaction time.

For agility, the players engage in various line drills around the court and many drills are designed to improve this component. Cardiovascular endurance is achieved by two- or three-mile runs a few times a week. Distance running is a great way to build stamina, especially in the preseason, but since tennis involves much stopping and starting and, therefore, heart rate recovery, interval training is also ideal. This form of training also greatly enhances speed. Sprints on the court, stressing quick starts and balance, are run regularly. As an alternative, you may run the lines of the court, always facing the net so you are forced to move up, back, and laterally.

The components of muscular endurance, strength, and power are developed through Nautilus, and the use of rubber bands and the Nick Bollettieri Tennis Handle, which involve resistance exercises to improve arm and leg strength. Every student at the academy goes through an individualized Nautilus program designed to improve specific weaknesses, be it arms, legs, stomach, strength, power, endurance, or whatever. Dramatic improvements have resulted following this program.

Flexibility is aided by stretching, which is done religiously prior to going on court. Both morning and afternoon programs begin and conclude with 20-minute stretches specific to tennis. Also, remedial classes are conducted each week for those needing specific help. A player with a high degree of flexibility has excellent range on the tennis court and is capable of reaching those hard to get wide and low shots. This player is also less susceptible to muscle pulls and tears.

To sharpen your reflexes, include five to ten minutes of jumping rope in your daily regimen. At the academy, for a change of pace, we often play "Follow the Leader" games in which the group must duplicate the hand and foot movements of the leader.

Aerobics (cardiovascular exercises to music) is a new form of conditioning. It is a great way to exercise and lots of fun. Our program begins with a warm-up going through all the muscle groups, loosening and stretching them. Then, the more vigorous activity begins! This includes exercises to improve cardiovascular endurance, agility, footwork, strength, muscular endurance, balance, and aids in injury prevention. The 45-minute session then concludes with a cool-down.

Once you have established a conditioning routine, you will feel stronger and quicker on the court. Make that new feeling of strength and quickness work for you by concentrating on improving your mobility during practice. Mobility is a crucial and often overlooked factor in tennis success. You may have the best strokes in the world, but what good are they if you do not reach the ball? So, during your on-court practice time, concentrate on the following keys in order to improve your mobility:

1. Watch the ball closely, so you can start sooner.

2. Keep your feet moving so you can push off in the right direction as soon as you see where the ball is going.

3. Never give up on a ball. Try for everything and you will gradually reach balls you never got before.

4. When you hit an offensive shot from your own baseline, anticipate a weak return and move up inside the baseline so you can more readily attack the short ball.

There are numerous other benefits gained from an off-court conditioning program. "Being physically fit" greatly reduces the chances of you

incurring an injury while playing tennis. Moreover, if you should happen to sustain an injury, being physically fit would help you to recover quickly and completely.

The confidence of a player is obviously helped when his or her condition is at the highest level. Remember, as you deteriorate physically during a match, you deteriorate mentally, too.

All these benefits mentioned in this chapter give a player a great psychological boost. And keeping fit increases enjoyment as it improves play.

Percentage Tennis (Accuracy and Consistency)

Until now we have concentrated on the foundation of tennis success: the body. Now, assuming that you are following a solid nutrition and conditioning program to prepare your body, it is time to consider the next step in the building process: the mind. Even the strongest, quickest athlete alive will fail miserably in tennis if he or she does not understand the percentages that underlie the game. Therefore, you must study percentage tennis and devise practice drills that encourage you to practice your strokes correctly physically *and* mentally.

The basis of percentage tennis can be summarized in three principles:

1. Keep the ball in play (consistency).

2. Keep the ball deep (accuracy).

3. Attack the short ball.

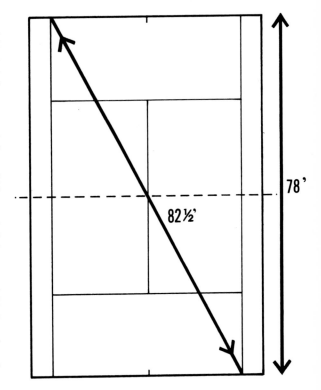

Difference in feet between crosscourt or down-the-line shot

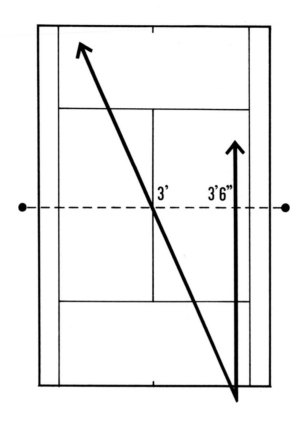

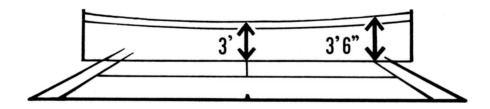

Difference in height of net for crosscourt or
down-the-line shot

Notice that these three principles combine both offense and defense. The successful junior player is one who recognizes that he or she must be adept at both.

The first and most important principle is to keep the ball in play. Almost all tennis matches are lost rather than won (errors always exceed winners), so your top priority must be keeping the ball in play at all costs. Two corollaries to the principle of keeping the ball in play are net clearance and hitting crosscourt. If you hit the ball into the net, you lose the point, whereas there is no penalty for hitting too high over the net. As Bjorn Borg demonstrated so well, the best way to achieve safe net clearance without sacrificing pace is the use of topspin. Once you are clearing the net consistently, you want to use as much of the court as possible. A shot hit directly (down the line) from one baseline to another can travel 78 feet before going out, while a ball hit *diagonally* (crosscourt) from baseline to baseline travels 82½ feet before going out. So, in addition to hitting high over the net to keep the ball in play, hit crosscourt as well. An additional benefit to hitting crosscourt is that your shot will cross the net at or near the center of the court, where the net height is only three feet high, compared to the height of the net at the sideline, which is three and one half feet high.

After you have successfully mastered the art of keeping the ball in play, you next want to become more selective in *how* you keep it in play. Keeping the ball in play is definitely of primary importance, but as the skill of the opposition improves, it may not be enough. If you hit weak and short shots too often, you will be giving your opponent too many chances for easy winners.

Therefore, the second principle of percentage tennis is to keep the ball deep (accuracy). Depth is often referred to as the main tactical weapon in tennis because depth restricts your opponent's offensive opportunities and, at the same time, forces your opponent to err or to hit short balls that you can attack. High net clearance is the best and easiest way to achieve depth without sacrificing consistency, and topspin is the ideal stroking technique to achieve that clearance.

Keeping the ball in play and keeping it deep will inevitably lead to errors by your opponent or numerous short-ball opportunities. In the case of errors, no more need be said. In the case of short balls, the third principle comes into play: attack the short ball. If you fail to attack the short ball when the opportunity arises, you will be giving your opponent more room in which to operate. He or she will soon begin to exploit your tentativeness by

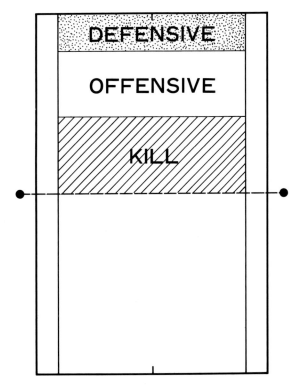

Court zones

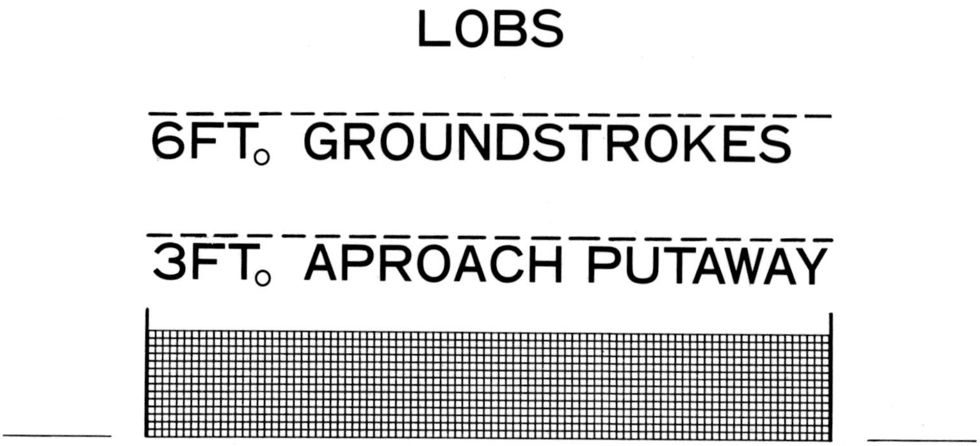

LOBS

6FT$_0$ GROUNDSTROKES

3FT$_0$ APROACH PUTAWAY

Net clearance

bringing you to the net with the dropshot and passing you or lobbing you. Also, by failing to treat the short ball offensively, you open yourself to successful counterattack by your opponent because of your vulnerable court position. So you must learn to attack the short ball. The ability to attack successfully is what separates the good player from the great player. In the accompanying diagram labeled "Court Zones," the court has been divided into three areas: defensive, offensive, and kill. Your objective, once you have succeeded in keeping the ball in play and deep, is to move into the offensive zone for an approach shot or groundstroke winner, and then into the kill zone for a volley putaway. If you can control the net, you will have many more choices of shot and should be able to control the match. Remember that the more of the court you can see over the net, the greater the variety of shots you can hit. In the next diagram, "Net Clearance," you can see the distinction between lobs, groundstrokes, approach shots, and volleys in net clearance. Lobs from the defensive zone clear the net by a great deal. Groundstrokes, from either the defensive or the offensive zone, usually clear the net by at least three feet. Approach shots, from the offensive zone, are hit within three feet of the top of the net, as are volleys from the kill zone. As a general rule, the closer you are to the net, the less clearance your shot will have. But as you get closer to the net,

you need less clearance because your chances for error (into the net) diminish, while your chances for winners (greater court surface available) increase.

As supplemental variations to the basics of percentage tennis previously outlined, top players will utilize dropshots, moon balls, and slices to confuse the opposition. Use of the dropshot can tire an opponent in less than excellent condition, can exploit poor up-and-back movement, and can bring the determined baseliner to a more vulnerable position at the net. Additionally, occasional dropshots add strength and diversity to your own baseline game because your opposition cannot afford to play deep, but most protect against the dropshot.

Judicious use of the moon ball (a very high shot, almost a lob, thrown into a groundstroke rally) can be another effective way to change the tempo of a rally and force the opponent to a deeper position behind the baseline.

The slice is a third way to change tempo, and a sliced underspin ball has the extra advantage of a low bounce. The combination of low bounce and underspin can often be disturbing to a power hitter who thrives on pace. Also, use of the slice's low bounce on the approach shot allows extra time to attain effective net position and forces your opponent to hit up to you at the net.

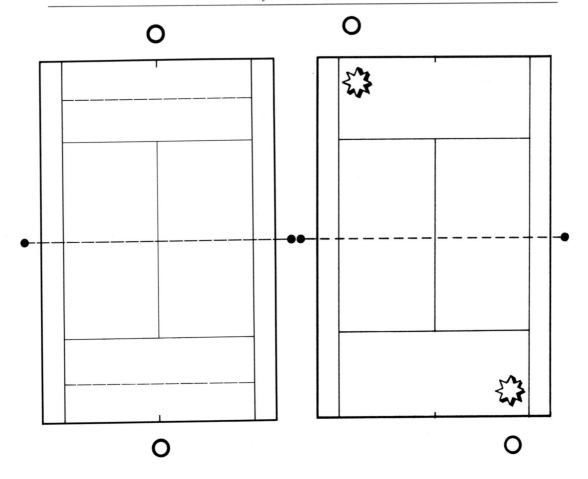

Height and Depth Drill   Target Drill

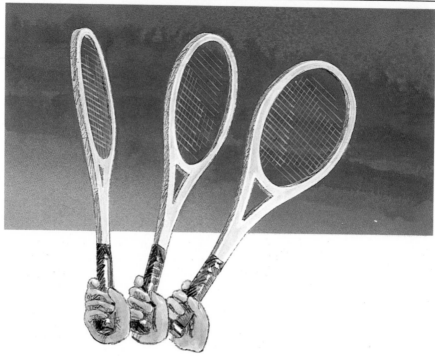

Plans and Drills

Although it is important to understand the principles of percentage tennis, it is equally as important to plan your practice sessions so that you are practicing your strokes in correct percentage situations. You should approach each practice session with the same commitment and determination you give to a match. How you practice often determines how you play. Therefore, make up your mind to give 100 percent on every ball. Practice the shots you use and situations you encounter in a match; work on your weaknesses; eliminate careless errors; and, remember to vary your routine periodically in order to avoid staleness.

A normal practice session might begin with some warm-up calisthenics, followed by light hitting to loosen up. After drilling the groundstrokes, volleys, overheads, serves, and returns, there is time for work on weak points and/or special shots. Then, both players may work on specific practice drills before playing points, games, or matches.

Practice drills designed to emphasize the principles of percentage tennis and to refine stroking techniques are a very important ingredient of a successful practice. Some popular drills at the academy are as follows:

1. Height and Depth Drill—Objective: to keep the ball in opponent's backcourt by hitting the ball high above the net. Operation: place targets six feet from baseline. Two play out points until opponent hits ball short of target. Games can be to 21 points.

2. Target Drill—Objective: to develop consistency from the baseline as well as increase accuracy. Operation: first place targets, either balls, ropes, tapes, etc., to form a four-foot square. Place the target two feet from both the baseline and the sideline. Then have the players hit either crosscourt or down the line. Keep the balls in play and have the players concentrate on hitting the targets.

3. Two-on-One from the Baseline—Objective: develop consistency and mobility. Operation: two players on baseline keep ball in play and move single player from side to side and up and back.

4. Forehand Weapon—Objective: to develop forehand by having student run around all short balls and hit hard forehands. Operation: used with two or more players and instructor. Instructor feeds short high ball to backhand side. Players run around backhand and hits offensive forehand. Player follows shot into the net. Instructor feeds volley.

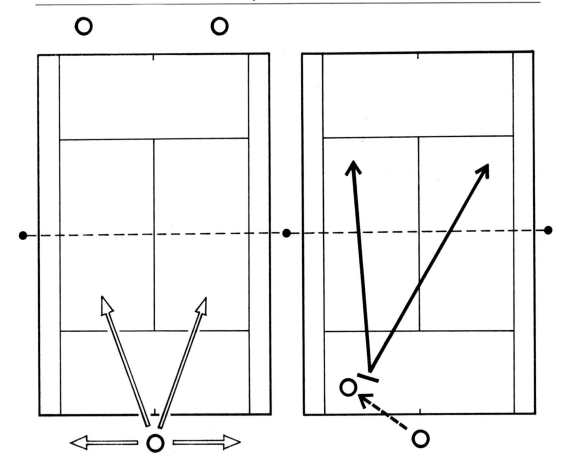

Two-on-one drill

Forehand Weapon

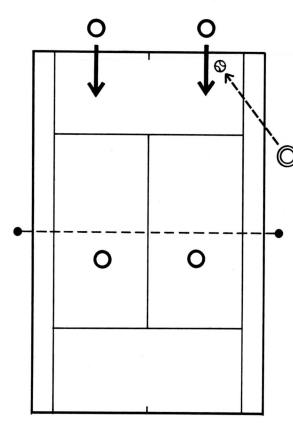

Two-on-Two Approach Drill

5. Two-on-Two Approach and Play Out Point —Objective: sharpen reflex volleys and approach shots. Operation: two players of one team stand at the net while opposing team is on the baseline. Ball is put into play by the instructor to the baseline team. Baseline team approaches and all players play out the point.

6. Quick Exchange Volley—Objective: shorten backswing in volley. Operation: one player stands with back against fence. The other player stands on the baseline. Players volley back and forth. Player with back to fence will have to have a short backswing or racket will hit the fence. After a few minutes, change players' positions.

The depth, target, and two-on-one drills emphasize the first principles of percentage tennis, keeping the ball consistently in play and placing it deep; while the forehand, two-on-two, and quick volley drills are intended to expand one's offensive techniques. Concentration throughout each practice session will make you more consistent from the baseline and more effective when you attack. Practice as you play, and play as you practice!

Percentage tennis involves more than just controlling the ball; it involves controlling your mind as well. You have to be able to play with adversity and bounce back from disappointing defeats. Self-discipline is essential and all players must learn to control their temper and concentrate throughout a match. The only way to master this is to practice concentration and self-control in practice just as you might practice a particular shot.

Tournaments

Tournaments provide the reward for long hours of practice and serve as a way to assess your progress as a player. Give yourself every possible chance to do well by preparing well in advance. Just as early preparation for a groundstroke gives you your best chance to hit it cleanly, so early preparation for a tournament allows you your best chance of winning.

In the days prior to the tournament, be sure to practice under conditions similar to those you will be playing in. Wear the same clothes, play on the same surface with the same balls, and use the shots and tactics you plan to employ in matches. Shorten the length of your practices as "day one" approaches, so you will be fresh and eager. Check all your equipment to be sure you are completely prepared for every eventuality. On the last day or two before the tournament, emphasize quick reaction drills for volleys and groundstrokes to sharpen your reflexes and shorten your reaction time.

On the opening day of the tournament, be sure you have correct directions to the site and arrive well before your starting time so you have sufficient time to check in, change, look around the site, do warm-up calisthenics, and practice hitting for 10 to 15 minutes if courts are available. When you go on court with your opponent, use the warm-up time to practice all your strokes. Concentrate on accuracy and consistency, rather than power.

Once the match starts, work to establish your rhythm so you are controlling your shots and the tempo of the match. Strive for consistency first, then depth, and exploit your short-ball opportunities. If you are winning most of the points, stick to your pattern and concentrate on closing out each point, each game, and each set. Do not experiment, maintain concentration. At set point and/or match point, remember what got you there and stay cool and collected.

If you are losing, try to determine whether the reason is your own faulty play or your opponent's strength. If the responsibility lies with you, tighten up your game. Be more determined to get every ball, to clear the net with plenty of height, to hit crosscourt, and to get your first serve in. If your opponent is playing too well for you, you will probably need to change your game a little in order to alter the balance of power. If your opponent has a big serve, concentrate on returning to the largest area of court available. If he or she is following serve to net effectively, go down the line with some returns, and/or attack the second serve yourself. In baseline exchanges, use underspin to slow the tempo of points and take a little more time between points and on changeovers to slow the tempo of the match as well. If all else fails, and you are still being outplayed, become more aggressive. Hit the ball a little harder from the backcourt and take the net more often. That extra bit of aggressiveness may be enough to throw your opponent off stride.

To summarize, in order to be an outstanding junior player you need to first establish a solid foundation with attention to nutrition and conditioning, and then learn the principles of percentage tennis (accuracy and consistency) and work on them diligently in practice. A combination of these principles, concentration and self-discipline, can prepare you to be at your best in tournament competition.

NICK BOLLETTIERI

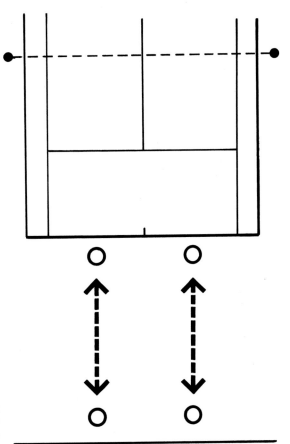

Quick Exchange Volley Drill

14

Choosing a Tennis Pro
and a Camp

Whether you are just beginning to play tennis or you are a veteran player wanting to correct some bad habits, a qualified tennis professional can help you to further your enjoyment of the game. Selection of the right professional is a difficult but important decision, largely because anyone can claim to be a tennis professional without any training or experience at all.

Therefore, the first step in making your selection is to get a list of the USPTA certified professionals in your area. This list can be obtained upon request from the USPTA national office at the following address:

USPTA at Saddlebrook
P.O. Box 7077
Wesley Chapel (Tampa), Florida 34249
813–973–3777

Although an outstanding tennis professional need not be a member of the USPTA, membership in USPTA does guarantee that a professional has passed an extensive written, teaching, and playing test to obtain certification. He or she has also met certain age, experience, and reference requirements. In addition, a member of the USPTA is kept continually informed on the latest teaching techniques through a variety of publications, educational workshops, and conventions.

You can select a certified pro from this list by several means. First you may ask friends or other tennis acquaintances for recommendations on professionals. Most tennis players have taken lessons and can offer helpful information. However, it is important to get specific reasons from your friends for liking or disliking a particular professional so that you can relate their reactions to your own situation. Their goals may have been different from yours.

Next look at potential candidates' playing and teaching backgrounds to see which ones have the type of credentials most suitable to your needs. For instance, if you are a strong junior player, which professionals have a record of working with and developing strong ranking juniors? Which professionals were ranked juniors themselves? On the other hand, some professionals may not be exceptional players but do have extensive teaching experience in relation to beginning adults.

Your next step is to observe your three or four top candidates giving a lesson. Do they have a style that you feel would motivate you? Does the pro project a professional appearance in his or her grooming and dress? Does the pro give full value by being punctual? Is the pro courteous and communicative in the lesson?

Finally, discuss with the final candidates their availability for lessons, their rates, and whether they recommend private, semi-private, or group lessons for you. (Group lessons are often best for beginners, for strategy lessons, and for drill sessions.)

Upon selecting your pro, you should discuss your tennis goals and clearly explain what you expect to accomplish during your lessons. The professional should give you an action play for accomplishing your goals. Concrete measures for gauging your improvement should be established. For example, you may be interested in improving the depth and consistency of your backhand. At the start of your lessons you can hit only three consecutive backhands deeper than the service line and fair. A reasonable goal might be to hit ten in a row after a month of once-a-week lessons supplemented by at least two prescribed practice sessions per week.

Continue to evaluate your tennis professional during your initial lessons. Does the pro mix his or her approach, using demonstrations, talk, and drills? Does he or she clearly communicate to you what you need to do and not just what you do not want to do? Is a summary of each lesson given at the end, with key checkpoints that you can remember? Does the pro assign practice sessions between lessons with specific drills? If you can answer yes to most or all of these questions, you have a professional who is genuinely interested in your improvement and has you on a path headed for success.

Selecting a Tennis Camp

The first step in selecting a tennis camp is to get a complete list of possibilities. Both *Tennis* magazine and *World Tennis Magazine* publish annual camp directories in January that can be obtained for a nominal fee by writing the magazines at the following addresses:

TENNIS
495 Westport Avenue
Box 5350
Norwalk, CT 06856

WORLD TENNIS MAGAZINE
CBS Consumer Publishing
1515 Broadway
New York, NY 10036

There are different types of camps, and you should initially decide which kind suits your needs.

For adults, there are camps at posh resorts that generally offer two to four hours of tennis instruction daily, plus excellent cuisine and numerous other activities. Alternatively, there are more intensive programs offering five to six hours of instruction daily with more available in the evening for the truly eager player. These programs are often available in less lavish locations (such as college campuses) and have fewer alternative activities, but have more instruction at a lower price. In addition, there are specialty camps targeted at certain groups (i.e., singles, couples, women) and/or concentrating on certain areas of tennis (i.e., doubles, mixed doubles, drills, advanced tactics) that may suit your needs better than a general program.

For juniors, tennis camps fall into three general categories. First, there is the more general type of camp which has a tennis emphasis. These camps often have two to three hours of instruction daily, high student/instructor ratios, programs aimed at beginners through intermediates, less experienced instructors, and lower fees.

The tennis specialty camp usually offers tennis exclusively during the day, with non-tennis activities available during the evening. Expect to find lower student/instructor ratios, more experienced staff, and higher fees at this type of camp. Beginners through advanced players are found in these programs.

In recent years, camps aimed at players wanting professional careers, college scholarships, better rankings, and/or better positions on school teams have sprung up. These "Tournament Prep Camps" usually include a large number of tournament newcomers as well as ranked players. Emphasis is on advanced techniques/tactics, conditioning, and match play. (A word of caution: these camps are geared to players who have strong basic strokes and the willingness to work very hard. Without these two basics, players attending this type of camp will usually be disappointed and/or unhappy.)

Getting a personal recommendation from friends who have attended a camp can be very helpful. Your local professional should also be consulted for his or her recommendation. Camps will provide phone numbers of past participants of the camp in your area. These people can also be helpful in your selection.

Surveying the literature provided by camp should provide answers to many important questions. If you still have unanswered concerns after reading this literature, call the camp and ask your questions of the camp operators.

The following are some key questions to consider:

1. Who is in charge? Does the camp director have credentials that reflect experience and success in camp operations as well as tennis instruction?

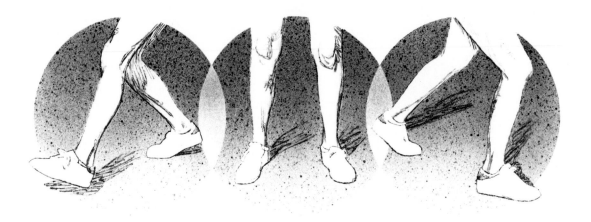

2. How long has the camp been in business? The longer the camp has been in operation the more likely that many start-up problems have been worked out successfully. Camps less than three years old should be carefully scrutinized.

3. What is the student/instructor ratio? Top camps usually offer no more than four or five students per instructor.

4. What are the staff's credentials? Staff members usually consist of the following:
   a. tennis coaches (college/high school).
   b. certified teaching professionals.
   c. college tennis players.
   d. school teachers with a tennis background.
   e. college students with a tennis background.
   f. counselors-in-training (CITS)—high school students with a tennis playing background.

Better quality camps have higher numbers of staff in categories *a* and *b*, plus few staff in categories *e* and *f*.

5. What is the average weekly enrollment? Although there is no perfect answer to this question, an average size of under 15 or over 100 should raise some concerns. Too few players makes it difficult to arrange compatible groupings and diversified competition. Large groups can raise problems about quality instruction control, adequate court time, and adequate supervision.

6. What is the daily schedule? Camps usually offer from two to six hours per day of instruction. During this time students can receive group instruction, demonstrations, video tape analysis, private instruction, match play (supervised and unsupervised), drilling segments, strategy sessions (on court or in classroom), stretching, and conditioning. Make sure the camp you select has the amount and type of instruction that you want. For instance, a beginner may want only two to four hours of instruction focussing on developing good stroke production through group instruction, video tape analysis, and drilling. On the other hand, an advanced player may be looking for a six-hour program, including a balanced program with emphasis on strategy development and advanced shotmaking techniques. In any case, make sure the format meets your needs.

7. What kind of non-tennis social activities are available? For adults these would include

planned cocktail parties or other functions as well as optional activities that are available at the camp or resort. The less intense the camp, the more important these amenities can be. If you plan to pursue a number of additional activities, you should ask what additional charges will be made.

For juniors a full scale of non-tennis evening activities are available at the better camps. This is particularly important for participants staying longer than one week.

8. What happens in the event of rain? If the camp has indoor courts, what kind of student-/court ratio is maintained? It takes expert organization to handle more than eight students per court for more than a short period of time while giving the students their full value.

Camps without indoor courts usually have one of the following policies:
   a. a refund is given for missed time.
   b. a raincheck is given, no refund.
   c. alternative activities are provided, no refund.

It is important to know the camp's policy before attending. Also, determine the likelihood of rain at the time and place you are going.

9. What special equipment is used? Most camps have both video tape and ball machines.

10. What kind of supervision is provided (junior camp only)? This is an important question to many concerned parents and one that should be diligently pursued. The best camp situations are ones that:
    a. have a camp layout that makes supervision easier.
    b. have all or most staff living with the students.
    c. have a strictly enforced time for lights out (generally around 10 p.m.).
    d. have a clearly explained set of camp rules that are fairly enforced.
    e. do not allow campers to leave camp without a member of the staff.

11. What is the cost? The answer to this is often better examined on a per hour of instruction basis. To get this figure, first subtract estimated charges for room, board, and other activities from the total cost. Then divide this figure by the number of instructional hours provided. Although cheaper does not necessarily mean better, the cost per hour of instruction offers you one more basis for comparing camps.

Finally, once you have selected a camp, make sure you attend in good physical condition and with a proper mental attitude, ready to experiment and to learn. If you do, you will find a good camp is an excellent way to improve your game and enjoy yourself in the process.

MIKE EIKENBERRY

15

Improving Your Tennis through Biomechanics

Among the tennis players on the tour, who do you think has the best form? Is it Chris Evert Lloyd, Martina Navratilova, Ivan Lendl, or Jimmy Connors? You might be surprised when I tell you that there really does not exist a *perfect way* to play tennis! Because of the numerous grips involved in the game and the different spins used to play effectively, many different methods of stroke production exist that are extremely effective and also efficient. But, how does all this apply to you? One question you need to ask yourself is, "What must I do to make my strokes more effective and efficient?" Some very basic physical laws apply to tennis that could help you become a better player.

One of the most important and most common of these principles is Newton's Third Law: for every action, there is an equal and opposite reaction. A good example of this is a ground reaction force. It is a fact that much of the force a player generates when hitting a shot comes from the ground. Any tennis player who tries to pulverize every shot by jumping into it is only looking for trouble. Although many players often jump when hitting high-velocity groundstrokes, the competitor pictured shows how skilled athletes do not leave the ground until the instant of impact. Therefore, they generate a high ground reaction force, and the jumping does not contribute that much to their strokes. Their main source of force comes from two other physical principles: linear and angular momentum.

Linear momentum results from transferring the body weight forward. When you were first learning tennis, your teacher probably told you to "step into the ball" on every shot. Your coach was telling you to "generate linear momentum." Once you have transferred your linear momentum forward, angular momentum should come into play. Angular momentum is produced by body rotation occurring at the hips and trunk. There are very few shots in tennis that can be effective without using angular momentum. To realize its importance, try hitting a forehand drive without rotating your trunk—it will not be one of your better shots.

Stability plays a large role in tennis. Anyone wishing to excel must strive to be balanced. This does not mean that you must be perfectly still each time you hit a ball nor does it mean that you should not hit a ball on the run. It simply means that your

body must be in control when swinging the racket toward impact. By lifting the shoulders too early in a stroke or by hitting off the back foot, you only increase the likelihood of making an error. Even when you hit a shot while running at full tilt, your upper body must be under control for you to bring the racket forward properly.

Once you understand these concepts, you need only one more to upgrade your mastery of the game. That principle is Newton's Second Law: Force = Mass × Acceleration. Since you have no control over your mass, it is always a constant. Therefore, force is directly proportional to acceleration. In other words, the greater the acceleration, the more force you will provide. But remember, tennis is not really a game of high-velocity shots as much as it is a game of control.

A good velocity/accuracy trade-off involves hitting a shot with a certain amount of speed, yet not so fast as to impede accuracy. Your stroke must depend on the velocity of your opponent's oncom-

Stepping into the ball and transferring weight

ing shot, where he or she is located on the court, and how you have to return the ball. If your opponent is at the net, for example, you would not want to hit a soft floater that clears the net by five or six feet. The shot you select to hit (whether it is a drive, lob, or even an angled dink shot) must be hit with the proper velocity to maintain maximal control. This requires good tennis stroke mechanics.

Obviously, there is more to the mechanics of tennis than Newton's Laws of Motion. However, this preliminary information will serve as a good foundation for the subsequent sections dealing with the mechanics of stroke production. By understanding these physical laws and applying them to your strokes, your game can improve significantly.

Your Body Should Act as a Linked System

It is amazing how many skilled tennis players seem to swing effortlessly when playing the game. As they stroke through the ball, it does not seem that they swing very hard, yet, when you try to return their shots, it seems as though the racket is almost knocked out of your hand. These players have learned to utilize their total body and effectively contact the ball. We have already discussed how a tennis player generates linear and angular momentum, but let us examine how the larger body parts can be utilized to allow the arm to work less.

When viewing a skilled player in action, it is not difficult to see how the body parts should work. Once the step forward is completed and linear momentum is transferred in the direction where impact will occur it is time for the body to *rotate* into position.

Few of us ever see the way a pro tennis player sets up to hit a groundstroke. It all happens too fast for the naked eye to catch. We only see the final product, when the professional athlete is facing the net in the follow-through. From the illustrations notice how, at the initiation of the stroke, the hips and trunk are turned to the side. Now watch as the player swings forward to make contact with the ball. As impact is approached, the hips and then the trunk rotate to bring the arm and racket into position for ball contact. The use of the larger body parts in this example assist an athlete in bringing the racket into the proper impact position without forcing the upper limb to do the majority of the work.

The Serve and Overhead Smash

Contrary to what many believe, the force provided by the body to hit an effective serve or overhead is

Tim Gullikson—serving

not developed at the trunk and upper arm. Most of the force is generated from the ground in the form of a ground reaction force. Remember Newton's Third Law: for every action, there is an equal and opposite reaction. When serving or hitting an overhead, the feet push against the ground and the ground pushes back with the same amount of force. Notice in the photo how Tim Gullikson (1979 Wimbledon quarterfinals) flexes and extends his knees to create a solid ground reaction force. Few tennis players use this principle to its fullest advantage. Obviously, the one thing that would increase the ground reaction force would be the correct use of knee flexion and extension. Two faults often prevent some players from correctly using the knees: (1) too little or too much knee flexion, and (2) improper timing of the knee movement relative to the rest of the stroke.

The proper amount of knee flexion is actually dependent on an individual's strength and coordination. Consider this example. If you were trying to jump vertically as high as possible, would you bend the knees just a little or would you go into a deep crouch? I doubt if you would do either. There is an optimum amount of knee flexion unique to each individual. Without enough knee bend, a poor ground reaction force will be generated, while too much knee flexion will result in excessive body motion and poor transfer of force from the ground.

The second problem encountered by many tennis players is poor timing of the knee action relative to the entire serving or overhead motion. Remember that the segments of the body act as a system of chain links. The force generated by one link, or body part, is transferred to the next link in succession. When the transfer of that force is not efficient, the outcome of the stroke will be poor. Since the knee bend is among the first of all body movements involved in the serve and overhead smash, it functions as the foundation for actions of the hips and trunk. Until recently, many athletes have questioned the involvement of the hips in hitting a serve or overhead and have, therefore, tended to overlook their importance. However, we now know that hip rotation may spell the difference between a great serve or overhead and a mediocre one. This is the area of the body where a skilled player transfers the linear and angular momentum generated by the legs to the trunk.

All agree that Roscoe Tanner has a great serve. Many think he hits the ball while the toss is rising and, because of his quick motion to do that, generates incredible racket velocity. First of all, he does not hit the ball on its way up! The ball is usually at the peak of the toss and is motionless when Tanner makes contact. This means that his reaction to the toss is not the reason for his high racket velocity. Tanner produces his racket speed from the way

he uses his legs and rotates his hips and trunk. Without the phenomenal timing of his hip rotation, even Roscoe Tanner's serve might only be average instead of one of the world's best.

Once the force is transferred effectively to the hips and they reach their maximum rotation velocity, the trunk is next in line. The amount of trunk rotation varies from player to player. Some players can generate a great deal of angular velocity (from rotation) with little trunk movement, but most good servers and smashers have a large degree of trunk rotation. In coiling the body, an athlete is able to create a great deal of angular momentum with the trunk.

Now the upper limb comes into play. Remember that serving and hitting an overhead are similar to throwing a ball. Therefore, the trunk imparts velocity to the arm which rotates at the shoulder, extends at the elbow, and "snaps through impact" with the wrist. As a final note, never hit down on your serve. Toss your ball in front of your body and hit the ball "straight out" to ensure net clearance.

The One-Handed and Two-Handed Backhand Drives: Is One Better?

Only recently have we begun to understand the mechanics of motion involved in the one-handed and two-handed backhand drives. For various rea-

Martina Navratilova—hip rotation

Chris Evert Lloyd—two-handed backhand

sons, players all over the world have generated strong feelings about which stroke they prefer and why. These reasons range from differences in reach, problems with muscular strength, disguise, and spin production. However, there are some things we can learn about the two strokes based on a mechanical analysis.

In the late 1970's I conducted a film study to examine the backhand techniques (both one-handed and two-handed) of 36 highly-skilled tennis players (18 for each stroke). One significant finding dealt with the number of body parts used in each stroke and how they are properly coordinated.

For the one-handed backhand, it was found that five distinct body parts are used prior to impact. When a player steps toward the ball, the hips turn slightly, transferring their momentum to the trunk which also begins slight rotation. Then the upper arm moves about the shoulder. This upper arm motion is transferred to slight forearm movement which, in turn, causes the hand and racket to reach correct position for ball contact. Ball contact must occur ahead of the front foot to ensure transfer of momentum along all these body parts and to orient the racket face vertically with respect to ball flight.

It is because five body parts are involved that many people have trouble playing tennis with a one-handed backhand. They really cannot coordinate all five segments. How many times have you seen individuals playing who lead with the elbow or drop the racket head to help hit the ball over the net? What happens is that those players can use the major body parts, but when it comes to transferring the momentum to the forearm through the elbow, they lose the coordinated pattern and lead with the elbow. Some can transfer the momentum through the elbow to the forearm well, but cannot get it by the wrist efficiently and severely drop the racket head, causing an awkward follow-through. The two-handed backhand is a different story.

The two-handed stroke only utilizes two body parts to swing the racket toward impact. After a player begins the forward transfer of linear momentum and steps toward the ball contact point, the hips begin to rotate. They in turn, cause the trunk to rotate *but*, the arms of both limbs rotate with the trunk with *no* movement at the elbows or wrists up to impact. That is, the trunk and arms rotate as one body part. After impact, any number of contortions occur for various body segments, depending on each player's own idiosyncracies.

It is important to understand that both the one-handed and two-handed backhands have specific characteristics and both can be used effec-

Two-handed backhand—two parts

tively. To say that one is better than the other would be absurd. However, there is one thing you should be aware of: the question about reach.

In a high-speed film study I conducted on 36 highly-skilled players, I could find no difference in reach between the two strokes. See for yourself by comparing the various views of one-handed and two-handed backhands illustrated. When the players in my study did not have to run for shot preparation, ball contact for each stroke occurred about the same distance from the body. •This statement usually brings the following question: What about the situation when a player is really stretched out for a backhand return? We can visualize how a pro with a one-handed backhand can lunge at a shot, but what about those players utilizing a two-handed backhand? Could they also reach the wide shot? My answer is *probably not!* However, how many of those lunging one-handed backhands have you seen hit for winners? Very few, I am sure. Most of those wide shots are returned as defensive underspin drives or lobs. They are *not* penetrating, offensive strokes. My point is that a player who has an effective two-handed backhand can learn to hit those one-handed lunges and develop a sound defensive underspin drive or lob. Therefore, there is really no rationale to avoid using a two-handed backhand due to a supposed lack of reach.

Spin Production

Anyone who has played tournament tennis knows the value of being able to vary spins on the ball when competing. Ball spin can be used for various reasons. Some players prefer to use underspin (or backspin) because they feel they can better control shot placement. Other players, who may attack the ball more aggressively, like to hit topspin on the ball because they feel it improves their control. Still other competitors have been seen to use sidespin on certain strokes. Therefore, it behooves anyone wishing to excel in the game to learn more about spin and why it is so important.

As a tennis ball travels toward the opponent, its flight is affected by the surrounding air. When the ball is spinning, the air has an even more significant effect on ball flight. For example, if a ball has topspin, the top of the ball is rotating in the direction the ball is traveling. You should be aware that, as the ball rotates, it carries a small boundary layer of air around with it. On top of the ball (where the ball is rotating in the same direction it is traveling), the boundary layer of air is going in the opposite direction as the airflow that is encountering the ball during its flight. This causes a high amount of turbulence above the ball which forces the ball downward, thus causing the looping effect commonly seen with topspin groundstrokes.

Contrast the reach involved in these one-handed and two-handed backhands.

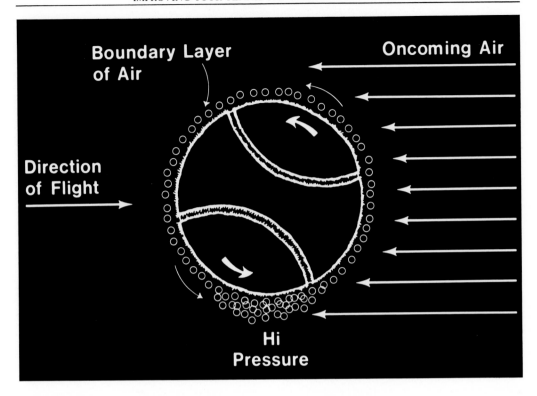

Underspin

The opposite effect is usually observed with underspin. Since the ball is spinning in the opposite direction, the bottom of the ball is rotating in the direction that the ball is traveling. Therefore, the interaction of the boundary layer of air with the oncoming air creates turbulence below the ball. The resultant effect is that the ball will tend to stay in the air longer as it travels across the net.

Spin also affects how a ball bounces. As the topspin shot rebounds off the opponent's court, the topspin tends to push backward against the court, causing the ball to rebound at a *lower* angle than the ball would have if it had no spin. The reason that so many topspin shots seem to have such a high bounce is due to their approach angle to the surface. Remember that the turbulence on top of the ball forces it downward, causing the approach angle to the court to be very steep. Therefore, even though the rebound angle of a topspin shot is lower than the rebound angle would have been had the ball been hit with no spin, the rebound of the topspin shot is still extremely high.

The bounce of a ball hit with underspin is different from that of topspin. Whereas the topspin shot causes the ball to bounce at a lower angle than a ball with no spin, the spin on a ball hit with underspin causes it to bounce at a *greater* angle under certain conditions. When the ball approaches the court at a steep approach angle, the underspin causes the ball to push *forward* against the court at contact which forces the ball to slow down and rebound more vertically than normal. However, the angle at which the underspin shot hits the court surface will also affect the rebound. A soft, lazy groundstroke hit with underspin will tend to have a steep approach angle to the court, causing the shot to "sit up." A sliced drive that just clears the net tends to approach the court at a very low angle, causing the ball to skid and take a low bounce. It is for this reason that the intent of most underspin groundstrokes is to *drive* the ball deep into the opponent's court with a low trajectory.

There is only one way to produce topspin on a tennis ball. The racket must be swung in a low to high pattern while the racket face maintains a vertical position through impact. The racket can be

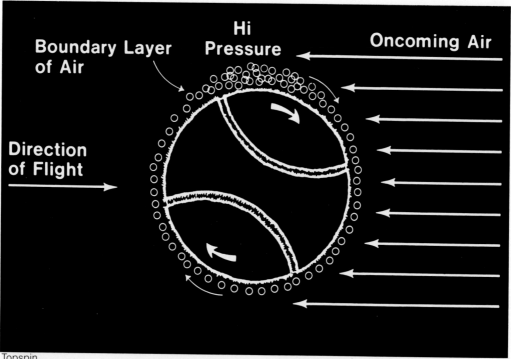

Topspin

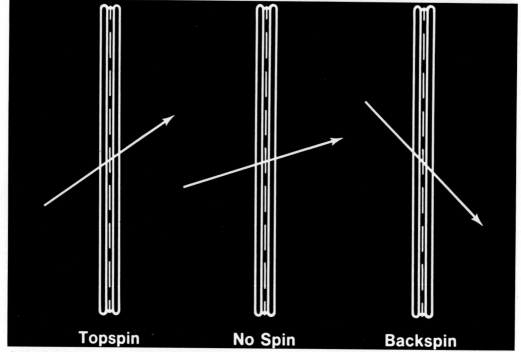

Angle of racket face for topspin, flat, and slice

opened or closed slightly but too much deviation of the racket head at impact will cause an errant shot. The more radical the motion of the racket head in an upward pattern, the more topspin you can produce on the ball. Since the ball is on the racket a very short time (.004 second), it is impossible to rotate the racket head while the ball is in contact with the racket. Therefore, attempting to produce additional topspin by "rolling over" the ball will not produce extra topspin, but might increase the possibilities of making a mistake.

To hit a ball with underspin, the backside of the ball must be struck in a downward fashion. This is usually done by taking the racket back in a position slightly higher than where impact will occur. Swinging the racket in a slight high to low pattern with a slightly open racket face will provide an ample amount of underspin on the ball. Be careful not to make the angle of the downward swing too steep, causing you to "chop" the ball, or to have the racket face too open at impact, which will then give the ball a high trajectory. However, kept low and deep, underspin is an extremely useful weapon.

DR. JACK L. GROPPEL

16

Adapting Your Game
to Court Conditions

Even the best of players find that they must change parts of their game occasionally in order to continue to improve, play better, and win. Adapting is the way a smart player survives.

Besides your opponent's shots, you will encounter sun, heat, wind, cold, different court surfaces, and indoor courts to which you will have to adapt. You will need to be able to handle all of these variables to become a better player.

Sun

The sun will affect mostly the serve and overhead because you will be looking up at the ball.

If your eyes catch even a brief glimpse of the sun while you are beginning your shot, you will most likely mishit, sending the ball out or into he net. To avoid this, you should, on the overhead, use the forearm and hand of your non-racket arm to block the sun from your eyes and get a better view of the ball. Another possibility is to let the ball bounce first and then hit a smash or a groundstroke when the sun will not be as great a factor. Keeping the ball further out in front of you will also help keep the brightness from temporarily blinding you during an overhead.

On your serve, the toss is critical when the sun is a factor. It must be aimed further out in front and lower than usual. This is to avoid the higher angle which will force you to look directly into those devastating rays. As you toss, lean in toward the net so that the lower, angled toss will not affect your serve to a great degree. Realize, however, that your body will be falling into the court. This action helps your first serve but not your second serve. You will not be able to use a spin serve very often if the sun is a strong factor. Slice serves, however, (depending on the angle of the sun) may be an effective weapon against your opponent. The general rule should be: if the sun is against you on the serve, hit flat by tossing the ball low and out in front.

Although bright sun mainly affects the serve and overhead, it can also affect court conditions. For example, if there are shadows on some parts of the court and bright sun on other parts, the ball's flight may be difficult to follow and its spin more difficult to read.

If you are in the sun and your opponent is in the shadows, the ball will seem to accelerate out of your opponent's court and into yours. The ball seems to move more quickly, hence, you must anticipate more in this situation.

On the other hand, if you are in the shadows and your opponent in the sun, many of your opponent's shots will appear to move more slowly as they come across the net, but then they will appear to speed up. In this situation, too, you must anticipate more.

When there is bright sun, you should try to lob your opponent often when he or she is on the side of the court facing the sun. Your lob offers a good opportunity to catch the other player off guard and move into the net. He or she will not be able to see well and has to worry more about the ball than about you. You will be able to hit a quick shot off your opponent's return.

Heat

Surviving the heat is mostly a matter of conditioning. Assuming you are in proper condition to play in the heat, there are three critical items to concentrate on: 1) evaluate your opponent's style, 2) pace yourself throughout the match, and 3) replace your lost water frequently.

To evaluate your opponent ask yourself: Is he or she an aggressive serve-and-volley style player, a baseline rallyer, or a mix of both?

If your opponent is an aggressive player, he or she will try to finish off the points quickly because his or her style will burn up a lot of energy in the heat. You should try to keep the points long with this player, lobbing frequently and moving the ball around the court.

If your opponent is a baseline rallyer, you may be in for a long match. Unless you have the skills to rally consistently from the baseline and feel you can out-rally this opponent, you should try to mix up your shots, bringing the baseliner to the net, then lobbing, moving the ball around the court, trying to upset his or her consistency.

Probably the hardest opponent to play in the heat is the kind of player you should try to be, an adaptable one. If your opponent can rally consistently from the baseline as well as play a serve-and-volley style occasionally, you will have to quickly try to take charge of the match. You should try to dictate the pace so that you get into a rhythm but your opponent does not.

Remember that as a general rule most rallies in the heat will last longer because the ball moves more slowly when it is hot, so you will have to pace yourself in order to have adequate strength at the end of the match. You do not want to run out of gas as you are about to win.

Pacing yourself is sometimes difficult because you do not know beforehand how your body is going to react to the heat on a particular day. You can, however, play so that you do not exhaust yourself. Do not try to overpower the ball on a hot day. Since the ball will travel through the air more slowly on hot days, your powerful shots will be blunted and you will use up valuable energy. Utilizing three-fourths of your power will be adequate

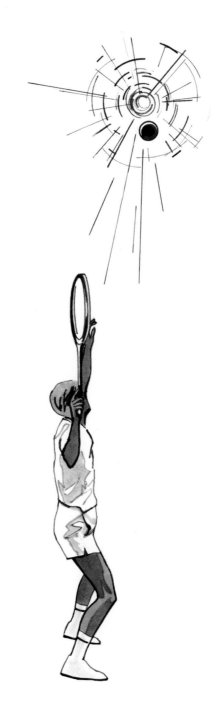

Adapting to sun

to end the points without sapping your strength.

When your opponent hits a great, well-angled shot during a match in normal weather, you try to get it. This is a good attitude under most conditions, but not in the heat. If you are going to give everything you have for one shot, it had better be the match point. A better plan of action would be to try hard for the shots you have a chance to get to and make, but let go the ones that are out of your reach. This will save some of the valuable energy you will need during the closing moments of the match.

Water loss is a great problem too during the heat. Players have been known to lose five to ten pounds of water in a match. If you do not replace the water you lose, you will not only lose energy, you will also feel faint and run the risk of suffering heat prostration.

Drink a few glasses of water before you go onto the court for your match and then drink a small amount of water at each changeover. This will act to replace the fluid you will be losing rapidly when the "heat is on."

Do not take salt tablets just prior to the match or during it. They can make you sick if taken at these times. Instead, eat bananas a couple of hours before match time. This will put potassium into your system, which will help prevent cramps from the heat.

Wind

Adapting to windy conditions requires you to make many adjustments in your game, adjustments that involve all of the strokes. The first adjustment involves the service toss. With the wind blowing, it is difficult to get a well-placed high toss. Try instead, to toss slightly lower than usual so the effect of the wind is reduced.

Since the wind will be blowing on the ball while it is traveling through the air, more spin will help in controlling your serve and will give the ball some action when it hits inside your opponent's service box.

Naturally, if the wind is at your back you should hit with less force, and if the wind is in your face you should hit a little harder. This is true of all the shots, not just the serve.

You can use the wind to your advantage if you know how it is going to affect your ball. You should use more spin on all your shots, not just topspin and backspin, but sidespin as well. This will allow you to hit into a cross-wind and still control the depth of your groundstrokes.

If the wind is blowing in your face, a ball hit with a topspin will drop sooner and a slice will rise

faster. If the wind is at your back, topspin will cause the ball to speed up and carry farther and a slice will also carry much farther. You should select your shots accordingly.

Overheads in the wind can be a source of dismay if not handled properly. You should let most lobs bounce first before hitting an overhead. The wind is going to be blowing the ball every which way and it is difficult to time the hit and judge the ball. If you let the ball bounce first, you will have more time to adapt to the wind and hit a good shot.

When you lob in windy conditions, the type of lob you choose depends upon the direction of the wind. If the wind is at your back, you should use a topspin lob to keep the ball from being carried too far out. If the wind is in your face, then an underspin lob works best because you can control the depth more easily. This should be hit fairly hard, however, to prevent the ball from falling short. If you have a cross-wind, you should try to lob into it, realizing that the ball will be carried back into the court. If you lob with this wind, your ball may be carried four courts away before it bounces.

Cold

Early spring, late fall, and indoors when the heat has not been turned on yet are times when the cold can affect your game.

The muscles do not perform as well in the cold and the "feeling" you will have for your racket will not be as precise. You have to dress so that you can stay warm and allow your muscles to do what you have trained them to do.

Wear a warm-up suit and a sweater and perhaps more layers, depending on the extremity of the temperature. (There is even a mitten designed for tennis players to keep their playing hand warm.)

Warm up your strokes slowly. Muscles pull very easily in the cold. Practice all strokes fully to get totally loose.

When you play in cold weather the ball will move through the air faster and travel farther than in warm temperatures. Becuase of this you must use more spin to keep the ball in the court, utilize a serve-and-volley style of play, and play more shots up the middle (in cold weather the balls will oftentimes sail wide).

Different Court Surfaces

It seems that each part of the world has a particular type of court surface that has achieved popularity. The best players are those who can adapt and play on all surfaces well. The varying surfaces you will encounter are: grass, clay, Fast-Dry, Har-Tru, cement, carpet, hard (or composition), plastic, and wood. These can be divided into three categories: 1) fast playing, 2) medium speed, and 3) slow playing. These categories refer to the speed of the bouncing ball.

Surfaces such as grass, plastic, and wood are considered "fast" courts. Wood courts, or "the boards" as they are sometimes called, are seldom played upon today but used to be the common surface indoors. There are still places today that maintain wood courts. Plastic courts have an interlocking grid with holes in the top surface and grass courts are cut short (not as short as a golf green, however) to the ground and rolled tight.

These "fast playing" courts require you to take the ball on the rise. You need to get off the baseline and up to the net quickly. Move in and stay low on the return of serve, hit hard quick serves, and shorten your backswing on all groundstrokes to play effectively on these surfaces.

"Medium speed" courts are those made of composition materials, carpet, and cement—although some cement courts will be considered fast. Composition, or "hard," courts have an asphalt base with an acrylic compound of some sort poured on top. The speed varies, depending upon how much acrylic is put down. Carpet courts use a material similar to indoor-outdoor carpet but specifically designed for tennis courts. The material is thicker than the average carpet. Cement courts are usually covered by an acrylic coating similar to that used on composition courts.

These are the "average" courts to play on, not favoring any particular style of play. Full swings should be used and all strokes are effective.

"Slow playing" courts are those made of clay and of a "fast-dry" material such as Har-Tru. Clay is the slower of the two. This is the surface used at the French and Italian Open tournaments.

On "slow" surfaces baseline rallies are common, serve-and-volley styles, rare. The ball bounces higher, so the premium is deep groundstrokes. The court surface will blunt the power on serves and overheads. These shots must be well-placed and well-angled to achieve full effect. Topspin is accentuated on these courts with the ball kicking high. Sliced shots tend to "sit" up more, rather than skid as they would on a "fast" surface.

Indoor Courts

The playing surface will vary from club to club but certain conditions will generally hold true at most indoor facilities. These are: the light is more diffused than that of the sun outdoors, the ceiling

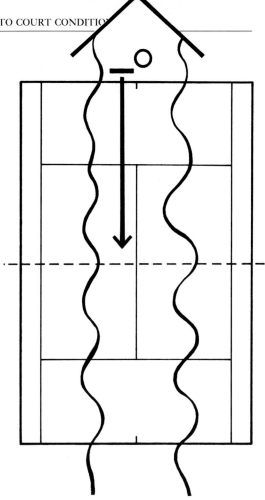

Adapting to wind

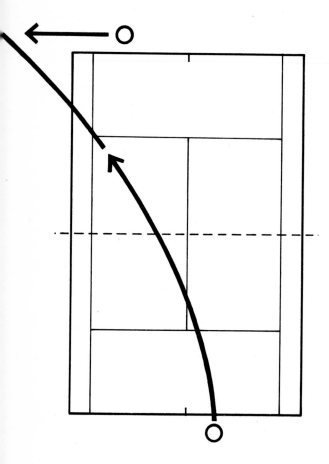

is in the way of lobs, and you have side netting separating the courts that can get in the way of some shots and in the way of some shot making.

The lighting takes some getting used to after playing outdoors. The first few times you play indoors try to get a full range of practice shots and notice how the lighting affects the way you hit and make the adjustments needed.

When you lob, you have to take great care to avoid the angled ceiling. Because of this, topspin lobs work better indoors than underspin ones; you can control the angle better.

The side netting can be used to your advantage instead of being a hindrance if you are smart. Use slice serves and spin serves to pull your opponent out of the court and into the side nets. He or she will be worrying about getting tangled up rather than concentrating on the return. When receiving serve, move in a bit so your opponent does not get away with the same tactic. On groundstrokes, a short angled shot will be effective in putting the other player into the "grasp" of the side net.

Adapting and changing to the varying conditions you find yourself playing in is necessary in achieving a winning record. It can be fun—a challenge to better your game. You may find some hidden skills that have been lying dormant within an unchanging game plan.

PAUL GAGON

Player slicing serve to pull opponent out of the court.

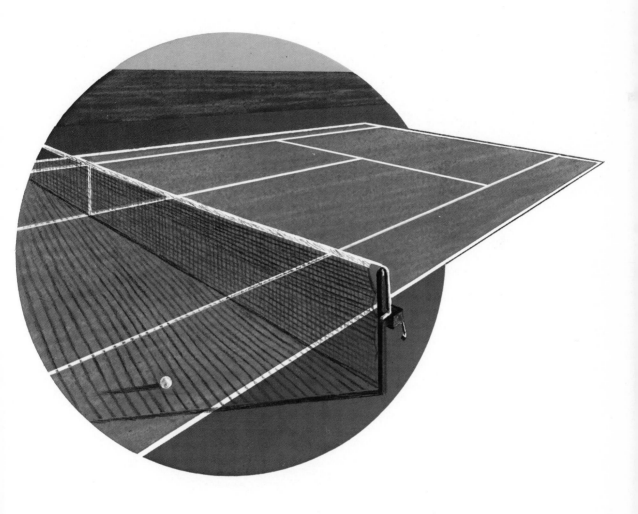

PART II

17

How to Become
a Teaching Professional

Teaching tennis can be a challenging and rewarding career, but in order to master your craft you must give many hours of preparation and many gallons of perspiration. Teaching professionals work hard, and with perseverance this hard work pays off. There are two routes one can take to become a teaching professional. First, you can work with a knowledgeable teaching professional either as an assistant or as a student. As you work under a teaching professional he or she can train you in the various areas of the profession. I recommend this route, for it gives first-hand experience in the three areas necessary for all teaching professionals to learn: execution, teaching, and business.

If you do not have the opportunity to train with a knowledgeable teaching professional, you must take the second route based on self-education and self-reliance. The following paragraphs outline the steps I recommend for "doing it on your own."

The execution phase of your education consists of learning to demonstrate each stroke with proper form. You should be able to show the various spins and perform each stroke with accuracy. If you start with the forehand you must demonstrate slice and topspin and be able to execute these crosscourt and down-the-line shots with accuracy. Next, work on the short angled slice and topspin passing shots. Finally, the preceding shots should

all be mastered with the backhand as well as the forehand.

On the volley you should be able to demonstrate the forehand and backhand approach and both the first volley and putaway volley. Next you can work on the drop volley. Finally, you should be able to maintain a nice and easy, consistent volley, which you need if you were teaching at the net and feeding someone at the baseline.

The lob, the overhead, the dropshot, and the serve must all be performed proficiently. Both an offensive and defensive lob should be worked on off the forehand and the backhand. The overhead should be executed both as a putaway moving into the net and with a scissors kick moving backwards. Your dropshot off both forehand and backhand side, should bounce three times before it leaves the service box. Finally, demonstrate the serve for accuracy and variety, including slice, topspin, and flat serve.

When you have mastered these strokes, you should be able to put them into practice on the court in a match situation. As a teaching professional you will have some left-handed students (maybe you are left-handed), so you should be able to demonstrate the strokes with your opposite hand. To complete the execution phase, you must be able to demonstrate the various grips and give their advantages and disadvantages.

An important skill, though it may appear trivial, is the ball feed. Teaching professionals feed countless balls to their pupils and the feed should be accurate with a comfortable pace and arc, so the student can have time to execute the stroke properly.

The second phase in your education, the teaching phase, is best acquired through reading and observing. There is a rich literature on the topic of teaching tennis, and I suggest you explore this. In addition, you can watch movies, listen to recordings, and attend the many workshops, conferences, and academies presented by various organizations.

You must develop your own manner of teaching strokes, strategy, and private and group lessons. I suggest you write down in detail the steps necessary to teach the various strokes to beginning, intermediate, and advanced players. Writing helps you organize your thoughts, and organized teaching makes for effective teaching. The same should be done for strategy and for private and group lessons: write out your thoughts and organize them so your lesson will flow smoothly.

The key to effective lessons is stroke diagnosis and correction. You must develop a plan to correct the various flaws in a stroke. Watch the student's racket throughout the entire stroke so you can see his or her stroke pattern. You must diagnose any flaws and prescribe the correction. In order to convey these corrections to the student, you will have to develop a vocabulary of clue words or phrases since different people respond to different phrases. Once again, by reading and observing you will broaden your understanding of effective teaching techniques. I cannot emphasize enough the importance of observing successful teaching professionals in order to see how they make a major or minor change in a player's stroke and what clue words they use to get their point across.

The final phase in your education as a tennis professional is the business phase. You can learn this phase by reading literature or by attending seminars, conferences, or courses on business. Here again, practical experience is desirable. If you work with an established professional or club manager, you can learn how to keep books, run a pro shop successfully, conduct tournaments, establish junior and adult programs, run tennis teams and leagues, and conduct a competitive ladder.

I would suggest spending time learning the operations of both indoor and outdoor facilities. Different facilities require different techniques for successful operation.

When you think you are ready to enter the tennis teaching profession, I advise you to take the USPTA's test. This test will evaluate your strengths and weaknesses in the execution, teaching, and business phases of professional tennis teaching.

Private Lessons

The very best private lessons are given by experienced professionals who make it a point to learn about their students and develop lesson plans geared to their needs and goals. Until you accumulate enough experience to interview and evaluate students in a few minutes before a lesson, it is a good idea to call them up to ask some questions in advance. It is also a good idea for beginning professionals to write up a detailed lesson plan to make sure they include all they intend to cover.

Good lesson plans include a logical progression of activity and are geared to the individual's needs. They should be organized for maximum success, and the drills selected should be appropriate for the student's level.

You need to do two things to plan effective lessons: talk to the individuals about their experience, and rally with them to establish their level. You will want to find out what their past experience is, whom they took lessons from, what their goals and objectives are, how they rate themself as tennis players, what their athletic ability is, and what other sports they have played (you may be able to use examples from these sports to illustrate the point you are making). You will also want to find out how much time they have to practice during the week, how many times a week they play, how many lessons they are interested in taking, and what they want their lessons to cover. Timing must be considered, too. If this is the only lesson the person is taking from you, if the student has a tournament the next day, or if he or she wants to achieve national ranking—each of these factors would affect your lesson plan. After introducing myself and talking with the students about their experience, I take them out on the court and rally with them. This gives me an opportunity to confirm their level, and gives them another chance to relax.

It is important for professionals to introduce themselves properly, put the students at ease, and establish a rapport. Remember that in order to project a professional image one must look professional. This includes neat, clean, well-fitted, and coordinated tennis clothes, and good grooming.

Once you know the student's goals and objectives and have established his or her level, you are ready to begin the lesson.

For beginners it is important to demonstrate the stroke and give the student a brief description of the various parts of the stroke. Make sure you position yourself so the person can see you when you are demonstrating. A beginner should be exposed to all parts of the stroke: the grip, ready position, stance, footwork, backswing, point of contact, and follow-through. Each professional should develop a system of teaching the various strokes·at the different levels of tennis. Although techniques may vary (some teaching pros like to teach the whole swing while others prefer to teach it in parts), each professional should prepare a progression to use for beginners, advanced beginners, etc.

With an intermediate or advanced student it is not necessary to demonstrate all the parts of the stroke. During the warm-up I normally analyze a student's stroke and pick out the biggest flaw. Then I concentrate the lesson on this one flaw, beginning with a demonstration of the way the student is executing the stroke and then demonstrating the correction we are going to work on.

Stroke explanations should be clear, concise, and direct. Keep it easy (some teaching professionals refer to the KISS theory: Keep It Simple Stupid). Remember the most important thing is for the student to understand the explanation.

You have to develop different ways of saying the same thing because different individuals respond to different clue words. If the problem is a late backswing some will respond to "racket back" as you feed them the ball, some to "the racket should point to the back fence by the time the ball crosses the net," and others to "as soon as your opponent hits the ball, take your racket back so you could drink a cup of coffee in your other hand while you are waiting for the ball to come to you." Good teaching professionals establish a library of clue words to use in their lessons. I suggest that inexperienced teachers start a card file of their clue words. Attending workshops, observing other professionals teaching, and reading articles and books can help you develop this library of words.

The best teachers are brief and to the point. They do not give a lecture but make a comment while they are having the student hit balls. Some teachers talk for fifteen minutes before the student hits a tennis ball. This is fine for a lecture before tennis professionals but not in a private lesson. The person taking the lesson should have an opportunity to hit a lot of tennis balls with the instructor, who gives constructive criticism.

Throughout the lesson it is important to maintain the rapport with your student you established initially. The most important thing to the person taking the lesson is his or her name. Make sure you use it all the time. Never give feedback to the individual without prefacing it with the name. Look your students in the eye when you talk to them. Get close to them if necessary; take their hand and lead them through the stroke if need be.

Always try to keep the lesson lively and light. Using humor helps, especially if the student is tense or makes a foolish mistake. A smile, too, can help the student stay relaxed. Variety in your speech and facial expressions will help emphasize points you are making.

You should develop two voices for teaching. One to use when you are close to the individual and another to use when you are on the other side of the net. Always project your voice when you make a point or congratulate your student. Your speech should be clear and concise; proper grammar is a must.

For me, diagnosing the problem and coming up with a cure is the main part of the lesson. The execution of a shot includes many factors, each of which affects the other, but the key to improving the stroke is to identify the *first cause* of the problem. The inexperienced teacher often confuses symptoms with the cause. I start by checking the student's grip and waiting position. This tells me a lot before I even feed a ball. Next I watch the shot preparation. How did the individual take the racket back and what footwork did he or she use in getting ready for the shot? Inexperienced teachers do not do this. They are used to watching the ball from their playing days and must retain themselves to watch the student instead. You should observe your student even after he or she has hit the ball to check the follow-through and balance.

Some tennis professionals say a different thing to the pupil after every swing (first: late backswing, second: wrist firm, third: weight forward, fourth: eye on ball, etc.). This keeps the student from concentrating on the necessary correction. Pick the primary cause and stick with it until your goal is accomplished—then go to the secondary factors that are giving the student trouble.

Beware of falling into the habit of changing for change's sake. You must have a reason for altering a person's stroke. A good player with an unorthodox stroke should be placed in a game situation with an advanced player to make sure that the stroke needs to be changed. Then you have to decide whether to make a major change or a minor adjustment. When suggesting a major change in a person's stroke, I explain that it is going to take a certain amount of time. The longer the student has played with an improper stroke, the longer the change will take. The student must be willing to go along with the change and able to take enough time

to practice in between lessons to work on it. I will take a player out of competition when making a major change. The player might revert to the old way of executing the stroke while playing.

Always find out if the person wants to go along with a major change. If not, you can suggest a minor adjustment that will help them. Be positive in your stroke correction, and be patient and persistent. You may have to look at the stroke again if you are not having success curing a flaw, because you may have missed the basic cause.

Going to opposite extremes sometimes helps in stroke correction. If a person is not getting the racket low enough for topspin, I will suggest touching the ground with the racket, then I will toss the ball and have the student hit a topspin forehand. At first players feel they cannot hit the ball with their racket so low, but then they discover it helps prepare them to get their racket under the ball. If you are making a major grip change, it is best to shift the grip a little at a time to help the person adjust gradually.

Another effective technique for stroke correction is to instruct the students to close their eyes, start to swing their rackets, and freeze at the moment of impact. Then take the rackets out of their hands and have them look through the strings to see where they were aiming. This is also useful for showing students the part of the stroke that needs to be corrected. Have them stop at the critical point to show them what needs to be changed.

Make sure you work on properly feeding your students the ball. You should give students a set-up ball that allows them time for preparation and to get into position for the shot. Make sure to feed underhand to put the right kind of spin on the ball for a natural bounce. Toss the ball so it is at its highest point when it reaches your student, after one bounce. Increase the pace only as the student improves the stroke. When a student is having trouble returning your feed you should reduce the distance between you and also reduce the speed of your toss. As the player improves the stroke, increase the distance and speed.

While skills and knowledge are important for teaching professionals, I have seen inexperienced teachers give an excellent lesson because of their enthusiasm. You should be excited about your lesson whether it is the first of the day or the last. You should be concerned and friendly. During the lesson make the person feel that he or she is the most important person in the world. What you lack in knowledge and expertise you can more than make up for with enthusiasm. If you want to become a teaching professional you should love to teach and

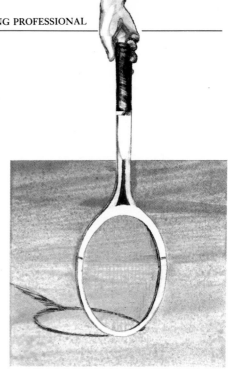

not just go through the motions. You should feel good that you helped someone improve during the lesson.

Keep safety in mind during lessons. The court should always be clear of tennis balls, and ball hoppers correctly placed. When you are using a ball machine make sure the student stays on the other side of the net until it is turned off, and do not get too close to a person showing you a stroke.

A good lesson ends with a proper review. Summarize the lesson and remind the individual of the critical points on which you want him or her to concentrate. Give some sound practical advice and homework. If possible give homework that can be done at home (such as practicing the service toss) as well as on the court. I ask students to keep a record of the days and amounts of time they practice, and the number of tips I have them working on. I always test them on their homework before starting the next lesson.

It is helpful to keep a card file system on which you record the student's name, address, phone number, and profile. For each lesson you record the date and time, the lesson's main subject, your diagnosis of the stroke, and the correction that was made. I also find it helpful to ask the person what I said or did that got my point across to them.

Some teaching professionals prefer giving private lessons in a series, and some will give a discount for paying in advance for a series. If you establish such a policy, put it and your fee in writing. You may also want to establish a cancellation policy. Some professionals require 24 hours notice of cancellation or they will charge for the lesson. You may want to print appointment cards with your name, phone number, and cancellation policy. If you use these cards you can write the individual's homework assignment on the back.

Group Lessons

The previous section contains my suggestions for private lessons. Many of these suggestions are useful for group lessons as well. For instance, be enthusiastic, be brief and concise, and always look your best. Ideally this section should be read in conjunction with the one on private lessons because all lessons can employ similar approaches and similar techniques.

All lessons, but especially group lessons, need to have a well-organized structure. The group lesson, like an educational book, needs a beginning, a middle, and an end which flow together smoothly to form a completed whole. The beginning is an introduction which puts the students at ease. The middle is the body of the lesson which conveys

knowledge, and the end concludes with review and homework drills for the next lesson. Each of these stages must be effective if a good lesson is to result. A well-organized lesson, then, is a necessity.

The lesson should be structured around a theme. The theme might be a stroke such as the topspin backhand or the slice serve, or the theme might be an aspect of the game such as concentration or strategy. Each drill is chosen to reinforce the theme, and the lesson is organized so that each drill is given enough time for proper attention.

In large groups with more than one teacher, the head professional should meet with the assistants and go over the teaching plan in advance of the lesson. Each assistant must know his or her responsibility for that lesson, and the head professional must be sure that all assistants use similar methods.

Group lessons are most effective when all of the members of the group are of similar ability. In your initial communication with the students, you should find out about their tennis background, experience, and goals so you can form groups of comparable ability. It is often helpful if the students form their own group because they can practice together between sessions.

Many students are self-conscious, nervous or embarrassed because of the social nature of a group lesson, so the introduction should help the students feel comfortable. A joke, an anecdote, or a brief story sets a comfortable tone that helps the students feel relaxed. Throughout the lesson, humor is essential to maintain this rapport. Humor also helps to sustain a high interest level, and interested students learn better. Using individuals' first names when you speak to them also sets them at ease, since this shows them that you recognize their individuality and importance.

In addition to putting the students at ease, the introduction should briefly review the previous lesson with a short drill.

In the body of the lesson you introduce new material to the students, usually in the form of a drill. After a brief talk and demonstration, the drill is practiced by everyone. It is important that everyone become involved with the activity. A lesson should be fun to encourage teacher and students to remain active throughout. It is also essential to spend equal time with each student.

One method I find particularly useful when working with a number of groups is the stations method. A teacher stays at each station while the group rotates from one station to the next. A different drill or stroke is used at each station. These drills can emphasize different aspects of one stroke or they can deal with different strokes altogether, depending on both the group's and your needs.

A second method I use with large groups is the tosser-hitter-shadow-retriever method. One person tosses the ball and another hits it; a third person shadows the stroke and timing, while the fourth person retrieves the ball. The group is periodically rotated through each position.

In a successful group lesson, all students should feel that they have received individual attention. On the other hand, do not take one person aside and explain something while the others are idle. Either give the others a drill to practice or make your comments applicable to everyone in the group by basing these comments on a more general principle.

It is during the primary drills that your responsibility is greatest. You must make sure the drill or stroke is done properly and you must correct any errors. A correct diagnosis of errors is essential. You must tell the students when they execute the stroke or drill properly so they can remember what the correct feeling is and repeat it. It is the students' responsibility to incorporate these changes into their game and to practice them until they become a habit.

To conclude the lesson, I find that a short, fun game puts everyone in a pleasant mood. With everyone in a positive state of mind a review of the lesson effectively reinforces the most important points of the lesson. Assign practice drills for the students to concentrate on during the week. The importance of these practice drills should be emphasized so that the group can move on to a new stroke or new facet of the game in the next lesson.

Throughout the lesson, safety is a paramount concern. You want no one hurt, so give each student, especially beginners, ample space and make sure this space is maintained throughout the lesson. The court should be cleared of any obstacles, such as loose balls or ball hoppers, which might cause ankle sprains. Finally, left-handed students should be placed so they can see the other students while they are hitting the ball.

GEORGE BACSO

18

Professional Ethics

Ethics should not be confused with the rules of tennis, but rather utilized as guidelines for those of us who have chosen to make tennis our profession. Ethical guidelines allow us to live and work smoothly among ourselves, the rest of the industry, and our most important asset—the client/player. Adherence to ethics projects the tennis professional to the top in his or her quest for excellence and recognition.

We have determined over the years that "awareness" of ethics guidelines breeds an increased respect among tennis professionals. This makes it important that even before a career decision is made, ethical guidelines are introduced. What, then, are ethics?

As we walk out on the court to give a lesson some things come to mind: Am I on time? Am I appropriately dressed? Do I belong on this court? We all know that the beginning of the end as a teacher is the day he or she starts to abuse lessons by not being on time. Likewise we know that a teacher's appearance will often impress on students, his or her degree of interest in them and professional skill. We also know that teachers cannot really teach well if they are at a facility (on a court) where they are not supposed to be plying their trade.

Am I teaching the game by the established rules? Does my own play/court conduct set the example? Do I enforce the rules? In these areas the teacher has a dramatic impact on the sport. We have all seen what happens when teaching professionals or coaches have not kept students within the written and unwritten rules of the game. The results are always unpleasant and erode the pleasures inherent in tennis.

Am I providing/recommending to my clients the best equipment? Do tennis equipment venders trust me and my ability? Am I considered a good account? We as teaching professionals deal constantly in the variables of equipment, the sport, and students. This allows us insights into what different students need in the way of equipment. We must use these insights to insure client satisfaction. Our suppliers of equipment must look forward to meeting with us and exchanging ideas. Sometimes these very important interactions are blunted when a professional does not honor financial obligations.

Am I loyal? Am I eagerly sought out by my clients for advice? Do I provide a program for all? Loyalty is often left behind in our fast-moving sport, but loyalty is often the most important factor to our employer, clients, and venders. Loyalty helps to make our extremely tough public relations work easier. Loyalty is often the "binder" for harmony with other employees. Our loyalty record seems to be a key factor when seeking positions. Loyalty gives us a common bond with clients that allows them to seek us out for advice and feel easy with us. Teaching professionals have the direction necessary to program for all. With their knowledge of the sport, facilities, and personnel, professionals mold a program to the needs/desires of their clientele. Professionals continually evaluate programs by watching participants' reactions, monitoring attendance, and soliciting feedback. In this manner, professionals can make changes as needed to maintain program viability.

What are my goals as a teaching professional? Do I communicate with my fellow professionals? Do I work to improve myself and my profession? Am I respected by other professionals and employers? When we set goals as professionals these alone often provide us parameters to work within and to guide us. We can learn a great many things about our profession from the frequent exchange of ideas with other professionals. The things we learn are not only about teaching tennis, but are also successful working habits and pitfalls to be avoided. The profession is a difficult one and is made a lot easier by communicating with other professionals who understand the difficulties and share your day-to-day concerns/needs. We gain respect of our fellow professionals by being open and forthright with them. Our open participation in all aspects of the sport and industry are signs to our fellow professionals and employers that we are truly professional, and earns us their respect. Now let us take a look at a set of professional ethics and discuss them briefly. One purpose of a professional organization such as the USPTA is to help establish ethical standards and then enforce them. Here is the "Code of Ethics" of the USPTA found as Article XVII of its bylaws:

Code of Ethics

"The name Tennis Professional must be and remain a synonym and pledge of honor, service and fair dealings. His professional integrity, fidelity to the game of tennis and a sense of his great responsibility to employers and to his brother professionals, must be of the highest. In accordance with these ideals and with the purposes of the Association, the USPTA enjoins upon its membership rigid observance of the following Code of Ethics:

1. A member shall not play or give or solicit, or give the appearance of soliciting lessons without informing the resident professional at any tennis facility and shall in no way cause embarrassment to any resident professional.

2. A member will not accept a position or appointment at a tennis facility in any but an honorable and ethical manner.

3. A member shall meet his financial obligations promptly.

4. A member shall not be guilty of conduct likely to injure the reputation and standing of the Association or any of its members.

5. A member shall not engage in any conduct which is contrary to or inconsistent with a policy adopted by the USPTA."

As you can see, the code is fairly general in nature and perhaps even a little vague. But, what you must understand is that this code, and basically all codes, must retain some flexibility in order to cover all circumstances and still remain viable.

The preamble paragraph of the code can best be summarized as an intent to bring pride and prestige to the teaching profession and a call for mutual respect within the entire industry.

Paragraph one deals with one pro soliciting or giving the appearance of soliciting lessons at a club that already has a resident pro. The visitor must first inform the resident of his or her intention to solicit lessons. Also, the former shall in no way cause embarassment to the latter. This paragraph does not forbid a pro from ever soliciting lessons at a tennis facility that has a resident pro. Generally, the law protects competition for customers. However, by requiring the visitor to tell the resident pro of his or her intention to solicit lessons, it affords the resident pro an opportunity to inform the visitor of any contractual rights which the resident might have. Often these include the sole right to solicit lessons at the facility. Such a clause is perfectly proper, and if the visitor does not respect it, this might result in a disciplinary proceeding being brought against him or her. Remember, club members and clients are not aware of these ethical considerations, so it is imperative that you explain them prior to any embarrassing situation arising.

Paragraph two states that a member's acceptance of a position of employment at a tennis facility must be in an honorable and ethical manner. Does this mean that a USPTA member may not seek a job at a club employing another member? No, not necessarily! Unless the pro has an employment contract with the tennis facility, this clause cannot be used to protect his or her job. Ordinarily, competition for employment must not be subject to pressure by a trade association. Where there is an employment contract, however, the situation is different. If the visitor induces the employer to breach his or her agreement with the resident pro, there is recognized legal cause of action against the visitor for interference with a contractual relationship. The resident pro might also have cause of action for breach of contract against the club. Many situations may arise because so many of the jobs for teaching professionals are handled by persons not familiar with the ethical standards of our trade. If the situation does not "feel" right, then make some inquiries. Do not undermine another professional. If you are the best for the job, then you will feel best if you earn the appointment.

Paragraph three requires the pro to meet his or her financial obligations promptly. Do not be mistaken and believe that this means the association will be a collection agency. It is best interpreted to mean that the association does not condone the mishandling of financial affairs, and that prompt payment of just debts will prevent any problems. Action by the association will normally come after legal determination has been made. Yes, we have all had difficulties during a change of job, severe winter, or illness, but these situations are known to businesspersons, and being open and honest with your accounts will bring you through your difficulty and gain your business respect. It only takes a card, letter, telephone call, or visit to keep financial harmony and maintain strong credit.

A catch-all provision of the Code of Ethics is paragraph four. It states that a professional shall not engage in any conduct which is likely to injure the reputation and standing of the association or any of its members. Here, as was stated earlier, there are as many interpretations as professionals. Tennis professionals, just like doctors, lawyers, and other professionals, have a sense of duty to their profession and all others practicing that profession—that they will do the best job they can and exercise care not to bring ill repute to either.

Paragraph five forbids a member from engaging in conduct contrary to or inconsistent with a policy adopted by the USPTA. This paragraph covers such matters as the use of the USPTA name or logo without prior national authorization, or scheduling a USPTA tournament without first securing national approval and paying a sanction fee. This also makes it imperative that each member become familiar with *all* the workings and policies of the association. Normally this is done by active participation. However, in this day of suits and counter-suits, you must be very careful as you "tiptoe" through ethics matters. This is why the USPTA and most associations retain counsel. Many times professionals and organizations get tunnel vision and must rely on objective counsel to ensure they do not get into legal difficulties.

As opposed to the practice of medicine, the law, or some other similar occupations, the teaching of tennis is completely unregulated. No governmental agency, either federal, state, or local, takes a hand in supervising tennis teaching. Do not let your feelings be hurt by this. It is not so much that you lack importance; rather, it is more that you are so far not recognized as being a menace to life and limb. But with the lack of governmental regulation, USPTA—as the only trade association in the profession—bears a real responsibility. A part of this responsibility is to promulgate a useful and meaningful Code of Ethics. As with all activities of the association, however, the administration of the code must be in accordance with the law. Trying to provide ethical standards for the profession takes time, effort, and money. A strong Code of Ethics, surely deserves the support and cooperation of all who have any connection with the game of tennis.

JACKIE JUSTICE

19

Tournament Organization

The most successful tournaments are those which have been thoroughly planned beforehand. Early preparation, scheduled planning meetings, plenty of volunteer help, and commitment to pre-arranged schedules, plans, and dates are crucial ingredients for tournament success. Over the long run, however, a tournament is only as successful as the skills, energy, and commitment of those most directly involved. Therefore, personnel and organization are the two most crucial aspects of any tournament.

Your tournament committee should consist of the tournament core—those people most committed to the tournament's success from "day one." Responsibilities of the tournament committee include obtaining the tournament sanction, appointing a referee, formulating and issuing the entry form, overseeing subsidiary committee operations, and generally supervising the entire organization of the tournament.

The referee (preferably a USTA or Grand Prix certified chair umpire or referee), appointed by the tournament committee or a member thereof, is responsible for guaranteeing impartiality and fair conditions of play. More specifically, the referee's responsibilities include seeding and making the draw, scheduling, supervising all aspects of play (including the courts, balls, ballboys and ballgirls, and officials), declaring defaults and other disciplinary actions, and acting as appeals judge for players defaulted by a chair umpire and/or player. If knowledgeable, capable, energetic people fill the spots on the tournament committee and appoint an experienced referee, the tournament is off to a good start.

Second in importance only to the tournament committee and the referee are the various committees needed to ensure a smooth-functioning event. A universal temptation of tournament committees is to take too much upon themselves. Good tournament management consists of thorough planning, successful recruitment of subsidiary personnel, proper delegation of tasks, and careful supervision and assistance—all of which should leave the tournament committee and referee unencumbered during the tournament so that they may deal calmly with the crisis which inevitably arise. If the tournament committee takes too much responsibility directly, crisis decisions may be made hastily and without careful thought, to no one's benefit.

Therefore, in order to ensure that the tournament continues to run smoothly from start to finish, the tournament committee must recruit, train, and supervise many different committees. The number of committees and volunteers will vary, depending on the complexity of the event. Some committee possibilities are: facilities, officials, ballboys and ballgirls, scorekeeping, hospitality,

VITT ORGANIZATIONAL CHART

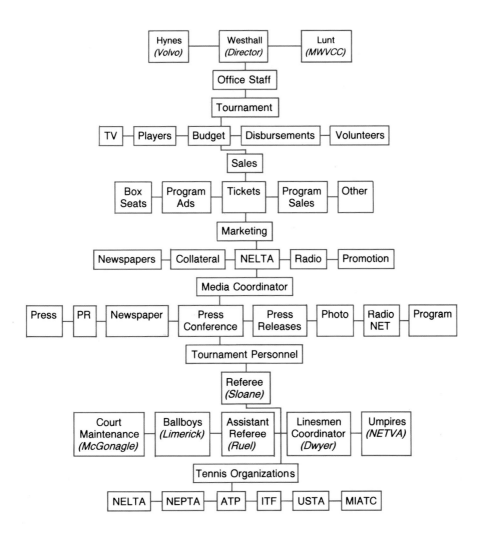

transportation, housing, publicity, legal, awards, and registration. Major events require even more committees. Remember, however, that all tournaments, large or small, will be successful only in proportion to the quality of their personnel and organizations. See the illustration for a chart of the Volvo International Grand Prix tournament in North Conway, New Hampshire.

Although there are literally hundreds of details to be considered and orchestrated for a successful tournament, the following are a few of the most important. *First*, be sure your entry blank is sent out well in advance and includes the following information on the top half, or on the first page:

1. Name of tournament.
2. Location.
3. Dates.
4. Events to be played and scoring to be used.
5. Fees.
6. Entry deadline.
7. Awards allocations.
8. Regulations (age limitations, USTA cards).
9. Check-in time.
10. Names of tournament committee members and referee.
11. How to make out entry check, address to send check to.
12. Tournament phone number.
13. Type of balls to be used.

Second, the bottom half of the entry blank, or the second page—which will be returned to the tournament along with the entry fee—should include:

1. Name.
2. USTA number.
3. Birthdate.
4. Address and phone numbers, home and work.
5. Events to be entered (singles, doubles, mixed doubles, age divisions).
6. Name of doubles partner.
7. Release of responsiblities and liability clause.
8. Player's signature, or parent's signature if a minor.
9. Seeding information.

Third, be sure you have acquired your tournament sanction well in advance, and order tennis balls and trophies as soon as your dates are set and confirmed. After entries are closed, calculate how many balls you will need and be sure you have an adequate supply, with a few extra in case of emergencies.

Fourth, be sure you have copies of the "Rules of Tennis" and "USTA Tournament Regulations" on hand at all times (the current *Official USTA Tennis Yearbook* will have both). Be sure to consult the appropriate procedures when making the draw. Rules for making the draw often change yearly, so reliance upon regulations and procedures from memory alone is unwise. As soon as the draw is completed, see that numerous copies are prepared for posting and distribution, otherwise you will have traffic jams. If feasible, it would be wise to pre-schedule matches on the draw sheet as soon as the draw is completed, including day, time, and court assignment.

Fifth, if you are utilizing different sites at any point, or plan to (for instance if rain forces you indoors), devise a clear-cut communications system between the tournament committee/referee and site directors well in advance, so every one understands the procedure when the time comes. Poor communications cause more problems at tournaments than any other single factor! Even a large single site can lead to communications' problems, especially if several things happen at once in different areas of the grounds.

Sixth, during the running of the tournament itself, all those involved should do their best to be courteous, cooperative hosts. People generally respond positively to positive treatment, even tournament players.

Finally, after the event is over, completed copies of the draw need to be sent immediately to appropriate sectional authorities (for seeding and ranking purposes) and to local, sectional, and national media for publicity. Thank-you letters should be sent promptly to all volunteers and a tournament report should be compiled, detailing strengths and weaknesses, so that next year's tournament can be PERFECT!

FERNANDO VELASCO

20

Junior Programs

As a tennis professional, one of your toughest responsibilities is to institute a good, well-rounded junior program. You must understand that the way you structure your program will have a definite impact on whether each junior continues on to make tennis a lifetime sport or goes to another activity which better suits his or her needs. Remember that the junior tennis players you work with today are the adult players of tomorrow.

What Makes a Good Junior Program?

Putting together a good junior program is like putting together a giant jigsaw puzzle. All the pieces must fit properly in order to obtain a finished product. The proper amount of lessons, competition, and social play, at the correct age and ability levels, will produce an excellent program.

In some programs too much emphasis is placed on lessons. Students have no organized play during which to work on skills, and they do not meet other players on their own level. In other programs competition is emphasized too heavily. Excessive competition is a major problem for those juniors who are not super athletes and who only want to have fun and enjoy tennis at this particular stage. Too much competition also places too much pressure to win on younger players.

When you are organizing your program, bear in mind that a great majority of your students will *not* become the superstars of tomorrow. Therefore, design your program for the majority, with supplemental programs for the tournament players.

Progressive Instruction

Since a good program calls for a mixture of instruction and play, let us discuss what to look for in a well-rounded progressive lesson program and how it will help the juniors learn. In order to keep their interest, you must always offer your students reasonable goals and other levels to which they can advance as their ability increases. In today's world, children are beginning all their activities at an early age, and it is no different with tennis. Therefore, the best starting point for a complete junior program would be the tiny tots program.

Tiny tot instruction for six- to nine-year-olds is the forgotten program at many clubs. One of the reasons is that it is not prepared with the right philosophy. Several key ingredients are necessary to run a smooth tot program. The clinic should show the children that tennis is a fun game and it should help them develop basic hand-eye coordination for tennis. Do not expect too much of them! Keep sessions short, and the number of students small. Since the attention span of children at this age is limited, you cannot expect them to listen and

lesson, a one-hour group lesson, a half-hour on the ball machine, and one and one-half hours of round-robin play each week. Scheduled at times convenient to the student, the "Four-Point Program" offers all the right ingredients in one package. It should only be offered to intermediate and advanced students, since they are obviously at the playing stage and this is a skill refinement program.

As juniors progress in their skill level toward tournament calibre, private lessons and drill sessions come into play. These two methods of teaching are used to refine strokes and strategy within a more personal professional/student relationship. Private lessons allow the professional to devote all of his or her attention to the individual student's problem areas. Drill sessions, usually consisting of three or four people, are designed to practice skills in a game situation over and over so that by the time the student has to hit that shot in a game, it will be second nature.

If you work at a club where there are few tournament players, do not be afraid to recommend good junior programs in the area where your tournament players can meet and practice with other top players. You are in a service business and your responsiblity is to help these students advance their skills any way possible, even if it means referring them to a program outside your club that better fits their needs.

By means of a "Progressive Instruction Program," juniors can improve their skill level to maximum potential. If they progress in stages they are working with attainable goals, and reaching goals gives them a sense of accomplishment that allows them to move forward to new levels of achievement.

Both clinics and private lessons are necessary to provide the instruction mix that makes a solid junior program. Clinics offer beginning students built-in practice partners. Once they reach the level where they need refinement of strokes, the private lessons become advantageous.

Activities for All Levels

Once a student begins an instructional program he or she needs a way to put these skills into play. This is where the combination of competitive and non-competitive activities must be planned. Let us talk first about some ideas for fun activities and then we will discuss how competition can be broken down to enable players to play at their own ability level.

For instance, a great way to start the summer is an "Opening Day Junior Circus." Boys and girls of any age or ability can try their luck at different tennis skill tests that have been set up on each court.

pay attention in a structured situation for two hours. A 45-minute session is usually about right to prevent them from becoming bored.

Since children this age require a lot of supervision, there should be no more than five students to a teacher. The major asset for a tiny tot program of this kind is an enthusiastic, patient, and very positive instructor. A capable instructor will make the program a pleasant new experience for these kids and will be careful not to push them too fast. Let young children choose when they want to learn. Parents should wait until their children show interest before entering them. Parents should also be ready to sustain their interest by tossing balls to them between lesson periods.

Juniors nine to sixteen years of age who are just starting to play tennis should first become involved through a camp or clinic situation. The attention span of this age group is considerably longer than that of the tiny tots, and their ability to learn tennis skills is greater. The clinic program also offers the most economical plan for parents. Parents always appreciate a moderately priced opportunity for their children to learn a new sport, especially when they will be meeting new friends in a pleasant environment. Since these juniors are older and their learning potential greater, clinics should focus on stroke production and basic strategy for both singles and doubles. There should be beginner and intermediate groups in order to give students more chances for progress.

An excellent instruction program is the "Four-Point Program," which gives students a combination of instruction, practice, and play. In this program the junior gets a half-hour private

Make sure that the skill tests are short and fun. Some possibilities might include serving blindfolded, hitting to areas or comic targets, or knocking empty tennis ball cans off a table. Follow the skill tests with relay races that incorporate tennis skills, such as running while bouncing a ball with a racket. Wind up the day with a doubles round robin, organized according to ability with a fun format such as "King-of-the-Hill." Four players begin play. When the first one makes a mistake, someone else from the sidelines rotates in. Each participant keeps score of his or her points won and at the end you have your "King-of-the-Hill." Move the games rapidly and keep the numbers low on each court, since the idea is to keep everyone active. Refreshments and a small gift for each participant is a nice finishing touch and everyone goes away a winner. They key to the success of this activity is to be imaginative, furnish early publicity, and have enthusiastic court attendants who will assist the kids during the skill tests.

Another way to ensure activity and provide juniors with a way to meet other juniors of their own age and ability level is to have periodic round robins of either singles or doubles, depending on the number of courts available. Since the idea is to meet as many other juniors as possible, a six- or eight-game set with changing partners is a beneficial format. Serve some light refreshments and have small prizes such as tennis pencils, shoelaces, or wristbands.

Competitive programs can be run so that everyone gets to play at his or her own level, making the game more enjoyable for everybody. With a little imagination, your programs can entice juniors to play more when they know their opponents will be approximately of the same calibre. The following competitive programs are some examples you can implement at your facility.

For the tiny tots, ages six to nine, start a "Minor League of Tennis," with matches played on a tot-sized court. If your club has a backboard, paint an area the size of a service court, and then put up a portable net about two feet high. If this is not possible, just use the service portion of a regular court. It stands to reason that small children relate better to a court more their size. This program should be set up as a team effort since we do not want youngsters at this age to face the pressure of head-to-head competition. Divide students into teams and play regular matches once a week. At the end of the season, have trophies for everyone, so there will be no losers. T-shirts with team names make a big hit. Balls should be provided, and a court attendant should be designated to supervise all matches. To participate in this league, tots must have gone through at least one tot clinic so they know the basics and how to keep score. A fee can be charged, or sponsors for the teams can be recruited to cover expenses.

Almost every club belongs to a league in which juniors play competitive matches against other clubs. The unfortunate thing about these leagues is that they cater to advanced players and these are the same juniors who are already playing regularly in local USTA tournaments. To find a place for the junior who is just below this echelon, add a "Little League of Tennis." Juniors in this category will benefit from the competition and it will provide a place for the tots to advance to when they are ready. As with the tots program, little tennis leaguers should be provided balls, T-shirts, and supervision. Little league play consists of a combination of singles, doubles, and mixed doubles, so the scoring emphasis is still on team effort. To get the juniors into this activity, select captains and let them have a player draft. It is a great way to give the up-and-coming juniors the opportunity to compete at their own level of ability and continue their progress as players.

One of the best ways to choose your "Inter-Club League Team" is through the use of ladder play. An active ladder provides the fairest way to decide who plays on the team each week. It also provides activity during possible slow times. You do, however, need an incentive to keep the juniors challenged. One incentive is, obviously, the chance to play on the team, but another incentive is to advertise a "Ladder Player of the Year" award. This award is not necessarily for the best player, but the most active. You should give points every time a player challenges, another point for each win, and a point for the number one player on the ladder at the end of each week. A big trophy on display will help to keep the challenge ladder active. There are two basic types of ladders: the straight ladder and the pyramid ladder. It is up to each club to decide which one works best. The rules for team qualifying, "Ladder Player of the Year," and challenges should be established early and made available to everyone concerned.

"Club Championships" are one of the mainstays of junior club programs. Since these are not sanctioned tournaments, use your imagination and set up the tournament so that juniors play opponents of approximately the same ability. Winners move on to the next level and losers go into a consolation event as in the following diagrams:

This system provides two winners in each age group. It also allows each player to play at least twice, and permits a player at the top echelon to have a chance at earning a trophy. Do not forget to run doubles and mixed doubles events in addition to the singles.

A "Member-Guest Tournament" could also be a most enjoyable junior event. Offer a girls' and boys' division, and also a mixed doubles' division. With eight teams participating, the following system gives each team a minimum of three matches, and every win or loss brings the teams closer to their own ability level. The following diagram shows the tournament draw and where players progress after each round.

As you can see, by the end of the tournament you have the teams ranked one through eight. This event can be run in three hours by using an eight-game pro set with a five-minute warm-up each round. A little award presentation combined with refreshments will top off a memorable day.

Overall, the key to a successful junior program is for each individual club to find the right mixture of programs and instruction. Some additional ingredients that go into a first-class junior program are to provide juniors with good used balls on a sign-out basis for random play, and to have used

rackets available for those juniors who decide to play at the last minute. Be sure to have some tiny tot rackets—it is tough for a ten-year-old to play with a 4⅝ medium.

The club should set aside junior time so that juniors have priority on the courts certain hours each weekday. There is no bigger turn-off for a junior than to be continually bumped by adults every time he or she attempts to play. The atmosphere should be positive and pro-junior. Children should not be treated as necessary evils. They are the members of tomorrow *if* we can keep them interested. Mail out a calendar at the beginning of the season so the juniors will know when all the activities are scheduled.

Other aspects of successful junior programs are the "Most Improved" and "Sportsmanship" awards. These awards are special in that they reward the attitudes we are trying to instill in each junior, in hopes they will stay with them the rest of their lives. Make every effort to make these awards special. For instance, prizes such as racket bags with the player's names and the names of the awards printed on them would be excellent gifts.

Your club has to decide what needs to be accomplished and how much should be offered. The

only way prospective members learn about your junior tennis program before they join is by talking to the professional, the activity director, or other members. Prospective members will be looking to see if their children can fit into your programs regardless of the differences in age and ability. Your programs should, therefore, not be geared strictly to the superstars because there are not many! Parents will expect you to have programs available that will allow room for their children to progress as they learn. If you offer the proper measures of instruction, programs, and extra incentives, you should have a tennis program that has something for everyone.

ROD DULANY

21

Team Coaching

Coaching a tennis team is complex, challenging, and satisfying when done well. However, the task of taking an individual sport and transferring it into a team situation is no easy one. The skills of the coach must be highly developed and continually honed to fit the pieces together in order to breed success for the group.

Since most coaches have other related duties as well, the amount of time spent coaching is often disproportionate to the salary earned. It is critical that an effective coach be well-organized and prepared so that time demands can be kept at a reasonable level.

The following description of factors involved in team coaching highlights all the responsibilities involved. The true professional will spend a career learning to deal with these facets, modify his or her approach based on experience, and strengthen personal areas of weakness. While this discussion of coaching cannot provide all the answers for you, it will at least expose the questions to be tackled.

Personnel

Coaching involves dealing with people in a variety of ways. The most effective coaches are not necessarily outstanding performers, tacticians, or diagnosticians, but rather individuals especially skilled in working with people.

If you think of the coach as the hub of a wheel, the various spokes represent the following people who work directly with him or her:

The athletic director or club manager.
Assistant coaches.
Team captain.
Team managers.
Players.

Each of these people has a distinct function to perform and can strengthen the overall effort or weaken it. From year to year, the tasks and responsibilities of these people can vary, depending on their talents and capabilities. However, here are some general suggestions for extracting the best out of these vital team members.

The *athletic director* (A.D.) or *club manager* is the coach's immediate supervisor. He or she can help greatly to facilitate the work of the coach. He or she assists in scheduling, travel arrangements, equipment purchasing and control, maintenance, and budget, with advice and input from the coach. It is critical to provide accurate, useful information so that your team can have the best support services permitted within your budget.

A regular meeting time between you and the

A.D. is important to review your needs and future plans. Good communication on a daily basis is also helpful and you should encourage him or her to visit your training and practice sessions regularly to keep in close touch.

The *assistant coach* (A.C.) can be anyone with an interest in tennis and/or young people. Typically, the A.C. is someone who serves for the opportunity to gain experience, someone eager to relieve the head coach of some of the load. To use assistants effectively, the coach should assign specific responsibilities so that the assistant coaches can take pride in their accomplishments. The head coach has to back assistants up and should expect the same loyalty and support from them. An A.C. can be assigned the role of drillmaster, junior varsity coach, conditioning specialist, or recruiter. This division of labor may be altered from year to year to bring along an assistant in every facet of coaching. Often players will grouse and complain to an assistant who seems sympathetic. This information, passed along, can help to keep the coach informed about team morale or developing trouble spots.

In general, team decisions are best made by agreement among the head coach, assistant coach, and the team captain. This method allows opinions from different perspectives and lets the players feel they have a voice in major decisions.

Team managers do the administrative detail work and free the coaches to be involved in the play. They assume responsibility for the equipment, scorekeeping, newspaper releases, court maintenance, and general troubleshooting for the coach. Perhaps the best manager is someone who truly loves tennis but is unable to play on the team for some reason. This kind of person can put in the long hours and accomplish the thankless jobs that are necessary.

The *team captain* is usually elected by the previous year's team. He or she can be tremendously helpful to the coach. The better a player the captain is, the more insight he or she will have into the legitimacy of teammates' complaints and concerns. The captain must be completely honest and forthright in dealing with the coach so that a feeling of trust emerges. Also, team players must feel that the captain is their voice in the decision-making process, and trust his or her judgment. An upperclassman has a decided advantage since he or she knows the ropes, the likely problems, and past solutions. You will find that the team captain often smooths over rough spots before the coach is even aware of them.

The *players* on the team are, of course, the beneficiaries of all the efforts discussed. They are often insecure, immature, and prone to make decisions based on transitory feelings. However, the pressure to perform athletically is great. A good coach can work with each player and learn to know him or her and his or her weaknesses as a person. And one day the coach rejoices in the maturing that takes place in the players.

A key ingredient in effective coach-player relationships is the player's knowledge that the coach has regard for him or her, first as a person and second as a tennis player. All players need to feel important, no matter what their skill level, and that the coach is genuinely interested in their improvement. This feeling can be instilled if the coach takes a personal interest in each person's background, family, school performance, social life, and future dreams.

An interesting, dynamic thing happens when young people get together on a team. The individual relationships that the coach has established with each player may now take a back seat to peer pressure or group decision. The coach must be ready for that development and forgive apparent violations of trust that sometimes result. On the other hand, positive results often occur when an intransigent team member is whipped into line by teammates who put pressure on him or her. Suffice it to say that the unexpected can happen with a group, and the coach should be prepared for anything.

Each of the previously mentioned people need to be aware of the contributions and functions of the others. Cooperative efforts toward common goals will help to establish this feeling, such as a fund raiser, a social outing, picnic, or tournament. Make sure all of these people know their roles and understand those of the others to prevent confusion and hurt feelings.

Coaching Style

Generally, coaches tend to adopt a style of coaching that emulates a successful coach they played for at some time. It is much better for a coach to develop an individual style based on his or her personality, taking into account the players to be dealt with on the team. There are three major coaching styles with variations: the authoritarian or "Lombardi" style, the laissez-faire style, and the democratic style. Each type of coaching has strengths and weaknesses, but in dealing with tennis players who are basically individuals the democratic style would seem to have the edge, and we have based our discussion of coaching personnel on that style.

Since most tennis coaches are not in a high pressure situation where their job hinges on the won-lost record, they can afford to give up some control to the players, more so than a football coach can. Athletes need to understand the style of the coach and what to expect in terms of response from him or her as the year progresses. The first team meeting is a good time to candidly discuss your view of the coach-player relationship.

The Coach as a Professional

While developing a coaching style that is comfortable, coaches, who aspire for self-improvement must build their personal skills in coaching along a well-thought out path. Assessment of your strengths and weaknesses will help you chart your path to improvement. If you lack understanding of racket technique, seek the help of an established tennis professional, perhaps during the summer. If the mental side needs attention, attend a seminar or workshop. Look to college courses in coaching for general administrative help. Join the professional tennis organizations, attend their workshops and clinics, and read every bit of printed material possible.

Planning the Year

It is helpful to think of your role as coach as a year-round assignment. The things you accomplish in the preseason and the postseason truly make the difference between top-flight programs and mediocre ones. The actual playing season is so short that players will not show much significant progress during this time. You need to map out, with them, the plans for an entire year so they understand the commitment necessary if they want to raise the level of their play.

The first task, for players and coach alike, is to set goals for the year. These should include long-range goals, intermediate goals, and short-term goals. Only in this way can success and progress be fairly measured, since so often we mistakenly measure success only by wins and losses. Obviously wins and losses are dependent on factors outside of the control of players and coaches, and give a misleading picture.

The group should establish team goals by consensus before the season begins. You might include such subjects as: team unity, respect for each individual, increased knowledge, top physical condition, loyalty to the group, and certainly fun. Full participation by each member of the group in formulating goals ensures a greater chance of acceptance and, therefore, effort than if the coach dictates to the group. The team rules and regulations for general conduct and play should follow goal-setting, and when "gray areas" are encountered during the season, a return to the spirit of the goals will often help clear up the cloudy areas.

Each player should set several levels of personal goals as well. Long-term goals may be dreams of a college scholarship or a professional tennis career—the aim should be high. Intermediate goals may include earning a higher position on the team ladder, improving last season's record, or achieving a winning record. Short-term goals are critical and must be readily attainable. They may include a commitment to hit 100 practice serves each day, improve personal fitness aims by 20 percent, or enter at least six tournaments during the summer. Each level should build in a logical sequence toward the long-range goals or dreams. It is a good idea for the players to write down these goals, share them with the coach, and post them in their room for regular progress checks and motivation.

Unit Planning

Once team and individual goals are set, it is up to the coaches (with advice from the team captain) to map out the specific plans to implement these goals. For ease in organization, it is helpful to think in terms of units of the year. The temptation to go with the flow during the season can be disastrous as you can easily end the season wondering where the time has gone.

Lay out, week by week, the schedule of practices and the topics to be covered in them. A logical order of presentation of strategy and tactics, combined with skill work, allows the players to improve at a faster rate. Be sure to include review time on key concepts, repetition of essential skills, and periodic evaluations of team progress so that revisions can be made.

It is important to assess your team and make decisions (based on the goals as set) concerning the proportion of time to be spent on the various parts of the game. If the tasks to be accomplished can be grouped into physical conditioning, racket skills, strategy and tactics, and mental training, a proportion of time must be allotted to each. The lower the level of skill of the group, the more emphasis you should place on basic strategy and racket skills. As skill levels increase, a relatively greater amount of time can be devoted to advanced tactics and mental training.

Written unit plans naturally develop into daily practice plans for the coach. He or she is the organizer who keeps all players active and focussed on specific tasks. The tendency to hit with players is self-defeating and should be done only after team workouts. These written plans, if kept from year to

year, provide a basic structure for future years and guard against the possibility of leaving out something important. Posting or duplicating copies of plans for each player also increases general understanding of the direction each is pursuing, and allows the players to plan personal time and responsibilities around team plans.

The Preseason

The preseason directly precedes the beginning of the competitive matches. Generally, this includes about four to six weeks before the first actual match. During this time, much has to be accomplished in the way of preparation in order for the competitive season to go smoothly.

In high school, the beginning date of practice is usually prescribed by your league or your school. Of course, weather is a factor in northern climates at any level. If the time allowed is shorter than four weeks, the days become even more precious and require careful planning.

Along with handling administrative tasks, the coach uses the preseason to select team members, determine team positions, institute a conditioning program, and schedule regular practices. The coach is responsible for four critical areas: physical conditioning, racket skills, strategy and tactics, and mental skills. The proportion of time spent on these four areas will depend on the level of coaching, the experience and talent of the players, and the total time available.

A wise coach will change the proportion each year to fit the current situation, while not neglecting any one area.

Physical Conditioning

There is no question that the development of physical strength and endurance is a long-term process that necessitates a year-round commitment. However, some significant progress can be made, during the preseason, provided that cardio-respiratory fitness has been established in the off-season. During the off-season, players should be encouraged to follow a regular program of long, slow distance running several times each week. This should be parallelled by a weight training program to strengthen the key muscles, the legs, and the upper body parts that are injury prone in tennis, such as elbow, shoulder girdle, and back.

During the short preseason, weight training and distance running will produce little significant gain. It is better instead to concentrate on short distances, working at maximum speed, using running patterns similar to those employed in tennis. Shuttle runs, agility drills, star patterns, and suicide sprints are typical effective drills.

An important task for the coach during this time is to teach players the benefits and techniques of stretching before activity. A regular pattern of static stretching will increase the range of motion at the joints, produce more efficient movement, increase power, and prevent injury. Young players are often reluctant to take the time to stretch adequately or warm up thoroughly before practice or play, so the coach must insist on the adoption of a team routine that is followed invariably.

Selecting a Team

This is often a difficult assignment for the coach. A planned program that ensures fairness and thoroughness should be developed each year. It is helpful for the coach to decide ahead of time the number of players that can effectively be part of the team. A good rule of thumb is to select no more than six players per court, and preferably four per court.

It should be made clear to the potential members which criteria will be used in the selection process. Physical condition can be tested by a fitness test the first day. An evaluation of racket skills can be made using a standardized skill test such as that used by the USPTA. At times, local teaching professionals are willing to assist coaches in judging relative racket skills of team candidates.

Once the players have established their abilities in the foregoing tests, match play of some type becomes the final test of ability. Rather than the traditional challenge ladder, which is unwieldy and time-consuming, try a round robin. Grouping players into quadrants of comparable skills, have them play one set versus each group member and keep total games won versus games lost. The player in each quadrant with the best record then moves up to the next higher level quadrant, and the player with the lowest total moves down to a less-skilled foursome. This method is fast and gives you a reading on how people play against different styles.

The question of doubles positions must wait until the singles positions are established, but the prudent coach will watch for the players who have doubles skills, yet are below standard for singles.

An evaluation of each player by the coach in person is the mature way to handle final decisions. In this way players know where they stand. For the younger players, helpful hints for practice can be important guidance for next year's tryouts. You might point out where they can get help, and suggest camps, tournaments, and lessons to bring them to a higher level.

Practice Sessions

Once the selection process has been completed, the actual preparation on court can begin. Each day should include some teaching of strategic concepts, drilling on skills, and competitive play. An orderly progression of skills and concepts should be developed, starting with the backcourt skills, moving to midcourt, and then net play. Review of the previous day's workout should be the first order of business after the warm-up each session.

It is important to demonstrate each playing concept as it is presented to the group, and explain the strategic principle behind it. If the coach is not skilled sufficiently to demonstrate, he or she should use veteran players as models. Be sure, also, to alternate hitting partners during practice to provide variety and fairness to players at different levels.

Drills are available in books, They can be adapted from those demonstrated at clinics, or invented to fit the situation. The key principles to keep in mind for drills are: use specific targets, make them vigorous, competitive, similar to a game situation, and vary them frequently. Stop drills when they are successful so that players look forward to them again, rather than run them into the ground.

Some time must be allotted to the development of mental skills as well, for the attitudes that are fostered in practice will carry over to matches. Discussion of behavior, concentration-relaxation techniques, and breathing regulation are critical. In addition, some drills that induce pressure in practice are a must to accustom players to dealing with uncomfortable situations.

Warm-up and stretching	10	minutes
Review of previous day	20	minutes
Demonstration and explanation	10	minutes
Drilling on skills	30	minutes
Match play	45	minutes
Conditioning	15	minutes
Total time	2 hours 10 min	

The Competitive Season

Once the competitive season is under way, the role of the coach and his or her functions change substantially. The task at hand is to enhance the ability of the players to perform at the peak of current ability most of the time. New skills, improvement in fitness, or major changes in style are not possible during the pressure of match play. Instead, the coach must now focus on emergency first-aid for strokes that break down, tactics to deal with different types of players, and mental skills to deal with pressure.

Mental Training Skills

As discussed earlier, a complete approach to competition must be established for the team. Methods of handling emotional arousal must be taught, attitudes toward winning and losing must be adjusted in some cases, and mental skills to deal with pressure must be introduced. Concentration skills can also be improved through drills and attention-focussing exercises. Practice time on rainy days, after hard matches, and at least once weekly should be allotted to discussion, practice, and learning of mental skills.

The basic strategy of match play should have been thoroughly covered in the preseason, but reminders and reinforcement throughout the season are essential. Your players must identify their own personal styles and learn to play within them. Drilling on patterns of play based on their chosen style is the essence of practice sessions. As they play each other, they will encounter varieties of style. You should expose them to tactics for playing left-handers, pushers, hard hitters, shotmaking artists, players with a big weapon, and all-court players.

It is often helpful, particularly with young players, to point out shot sequences or patterns that they can do naturally, and urge them to practice them to achieve success a majority of the time. A pattern such as hitting deep to one side, then short to the other will work against the baseliner opponent. Perhaps the "moon ball" approach shot will be a useful weapon. You might recommend a balance between serve-and-volley tennis and baseline play to keep an opponent off balance. Probably success can best be reached by limiting the options of young players and striving for quality of execution, rather than by suggesting a wide variety of options that breeds uncertainty.

Singles versus Doubles

Depending on your team, the same players may have to play both singles and doubles, Both games should be practiced and learned so that versatile players are developed from year to year. No favors are done for the high school player who plays only singles, when college later demands doubles too.

Doubles play can be influenced by the coach more than singles, and strong emphasis should be placed on doubles skills. Practice time each day should normally be allotted to both singles and doubles skill work. Doubles teams must be paired. The primary requirement usually is that the two players like to play together. The wise coach will work with each team to develop its best style and to help the players to complement each other's individual strengths. Pride in strong doubles teams fosters team spirit and produces an espirit de corps that singles players often lack.

If court space is a problem for singles play, partner singles can fill the need, weekends can be used for additional play, or groups of six can drill on one court to free another for one-on-one play.

Practice Sessions

Throughout the season the same pattern for daily practice should be followed: teach a concept, drill it, and then incorporate it into playing points. As the season wears on, the practice sessions should be shortened in order to prevent boredom and staleness. Days off after tough matches are also a welcome relief for both coaches and players. The really hard work should be done in the off-season and preseason, while energy and effort are conserved during the season for matches.

The key to maintaining interest in practice is to vary the drills each day. Coaches tend to adopt favorites, which eventually bores players and produces sloppy play. Use the same basic principles, but be inventive in creating drills to accomplish specific tasks.

Challenge matches for position are probably a poor idea once the season has begun. Rather, players should be evaluated by their play in matches and adjustments in placement in the lineup made accordingly. Too many challenge matches within the team changes the focus to defeating each other rather than the opposing team.

The Performance Autopsy

After the conclusion of a match, or perhaps the next day, coaches and players need to assess the performance. Without placing blame, an objective evaluation should be made. Results should be measured against each player's ability and how closely they came to using it to its fullest. Wins and losses are often a capricious measure because they depend upon the opponents.

Since the coach needs to develop self-sufficient players, the primary responsibility for this evaluation should be upon the player. Then the coach adds or suggests items overlooked. If shot charting or video taping can be done occasionally, the critique is enhanced significantly. Recollections of players are often hazy, clouded, or too general to be meaningful. Coaches must bring the performance into focus and pull out specific areas that need attention.

Problems of Players

During the season, most players will experience peaks and valleys of performance. The role of the coach is to minimize the effect of prolonged slumps, strive for consistent performances, and hope that peak performances occur once in a while. Interference from schoolwork, family problems, or personal problems may be at the root of poor performances. Be ready to listen, advise when asked, or suggest where help can be obtained. Performance cannot be separated from the total person, so all factors in life affect results.

Coaching styles may have to be altered to deal with certain types of athletes. Firmness for one player and compassion for another may be necessary. Skill in coaching develops from handling people under stress. Study and experience will improve your abilities to produce results.

Assuming that you have players who are subvarsity, care must be taken to keep them challenged and interested. They will be your team of the future and deserve attention. Treat them as valuable and worthwhile persons even if their skill is inferior. Ask the top players to work with them, drill with them, and encourage them. Try to schedule some meaningful matches for the junior varsity so they can try out their skills. Use the top players as assistant coaches in arranging or handling these matches.

Sometime during the season, recall and reassessment of individual and team goals must be accomplished. The pressure of matches tends to obscure the objectives set before the season. Keep the goals in mind, stay on course, and modify obviously unrealistic aims. A coach can use his or her perspective, maturity, and value structure to affect young people during their critical periods. Keep in mind that the whole adventure should be fun, which comes from acceptance of a challenge and overcoming obstacles. A sense of humor can get players through even the most trying times.

The Postseason

The end of the competitive season often brings a sigh of relief from players and coaches alike. Yet this is the time to make plans for the next year and to begin the work that will pay off 12 months from now.

The first task for the coach is to evaluate the efforts of the past year, evaluate the total program, and ask for help in the assessment from players, assistant coaches, and the athletic director. Recognition of each player's contribution to the successes of the past year are also important. Most valuable player awards, most improved awards, and election of next year's team captain should take place now. Newspaper publicity noting outstanding achievements will thrill players and parents, and build pride in team and individual accomplishments. A team dinner, picnic, or banquet, no matter how inexpensively staged, is a fine culmination and marks the end of one year and the beginning of another.

Physical Conditioning

Under the care of athletic trainers, athletes should embark upon a program of fitness that will strengthen muscles, build endurance, and rehabilitate injury areas. Long, slow distance running is appropriate here as well as weight training using a Nautilus or Universal system. Goals for the coming year for each player can be set and checked at regular intervals.

Stroke Development

With the pressure of matches behind them, this is the time for players to make significant changes or additions to their game. Coaches can schedule individual lessons, recommend a competent local teaching professional, or suggest summer camps.

In addition to stroke development, players may need more match play to test their shots and experience varying styles of play. Summer tournament play is the answer, either in USTA sanctioned tournaments or local club and municipal ones.

The key point here it that teams improve most dramatically in the off-season, not during the season. The coach must, therefore, motivate and assist players in planning and executing their schedules during this time. Availability of coaches is crucial so that players can check in at regular intervals to discuss their progress, receive encouragement, and keep the coach informed of trouble spots.

The Indoor Season

In cold weather climates, the winter months used to be lost for tennis players. There is absolutely no need for this any longer. Indoor clubs are anxious to work with school programs to fill their slow times, and they know these kids will be their future customers. Decide what would be good for your people, approach a local club, and discuss the benefits to them. Regular court rental may be very expensive, but look to slack hours on weekends or early mornings to get a price break. Some clubs have programs of drilling, round-robin play, or instruction for high school teams. If money is the obstacle, consider fund raisers by the team for court time.

Recruiting

No matter what the level, it is up to the coach to establish an on-going program of development to ensure the presence of good players from year to year. The junior varsity players should be the first to consider for the next year. If a good job has been done with them, your problems are solved for the moment. However, over the long term, the secondary school coach must create summer leagues, junior programs, community recreation programs, and tournaments in order to raise the standard of tennis play in the community. Some coaches even run for town council in order to gain a voice on the expenditure of recreational monies so that they include tennis courts and programs. At the same time, the coach can provide income for himself or herself during the summer by developing an instructional program.

At the college level, coaches must recruit prospective players. Even if athletic scholarships are not involved, attracting players to your school is necessary. This function of the coach must be year round, intensive at the critical times when young people make college decisions. It requires constant follow-up.

You need to thoroughly understand your school, its advantages over others, and the most attractive features that can be highlighted. These may include cost, location, variety of academic programs, excellence of academics, physical setting,

size, tradition, career placement record, reputation, and excellence of the tennis program. Most recruits want a school where they can be assured of improving their ability, and the team must be neither too strong nor too weak.

The effective recruiter will produce a steady stream of freshmen each year of moderate ability who can improve with coaching and competition. Some years, the exceptional athletes may come to you, but do not hold your breath. It takes luck and hard work for that to occur. Above all, the recruiter must study the problems faced, plan strategies, maintain a positive outlook, and not take rejection personally when a young person makes another choice. Work with your admissions people. Get to know them and learn their strategies and skills. They are the professionals in this field and can teach you as situations arise. There is no better ally than the Dean of Admissions.

Improving Your Coaching

Simply said, you must improve your coaching every year or the competition will pass you by. Younger, better-trained, innovative coaches will outcoach you unless you plan every year to add to knowledge of the job. Consider the following areas for updating or in-depth study:

Physical training.
Mental training skills.
Administrative skills.
Racket technique.
Strategy and tactics.
Public relations.
Group dynamics.
Handling problem athletes.
Understanding adolescents.
Practice variety and drills.
Goal setting and adjustment.
Fundraisers.
Recruiting.
Off-season programs.

Stay alert to inexpensive opportunities at nearby colleges, to clinics, workshops, USPTA affiliations, publications, new books, internships with outstanding teaching professionals, and visits to spend time with successful coaches. Set personal goals for your own career in coaching, evaluate your progress each year, and exult in the challenge of a demanding, yet satisfying profession.

RON WOODS

22

Pro Shop Development
and Management

You would be surprised how many people call the USPTA and ask for advice on how to start and manage a pro shop. For some reason they speak with reverence of a "pro shop" and seem to imply that it is different from a lingerie store, a book shop, a dress shop, or any other small retail business. But that is precisely what it is—a retail business.

It is a business that requires precise construction, exact procedures, detailed recordkeeping, and carefully planned management. The sooner you realize this the more likely you are to achieve success.

The subject is so extensive that it cannot be covered completely in the space available here. But I will systematically explore, step by step, the general areas involved in developing and managing a retail store. I will assume that you are starting from scratch. Along the way, recommendations will be made for further specific study.

Location

This may or may not be flexible. In the case of a club tennis professional, the store is already in place and moving it for the sake of traffic flow or other reasons might not be cost-justified. Should flexibility exist (as in the case of a shop yet to be constructed), the key features to be considered are:

1. Flow of traffic.
2. Projected income vs. cost of prime location.
3. Competition in the area.
4. Accessibility to supplemental amenities (courts, etc.).
5. Availability of labor.

Financing

I assume that you were born of normal means and will need financing. (Those born into money can skip this section.) You, however, will need to be armed with certain documents when you visit a sympathetic banker:

1. PRO FORMA INCOME STATEMENT: This is a statement of your expectations related to the profitability of your new business venture. It is prepared according to a standard procedure, showing expected revenues and expenses along with projections intended to gain the banker's confidence. (For specific details and descriptions of types of format available, consult a book dealing specifically with this subject.) Sometimes overlooked in books, however, are ways in which you can determine projected figures and statistics to fit into the pro forma. These cannot be pulled from a hat, so here are a few common sense ways to produce them:

a. Speak to the person who had the store ahead of you. His or her figures would be the most accurate to go by.

b. Ask the help of other people in similar businesses.

c. Discuss traffic, sales volume, and business trends with nearby merchants, even if they own different types of retail outlets.

d. Read consumer trend publications. Use copies of these to convince your banker of the sound concept of your business.

2. RESUMÉ: A well-prepared resumé will increase your credibility in the eyes of the banker. This should be specifically researched and professionally prepared.

3. ATTITUDE AND APPEARANCE: The correct attitude is very important to your banker. If you cannot act confidently in his or her presence, why should he or she expect you to have the charisma and qualifications to handle the retail public? Your dress and grooming during the interview will also be indicative of how you plan to face the public.

4. BANKER: It is often useful to choose a banker who plays and understands tennis. This will give you an immediate common ground. Above all, realize that your banker is human and someone you should get to know as a confidant. Regardless of the statistics in your pro forma income statement, a part of the decision to finance the business will depend on your banker's impression and confidence in you as a person.

Accounting

An experienced accountant will be most important to your business. You will not only need help with your taxes, but questions will arise about incorporating, business expenses, and capital expenditures, to name a few. An accountant can also participate in preparing your profit and loss statement, which will be the most important management tool in your business.

A monthly profit and loss statement is a must for any business, whether you produce it yourself or have it done through an accounting firm. You can also use an outside data processing company to produce it. Your decision on which way to produce it will be determined by evaluating the two factors which help you make most business decisions—time and expense. In this instance, ask yourself if you can afford the time to do it yourself or would it be more cost efficient to have it farmed out?

Before developing a profit and loss statement you will need to design a budget showing monthly income and expense projections. These projections can be determined by following the methods used to prepare your pro forma income statement, such as consulting last year's performance, the previous owner, and people in a similar business as well as studying traffic, buying habits, etc. Budgets improve over the years as you gain knowledge from actual performance.

Once you have a budget, you should make every effort to live within it or, at least, set up systems to justify any variances. When you can compare your actual income and expense on your monthly profit and loss statement with the projected budget, you will have an exceptional management tool.

Purchase an accounting manual that deals with budgeting and profit and loss statements. The forms and styles of operation may vary; however, the basic principles are the same.

Many small business owners are purchasing microcomputers. Accounting packages are available for most computers which will handle all of your needs, including accounts receivable, accounts payable, general ledger, inventory control, and more. Your accountant can best advise you on the details of these items.

The accounting aspects of your business should not be underestimated. In order to make a profit you must be aware from day to day of your financial situation. Many shop operators mistakenly believe that the fun side of the business is buying and selling, and people contact. Let me assure you that if you handle your accounting well, you will have even more fun making two trips a day to the bank.

Business Credentials

You will soon find out, when you are about to enter into a new business that, like it or not, you have a partner. Your new silent partner will be "Uncle Sam." State sales taxes and store licenses (where applicable) are two ways he can dip into your cashbox. These, of course, are state-controlled taxes. Since state laws vary throughout the U.S., you will need to investigate those which are applicable in your particular state. Generally, however, you will need to secure the following:

1. ASSUMED OR FICTITIOUS NAME FOR THE NEW BUSINESS: The method of acquiring an assumed or fictitious name for your business will vary slightly from state to state. In most cases, you will visit the Occupational License Department at the country courthouse and fill out an applica-

tion. Some states have an updated computer readout showing all previously claimed names. If the name you have chosen is not listed, you are registered immediately. Other states may use different systems. For example, in Florida you are required to advertise the intended name of your business in the local newspaper for four consecutive weeks. If no one objects, the newspaper gives you a certificate of verification to present to the Occupational License Department, and you are then granted that name.

2. SMALL BUSINESS LICENSE: Most states require a small business license that can be purchased from the Occupational License Department at the county courthouse.

3. LIMITED SALES TAX NUMBER: This is needed to exempt you from paying sales tax on items that you purchase for resale in your store. It is also used to report the tax that you charge the consumer and must pass on to the state. To acquire a limited sales tax number, apply to your state's Department of Revenue and fill out the necessary applications in the name of your business.

"Uncle Sam" holds out his federal hand in several ways as well, such as, FEDERAL INCOME TAX REPORTING. You will need to apply to the Internal Revenue Service for an identification number to be used when reporting employee earnings and withholding taxes.

Establishing Credit and Venders

The financial nod from your banker is only the first step in getting your business off the ground. You will also need short-term financing that allows you to operate comfortably while purchasing goods for resale from various venders. This is referred to as credit and it is granted by the respective venders themselves. Credit is meant to expedite your ordering and receiving of goods in good faith with the stipulation that you will pay for the goods shortly after receipt. If you do not make prompt payments to your venders, you are, in essence, forcing them to lend you the goods at no interest out of the kindness of their hearts. And, there are not too many venders with hearts that kind.

Credit is essential for your business and there are a few helpful ways to establish it quickly:

1. Secure a Dunn and Bradstreet (D & B) credit rating if possible. Call D & B for details on how to qualify for this.

2. Prepare a one-page profile of yourself and your business, listing your current personal data and business references, your banking officer's name, etc. Include other general information you might expect to see on a credit application. This form will expedite your credit and leave the prospective vender with a good first impression of your preparedness.

3. Submit a letter of financial responsibility from your banker.

Choosing the appropriate venders is sometimes a little more tricky. There are several considerations involved in this task:

1. Understanding your clientele, their income range, and their buying habits is probably the most important. Buying from a high-priced fashion line vender for a middle-income clientele could spell disaster. You must research this carefully.

2. Service and attitude of the vender should play a large role in your choice. If the vender has acceptable credit policies, visits you regularly, stands behind defective merchandise, and delivers as promised, you will have a successful relationship.

3. Deal with venders who do an appropriate amount of advertising and promotion to bring the product in front of the public.

Buying and Inventory Control

The best advice to someone without previous buying experience is "do not do it yourself." Find somebody with knowledge of styles, volume control, fabrics, and prices to do your buying or look over your shoulder while you do it.

One of the big surprises in my life occurred shortly after my first merchandise orders started rolling in. It was inconceivable to me that all of those beautiful see-through, flowery dresses in sizes six and eight (with cut-outs in all the right places) kept hanging on the rack month after month. It was only after I hired someone with buying experience that I realized that stylish dresses, designed in good taste in sizes larger than eight commanded a large portion of the market share.

One of the pitfalls in retailing is overbuying. A good buyer will not go on a buying trip without establishing an "Open-to-Buy." In simple terms, this is the amount of money that can responsibly be spent on new merchandise at any given time. It can be arrived at by using a formula that deals with your acceptable maximum inventory and the volume of incoming and outgoing merchandise. These factors are clarified in the following example:

Open-to-Buy

STORE: Fred and Myrtle's Family Tennis Shop

SEASON: Fall   **O.T.B. DATE: 01-01-84**

DEPARTMENT: Shoes

		Quantity	Dollar Volume
1.	Maximum acceptable inventory (determined in advance and estimated after considering all factors)	100 pr	$4,000.00
2.	Actual inventory in stock	62 pr	$2,480.00
3.	Inventory on order (this will reduce your open-to-buy since it has already been ordered and will soon be delivered)	20 pr	$ 800.00
4.	Combined inventory in-stock plus on-order (2 plus 3)	82 pr	$3,280.00
5.	Current open-to-buy (if delivery could be made today) (1 minus 4)	18 pr	$ 720.00
6.	Estimated sales before delivery of purchase about to be ordered. (This quantity will be considered as sold by delivery date and will increase your present open-to-buy by that amount	50 pr	$2,000.00
7.	Estimated inventory on delivery date (on hand immediately prior to delivery of purchase about to be made) (4 minus 6)	32 pr	$1,280.00
*8.	Actual open-to-buy (taking into consideration date of delivery and all interim sales) (1 minus 7)	68 pr	$2,720.00

*To a degree this has been oversimplification in an effort to deal with a complex topic in an allotted space. The intention, however, is to explain a concept of management which you will expand on with your own buying experience.

It is wise to do the buying for your store at special trade shows that are designed for that purpose. In this way you will have the advantage of making comparisons and watching more experienced buyers in action. It also permits you to see trends and make better business judgments.

To help you control inventory, there are many systems available, ranging from manual to computerized. This is a subject unto itself and is worth a trip to the library or book store to read up on. Obviously, inventory control goes hand-in-hand with successful buying, as seen from the description of "Open-to-Buy." You need some form of inventory control system, however simple. Without it, you are driving a car without a gas gauge—not knowing when or where you might run out of gas.

Shop Design and Display

The design of a shop—like its location—may not be totally flexible, particularly in the case of a tennis shop at a club. All shop owners fantasize about designing their store from scratch. If they could, the master plan might go like this:

1. FLOOR SPACE: The shop should have enough floor space to be adequately departmentalized. It might surprise the men reading this chapter to learn that women do not like to do their shopping with men around nearly as much as the opposite. It is also unappealing to have to side-step the stringing machine in order to reach the dress rack.

2. STORAGE: A large storeroom should be available, not just for bulk storage but also as a work room. There should be a work counter and hanging rack for marking merchandise prior to distributing it to the sales floor.

3. POINT OF SALES AREA: This should provide adequate space for all required purposes. The layout should permit facilities for other functions, such as court reservations and reception or any other club matters not necessarily related to merchandise sales. There should be excellent visual and physical control of the shop from this position.

4. SEPARATE AND/OR JOINT ACCESS TO OTHER CLUB AMENITIES: If possible, the shop should be designed so that, at times, it can be opened and closed independently of the other club amenities. This may later produce financial savings if it becomes obvious that shop sales at certain hours do not warrant staying open while other amenities, such as tennis courts, need to.

5. DRESSING ROOMS: Several dressing rooms are desirable. Nothing can be a bigger turn-off to a customer than having to wait in line to try on something.

6. STRINGING ROOM: The stringing area should be separated from the sales floor. If not, it imparts an unfashionable impression. On the other hand, people are sometimes intrigued by watching a good stringer in action, much as they enjoy watching any expert craftsman. It would be ideal if the stringing room could be seen through a glass window or through a doorway.

7. INTERIOR DECORATING: The shop interior should reflect seasonable, light colors. A short-piled carpet that will not hold granular dirt is highly desirable, especially at tennis clubs with soft court surfaces. Lighting should be designed for optical comfort and track lights should be considered over display areas. An adequate number of mirrors should be available for decorative and practical purposes.

The art of proper store display is a subject by itself. It is a fact that stores with good displays sell more merchandise. You might try some of the following ways to get good ideas for displaying your wares:

1. Visit any large shopping mall and steal ideas from the displays there. You will be surprised to realize how inexpensive some displays are. You do not need expensive mannequins. Just check around and you will see cardboard, posterboard, old crates, wheelbarrows, old horse-collars, farm tools, and many other potential props. With any variety of odds and ends, some long display pins, and clear nylon fishing tackle, a store owner can soon become a good display technician. Most cities have companies that deal in renting display items, so a store owner can change displays often and can decorate for a particular season or special occasion.

2. You might consider hiring a display specialist to decorate your store once a month or once every two months. A good place to locate such a person is through your favorite department

store. Many of the display specialists do free-lance work in their spare time.

3. Look for new ideas in trade magazines.

4. There are several books on creative store display which can be purchased at your local book store.

Insurance

After all of this investment in time and money, it would be tragic to loose it all due to one of numerous possible mishaps.

Fire, flood, storm damage, theft, and vandalism all seem so distant until they actually happen to you. The thought of you accidentally causing injury or harm to someone else seems impossible until you "accidentally" find yourself faced with a lawsuit. And, of course, you would never anticipate taking off for the pearly gates and leaving your spouse loaded down with your earthly debts.

The best advice for you at this point, if you have not already done so, is to visit your insurance agent and design a plan to cover all of these potential hazards.

Security

In line with the previous paragraphs, security is something you will never miss until it is too late. Your insurance rates can be significantly reduced if you apply security measures that might avert possible mishaps.

In the case of a store, these preventive devices include but are not limited to:

1. Burglar alarm systems.
2. Fire alarm systems.
3. Special window and door locks.
4. Window bars.
5. Security guard services.

There are numerous companies that deal in security systems. Have a few of them make presentations to you and make the most sensible decision based on cost versus anticipated risk.

Theft of merchandise by shoppers is also a security problem, and there are many methods used to deter this. Some of these include:

1. Tags on merchandise that trip an electronic buzzer as they pass a special sensor near the door.

2. Long, plastic-coated, stainless steel cables which pass through the armholes of various items and are then locked to a permanent fixture. (This is a very cumbersome system.)

3. Most stores staple a sales ticket to the top of a package which seals the package simultaneously.

4. Placing the point-of-sale counter in a strategic observation position.

5. Video cameras that scan the hard-to-see areas of the store and send the picture back to a security monitor. (These machines can also record single-frame pictures of their surveillance which can be reviewed later in case of a theft.)

6. Mirrors are often placed in hard-to-secure areas in some stores. (This allows sales personnel to view those areas by reflection.)

Needless to say, all of these systems are distasteful and should be avoided unless definite shortages are noticed. In making a decision on a system, you should analyze your shortages through your inventory program and determine if the cost of your losses justifies the cost of the proposed security system.

Staffing

Staffing your new business correctly is one of the most important functions you will ever have to deal with. Your customers will form an image of you through the actions of your employees; this is one thought that will keep you awake at night after you have made your first wrong choice. Unfortunately, making correct choices more often than not requires years of experience, which is why most large institutions have personnel departments with highly trained specialists to screen prospective employees.

1. FINDING EMPLOYEES: Depending on the job market at a given time, you might have luck with at least one of the following ways to find employees:

   a. *Newspaper advertising:* A short, well-worded advertisement will generally receive a favorable response. It is less bothersome and time-consuming if you ask for a resumé to be sent to you. You can then screen out the good applicants and not have to deal with every Tom, Dick, and Jane on the phone.

   b. *Employment agencies:* These companies act as a paid personnel department and screen and recommend employees for your respective positions. Their reputations often depend on

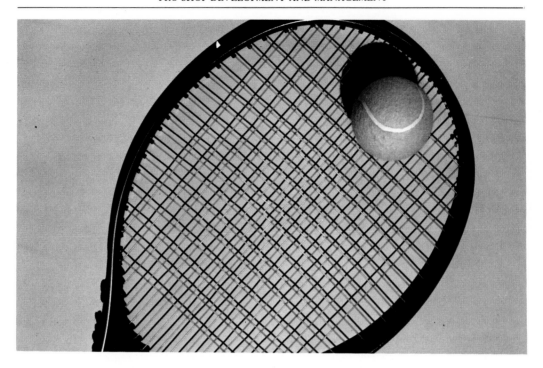

the quality of applicants they send out. But since their payment depends on their filling the position at hand, some agencies unfortunately have been known to shovel bodies into interviews with hopes of hitting the right combination. The companies with better reputations, however, are generally trustworthy.

c. *Word of mouth:* This is often an effective means of soliciting good help. Let the word out to other employees at the tennis club or in the shopping center. Good employees of other businesses often have friends who are similarly motivated.

2. INTERVIEWING: Before starting your interviews, it would be wise to have certain tools prepared:

   a. A job description for the position in question.

   b. A list of pertinent interview questions.

   c. Be prepared to answer questions asked by interviewees, i.e., availability of benefits, etc.

There are informative books available that suggest interview questions and recommend qualities to evaluate during an interview.

3. HIRING: Before agreeing to employ anyone, be sure you both understand the agreement. The salary, potential raises, insurance, vacations, hours, job descriptions, and attitude expectations should be made clear. It is also wise to stipulate that the first 90 days is a trial period and that at the end of 90 days there will be an evaluation of your mutual needs. Should either party wish to terminate at that point, it can be done with no hard feelings.

4. PROMOTION: Part of your yearly budget should include a planned expense for store promotion. Promotion can fit into a wide range from advertising to subtle word of mouth. The location of your store and clientele will determine the best use of your promotion dollars. For instance, a tennis shop at a club will require little if any paid advertising since it has a limited and often closed clientele. Your promotion budget in this case would best be directed to in-club programs along the following lines:

   a. *Birthday discounts:* A printed birthday card can be sent to members in the month of their birthday, offering them a special store discount. You can take the birthdates from the club's membership applications or computer.

b. *Newsletter promotion:* Always take advantage of opportunities to write for the club's newsletter and promote your store tastefully.

c. *Personal advice on purchases:* Most club members regard the pro or pro shop owner as the merchandise expert. Be visible and share your time.

d. *Pamphlets:* Since you are the most knowledgeable person in your business, do not leave technical advice to an employee who cannot express it with your expertise. Sensitive areas of importance such as: (1) types of strings, (2) differences in rackets, (3) fabrics, (4) lesson programs and rates, and (5) return policies on merchandise, etc, should be neatly typeset in an attractive pamphlet. Your employees can then hand out this pamphlet written in your own words and they will have on hand an accurate guide to explain any additional details requested of them.

e. *Localized advertising:* If your club or tennis shop is open to the public, you may receive favorable trade from non-members within your area. You can reach them by inexpensive advertising in neighborhood newspapers or similar outlets.

These are just a few ideas to get you thinking about promotions. Each club is different, and if you watch the promotion of other stores you can pick up ideas that will work for your specific area.

Conclusion

You probably feel that you have just gone through a crash course in brain surgery. What started out to be a few helpful hints on pro shop development and management has turned into a fairly lengthy treatise. Yet, I have done no more than offer tested suggestions. There is so much that goes into developing a retail business that considerable research and further reading is vital for success. Operating a retail store can be rewarding if it is done properly and with respect for the business. My final advice is that if you do not plan to do it with those intentions, *do not do it at all!*

TIM HECKLER

23

Court Maintenance

There are two basic types of court surfaces: soft courts and hard courts. A soft court has a green, granular, porous surface with a stone base. Trade names for soft courts include Fast-Dry, Har-Tru, Rubico, and Teniko. Hard courts are non-porous. They are made with an asphalt or cement base and then topped with acrylic or polyurethane coatings, either sprayed or rolled on. Lay-kold, Plexipave, and Deco-Turf are among the brand names for hard courts. Keep in mind the preceding characteristics and it will make it easier to understand how to maintain these surfaces.

Court maintenance should be a prime consideration before deciding on the type of surface to install. When investigating surfaces, ask yourself several questions. "What is the initial cost versus the long-range cost?" "Do I have an adequate maintenance budget and a dependable maintainance employee?" "How will the weather in my area affect the type of court I install?" "Which courts will give me the longest playing season?" "What kind of bounce and what speed will my members want?"

Comparing the initial cost to the long-range cost is important in determining how much money you will be spending over the next three to five years. When you obtain your initial bids, you will be surprised to find that soft courts are 50–60 percent cheaper to install than hard costs. This figure

alone is deceiving. The maintenance cost for soft courts will be high, due to man-hours required, court material, water usage, and equipment. Hard courts, however, are virtually maintenance free. Over the long run, the overall expenditure usually balances out.

Soft court maintenance requires a dependable and knowledgeable technician. The tennis professional should have a working knowledge of the courts, but he or she does not have time to put in three hours a day necessary for a well-maintained court.

There are experts in the field who will be glad to consult with you on any problems or questions you might have pertaining to your type of surface. These court builders will be your very best source of information regarding the effects your particular locale and weather conditions will have on certain surfaces. They will advise you on all aspects of court maintenance.

To keep a soft court in good playing condition an extensive spring maintenance operation is necessary in addition to daily maintenance. Daily maintenance is a fairly routine procedure of watering, brushing, sweeping lines, and rolling when needed. How often this routine is needed each day varies with the weather and amount of play. Watering the courts is the single most important part of the maintenance procedure since these courts thrive on lots of water. You should water at night after you close the courts, and again during midday, as the play gets heavier and the day get hotter. Evening watering is the most critical since you have time to flood the courts, letting the water soak in before the next morning's play. By flooding the courts we mean that water should be standing on the entire surface. If you have an automatic sprinkling system, you might want to experiment with two separate waterings in smaller doses at night so that you do not lose a lot of water and material from an overflow. You can begin the first watering cycle as soon as the courts close and a second small one at 1 or 2 a.m. The key is to time it so the courts will not be too wet in the morning. This two-phase method seems to be the most efficient use of water and eliminates, to a great extent, the run-off of material and excess water. Also, since there is no run-off the water keeps the base damp and free from cracking. Before watering I would recommend brushing to help level the surface. Having the proper sprinkling system is a necessity. Therefore, check with your local soft court representative and investigate a system with a sufficient water spread.

Brushing the courts and sweeping the lines are the leveling, smoothing, and cosmetic part of daily maintenance. This should be done before and after each watering. You should also sweep just before the evening crowd arrives. Even though brushing tends to dry out the material, it greatly enhances the appearance and the playability, and takes out the bad bounces. You should arrange your watering to keep a dark, rich color.

Throughout the season, the maintenance crew should be looking for build-up of dead material and low spots on the courts. Both of these minor problems need attention when they first appear so that they do not become major ones. Dead material should be scraped off periodically and replaced with new material that binds. When you find a low spot fill it with new material until it is level. Identify the area, level, water lightly, roll, water more deeply, roll again and the spot should be ready for play. If it is a bad depression then you need to get advice from your court representative, since this could mean extensive repair.

Certain steps should be taken at the end of the outdoor season to keep the courts in the best shape possible through the winter and to make your spring opening procedure easier. Store the nets, take up the line tapes, and remove the nails. You will not be able to use the nails again, but you can sometimes get two or three seasons out of the tapes if you get them up before winter. Clean the tapes,

roll and tag them, and store them for the winter. If you leave the tapes in, not only will the climate damage them, but the constant freezing and thawing process will cause the nails to pop up which will in turn pull up some of the underbase.

Most watering systems are sloped to enable them to be drained for the winter. For extra protection, use an air compressor and blow out the lines thoroughly to prevent any chance of the pipes freezing and breaking.

Winter is a perfect time for an equipment check, such as preventive maintenance on your roller. It is a good idea to hose down your windscreens, allowing them to dry thoroughly before storing. Remember to tag them according to their previous fence positions. Also during the winter months, your maintenance people can repair and paint benches and chairs. It will be to your benefit to place your order for materials and equipment ahead of the spring rush to take advantage of any price breaks and to insure prompt delivery. It pays to plan ahead.

The first warm day in the spring will find everyone clamoring to play on the soft courts. The professional should not get too caught up in the enthusiasm and start resurfacing too early, because a new siege of cold weather could spoil his or her efforts. It is best to wait until after the last freeze to begin preparing your courts for the summer season. Since you have taken up the tapes and ordered your material during the winter, you have already speeded up your opening process.

Each court will need between one and a half and three tons of material, depending on the amount of lost and dead material caused by the winter. Keep about one inch thickness for best results. Remove the dead material by scraping it into piles and then remove in bulk. Once the dead material is removed, patch any holes in the court surface made from the nails or underbase that has come up over the winter. Roll the courts several times to help set a solid and smooth base to work with. Now that the area is prepared, patch the larger depressions and spread the material. Once the material is down, brush it both ways to get a smooth, even texture. Then lightly hand water the material to help promote the binding process. Once it drys, roll the surface again. Since the material is sticky when wet, be careful of its sticking to the roller. After you roll, water a little more heavily with the sprinkler system. Do not flood the court. Water less than five minutes. Later in the day brush and roll again. For an even distribution of material, alternate the direction each time you roll and sweep.

During the evening, water for about ten minutes. Roll and brush the next morning. Install the tapes, put up the nets, and you are ready to play. The courts will still be soft, so keep an eye on them and replace divots. The courts will need to be rolled daily for the first two to four weeks to make them solid, after which you will use your judgement as to their playability.

If you do not have a sufficient crew for spring opening, contact your local soft court company. Most of these companies will do your spring reconditioning for a fee, which might be cheaper for you in the long run, with less headaches.

Hard court maintenance is not so time consuming. As a safety precaution and for better playability, keep the courts free of leaves and sand. In the spring sand may blow on the courts, making them slick. In the fall, leaves must be removed as soon as possible to prevent staining and for court safety. It is a good idea to hose down hard courts every two to three weeks.

While your own maintenance people can usually correct problems in soft courts, problems such as cracks in hard courts require professional service. Continually check for cracks, and call in a consultant as soon as any become evident. If left unattended over the winter, the cracks will expand.

The advantage of a hard court is that it can be open year-round. Of course, a longer playing period results in more wear and tear on the surface, nets, and posts. Weather conditions and heavy play can also increase the speed of the court. This means that every three to four years you may want to have the hard court company apply another layer of topping to keep it at medium speed.

Different surfaces in different locales will display their own individual problems. It is important to choose the right court for your own particular situation. Examine your options carefully before choosing a court surface and investigate all maintenance requirements. Preventive maintenance is the key to court preservation.

Rod Dulany

PART III

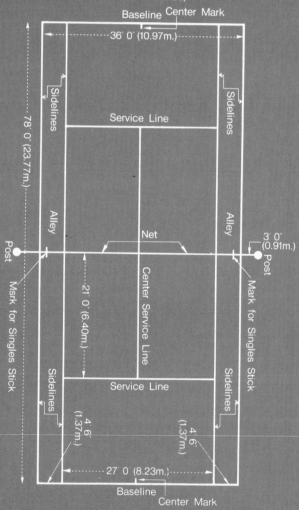

PLAN OF THE COURTS
(See Rules 1 and 35)

Rules of Tennis
and Cases
and Decisions 1984

Rules of Tennis
EXPLANATORY NOTE

The following Rules and Cases and Decisions are the official Code of the International Tennis Federation, of which the United States Tennis Association is a member. USTA Comments and USTA Cases and Decisions have the same weight and force in USTA tournaments as do ITF Cases and Decisions.

When a match is played without officials the principles and guidelines set forth in the USTA Publication, The Code, shall apply in any situation not covered by the rules.

Except where otherwise stated, every reference in these Rules to the masculine includes the feminine gender.

A vertical line in the margin indicates a change or amendment made by the ITF at their Annual General Meeting in June 1983, and which took effect January 1, 1984.

THE SINGLES GAME
Rule 1

The Court
The court shall be a rectangle 78 feet (23.77m.) long and 27 feet (8.23m.) wide. USTA COMMENT: See Rule 34 for a doubles court.

It shall be divided across the middle by a net suspended from a cord or metal cable of a maximum diameter of one-third of an inch (0.8cm.), the ends of which shall be attached to, or pass over, the tops of two posts, which shall be not more than 6 inches (15cm.) square or 6 inches (15cm.) in diameter. The centres of the posts shall be 3 feet (0.914m.) outside the court on each side and the height of the posts shall be such that the top of the cord or metal cable shall be 3 feet 6 inches (1.07m.) above the ground.

When a combined doubles (see Rule 34) and singles court with a doubles net is used for singles, the net must be supported to a height of 3 feet 6 inches (1.07m.) by means of two posts, called "singles sticks," which shall be not more than 3 inches (7.5cm.) square or 3 inches (7.5cm.) in diameter. The centres of the singles sticks shall be 3 feet (0.914m.) outside the singles court on each side.

The net shall be extended fully so that it fills completely the space between the two posts and shall be of sufficiently small mesh to prevent the ball passing through. The height of the net shall be 3 feet (0.914m.) at the centre, where it shall be held down taut by a strap not more than 2 inches (5cm.) wide and completely white in colour. There shall be a band covering the cord or metal cable and the top of the net of not less than 2 inches (5cm.) nor more than two and a half inches (6.3cm.) in depth on each side and completely white in colour.

There shall be no advertisement on the net, strap, band or singles sticks.

The lines bounding the ends and sides of the Court shall respectively be called the base-lines and the side-lines. On each side of the net, at a distance of 21 feet (6.40m.) from it and parallel with it, shall be drawn the service-lines. The space on each side of the net between the service-line and the side-lines shall be divided into two

equal parts called the service-courts by the centre service-line, which must be 2 inches (5cm.) in width, drawn half-way between, and parallel with the side-lines. Each base-line shall be bisected by an imaginary continuation of the centre service-line to a line 4 inches (10cm.) in length and 2 inches (5cm.) in width called the centre mark drawn inside the Court, at right angles to and in contact with such base-lines. All other lines shall be not less than 1 inch (2.5cm.) nor more than 2 inches (5cm.) in width, except the base-line, which may be 4 inches (10cm.) in width, and all measurements shall be made to the outside of the lines. All lines shall be of uniform colour.

If advertising or any other material is placed at the back of the court, it may not contain white or yellow, or any other light colour.

If advertisements are placed on the chairs of the Lines-men sitting at the back of the court, they may not contain white or yellow.

NOTE: In the case of the International Tennis Championship (Davis Cup) or other Official Championships of the International Tennis Federation, there shall be a space behind each base-line of not less than 21 feet (6.4m.), and at the sides of not less than 12 feet (3.66m.).

USTA COMMENT: *It is important to have a stick 3 feet, 6 inchs long, with a notch cut in at the 3-foot mark for the purpose of measuring the height of the net at the posts and in the center. These measurements always should be made before starting to play a match.*

Rule 2

Permanent Fixtures
The permanent fixtures of the Court shall include not only the net, posts, singles sticks, cord or metal cable, strap and band, but also, where there are any such, the back and side stops, the stands, fixed or movable seats and chairs round the Court, and their occupants, all other fixtures around and above the Court, and the Umpire, Net-cord Judge, Foot-fault Judge, Linesmen and Ball Boys when in their respective places.

NOTE: For the purpose of this Rule, the word "Umpire" comprehends the Umpire, the persons entitled to a seat on the Court, and all those persons designated to assist the Umpire in the conduct of a match.

Rule 3

The Ball
The ball shall have a uniform outer surface and shall be white or yellow in colour. If there are any seams, they shall be stitchless.

The ball shall be more than two and a half inches (6.35cm.) and less than two and five-eighths inches (6.67cm.) in diameter, and more than two ounces (56.7 grams) and less than two and one-sixteenth ounces (58.5 grams) in weight.

The ball shall have a bound of more than 53 inches (135cm.) and less than 58 inches (147cm.) when dropped 100 inches (254cm.) upon a concrete base.

The ball shall have a forward deformation of more than .220 of an inch (.56cm.) and less than .290 of an inch (.74cm.) and a return deformation of more than .350 of an inch (.89cm.) and less than .425 of an inch (1.08cm.) at 18 lb. (8.165kg.) load. The two deformation figures shall be the averages of three individual readings along three axes of the ball and no two individual readings shall differ by more than .030 of an inch (.08cm.) in each case.

All tests for bound, size and deformation shall be made in accordance with the Regulations in the Appendix hereto.

Rule 4

The Racket
Rackets failing to comply with the following specifications are not approved for play under the Rules of Tennis:

(a) The hitting surface of the racket shall be flat and consist of a pattern of crossed strings connected to a frame and alternately interlaced or bonded where they cross; and the stringing pattern shall be generally uniform, and in particular not less dense in the centre than in any other area.

(b) The frame of the racket shall not exceed 32 inches (81.28cm.) in overall length, including the handle and 12½ inches (31.75cm.) in overall width. The strung surface shall not exceed 15½ inches (39.37cm.) in overall length, and 11½ inches (29.21cm.) in overall width.

(c) The frame, including the handle, and the strings:

(i) shall be free of attached objects and protrusions, other than those utilised solely and specifically to limit or prevent wear and tear or vibration, or to distribute weight, and which are reasonable in size and placement for such purposes; and

(ii) shall be free of any device which makes it possible for a player to change materially the shape of the racket.

The International Tennis Federation shall rule on the question of whether any racket or prototype complies with the above specifications or is otherwise approved, or not approved, for play. Such ruling may be undertaken on its own initiative, or upon application by any party with a bona fide interest therein, including any player, equipment manufacturer or National Association or members thereof. Such rulings and applications shall be made in accordance with the applicable Review and Hearing Procedures of the International Tennis Federation, copies of which may be obtained from the office of the Secretary.

Rule 5

Server and Receiver
The players shall stand on opposite sides of the net; the player who first delivers the ball shall be called the Server, and the other the Receiver.

Case 1. Does a player, attempting a stroke, lose the point if he crosses an imaginary line in the extension of the net,
(a) before striking the ball,
(b) after striking the ball?
Decision. He does not lose the point in either case by crossing the imaginary line and provided he does not enter the lines bounding his opponent's Court (Rule 20(e)). In regard to hindrance, his opponent may ask for the decision of the Umpire under Rules 21 and 25.

Case 2. The Server claims that the Receiver must stand within the lines bounding his Court. Is this necessary?
Decision. No. The Receiver may stand wherever he pleases on his own side of the net.

Rule 6

Choice of Ends and Service
The choice of ends and the right to be Server or Receiver in the first game shall be decided by toss. The player winning the toss may choose or require his opponent to choose:

(a) The right to be Server or Receiver, in which case the other player shall choose the end; or

(b) The end, in which case the other player shall choose the right to be Server or Receiver.

USTA COMMENT: *These choices should be made promptly and are irrevocable.*

Rule 7

The Service
The service shall be delivered in the following manner. Immediately before commencing to serve, the Server shall stand with both feet at rest behind (i.e., further from the net than) the base-line, and within the imaginary continuations of the centre-mark and side-line. The Server shall then project the ball by hand into the air in any direction and before it hits the ground strike it with his racket, and the delivery shall be deemed to have been completed at the moment of the impact of the racket and the ball. A player with the use of only one arm may utilize his racket for the projection.

USTA COMMENT: *The service begins when the Server takes a ready position and ends when his racket makes contact with the ball, or when he misses the ball in attempting to serve it.*

Case 1. May the Server in a singles game take his stand behind the portion of the base-line between the side-lines of the Singles Court and the Doubles Court?
Decision. No.

Case 2. If a player, when serving, throws up two or more balls instead of one, does he lose that service?
Decision. No. A let should be called, but if the Umpire regards the action as deliberate he may take action under Rule 21.

USTA Case 3. May a player serve underhand?
Decision. Yes. There is no restriction regarding the kind of service which may be used; that is, the player may use an underhand or overhand service at his discretion.

Rule 8

Foot Fault
The Server shall throughout the delivery of the service:

(a) Not change his position by walking or running.

(b) Not touch, with either foot, any area other than that behind the base-line within the imaginary extensions of the centre mark and side-lines.

NOTE: The following interpretation of Rule 8 was approved by the International Tennis Federation on 9th July, 1958:

(a) The Server shall not, by slight movements of the feet which do not materially affect the location originally

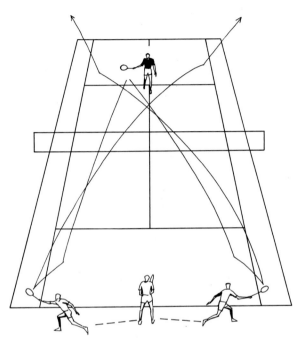

taken up by him, be deemed "to change his position by walking or running."

(b) The word "foot" means the extremity of the leg below the ankle.

USTA COMMENT: *This rule covers the most decisive stroke in the game, and there is no justification for its not being obeyed by players and enforced by officials. No official has the right to instruct any umpire to disregard violations of it. In a non-officiated match, it is the prerogative of the Receiver, or his partner, to call foot faults, but only after all efforts (appeal to the server, requests for an umpire, etc.) have failed, and the foot faulting is so flagrant as to be clearly perceptible from the Receiver's side.*

Rule 9

Delivery of Service

(a) In delivering the service, the Server shall stand alternately behind the right and left Courts beginning from the right in every game. If service from a wrong half of the Court occurs and is undetected, all play resulting from such wrong service or services shall stand, but the inaccuracy of station shall be corrected immediately it is discovered.

(b) The ball served shall pass over the net and hit the ground within the Service Court which is diagonally opposite, or upon any line bounding such Court, before the Receiver returns it.

Rule 10

Service Fault

The Service is a fault:

(a) If the Server commits any breach of Rules 7, 8 or 9;

(b) If he misses the ball in attempting to strike it;

(c) If the ball served touches a permanent fixture (other than the net, strap or band) before it hits the ground.

Case 1. After throwing a ball up preparatory to serving, the Server decides not to strike at it and catches it instead. Is it a fault?

Decision. No. **USTA COMMENT:** As long as the Server makes no attempt to strike the ball, it is immaterial whether he catches it in his hand or racket or lets it drop to the ground.

Case 2. In serving in a singles game played on a Doubles Court with doubles posts and singles sticks, the ball hits a singles stick and then hits the ground within the lines of the correct Service Court. Is this a fault or a let?

Decision. In serving it is a fault, because the singles stick, the doubles post, and that portion of the net, or band between them are permanent fixtures. (Rules 2 and 10, and note to Rule 24.)

USTA COMMENT: *The significant point governing Case 2 is that the part of the net and band "outside" the singles sticks is not part of the net over which this singles match is being played. Thus such a serve is a fault under the provisions of Article (c) above . . . By the same token, this would be a fault also if it were a singles game played with permanent posts in the singles position. (See Case 1 under Rule 24 for difference between "service" and "good return" with respect to a ball's hitting a net post.)*

USTA COMMENT: *In matches played without umpires each player makes calls for all balls hit to his side of the net. In doubles, normally the Receiver's partner makes the calls with* respect to the service line, with the Receiver calling the side and center lines, but either partner may make the call on any ball he clearly sees out.

Rule 11

Second Service

After a fault (if it is the first fault) the Server shall serve again from behind the same half of the Court from which he served that fault, unless the service was from the wrong half, when, in accordance with Rule 9, the Server shall be entitled to one service only from behind the other half.

Case 1. A player serves from a wrong Court. He loses the point and then claims it was a fault because of his wrong station.

Decision. The point stands as played and the next service should be from the correct station according to the score.

Case 2. The point score being 15 all, the Server, by mistake, serves from the left-hand Court. He wins the point. He then serves again from the right-hand Court, delivering a fault. This mistake in station is then discovered. Is he entitled to the previous point? From which Court should he next serve?

Decision. The previous point stands. The next service should be from the left-hand Court, the score being 30/15, and the Server has served one fault.

Rule 12

When To Serve

The Server shall not serve until the Receiver is ready. If the latter attempts to return the service, he shall be deemed ready. If, however, the Receiver signifies that he is not ready, he may not claim a fault because the ball does not hit the ground within the limits fixed for the service.

USTA COMMENT: *The Server must wait until the Receiver is ready for the second service as well as the first, and if the Receiver claims to be not ready and does not make any effort to return a service, the Server may not claim the point, even though the service was good.*

Rule 13

The Let

In all cases where a let has to be called under the rules, or to provide for an interruption to play, it shall have the following interpretations:

(a) When called solely in respect of a service that one service only shall be replayed.

(b) When called under any other circumstance, the point shall be replayed.

USTA COMMENT: *A service that touches the net in passing yet falls into the proper court (or touches the receiver) is a let. This word is used also when, because of an interruption while the ball is in play, or for any other reason, a point is to be replayed. A spectator's outcry (of "out," "fault" or other) is not a valid basis for replay of a point, but action should be taken to prevent a recurrence.*

Case 1. A service is interrupted by some cause outside those defined in Rule 14. Should the service only be replayed?

Decision. No, the whole point must be replayed.

USTA COMMENT: *The phrase "in respect of a service" in (a) means a let because a served ball has touched the net before landing in the proper court, OR because the Receiver was not ready ... Case 1 refers to a second serve, and the decision means that if the interruption occurs during delivery of the*

second service, the Server gets two serves. Example: On a second service a linesman calls "fault" and immediately corrects it (the Receiver meanwhile having let the ball go by). The Server is entitled to two serves, on this ground: The corrected call means that the Server has put the ball into play with a good service, and once the ball is in play and a let is called, the point must be replayed ... Note, however, that if the serve is an unmistakable ace—that is, the Umpire is sure the erroneous call had no part in the Receiver's inability to play the ball—the point should be declared for the Server.

Case 2. If a ball in play becomes broken, should a let be called? *Decision.* Yes.

USTA COMMENT: *A ball shall be regarded as having become "broken" if, in the opinion of the Chair Umpire, it is found to have lost compression to the point of being unfit for further play, or unfit for any reason, and it is clear the defective ball was the one in play.*

Rule 14

The "Let" in Service

The service is a let:

(a) If the ball served touches the net, strap or band, and is otherwise good, or, after touching the net, strap or band, touches the Receiver or anything which he wears or carries before hitting the ground.

(b) If a service or a fault is delivered when the Receiver is not ready (see Rule 12).

In case of a let, that particular service shall not count, and the Server shall serve again, but a service let does not annul a previous fault.

Rule 15

Order of Service

At the end of the first game the Receiver shall become Server, and the Server, Receiver; and so on alternately in all the subsequent games of a match. If a player serves out of turn, the player who ought to have served shall serve as soon as the mistake is discovered, but all points scored before such discovery shall be reckoned. If a game shall have been completed before such discovery, the order of service remains as altered. A fault served before such discovery shall not be reckoned.

Rule 16

When Players Change Ends

The players shall change ends at the end of the first, third and every subsequent alternate game of each set, and at the end of each set unless the total number of games in such set is even, in which case the change is not made until the end of the first game of the next set.

If a mistake is made and the correct sequence is not followed the players must take up their correct station as soon as the discovery is made and follow their original sequence.

Rule 17

The Ball in Play

A ball is in play from the moment at which it is delivered in service. Unless a fault or a let is called it remains in play until the point is decided.

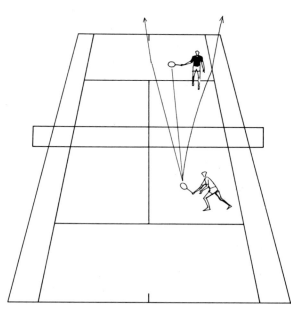

A point is not "decided" simply when, or because, a good shot has clearly passed a player, or when an apparently bad shot passes over a baseline or sideline. An outgoing ball is still definitely "in play" until it actually strikes the ground, backstop or a permanent fixture, or a player. The same applies to a good ball, bounding after it has landed in the proper court. A ball that becomes imbedded in the net is out of play.

Case 1. A player fails to make a good return. No call is made and the ball remains in play. May his opponent later claim the point after the rally has ended?

Decision. No. The point may not be claimed if the players continue to play after the error has been made, provided the opponent was not hindered.

USTA COMMENT: *To be valid, an out call on A's shot to B's court, that B plays, must be made before B's return has either gone out of play or has been hit by A. See Case 3 under Rule 29.*

USTA Case 2. A ball is played into the net; the player on the other side, thinking that the ball is coming over, strikes at it and hits the net. Who loses the point?

Decision. If the player touched the net while the ball was still in play, he loses the point.

Rule 18

Server Wins Point

The Server wins the point:

(a) If the ball served, not being a let under Rule 14, touches the Receiver or anything which he wears or carries, before it hits the ground;

(b) If the Receiver otherwise loses the point as provided by Rule 20.

Rule 19

Receiver Wins Point

The Receiver wins the point:

(a) If the Server serves two consecutive faults;

(b) If the Server otherwise loses the point as provided by Rule 20.

Rule 20

Player Loses Point

A player loses the point if:

(a) He fails, before the ball in play has hit the ground twice consecutively, to return it directly over the net (except as provided in Rule 24(a) or (c)); or

(b) He returns the ball in play so that it hits the ground, a permanent fixture, or other object, outside any of the lines which bound his opponent's Court (except as provided in Rule 24(a) or (c)); or

USTA COMMENT: *A ball hitting a scoring device or other object attached to a net post results in loss of point to the striker.*

(c) He volleys the ball and fails to make a good return even when standing outside the Court; or

(d) In playing the ball he deliberately carries or catches it on his racket or deliberately touches it with his racket more than once; or

USTA COMMENT: *Only when there is a definite "second push" by the player does his shot become illegal, with conse-*

quent loss of point. It should be noted that the word "deliberately" is the key word in this Rule and that two hits occurring in the course of a single continuous stroke would not be deemed a double hit.

(e) He or his racket (in his hand or otherwise) or anything which he wears or carries touches the net, posts, singles sticks, cord or metal cable, strap or band, or the ground within his opponent's Court at any time while the ball is in play; or

USTA COMMENT: *Touching a pipe support that runs across the court at the bottom of the net is interpreted as touching the net; See USTA Comment under Rule 23.*

(f) He volleys the ball before it has passed the net; or

(g) The ball in play touches him or anything that he wears or carries, except his racket in his hand or hands; or

USTA COMMENT: *This loss of point occurs regardless of whether the player is inside or outside the bounds of his court when the ball touches him. Except for a ball used in a first service fault, a player is considered to be "wearing or carrying" anything that he was wearing or carrying at the beginning of the point during which the touch occurred. Exception: If an object worn or carried by a player falls to the ground and a ball hit by his opponent hits that object, then (1) if the ball falls outside the court, the opponent loses the point; (2) if the ball falls inside the court, a let is to be called.*

(h) He throws his racket at and hits the ball; or

(i) He deliberately and materially changes the shape of his racket during the playing of the point.

Case 1. In delivering a first service which falls outside the proper Court, the Server's racket slips out of his hand and flies into the net. Does he lose the point?

Decision. If his racket touches the net whilst the ball is in play, the Server loses the point (Rule 20 *(e)*).

Case 2. In serving, the racket flies from the Server's hand and touches the net before the ball has touched the ground. Is this a fault, or does the player lose the point?

Decision. The Server loses the point because his racket touches the net whilst the ball is in play (Rule 20 *(e)*).

Case 3. A and B are playing against C and D, A is serving to D, C touches the net before the ball touches the ground. A fault is then called because the service falls outside the Service Court. Do C and D lose the point?

Decision. The call "fault" is an erroneous one. C and D had already lost the point before "fault" could be called, because C touched the net whilst the ball was in play (Rule 20 *(e)*).

Case 4. May a player jump over the net into his opponent's Court while the ball is in play and not suffer penalty?

Decision. No. He loses the point (Rule 20 *(e)*).

Case 5. A cuts the ball just over the net, and it returns to A's side. B, unable to reach the ball, throws his racket and hits the ball. Both racket and ball fall over the net on A's Court. A returns the ball outside of B's Court. Does B win or lose the point?

Decision. B loses the point (Rule 20 *(e)* and *(h)*).

Case 5. A player standing outside the service Court is struck by a service ball before it has touched the ground. Does he win or lose the point?

Decision. The player struck loses the point (Rule 20 *(g)*), except as provided under Rule 14 *(a)*.

Case 7. A player standing outside the Court volleys the ball or catches it in his hand and claims the point because the ball was certainly going out of court.

Decision. In no circumstances can he claim the point:

(1) If he catches the ball he loses the point under Rule 20 *(g)*.

(2) If he volleys it and makes a bad return he loses the point under Rule 20 *(c)*.

(3) If he volleys it and makes a good return, the rally continues.

Rule 21

Player Hinders Opponent

If a player commits any act which hinders his opponent in making a stroke, then, if this is deliberate, he shall lose the point or if involuntary, the point shall be replayed.

USTA COMMENT: *"Deliberate" means a player did what he intended to do, although the resulting effect on his opponent might or might not have been what he intended. Example: a player, after his return is in the air, gives advice to his partner in such a loud voice that his opponent is hindered. "Involuntary" means a non-intentional act such as a hat blowing off or a scream resulting from a sudden wasp sting.*

Case 1. Is a player liable to a penalty if in making a stroke he touches his opponent?

Decision. No, unless the Umpire deems it necessary to take action under Rule 21.

Case 2. When a ball bounds back over the net, the player concerned may reach over the net in order to play the ball. What is the ruling if the player is hindered from doing this by his opponent?

Decision. In accordance with Rule 21, the Umpire may either award the point to the player hindered, or order the point to be replayed. (See also Rule 25).

Case 3. Does an involuntary double hit constitute an act which hinders an opponent within Rule 21?

Decision. No.

USTA COMMENT: *Upon appeal by a competitor that an opponent's action in discarding a "second ball" after a rally has started constitutes a distraction (hindrance), the Umpire, if he deems the claim valid, shall require the opponent to make some other and satisfactory disposition of the ball. Failure to comply with this instruction may result in loss of point(s) or disqualification.*

Rule 22

Ball Falls on Line

A ball falling on a line is regarded as falling in the Court bounded by that line.

USTA COMMENT: *In matches played without officials, it is customary for each player to make the calls on all balls bit to his side of the net, and if a player cannot call a ball out with surety he should regard it as good. See The Code.*

Rule 23

Ball Touches Permanent Fixture

If the ball in play touches a permanent fixture (other than the net, posts, singles sticks, cord or metal cable, strap or band) after it has hit the ground, the player who struck it wins the point; if before it hits the ground, his opponent wins the point.

Case 1. A return hits the Umpire or his chair or stand. The player claims that the ball was going into Court.

Decision. He loses the point.

USTA COMMENT: *A ball in play that after passing the net strikes a pipe support running across the court at the base of the net is regarded the same as a ball landing on clear ground. See also Rule 20(e).*

Rule 24

A Good Return
It is a good return:

(a) If the ball touches the net, posts, singles sticks, cord or metal cable, strap or band, provided that it passes over any of them and hits the ground within the Court; or

(b) If the ball, served or returned, hits the ground within the proper Court and rebounds or is blown back over the net, and the player whose turn it is to strike reaches over the net and plays the ball, provided that neither he nor any part of his clothes or racket touches the net, posts, singles sticks, cord or metal cable, strap or band or the ground within his opponent's Court, and that the stroke is otherwise good; or

(c) If the ball is returned outside the posts, or singles sticks, either above or below the level of the top of the net, even though it touches the posts or singles sticks, provided that it hits the ground within the proper Court; or

(d) If a player's racket passes over the net after he has returned the ball, provided the ball passes the net before being played and is properly returned; or

(e) If a player succeeds in returning the ball, served or in play, which strikes a ball lying in the Court.

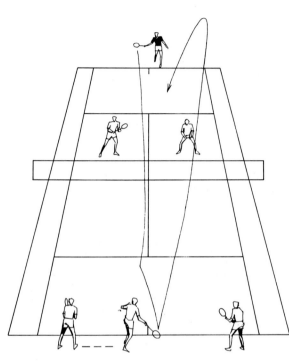

USTA COMMENT: *i.e., on his court when the point started; if the ball in play strikes a ball, rolling or stationary on the court, that has come from elsewhere after the point started, a let should be called. See USTA Comment under Rule 20(g).*

NOTE TO RULE 24: In a singles match, if, for the sake of convenience, a doubles Court is equipped with singles sticks for the purpose of a singles game, then the doubles posts and those portions of the net, cord or metal cable and the band outside such singles sticks shall at all times be permanent fixtures, and are not regarded as posts or parts of the net of a singles game.

A return that passes under the net cord between the singles stick and adjacent doubles post without touching either net cord, net or doubles post and falls within the area of play, is a good return. **USTA COMMENT:** *But in doubles this would be a "through"—loss of point.*

Case 1. A ball going out of Court hits a net post or singles stick and falls within the lines of the opponent's Court. Is the stroke good?

Decision. If a service: no, under Rule 10(c). If other than a service: yes, under Rule 24(a).

Case 2. Is it a good return if a player returns the ball holding his racket in both hands?

Decision. Yes.

Case 3. The service, or ball in play, strikes a ball lying in the Court. Is the point won or lost thereby?

USTA COMMENT: *A ball that is touching a boundary line is considered to be "lying in the court."*

Decision. No. Play must continue. If it is not clear to the Umpire that the right ball is returned a let should be called.

Case 4. May a player use more than one racket at any time during play?

Decision. No; the whole implication of the Rules is singular.

Case 5. May a player request that a ball or balls lying in his opponent's Court be removed?

Decision. Yes, but not while a ball is in play.

USTA COMMENT: *The request must be honored.*

Rule 25

Hindrance of a Player

In case a player is hindered in making a stroke by anything not within his control, except a permanent fixture of the Court, or except as provided for in Rule 21, a let shall be called.

Case 1. A spectator gets into the way of a player, who fails to return the ball. May the player then claim a let?

Decision. Yes, if in the Umpire's opinion he was obstructed by circumstances beyond his control, but not if due to permanent fixtures of the Court or the arrangements of the ground.

Case 2. A player is interfered with as in Case No. 1, and the Umpire calls a let. The Server had previously served a fault. Has he the right to two services?

Decision. Yes: as the ball is in play, the point, not merely the stroke, must be replayed as the Rule provides.

Case 3. May a player claim a let under Rule 25 because he thought his opponent was being hindered, and consequently did not expect the ball to be returned?

Decision. No.

Case 4. Is a stroke good when a ball in play hits another ball in the air?

Decision. A let should be called unless the other ball is in the air by the act of one of the players, in which case the Umpire will decide under Rule 21.

Case 5. If an Umpire or other judge erroneously calls "fault" or "out," and then corrects himself, which of the calls shall prevail?

Decision. A let must be called unless, in the opinion of the Umpire, neither player is hindered in his game, in which case the corrected call shall prevail.

Case 6. If the first ball served—a fault—rebounds, interfering with the Receiver at the time of the second service, may the Receiver claim a let?

Decision. Yes. But if he had an opportunity to remove the ball from the Court and negligently failed to do so, he may not claim a let.

Case 7. Is it a good stroke if the ball touches a stationary or moving object on the Court?

Decision. It is a good stroke unless the stationary object came into Court after the ball was put into play in which case a let must be called. If the ball in play strikes an object moving along or above the surface of the Court a let must be called.

Case 8. What is the ruling if the first service is a fault, the second service correct, and it becomes necessary to call a let either under the provision of Rule 25 or if the Umpire is unable to decide the point?

Decision. The fault shall be annulled and the whole point replayed.

USTA COMMENT: *See Rule 13 and Explanation thereto.*

Rule 26

Score in a Game

If a player wins his first point, the score is called 15 for that player; on winning his second point, the score is called 30 for that player; on winning his third point, the score is called 40 for that player, and the fourth point won by a player is scored game for that player except as below:

If both players have won three points, the score is called deuce; and the next point won by a player is scored advantage for that player. If the same player wins the next point, he wins the game; if the other player wins the next point the score is again called deuce; and so on, until a player wins the two points immediately following the score at deuce, when the game is scored for that player.

USTA COMMENT: *In matches played without an umpire the Server should announce, in a voice audible to his opponent and spectators, the set score at the beginning of each game, and (audible at least to his opponent) point scores as the game goes on. Misunderstandings will be avoided if this practice is followed.*

Rule 27

Score in a Set

(a) A player (or players) who first wins six games wins a set; except that he must win by a margin of two games over his opponent and where necessary a set is extended until this margin is achieved.

(b) The tie-break system of scoring may be adopted as an alternative to the advantage set system in paragraph (a) of this Rule provided the decision is announced in advance of the match.

USTA COMMENT: *See the Tie-Break System in the appendix of this book.*

In this case, the following Rules shall be effective:

The tie-break shall operate when the score reaches six games all in any set except in the third or fifth set of a three set or five set match respectively when an ordinary advantage set shall be played, unless otherwise decided and announced in advance of the match.

The following system shall be used in a tie-break game.

Singles

(i) A player who first wins seven points shall win the game and the set provided he leads by a margin of two points. If the score reaches six points all the game shall be extended until this margin has been achieved. Numerical scoring shall be used throughout the tie-break game.

(ii) The player whose turn it is to serve shall be the server for the first point. His opponent shall be the server for the second and third points and thereafter each player shall serve alternately for two consecutive points until the winner of the game and set has been decided.

(iii) From the first point, each service shall be delivered alternately from the right and left courts, beginning from the right court. If service from a wrong half of the court occurs and is undetected, all play resulting from such wrong service or services shall stand, but the inaccuracy of station shall be corrected immediately it is discovered.

(iv) Players shall change ends after every six points and at the conclusion of the tie-break game.

(v) The tie-break game shall count as one game for the ball change, except that, if the balls are due to be changed at the beginning of the tie-break, the change shall be delayed until the second game of the following set.

Doubles

In doubles the procedure for singles shall apply. The player whose turn it is to serve shall be the server for the first point. Thereafter each player shall serve in rotation for two points, in the same order as previously in that set, until the winners of the game and set have been decided.

Rotation of Service

The player (or pair in the case of doubles) who served first in the tie-break game shall receive service in the first game of the following set.

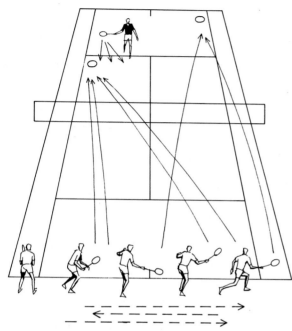

Case 1. At six all the tie-break is played, although it has been decided and announced in advance of the match that an advantage set will be played. Are the points already played counted?

Decision. If the error is discovered before the ball is put in play for the second point, the first point shall count but the error shall be corrected immediately. If the error is discovered after the ball is put in play for the second point the game shall continue as a tie-break game.

Case 2. At six all, an advantage game is played, although it has been decided and announced in advance of the match that a tie-break will be played. Are the points already played counted?

Decision. If the error is discovered before the ball is put in play for the second point, the first point shall be counted but the error shall be corrected immediately. If the error is discovered after the ball is put in play for the second point an advantage set shall be played.

Case 3. If during the tie-break in a doubles game a partner receives out of turn, or a player serves out of rotation, shall the order of receiving, or serving as the case may be, remain as altered until the end of the game?

Decision. Yes.

Rule 28

Maximum Number of Sets

The maximum number of sets in a match shall be 5, or, where women take part, 3.

Rule 29

Role of Court Officials

In matches where an Umpire is appointed, his decision shall be final; but where a Referee is appointed, an appeal shall lie to him from the decision of an Umpire on a question of law, and in all such cases the decision of the Referee shall be final.

In matches where assistants to the Umpire are appointed. (Linesmen, Net-cord Judges, Foot-fault Judges) their decisions shall be final on questions of fact except that if in the opinion of an Umpire a clear mistake has been made he shall have the right to change the decision of an assistant or order a let to be played. When such an assistant is unable to give a decision he shall indicate this immediately to the Umpire who shall give a decision. When an Umpire is unable to give a decision on a question of fact he shall order a let to be played.

In Davis Cup matches or other team competitions where a Referee is on Court, any decision can be changed by the Referee, who may also instruct an Umpire to order a let to be played.

The Referee, in his discretion, may at any time postpone a match on account of darkness or the condition of the ground or the weather. In any case of postponement the previous score and previous occupancy of Courts shall hold good, unless the Referee and the players unanimously agree otherwise.

Case 1. The Umpire orders a let, but a player claims that the point should not be replayed. May the Referee be requested to give a decision?

Decision. Yes. A question of tennis law, that is an issue relating to the application of specific facts, shall first be determined by the Umpire. However, if the Umpire is uncertain or if a player appeals from his determination, then the Referee shall be requested to give a decision, and his decision is final.

Case 2. A ball is called out, but a player claims that the ball was good. May the Referee give a ruling?

Decision. No. This is a question of fact, that is an issue relating to what actually occurred during a specific incident, and the decision of the on-court officials is therefore final.

Case 3. May an Umpire overrule a Linesman at the end of a rally if, in his opinion, a clear mistake has been made during the course of a rally?

Decision. No, unless in his opinion the opponent was hindered. Otherwise an Umpire may only overrule a Linesman if he does so immediately after the mistake has been made.

USTA COMMENT: *See Rule 17, Case 1.*

Case 4. A Linesman calls a ball out. The Umpire was unable to see clearly, although he thought the ball was in. May he overrule the Linesman?

Decision. No. An Umpire may only overrule if he considers that a call was incorrect beyond all reasonable doubt. He may only overrule a ball determined good by a Linesman if he has been able to see a space between the ball and the line; and he may only overrule a ball determined out, or a fault, by a Linesman if he has seen the ball hit the line, or fall inside the line.

Case 5. May a Linesman change his call after the Umpire has given the score?

Decision. No. If a Linesman realises he has made an error, he must call "correction" immediately so that the Umpire and players are aware of his error before the score is given.

Case 6. A player claims his return shot was good after a Linesman called "out." May the Umpire overrule the Linesman?

Decision. No. An Umpire may never overrule as a result of a protest or an appeal by a player.

Rule 30

Continuous Play and Rest Periods

Play shall be continuous from the first service till the match be concluded.

(a) notwithstanding the above, after the third set, or when women take part the second set, either player is entitled to a rest, which shall not exceed 10 minutes, or in countries situated between Latitude 15 degrees North and Latitude 15 degrees South, 45 minutes and furthermore, when necessitated by circumstances not within the control of the players, the Umpire may suspend play for such a period as he may consider necessary.

If play is suspended and is not resumed until a later day the rest may be taken only after the third set (or when women take part the second set) of play on such later day, completion of an unfinished set being counted as one set.

If play is suspended and is not resumed until 10 minutes have elapsed in the same day the rest may be taken only after three consecutive sets have been played without interruption (or when women take part two sets), completion of an unfinished set being counted as one set.

Any nation and/or committee organising a tournament, match or competition, other than the International Tennis Championships (Davis Cup and Federation Cup), is at liberty to modify this provision or omit it from its regulations provided this is announced before play commences.

USTA Rules Regarding Rest Periods

Regular MEN's and WOMEN's, and MEN's and WOMEN's Amateur—Paragraph (a) of Rule 30 applies, except that a tournament using tie-breaks may eliminate rest periods provided advance notice is given.

BOYS' 18—All matches in this division shall be best of three sets with NO REST PERIOD, except that in interscholastic, state, sectional and national championships the FINAL ROUND may be best-of-five sets. If such a final requires more than three sets to decide it, a rest of 10 minutes after the third set is mandatory. Special Note: In severe temperature-humidity conditions the Referee may rule that a 10-minute rest may be taken in a Boys' 18 best-of-three before the third set. However, to be valid this must be done before the match is started, and as a matter of the Referee's independent judgment.

BOYS' 16, 14 and 12, and GIRLS' 18, 16, 14 and 12 —All matches in these categories shall be best of three sets. A 10-minute rest before the third set is MANDATORY in GIRLS' 12, 14 and 16, and BOYS' 12 and 14. The rest period is OPTIONAL in GIRLS' 18 and BOYS' 16. (Optional means at the option of any competitor.)

All SENIOR divisions (35 and over), Mother-Daughter, Father-Son and similar combinations: Under conventional scoring, all matches best of three sets, with rest period at any player's option.

When "NO-AD" scoring is used in a tournament the committee may stipulate that there will be no rest periods. Two conditions of this stipulation are: (1) Advance notice must be given on entry blanks for the event, and (2) The Referee is empowered to reinstate the normal rest periods for matches played under unusually severe temperature-humidity conditions; to be valid, such reinstatement must be announced before a given match or series of matches is started, and be a matter of the Referee's independent judgment.

USTA COMMENT: *When a player competes in an event designated as for players of a bracket whose rules as to intermissions and length of match are geared to a different physical status, the player cannot ask for allowances based on his or her age, or her sex. For example, a female competing in an intercollegiate (men's) varsity team match would not be entitled to claim a rest period in a best-of-three-sets match unless that were the condition under which the team competition was normally held.*

(b) Play shall never be suspended, delayed or interfered with for the purpose of enabling a player to recover his strength or his breath.

(c) A maximum of 30 seconds shall elapse from the moment the ball goes out of play at the end of one point to the time the ball is struck for the next point. In the event such first serve is a fault, then the second serve must be struck by the Server without delay.

The Receiver must play to the reasonable pace of the Server and must be ready to receive when the Server is ready to serve within the permitted time.

When changing ends a maximum of one minute thirty seconds shall elapse from the moment the ball goes out of play at the end of the game to the time the ball is struck for the first point of the next game.

The Umpire shall use his discretion when there is interference which makes it impossible for the server to serve within that time.

These provisions shall be strictly construed. The Umpire shall be the sole judge of any suspension, delay or interference, and after giving due warning he may disqualify the offender.

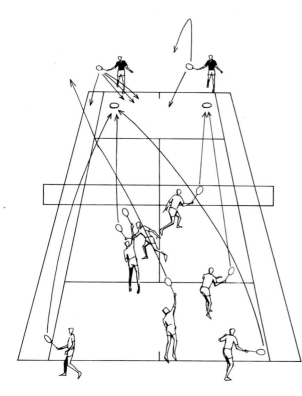

NOTE: A Tournament Committee has discretion to decide the time allowed for a warm-up period prior to a match. It is recommended that this does not exceed five minutes.

Case 1. A player's clothing, footwear, or equipment (excluding racket) becomes out of adjustment in such a way that it is impossible or undesirable for him to play on. May play be suspended while the maladjustment is rectified?

Decision. If this occurs in circumstances outside the control of the player, a suspension may be allowed. The Umpire shall be the sole judge of whether a suspension is justified and the period of the suspension.

Case 2. If, owing to an accident, a player is unable to continue immediately, is there any limit to the time during which play may be suspended?

Decision. No allowance may be made for natural loss of physical condition. In the case of accidental injury the Umpire may allow a one-time, three minute suspension for that injury. Play must resume in three minutes. However, the organizers of international circuits and team events recognized by the ITF may extend this if treatment is necessary.

USTA COMMENT: *Case 2 refers to an important distinction that should be made between a disability caused by an accident during the match, and disability attributable to fatigue, illness or exertion (examples: cramps, muscle pull, vertigo, strained back). Accidental loss embodies a sprained ankle or actual injury from such mishaps as collision with netpost or net, a cut from a fall, contact with chair or backstop, or being hit with a ball, racket or other object. An injured player shall not be permitted to leave the playing area. If, in the opinion of the Umpire, there is a genuine toilet emergency, a bona fide toilet visit by a player is permissible and is not to be considered natural loss of condition.*

Case 3. During a doubles game, may one of the partners leave the Court while the ball is in play?

Decision. Yes, so long as the Umpire is satisfied that play is continuous within the meaning of the Rules, and that there is no conflict with Rules 35 and 36.

USTA COMMENT: *When a match is resumed following an interruption exceeding 10 minutes necessitated by weather or other unusual conditions, it is allowable for the players to engage in a "re-warm-up," using the balls that were in play at the time of the interruption, with the time for the next ball change not being affected. The duration of the re-warm-up will be as follows: 0–10 minutes delay, no warm-up; 11–20 minutes delay, 3 minutes warm-up; more than 20 minutes delay, 5 minutes warm-up.*

Rule 31

Coaching

During the playing of a match in a team competition, a player may receive coaching from a captain who is sitting on the court only when he changes ends at the end of a game, but not when he changes ends during a tie-break game.

A player may not receive coaching during the playing of any other match.

The provisions of this rule must be strictly construed. After due warning an offending player may be disqualified.

Case 1. Should a warning be given, or the player be disqualified, if the coaching is given by signals in an unobtrusive manner?

Decision. The Umpire must take action as soon as he becomes aware that coaching is being given verbally or by signals. If the

Umpire is unaware that coaching is being given, a player may draw his attention to the fact that advice is being given.

Case 2. Can a player receive coaching during the ten minute rest in a five set match, or when play is interrupted and he leaves the court?

Decision. Yes. In these circumstances, when the player is not on the court, there is no restriction on coaching.

NOTE: The word "coaching" includes any advice or instruction.

Rule 32

Changing Balls

In cases where balls are changed after an agreed number of games, if the balls are not changed in the correct sequence the mistake shall be corrected when the player, or pair in the case of doubles, who should have served with new balls is next due to serve.

THE DOUBLES GAME
Rule 33

The above Rules shall apply to the Doubles Game except as below.

Rule 34

The Doubles Court

For the Doubles Game, the Court shall be 36 feet (10.97m.) in width, i.e., 4½ feet (1.37m.) wider on each side than the Court for the Singles Game, and those portions of the singles side-lines which lie between the two service-lines shall be called the service side-lines. In other respects, the Court shall be similar to that described in Rule 1, but the portions of the singles side-lines between the base-line and service-line on each side of the net may be omitted if desired.

USTA Case 1. In doubles the Server claims the right to stand at the corner of the court as marked by the doubles sideline. Is the foregoing correct or is it necessary that the Server stand within the limits of the center mark and the singles sideline?

Decision. The Server has the right to stand anywhere back of the baseline between the center mark extension and the doubles sideline extension.

Rule 35

Order of Service in Doubles

The order of serving shall be decided at the beginning of each set as follows:

The pair who have to serve in the first game of each set shall decide which partner shall do so and the opposing pair shall decide similarly for the second game. The partner of the player who served in the first game shall serve in the third; the partner of the player who served in the second game shall serve in the fourth, and so on in the same order in all the subsequent games of a set.

Case 1. In doubles, one player does not appear in time to play, and his partner claims to be allowed to play single-handed against the opposing players. May he do so?

Decision. No.

Rule 36

Order of Receiving in Doubles

The order of receiving the service shall be decided at the beginning of each set as follows:

The pair who have to receive the service in the first game shall decide which partner shall receive the first service, and that partner shall continue to receive the first service in every odd game throughout that set. The opposing pair shall likewise decide which partner shall receive the first service in the second game and that partner shall receive the first service in the second game and that partner shall continue to receive the first service in every even game throughout that set. Partners shall receive the service alternately throughout each game.

Case 1. Is it allowable in doubles for the Server's partner to stand in a position that obstructs the view of the Receiver?

Decision. Yes. The Server's partner may take any position on his side of the net in or out of the Court that he wishes.

USTA COMMENT: *The same is true of the Receiver's partner.*

Rule 37

Service Out of Turn in Doubles

If a partner serves out of his turn, the partner who ought to have served shall serve as soon as the mistake is discovered, but all points scored, and any faults served before such discovery, shall be reckoned. If a game shall have been completed before such discovery, the order of service remains as altered.

USTA COMMENT: *For an exception to Rule 37 see Case 3 under Rule 27.*

Rule 38

Error in Order of Receiving in Doubles

If during a game the order of receiving the service is changed by the Receivers it shall remain as altered until the end of the game in which the mistake is discovered, but the partners shall resume their original order of receiving in the next game of that set in which they are Receivers of the service.

Rule 39

Service Fault in Doubles

The service is a fault as provided for by Rule 10, or if the ball touches the Server's partner or anything which he wears or carries; but if the ball served touches the partner of the Receiver, or anything which he wears or carries, not being a let under Rule 14(a) before it hits the ground, the Server wins the point.

Rule 40

Playing the Ball in Doubles

The ball shall be struck alternately by one or other player of the opposing pairs, and if a player touches the ball in play with his racket in contravention of this Rule, his opponents win the point.

USTA COMMENT: *This means that, in the course of making one return, only one member of a doubles team may hit the ball. If both of them hit the ball, either simultaneously or consecutively, it is an illegal return. The partners themselves do not have to "alternate" in making returns. Mere clashing*

of rackets does not make a return illegal, if it is clear that only one racket touched the ball.

If you have a rules problem, send full details, enclosing a stamped self-addressed envelope, to Nick Powel, USTA Tennis Rules Committee, 3147 South 14th Street, Arlington, Virginia, 22204, and you will be sent a prompt explanation.

APPENDIX

Regulations for Making Tests Specified in Rule 3

1. Unless otherwise specified all tests shall be made at a temperature of approximately 68° Fahrenheit (20° Centigrade) and a relative humidity of approximately 60 per cent. All balls should be removed from their container and kept at the recognized temperature and humidity for 24 hours prior to testing, and shall be at that temperature and humidity when the test is commenced.

2. Unless otherwise specified the limits are for a test conducted in an atmospheric pressure resulting in a barometric reading of approximately 30 inches (76cm.).

3. Other standards may be fixed for localities where the average temperature, humidity or average barometric pressure at which the game is being played differ materially from 68° Fahrenheit (20° Centigrade), 60 per cent and 30 inches (76cm.) respectively.

Applications for such adjusted standards may be made by any National Association to the International Tennis Federation and if approved shall be adopted for such localities.

4. In all tests for diameter a ring gauge shall be used consisting of a metal plate, preferably non-corrosive, of a uniform thickness of one-eighth of an inch (.32cm.) in which there are two circular openings 2.575 inches (6.54cm.) and 2.700 inches (6.86cm.) in diameter respectively. The inner surface of the gauge shall have a convex profile with a radius of one-sixteenth of an inch. (.16cm.). The ball shall not drop through the smaller opening by its own weight and shall drop through the larger opening by its own weight.

5. In all tests for deformation conducted under Rule 3, the machine designed by Percy Herbert Stevens and patented in Great Britain under Patent No. 230250, together with the subsequent additions and improvements thereto, including the modifications required to take return deformations, shall be employed or such other machine which is approved by a National Association and gives equivalent readings to the Stevens machine.

6. Procedure for carrying out tests.

(a) Pre-compression. Before any ball is tested it shall be steadily compressed by approximately one inch (2.54 cm.) on each of three diameters at right angles to one another in succession; this process to be carried out three times (nine compressions in all). All tests to be completed within two hours of pre-compression.

(b) Bound test (as in Rule 3). Measurements are to be taken from the concrete base to the bottom of the ball.

(c) Size test (as in paragraph 4 above).

(d) Weight test (as in Rule 3).

(e) Deformation test. The ball is placed in position on the modified Stevens machine so that neither platen of the machine is in contact with the cover seam. The contact weight is applied, the pointer and the mark brought level, and the dials set to zero. The test weight equivalent to 18 lb. (8.165kg.) is placed on the beam and pressure applied by turning the wheel at a uniform speed so that five seconds elapse from the instant the beam leaves its seat until the pointer is brought level with the mark. When turning ceases the reading is recorded (forward deformation). The wheel is turned again until figure ten is reached on the scale (one inch [2.54 cm.] deformation). The wheel is then rotated in the opposite direction at a uniform speed thus releasing pressure) until the beam pointer again coincides with the mark. After waiting ten seconds the pointer is adjusted to the mark if necessary. The reading is then recorded (return deformation). This procedure is repeated on each ball across the two diameters at right angles to the initial position and to each other.

The Tie-break System

A tournament committee must announce before the start of its tournament the details concerning its use of tie-breaks. A tournament that has been authorized by the USTA or by a USTA Section to use VASSS No-Ad scoring may use the 9-point tie-break in any set played under No-Ad; it may change to the 12-point tie-break in its later rounds. No-Ad scoring is authorized for tournaments held at the Sectional Championship level and below, and for consolation matches in any tournament (excluding any USTA National Junior Championship). Other than the foregoing exceptions, all sanctioned tournaments using tie-breaks will use only the 12-point tie-break. Rule 27 establishes the procedure for the 12-point tie-break game. For a more detailed explanation see below.

If a ball change is due on a tie-break game it will be deferred until the second game of the next set. A tie-break game counts as one game in reckoning ball changes. The score of the tie-break set will be written 7–6 (x) or 6–7 (x), with the score of the winner of the match entered first, followed by the score of the tie-break game in parentheses, such as (10–8) or (8–10), with the score of the winner of the match again entered first. Changes of ends during a tie-break game are to be made within the normal 30 seconds allowed between points.

The 12-Point Tie-Break

Singles: A, having served the first game of the set, serves the first point from the right court; B serves points 2 and 3 (left and right), A serves points 4 and 5 (left and right); B serves point 6 (left) and after they change ends, point 7 (right); A serves points 8 and 9 (left and right); B serves points 10 and 11 (left and right), and A serves point 12 (left). A player who reaches 7 points during these first 12 points wins the game and set. If the score has reached 6 points all, the players change ends and continue in the same pattern until one player establishes a margin of two points, which gives him the game and set. Note that the players change ends every six points, and that the player

who serves the last point of one of these 6-point segments also serves the first point of the next one (from right court). For a following set the players change ends, and B serves the first game.

Doubles: This follows the same pattern, with partners preserving their serving sequence. Assume A-B versus C-D, with A having served the first game of the set. A serves the first point (right); C serves points 2 and 3 (left and right); B serves points 4 and 5 (left and right); D serves point 6 (left) and the teams change ends. D serves point 7 (right); A serves points 8 and 9 (left and right); C serves points 10 and 11 (left and right); B serves point 12 (left). A team that wins 7 points during these first 12 points wins the game and set. If the score has reached 6 points all, the teams change ends. B then serves point 13, (right) and they continue until one team establishes a two-point margin and thus wins the game and set. As in singles, they change ends for one game to start a following set, with team C-D to serve first.

The 9-Point Tie-Break

Singles: With A having served the first game of the set, he serves points 1 and 2 (right court and left); then B serves points 3 and 4 (right and left). Players change ends. A serves points 5 and 6 (right and left), and B serves points 7 and 8 (right and left). If the score reaches 4 points all B serves point 9 (right or left) at the election of A. The first player to win 5 points wins the game and set. The players stay for one game to start the next set, and B is the first server.

Doubles: The same format as in singles applies, with each player serving from the same end of the court in the tie-break game that he served from during the set. (Note that this operates to alter the sequence of serving by the partners on the *second*-serving team. With A-B versus C-D, if the serving sequence during the set was A-C-B-D the sequence becomes A-D-B-C in the tie-break.)

VASSS No-Ad Scoring

The No-Ad procedure is simply what the name implies: the first player to win four points wins the game, the 7th point of a game becoming a game point for each player. The receiver has the choice of advantage court or deuce court to which the service is to be delivered on the 7th point. If a No-Ad set reaches 6 games all a tie-break shall be used which is normally the 9-point tie-break.

NOTE: The score-calling may be either in the conventional terms or in simple numbers, i.e., "zero, one, two, three, game."

Cautionary Note

Any ITF-sponsored tournament should get special authorization from ITF before using No-Ad.

Reprinted with the permission of the United States Tennis Association. A copy of the *Rules of Tennis and Cases and Decisions 1984* in booklet form may be purchased for $.50 plus $.50 for postage and handling from the USTA Education and Research Center, 729 Alexander Road, Princeton, NJ 08540, 609-452-2580.

The Code

1. Before reading this pamphlet you might well ask yourself: Since we have a book which contains all the rules of tennis, why do we need a code? Isn't it sufficient to know and understand all the rules?

2. An answer to these questions could come from this hypothetical situation. Two strangers, A and B, are playing a tightly contested tournament match without officials. On one of B's shots A says: "I can't be sure if it was in or out; therefore, the point is yours." Three games later, on one of A's shots B says: "I'm not sure how it was; let's play a let." In two identical situations there are different decisions. If no one else is in favor of a code that works the same on both sides of the net, you can be sure that A is!

3. There are a number of things not specifically set forth in the rules that are covered by custom and tradition only. For example, everybody knows that in case of doubt on a line call your opponent gets the benefit of the doubt, but can you find that in the rules? Further, custom dictates the standard procedures that players will use in reaching decisions. These, then, plus some other similar ones, are the reasons why we need a code, the essential elements of which are set forth here.

4. One of the difficult aspects of tennis is that when a match is played without officials the players themselves have the responsibility for making decisions, particularly line calls; but there is a subtle difference between their decisions and those of an umpire or a linesman. A linesman does his best to resolve impartially a problem involving a line call with the interests of both players in mind, whereas a player must be guided by the unwritten law that any doubt must be resolved in favor of his opponent.

5. A corollary of this principle is the fact that a player in attempting to be scrupulously honest on line calls will find himself frequently keeping in play a ball that "might have been out" and that he discovers—too late—*was* out. *Even so, the game is much better played this way.*

6. In making a line call a player should not enlist the aid of a spectator. In the first place, the spectator has no part in the match and putting him in it may be very annoying to an opponent; in the second, he may offer a call even though he was not in a position to see the ball; in the third, he may be prejudiced; and in the fourth, he may be totally unqualified. All these factors point decisively toward keeping out of the match all persons who are not officially participating.

7. It is both the obligation and prerogative of a player to call all balls on his side, to help his opponent make calls *when the opponent requests it,* and to call against himself (with the exception of a first service; see par. 32) any ball that he clearly sees out on his opponent's side of the net.

8. The prime objective in making line calls is accuracy, and all participants in a match should cooperate to attain this objective. *When a player does not call an out ball (with the exception of a first serve) against himself when he clearly sees it out—whether he is requested to do so by his opponents or not—he is cheating.*

9. All players being human, they will all make mistakes, but they should do everything they can to minimize these mistakes, including helping an opponent. No player should question an opponent's call unless asked, but a player should *always* request his opponent's opinion when the opponent is in a better position to see a ball;

and once the opponent has given a positive opinion it must be accepted; if neither player has an opinion the ball is considered good. Obviously, aid from an opponent is available only on a call that terminates a point. In accordance with the laws of parallax, the opinion of a player looking *down* a line is much more likely to be accurate than that of a player looking *across* a line.

9.1. When you are looking *across* a line don't call a ball out unless you can clearly see part of the court between where the ball hit and the line. This means if you are half a court or so away and a ball lands within two inches of a line it is almost impossible for you to call it with accuracy. A player who stands on one base line and questions a call concerning a ball that landed near the other base line is probably being ridiculous.

9.2. Unless you have made a local ground rule designed to save chasing balls that are obviously going out, when you catch in the air a ball that is in play you have lost the point, regardless of whether you are inside or outside the court.

10. Any call of "out," "let," or "fault" must be made instantaneously; otherwise, the ball is presumed good and still in play. In this connotation "instantaneously" means that the *call is made before either an opponent has hit the return or the return has gone out of play. Most important: a ball is not out until it is called out.*

11. The requirement for an instantaneous call will quickly eliminate the "two chance" option that some players practice. To illustrate, C is advancing to the net for an easy putaway when he sees a ball from an adjoining court rolling towards him. He continues his advance and hits the shot, only to have his supposed easy putaway fly over the baseline. C then makes a claim for a let, which is obviously not valid. C could have had a let had he stopped when he first saw the ball rolling towards him, but when he saw it and then continued on to hit the easy shot he forfeited his right to a let. He took his chance to win or lose, and he is not entitled to a second one.

12. Another situation eliminated by the instantaneous call requirement is that in which a player returns the ball, at the same time yelling: "I don't know." This sort of call constitutes a puzzle which should not be thrown at any opponent.

13. In living up to the instantaneous call requirement it is almost certain that there will be out balls that are played. On a fast first service, for example, sometimes the ball will be moving so rapidly that the receiver has hit the ball and it has gone into play (maybe for a placement) or into the net before an out call can be made. *In such cases, the receiver is considered as having taken his chance, and he is entitled to only one, whether he made a putaway or an error.* Likewise, when the server and his partner *thought* to be out the ball which *was* good and didn't play their opponents' return, they lose the point. The purists' argument that a ball that is out cannot be played under any circumstances falls before the practicality of the player's responsibility to make calls. Otherwise, after a point involving a long rally had been concluded a player could

discover an out mark made at the beginning of the point and ask that the point he had just lost be awarded to him. It is only fair that any time you cause your opponent to expend energy he should have a chance to win the point; and when you fail in your duties as a linesman you pay by letting an out ball stay in play. *From strictly the practical view, the instantaneous call rule will eliminate much indecision and unpleasantness.*

14. Any ball that cannot be called out is presumed to have been good, and a player cannot claim a let on the basis that he did not see a ball. If this were not so, picture your opponent at the net ready to tap away a sitter. As he does so your back is to him. Can you ask for a replay because you didn't see where his shot landed? If you could, the perfect defense has been found against any shot that is out of reach: close your eyes before it touches the court.

15. One of tennis' most infuriating moments occurs when after a long hard rally a player makes a clean placement and hears his opponent say: "I'm not sure if it was good or out. Let's play a let." Remember that it is each player's responsibility to call all balls on his side of the net, and if a ball can't be called out with surety, it is good. When you ask for a replay of a point because you say your opponent's shot was really out but you want to give him "a break," you are deluding yourself; you *must* have had some small shred of doubt, and that doubt means the point should be your opponent's. *Further, telling your opponent to "take two" is usually not so generous as it might sound.*

16. When time and the court surface permit, a player should take a careful second look at any *point-ending placement* that is close to a line. Calls based on a "flash look" are often inaccurate, and the "flash look" system has a high probability of being unfair to an opponent.

17. In doubles when one partner calls a ball out and the other one good, the doubt that has been established means the ball must be considered to have been good. The reluctance that some doubles players have to overrule their partners is secondary to the importance of not letting your opponents suffer from a bad call. The tactful way to achieve the desired result is to tell your partner quietly that he has made a mistake and then let him overrule himself. If it comes to a showdown, untactful honesty is preferable to tactful dishonesty.

18. Normally, asking for a replay of a point is a sign of weakness and of failure to exercise line calling responsibilities, and should occur only on rare occasions. One of these is as follows. Your opponent's ball appears out and you so call, but return the ball to his court. Inspection reveals that your out call, which stopped play, is in error. Since you actually returned the ball a let is authorized. Had you not returned the ball the point would have been your opponent's. (See last sentence in par. 19.) Another possible replay situation occurs when, just as C is returning A's good shot, A's overzealous partner, B, calls A's shot out. If C hits a placement he wins the point; otherwise, the point should be replayed.

18.1. When you are hindered attempting to return a shot that you could not have returned even had there been no hindrance, a let is not authorized. Incidentally, a request for a let does not mean that the let is automatically granted. For example, a request for a let because you have tripped over your own hat should be denied.

19. Once an out, fault, or let call is made play stops, regardless of what happens thereafter. This policy is sound, though sometimes maddening. For example, with you at the net your partner serves a bullet that the receiver barely gets to the net for an easy setup which you whack away, but the receiver has yelled "fault" as he was returning the service. Inspection reveals that the service was good. You first feel that your putaway shot should count for the point. But suppose that you had missed the putaway. Your immediate cry would have been for a let because the out call distracted you and made you miss. A rule can't work one way one time and work another way another time. It is unfortunate that a miscall was made on such a good service, but you must trust your opponent's intentions to be fair, remember that since they are human they are going to make some mistakes, and realize that since they returned the service a let may be called. The validity of the principle here notwithstanding, most good players who have made a weak giveaway type of return because of an opponent's good forcing shot will give the opponent the point in spite of the out call.

20. All points in a match should be treated with the same importance, and there is no justification for considering a match point differently than the first point. Also, some players will insist that on occasion even though a ball is good they *want* it to be out so badly that they will unconsciously call it out; this reasoning is difficult for a strong-willed fair-minded player to accept.

21. As a driven ball—in contrast to a ball dropping vertically—strikes the ground (or asphalt or cement, but *not* grass) it will leave a mark in the shape of an ellipse. If this ellipse is near a line and you cannot see court surface *between* the ellipse and the line, the ball is good. If you can see only part of an ellipse on the ground this means that the missing part is on the line or tape. Some players will call a ball of this kind out on the basis that all of the mark they can see is outside the line; this thinking is fallacious. An ellipse tangent to a line (literally, touching the line at only one point) still represents a good ball; this is tantamount to saying that a ball 99% out is 100% good.

22. Notwithstanding the ellipse theory, on courts which have tapes for lines, occasionally a ball will strike the tape, jump an inch, then leave a full ellipse. This is frequently the case with a hard service when the server will see a clear white spot appear on the service tape, only to have the receiver call "fault" and point to an ellipse an inch back of the line. To attain accuracy in such situations is difficult. The best that the receiver can do is to listen for the sound of the ball touching the tape and look for a clean spot on the tape directly between the server and the ellipse; if these conditions exist he should give the point to his opponent. Sometimes sound alone can be

misleading, particularly when the hearer is some distance —across the net or otherwise—from the sound. Also, an inch and a half is about the maximum that a ball will jump off the tape.

23. In returning service the partner of the receiver should call the service line for him, with the receiver calling the center line and the side line. It is difficult for the receiver, who is looking *across* the service line, to call with accuracy a shot that lands near that line. This is the reason why in singles a receiver will frequently find himself unsure of a serve and put it in play even though later it is determined that it was out.

24. Returning a service that is obviously out (accompanied by an out call) is a form of rudeness, and when the receiver knows that in making these returns he bothers the server it is gamesmanship. At the same time it must be expected that a fast service that just misses the line will frequently with justification be returned as a matter of self-protection, even though an out call is made. The speed of deliveries is such that if the receiver waited for a call before he started to make a return he would be overpowered. Probably the most difficult shot in tennis to call accurately is a hard flat service, aimed directly at the receiver, that hits within an inch of the service line in a grass court singles match.

24.1. Returning a first service that is obviously out *without* an out call in an attempt to catch an opponent off guard is cheating. At the same time, if the receiver in good faith gives the server the benefit of the doubt and returns an out ball, the server is not entitled to refuse the benefit of the doubt and ask for a let on the basis that since he saw the serve out the return caught him by surprise.

25. A USTA rule interpretation authorizes the receiver or his partner to call footfaults on the server after the server has been warned once. This call should be made only when the caller is *absolutely* certain. While in doubles the partner of the receiver may be in a fair position to call a normal footfault, in either singles or doubles the receiver himself would be able to make this call only in *flagrant* cases.

25.1. When you feel that your opponent, a netrusher, is footfaulting but his violations are not sufficiently flagrant for you to be sure and to call, the situation can be irritating. Compliance with the footfault rule is very much a function of a player's personal honor system. The plea that he only touches the line and doesn't rush the net is not acceptable. If he doesn't footfault when there is an umpire but does when there is no umpire, the time has come for him to examine his own sense of fair play to see if he is the type of person who will cheat provided he thinks he can go undetected or unpunished, and, if he is, to try to make a change. *Footfaulting is just as surely cheating as is making a deliberate bad line call.*

26. Even if no ethics were involved, from the practical view it behooves a player to avoid footfaults. It is not uncommon in a match having officials for a chronic footfaulter to become so upset by the frequent footfault calls against him that his whole game disintegrates.

27. A player who hits a weak shot and then, *when the ball is moving towards his opponents' court,* utters an exclamation such as "back, partner!" has violated the ethics of good play. His opponent is clearly entitled to *at least a let, and quite possibly the point,* on the grounds of interference. However, if the opponent goes ahead and plays the ball and misses, the "two chance" rule holds. There is such a thing as the exclamation coming forth just as the opponent is making his shot. It is then properly a matter for the opponent to determine whether or not he is entitled to a let, for *only* he can judge if the hindrance came *before* his shot, *after* it, or *simultaneously* with it. If he is going to request a let he should try to make the claim before he sees the outcome of his shot, though this is not always possible. A certain type of player will wait and request a let if he has made an error, but will forget about the let if his shot has turned into a freak placement; this practice is not ethical. The main thing is that if the opponent was hindered, then had an option to stop or to make the shot, then attempted the shot, whether he missed it or not is immaterial; he is considered to have played the ball and there is no basis for a let.

28. In general, any conversation between partners while the ball is moving *toward* their opponents' side of the net is taboo; once either you or your partner has hit the ball, don't say anything until an opponent has hit it. Even when a ball is moving toward two partners conversation between them should be minimized, with about the only words permitted being such exhortations as to try hard for a ball ("run!") or to let one pass ("out!"), etc. Incidentally, "out" as advice to a partner to let the ball drop does not suffice for the normal "out" call necessary when a ball has landed outside the court.

29. With respect to a player moving when a ball is in play or about to be in play, in general he is entitled to feint with *his body* as he wishes. He may change position on the court at any time including while the server is tossing the ball to serve. He may not wave his racket or his arms nor may he talk or make noise in an attempt to create a distraction.

30. A ball from your court going into an adjoining court or a ball from an adjoining court coming into your court can provide the basis for a let. In handling these balls here are some things to remember. When play is in progress don't go behind another court to retrieve a ball or hit a loose ball to that court; this may mean holding a ball for several seconds while a point is being finished. Don't ask for one of your balls until the point in play on the adjoining court has stopped. *In returning a loose ball to another court don't hit it aimlessly as if you didn't care where it goes as long as it leaves your court.* Instead, pick up the ball and hit it so that it goes directly to one of the players on the other court, *preferably the server, on the first bounce;* this might be termed "Rule One" of court etiquette. As a corollary to this rule, when changing ends collect your match balls on your side of the net and give them to the next server.

31. In the general area of common courtesy and consideration for others violations are too frequent. Some players in loud tones have a post mortem on each point, to the dismay of the players on the adjoining courts. Some players complain of the type of shots an opponent hits (e.g., too many lobs); what he hits is his business as long as they are legal. Don't embarrass a weak opponent by being overly gracious or condescending. Don't spoil the game for your partner or opponents by losing your temper and using vile language or throwing your racket. After losing a point don't slam a ball in anger; a ball boy once lost an eye from this sort of action. And don't sulk when you are losing; instead, praise your opponent's good shots. Above all, try to make tennis a fun game for all participants.

31.1. Be neat in your dress, and wear proper tennis clothing: no blue jeans, loud sport shirts, or jogging shoes. If you are going to a strange club with whose rules you are not familiar you can never be wrong dressing in all-white. Carry a spare racket; if one breaks you are not allowed a delay to find a replacement, but instead must continue with what you have courtside, broken or not.

32. As mentioned in paragraph 7, neither the server nor his net man should make an out call on a *first* service even though he thinks it is out, because the receiver, not being sure of the ball, may give the server the benefit of the doubt and then hit a placement. In this instance the prerogative of the receiver to give the benefit of the doubt and make a return should not be usurped. However, either the server or the net man should volunteer a call on any *second* service he clearly sees to be out for his call terminates the point. In doubles the net man is usually in the best position to hear a service touch the net, though custom supports the calling of a let by any player who hears an otherwise good serve touch the net.

33. Calls involving a ball's touching a player, a player's touching the net, a player's touching his opponent's court (invasion), hitting an opponent's return before it has passed the net, and a double-bounce, can be very difficult to make. Any player who becomes aware that he has committed a violation in one of these areas should announce the violation immediately.

33.1 *In all of the above areas the prerogative of decision belongs to the player involved.* To illustrate, A thinks B's shot is a double-bounce, catches B's shot and claims the point. B, however, feels sure there was no double-bounce; since B has the prerogative of decision the point is B's. On occasion even though B thinks there was no double-bounce he will defer to A's judgment because A was in a better position to see what happened.

33.2. After a point has been finished A might give B an opportunity to admit, for example, a double-bounce that was not called during the point. If B accepts A's thinking he should give him the point, even at that late time. The decision, of course, is still B's. A better example would be where A thinks that B has invaded A's court, but B hasn't called the invasion. After the point is over, if A can point out half of one of B's footprints under the net it would be difficult for B to refuse to give A the point.

33.3. Done without deliberation and with one continuous forward swing of the racket, a double-hit and a carry are legal shots. When done with deliberation, or when there is a definite "second push" of the racket, each of these shots is illegal, with consequent loss of point that the striker should call on himself.

34. Some players confuse "warm-up" and "practice." A player should provide his opponent five minutes of warm-up, making a special effort to hit his shots directly to his opponent. Five minutes warm-up is adequate even on a chilly day, although it may not be adequate for him to *practice* his shots as much as he would like. If he wants to practice more than five minutes he should do it prior to the match. Courtesy dictates that you not practice your service return when your opponent practices his serve. Incidentally, even a windy day does not justify taking warm-up serves from both ends of the court.

34.1. Many players want to practice or to warm-up their serves just before they serve the first time, even though the match is then one game or more old. Once a match has started there is no basis for further practice or warm-up. It would be just as logical to hit practice serves before the tenth game as it would be to hit them before the second game.

35. If you feel that you, as a receiver, are being victimized by a server who serves without hesitation (frequently, a server who serves when you are *getting* ready rather than when you *are* ready) the person to blame is most likely yourself. This is true because in any discussion over whether a receiver was ready or not the sole criterion is the receiver's own statement, and if he wasn't ready a let is in order. Obviously, the receiver can't signal by word or position that he is ready and then, just as the server delivers, become "unready" and get a let. *In reality, while there are unsmart receivers, there is no such thing as a quick server.*

36. The receiver should make no effort to return a serve when he is not ready if he wishes to maintain valid his right to a let. On the other hand the server is protected from the "two chances" receiver under the same rule; this rule states that if a receiver makes any attempt to return a service he is *presumed* to have been ready.

37. Some receivers indicate they are ready and then, as the server tosses the ball, become "unready" in an attempt to upset him. This is gamesmanship at its worst. The remedy is for the server to ask "ready" before each serve, a practice (particularly on a second serve) which detracts from the game and can become annoying.

38. When the receiver has indicated that he is ready and the server serves an ace, the receiver's partner cannot claim a let because he (the partner of the receiver) was not ready. The receiver's indication of being ready is tantamount to indicating that his team is ready. While no server should serve if he sees either of his opponents is not ready, he is not expected to check both opponents before each serve. It is the receiver's responsibility to signal ready only when *both* he and his partner are ready.

39. When a server requests three balls to be in his hand prior to each point he is to serve, the receiver should comply with this wish when the third ball is readily available. Since only two balls are normally needed for a service, the receiver should not be required to get the third when it is some distance away, nor, under the continuous play rule, should a server during a game be permitted to retrieve a distant third ball himself. The distant balls should be retrieved at the end of a game.

40. In any argument about *facts* it should be remembered that the position of each side has equal weight. For example, regardless of how sure you are that the score is thirty-forty, your opponent may be just as sure that it is forty-thirty (or five games to three versus four games all). One method of settling a score dispute is to go back to the last score on which there was agreement, then resume play from that point. If no agreement can be reached in a dispute, whatever the disagreement may be, it should be settled by tossing a racket. Certainly, it would be undesirable to have the players depart in a huff.

40.1. To eliminate arguments about the score the server should announce the set score (e.g., 5-4) prior to his first serve and the game score (e.g., thirty-forty) prior to serving each point. *This is important.*

40.2. No matter how obvious it may be to you that your opponent's shot is out, it may not be obvious to him. He is entitled to a prompt hand signal or call; give it to him.

41. You have had contact with the primary form of stalling when your opponent in an offical match purposely arrives 25 minutes late, hoping that those 25 minutes will have provided you with ample opportunity to tense up. Some opponents attempt an excessively long warm-up to achieve the same result. Another form of stalling is provided by the player who walks and plays at about one-third his normal rate, thereby, among other things, taking much of the fun out of the match. Another form is the excess time taken between games when the authorized delay is doubled due to extra toweling, drinking, taking of pills, and sitting down. Another form is the taking of time at the end of a 6-4 first set; the rules say play shall be continuous except for specified breaks, which do not include one at the end of the first set that ends on an even number of games. Another form is the server's waiting at the net—instead of going to the base line—while the receiver is retrieving a ball to give to him. Another form is taking more time than the authorized ten minute break at the end of the second set in a three-set match. Another is the starting of a discussion to permit a player to catch his breath. Another is the action of the receiver in clearing an out first service that doesn't need to be cleared, such as one that ends up six inches from the backstop. Another is bouncing the ball ten times before each serve. These are some of the more common forms of stalling, a type of gamesmanship aimed at upsetting an opponent. What is the answer to the problem? Again, like footfaulting, it is a matter of a player's personal honor system. From a practical view, if you try to outstall a staller you may upset yourself even more, and from an ethical view you may damage your own reputation. With

it all, you can be firm in waiting for a late opponent only a reasonable period (as you interpret the meaning of the word under the circumstances involved) before departing, and in other cases refusing to continue play without an official. The best players are not known as stallers.

41.1. If you opponent is a chronic footfaulter or makes a larger number of what you feel sure are bad calls, what should you do? There is only one answer: calmly call for an umpire and refuse to continue until the umpire arrives. While normally a player may not leave the playing area during a match, an expeditious visit to the referee to request an umpire is authorized. Incidentally, also authorized is a bona fide toilet visit.

41.2. Grunting (or other loud noises) can be the basis for a let or a hindrance, and should be avoided. Fortunately, a player can usually adjust to his opponent's grunting so that it does not become a distraction; unfortunately, grunting can be an annoyance to players on an adjacent court.

41.3. Don't enter a tournament and then withdraw when you discover some tough opponents have also entered. Don't be a cup hunter and search for tournaments where all the entrants will be of a much lower caliber than yourself. If you must default a match notify the referee at once so that your opponent may be saved a trip. If you withdraw from a tournament don't expect the return of your entry fee if your name appears in the draw.

42. When your serve hits your partner stationed at the net is it a let, fault, or loss of point? Likewise, what is the ruling when your serve before touching the ground hits an opponent who is standing *back* of the base line? The answers to these questions are obvious to anyone who knows the fundamentals of tennis, but it is surprising the number of players who don't know these fundamentals. All players have the responsibility of being familiar with the basic rules and customs. Further, it can be distressing to your opponent when he makes a decision in accordance with a rule and you protest with the remark: "Well, I never heard of that rule before!" Ignorance of the rules constitutes a delinquency on the part of a player and often spoils an otherwise good match.

43. What has been written here constitutes the essentials of "The Code," the summarization of procedures and unwritten rules which custom and tradition dictate all players should follow. No system of rules will cover every specific problem situation that may arise, but if players of good will follow the principles of The Code they should always be able to reach an agreement, at the same time making tennis a better game and more fun for all participants.

Reprinted with permission of Colonel Nick Powel

© N.E. Powel, 1981
Copies available from USTA,
Education and Research Center
729 Alexander Rd.
Princeton, N.J. 08540

USPTA Members

USPTA Members

If you wish to contact a USPTA professional in your area for instruction, please consult your telephone directory for address and telephone number. For further information regarding the USPTA or accredited members, write to national headquarters at this address:

Tim Heckler
USPTA
Saddlebrook, The Golf and Tennis Resort
P.O. Box 7077
Wesley Chapel (Tampa), Florida, 34249

ALABAMA

Anniston	Henry, Allan D
Auburn	Thomson, Hugh
Birmingham	Cascarano, Tom
Birmingham	Everly, Roger B
Birmingham	Herren, Wade L
Birmingham	Irwin, Scott Richard
Birmingham	Justice, Jack
Birmingham	Longshore, Leslie Jr
Birmingham	Moore, Ballard J
Birmingham	Morgan, Patricia A
Birmingham	Perrin, Patrick
Birmingham	Phillips, Chas D
Birmingham	Warren, Joan S
Blue Mountain	Gold Medal Rec. Products
Cullman	Swindoll, Keith
Cullman	Trinchitella, John Howard
Eufaula	Wise, John S
Fairhope	Overton, Wesley G
Florence	Vinson, Jack
Gadsden	Jacques, Ed
Gadsden	Stewart, Ernest (Buster)
Gadsden	Stewart, Paula
Glencoe	Loconto, Nancy
Guntersville	Sahag, Edmond R
Hokes Bluff	Sims, Tim D
Homewood	Badger, Charles
Hoover	Gardner, Coney
Huntsville	Dinwiddie, Rusty
Huntsville	Liston, Nancy L
Huntsville	Schiffman, Leo Jr
Huntsville	Tym, Bill
Huntsville	Warden, G E Jr
Killen	Edgar, James L
Mobile	Beaumier, Gaston
Mobile	Cook, Ronald A
Mobile	Cooper, Tom D Jr
Mobile	Cox, Ernest J
Mobile	Cox, James Newton
Mobile	Gray, Jeff
Mobile	Hilley, Greg
Mobile	Lubel, Marilyn
Mobile	Masterson, Lucy
Montgomery	Johns, James A
Montgomery	Lane, Charles A
Montgomery	Nieminen, Cecelia (CEC)
Montgomery	Roberson, Mike
Montgomery	Roberson, Mimi
Montrose	Bashinsky, Gayle H
New Hope	Holaday, Jan
New Hope	Holaday, Matthew
Selma	McWilliams, John H
Selma	Sewell, Bernard
Tuscaloosa	Keeney, Curtiss W
Tuscaloosa	Scott, Randy
University	Gaiser, Karin Sue
University	Heffernan, Peter

ALASKA

Anchorage	Lindgren, John A

ARIZONA

Bella Vista	Sheely, Thomas H
Carefree	Neuhart, David
Carefree	Schuler, Frank X
Chandler	Cheney, Brian
El Dorado	Phillips, Suzanne B
Fayetteville	Carrigan, Kathy
Fayetteville	Carrigan, Mike
Flagstaff	Carver, Kevin
Ft. Smith	Strassle, James
Hot Springs	Palafox, Victor A
Hot Springs Village	Burns, James P
Lake Village	Copete, Eddie
Little Rock	Kostin, Paul
Little Rock	Labat, Delane

Little Rock	New, Rick	*Alameda*	Coyne, Jim
Magnolia	Downs, Ann	*Alameda*	Murphy, Matthew P
Mesa	King, Mary Kennerty	*Altadena*	Whitfield, Greg
Morristown	Erie, Al	*Anaheim*	Burt, Jack Ed
N. Little Rock	Snively, Darrel D	*Anaheim*	Okizaki, Ronnie S
Peoria	Sarten, Beverly	*Apple Valley*	Grisham, James R
Phoenix	Allen, Jim	*Apple Valley*	Kruse, Gregory W
Phoenix	Blanchard, Mike	*APO San Francisco*	Pagano, Mijai
Phoenix	Brown, Russell Alan	*Aptos*	Owens, Devon
Phoenix	Byron, John	*Bakersfield*	Davidson, Andy
Phoenix	Cotten, Lucky	*Bakersfield*	Hodges, Alan
Phoenix	Douglas, William C	*Bakersfield*	Perreira, Gary
Phoenix	Eck, Bryan	*Barstow*	Brown, Theris
Phoenix	Fait, Joseph F	*Berkeley*	Brown, Alex
Phoenix	Howard, John	*Berkeley*	Saxton, Garrett M
Phoenix	Kelly, Jack	*Berkeley*	Shafer, Samuel R
Phoenix	Kilgard, Barbara	*Beverly Hills*	Olmedo, Alex
Phoenix	Michalko, Jack	*Bonsall*	Brillant, Philippe
Phoenix	Mickler, Carl Thomas	*Boulder Creek*	Bradley, Christopher
Phoenix	Mulligan, Mike	*Burlingame*	Reed, John M
Phoenix	Munsil, James	*Calabasas*	Heinberg, Craig
Phoenix	Ryan, Paul	*Calexico*	Armendariz, Jose
Phoenix	Vacchina, Michael X	*Camarillo*	Bryan, Wayne
Phoenix	Wilkinson, Michael G	*Campbell*	Sanfilippo, Charles
		Canoga Park	Mitchell, Patricia K
Phoenix	Young, Ray	*Canoga Park*	Mitchell, Robert (Bob)
Scottsdale	Arnold, Glenn G		
Scottsdale	Belken, Louis	*Canoga Park*	Morett, Don
Scottsdale	Breece, Tom	*Canoga Park*	Shoemaker, Kirk
Scottsdale	Druliner, George	*Canoga Park*	Stubblefield, Steve
Scottsdale	Hecht, Robert	*Cardiff by the Sea*	Bryant, John A
Scottsdale	Hoffman, Mark A	*Cardiff by the Sea*	Hightower, Don R
Scottsdale	Kanter, Dave	*Cardiff by the Sea*	Marvin, James C
Scottsdale	Lenoir, Bill	*Cardiff by the Sea*	Spies, Daniel A
Scottsdale	Nielson, Dean	*Carlsbad*	Mayer, Jim
Scottsdale	Van Dusen, Mary E	*Carlsbad*	Millikan, William B
Sun Lakes	Earle, Fred A Jr	*Carlsbad*	Peterson, Nels C
Tempe	Pittman, Anne M	*Carlsbad*	Rapp, David Erle
Tucson	Anderson, Gregory	*Carlsbad*	Segura, Pancho
Tucson	Bennett, Terry H	*Carlsbad*	Tilton, Art
Tucson	Blake, Anthony	*Carlsbad*	Williams, Rod
Tucson	Campbell, Donald Jr	*Carmel*	Batchelder, Philip
Tucson	Chotichuti, Adej	*Carmel*	Lehman, Gregory
Tucson	Ciulla, Sam	*Carmel*	Stanton, Doug
Tucson	Davis, John P	*Carmel Valley*	Drumheller, Ralph
Tucson	Dickenson, Donald J	*Carmel Valley*	Gardiner, John
Tucson	Feldhausen, E Brittin	*Carmichael*	Leles, John G
		Carmichael	Moulton, James S
Tucson	Hall, H Joseph	*Carson*	Perez, Manny
Tucson	Hardy, Craig	*Cathedral City*	Pachacki, Mark
Tucson	Hunt, Susan W	*Chico*	Runquist, Doug
Tucson	Leavitt, Genevieue	*Chula Vista*	Campbell, John (Jack) P
Tucson	Little, John M		
Tucson	Long, Dale H	*Citrus Heights*	Provines, Lt. Col. Jim
Tucson	Moreno, Andrew Matthew		
Tucson	Morse, Michael	*Claremont*	Coats, Ellis
Tucson	Murphy, Bill	*Corona Del Mar*	Bernstein, Robert Marc
Tucson	Newton, Edward B	*Coronado*	Daniels, Robert J
Tucson	Peterson, Norman	*Coronado*	Henreid, Mimi
Tucson	Pfordt, Katherine E	*Coronado*	McInerney, Robert E
Tucson	Present, Robert	*Coronado*	Meade, Pike
Tucson	Reffkin, Jim	*Costa Mesa*	Bogatay, Duke V
Tucson	Salant, Robb	*Costa Mesa*	Hirtler, Mark
Tucson	Schroeder, Pam J	*Costa Mesa*	Murry, Dennis M
Tucson	Shuman, Donald	*Costa Mesa*	Roobian, Lowery
Tucson	Touche, Perri S	*Cupertino*	Abalateo, Eric A
Tucson	Vasile, John	*Cupertino*	Roeske, Gary
Tucson	Yuhas, George F	*Cupertino*	Sharpe, John
W. Sedona	Landin, Bill	*Dana Point*	Lynch, Richard A
W. Sedona	Siegert, Gunter	*Danville*	Elliott, Mark
		Danville	Zwieg, John
		Davis	Atkinson, Doug
		Del Mar	U.S. Racquet Stringer
CALIFORNIA			
Agoura	Kerr, David W	*Diamond Springs*	Borowiak, Scott
Alameda	Ballard, Janis Sherer	*Downey*	Ashbrooke, Norman

El Cajon	Gomsi, Donald	Los Angeles	Elkins, Henri
El Cerrito	Bleckinger, Chuck	Los Angeles	Esse, Clayton J
El Granada	Kerhoulas, Dion P	Los Angeles	Everett, Silas K
Encinitas	Humphreys, Brad	Los Angeles	Greens, Philip
Encinitas	Kramer, Don	Los Angeles	Grossman, Jerry
Encinitas	Pursley, Peter	Los Angeles	Kramer, Jack
Escondido	Dollins, Dave	Los Angeles	Marz, Don
Escondido	Smith, Raymond E	Los Angeles	Montz, Frederick J M.D.
Fairfield	Young, Barry		
Fallbrook	Greenwald, Jan S	Los Angeles	Reedy, Dennis C
Flintridge	Stewart, Charles	Los Angeles	Saunders, Richard
Foster City	Aillery, Jerry	Los Angeles	Secunda, Al
Foster City	Miller, Stephen	Los Angeles	Spencer, Nancy
Fountain Valley	Moore, Cheryl Kunkel	Los Angeles	Stanley, William
		Los Angeles	Thurm, Andrew
Fountain Valley	Moss, Denis S	Los Angeles	Toley, George
Fountain Valley	Roth, Bill	Los Angeles	Wintroub, Barbara
Fremont	Cowan, Ada E	Los Gatos	Collins, Gordon
Fresno	Belman, Mark	Los Gatos	Darley, Charles F
Fresno	Doerner, Cynthia	Los Gatos	Marston, Arthur A
Fresno	Doerner, Peter	Los Gatos	Sunderland, Tim
Fresno	Jizmejian, Mike	Los Osos	Napoli, Michael
Fresno	Legler, Cuyler	Malibu	Drobnick, Louis III
Fresno	Roberts, Coby	Mammoth Lakes	Yorkey, Michael W
Gardena	Sportsman Intl (Suzuki)	Manhattan Beach	McQuady, Chuck
		Marina Del Rey	Allison, Ronald L
Glendale	Sanders, Phronie	Martinez	Draisin, Lee H
Glendale	Starleaf, Steve	Martinez	Guilfoyle, Rosalind
Granada Hills	Kerr, Edwin	Maywood	Worley, John
Granada Hills	Stewart, Pamela	Mendocino	Daoust, Penny C
Greenbrae	Phillips, Patty	Mendocino	Daoust, Robert
Half Moon Bay	Regan, Peter F	Menlo Park	Gould, Dick
Hermosa Beach	Parker, Bob	Menlo Park	Hyams, David S
Hermosa Beach	Whittle, Judy	Menlo Park	Kurnoff, Shirley
Hollywood	Butcher, Barry R	Merced	Hom, Kimberly J
Huntington Beach	Litrich, Robert	Merced	Vrana, Leo E
Huntington Beach	Paster, Patrick	Mill Valley	Peters, Jerry
Huntington Beach	Winn, Inc.	Mill Valley	Stewart, David W
Indian Wells	Wheatley, Robert Jr	Modesto	Collier, George J
Indio	Violette, Joseph D Jr	Modesto	Earl, Keith R
		Modesto	Earle, Fred A III
Irvine	Adams, Edward	Modesto	Kuntz, Gregory M
Irvine	Cady, Bill	Modesto	Lackey, Jack
Irvine	Hovde, Rebecca L	Modesto	Stanley, Larry D
Irvine	Moore, John W Jr	Modesto	Weir, Mark
Irvine	Petchul, Dane A	Monta Vista	Parker, Christine
Kentfield	Nelson, John M	Monterey	Ruff, Lt. David C
Kenwood	Riebel, Suzan	Montrose	Muscare, Michael
La Habra	Tiberg, Michael W	Morgan Hill	Hooks, Van W
La Jolla	Bacon, Robert C	Murrieta	Maples, Timothy
La Jolla	Bell, Greg	Napa	Jamison, Howard
La Jolla	Bond, William E	Napa	Stefanki, Steve
La Jolla	Mott, Stephen G	Napa	Stow, Tom D
La Jolla	Schroeder, F R (Ted)	Newport Beach	Brown, Vic
		Newport Beach	Burchett, Jay
La Jolla	Walts, Patricia	Newport Beach	Emerson, Roy
La Quinta	Mohler, Daniel B	Newport Beach	Hibbs, Kerry
Laguna Hills	Bard, Muriel A	Newport Beach	O'Shaughnessy, Julia E
Laguna Hills	Smith, Douglas John		
Lagunitas	Jilot, Russell	Newport Beach	Ray, Robyn
Laquinta	Cooper, Jackie	Newport Beach	Robins, Gregory J
Larkspur	Heckelman, Rod	Novato	Parkerson, Gregory W
Lodi	Chiene, Robert S		
Lodi	Solari, Jonathon J	Oakland	Kahn, Roger
Lodi	Tiffin, Steven	Oakland	Siegel, Linda
Lomita	DeYoung, Lee	Oceanside	Smith, Edward A
Long Beach	Boyle, Chris	Ojai	Nielson, Ron
Long Beach	Bray, Al	Olivenhain	Staats, Neal
Los Altos	Brennan, Frank	Orinda	King, Douglas S
Los Altos	Gulick, Edward S	Orinda	Murphy, Chet
Los Angeles	Arthur, Charles	Pacific Palisades	Schoop, Mary
Los Angeles	Bailin, Jonathan Lee M.A.	Palm Desert	Germain, Henry
		Palm Desert	Leoncio, Collas
Los Angeles	Brennan, John M	Palm Desert	Woods, Conrad
Los Angeles	Brown, Ulysses	Palm Springs	Goldsmith, Pamela
Los Angeles	Calhoun, Allen Ray	Palm Springs	Haas, Carol
Los Angeles	D'Avlan, Anna Maria	Palm Springs	Kast, Larry
Los Angeles	Dundis, Tom P	Palm Springs	Palcich, Stan

Palm Springs	Rose, William	*San Diego*	Perry, Robert M
Palm Springs	Schroeder, Carl	*San Diego*	Pigorsch, Mitchell
Palm Springs	Seymore, Jack E		Ben
Palm Springs	Smith, Kenneth E	*San Diego*	Poliakoff, Gaylee
Palm Springs	Sockolov, Maurice L	*San Diego*	Porzak, Melissa A
Palm Springs	Steidel, Ken	*San Diego*	Press, Ben
Palm Springs	Tamura, Stan	*San Diego*	Radtke, Dan
Palm Springs	Tovey, Perry	*San Diego*	Ray, Lynn L
Palo Alto	Delaney, William J	*San Diego*	Richardson, Dr.
Palo Alto	Jacobson, Rick		Edward
Pasadena	Davila, Fermin	*San Diego*	Rivera, Cindy
Pasadena	Hoag Company	*San Diego*	Scott, Sherry J
Pasadena	Jackson, Michael	*San Diego*	Smith, Christopher S
Pebble Beach	Briant, Andy	*San Diego*	Standlee, Scott
Playa Del Rey	Bellefeuille, Richard	*San Diego*	Steinhauser, Aaron
Porterville	Guevara, John L.	*San Diego*	Stewart, Patricia
Portola Valley	Beatty, Susan	*San Diego*	Temple, Ken
Portola Valley	Parker, Larry	*San Diego*	Thurston, Peggy L
Poway	Bennett, John H	*San Diego*	Walts, Kenneth
Poway	Navratil, Paul	*San Diego*	Wesson, Joe
Pt. Loma	Williamson, H Mace	*San Diego*	Wichary, Hans
Ramona	Askin, Margie Boone	*San Dimas*	Eugenio, Glen L
Ramona	Colton, David	*San Francisco*	Axtell, Lawrence
Ramona	Fuchs, Axel	*San Francisco*	Gilbert, Barry
Rancho Mirage	Casey, Mike	*San Francisco*	Mattimore, Patrick
Rancho Mirage	Smith, Bill Jr	*San Francisco*	Morales, Jose L
Rancho Mirage	Trabert, Tony	*San Francisco*	Moseley, Susan
Rancho Palos		*San Francisco*	N. California Tennis
Verdes	Winkler, Robert E		Assoc.
Rancho Santa Fe	Hathaway, Joe	*San Francisco*	Reese, J Weston
Rancho Sante Fe	Bennett, Dave	*San Francisco*	Shein, Keith
Redding	Sullens, Terry Lee	*San Francisco*	Tennis Outings
Redlands	George, Gary J	*San Francisco*	Washauer, Bill
Redlands	Verdieck, James E	*San Jose*	Davis, Craig
Redondo Beach	Abbey, Jeff	*San Jose*	Elices, Mark
Redondo Beach	Ellis, F Stan	*San Jose*	Fitzsimons, B
Redondo Beach	Klene, Brian C		Hashman
Redondo Beach	Little, Del	*San Jose*	Gildemeister, Diane
Redondo Beach	Lolley, Rodger	*San Jose*	Gildemeister, Fritz
Redondo Beach	Mackure, Joseph	*San Jose*	Romera, James
Rescue	Hawkins, Jeff	*San Jose*	Seandel, Dana
Riverside	Nelson, Michael J	*San Juan*	
Roseville	Schulman, Steven	*Capistrano*	Canfield, Robert B.
S. Pasadena	Leonard, H Thomas	*San Leandro*	Del Moral, Jorge
Sacramento	Fong, Dexter	*San Luis Obispo*	Phelps, Miguel A
Sacramento	Vosburgh, Bob	*San Marino*	Eisenhardt, Ted
Salinas	King, David F	*San Marino*	Risinger, Robert
San Bruno	Kasavage, Peter C	*San Mateo*	Thomas, John M
San Carlos	Kernan, Philip Jr	*San Rafael*	Fraser-Edwards
San Carlos	Robinson, Ken		Sports
San Carlos	Show, Jerry	*San Rafael*	Zahorsky, George
San Clemente	Lemberg, Barbara	*San Ramon*	Overstreet, Dick
San Diego	Ahrens, Shirl J	*San Ramon*	Schnarr, Joan
San Diego	Barnes, Van	*Santa Ana*	Baker, Robert A
San Diego	Barr, Bruce A	*Santa Ana*	Pate, Chuck Jr
San Diego	Bartoe, David	*Santa Ana*	Puzzo, Santo
San Diego	Beckett, Lisa M	*Santa Barbara*	Detrich, William
San Diego	Berner, Mark	*Santa Barbara*	Druckman, Gary
San Diego	Blankenship, Powell	*Santa Barbara*	Hutchison, Stuart
San Diego	Cadel, Sandy	*Santa Barbara*	Kinsella, John P
San Diego	Cheesebro, R Alan	*Santa Barbara*	Mousouris, Larry
San Diego	Collins, Ed	*Santa Clara*	Carroll, Patricia Ann
San Diego	Creagh, Timothy H	*Santa Margarita*	Vane, Robert Castle
San Diego	D'Acri, Rebecca	*Santa Monica*	Leblanc, Yvon
	Edles	*Santa Monica*	Middleton, Alice
San Diego	Galloway, Robert L	*Santa Monica*	Roberti, Bill
San Diego	Gerrick, H Renee	*Saratoga*	Babcock, Clay
San Diego	Grout, Montgomery	*Saratoga*	Stepovich, Arline
	B	*Sausalito*	La Rocca, Vincent
San Diego	Haber, Tony	*Seal Beach*	Boyle, Chuck
San Diego	Hignight, Joe	*Seal Beach*	Gibbons, Gary
San Diego	Johnson, Clay	*Seal Beach*	Sanderson, Peter
San Diego	Lopez, Angel	*Sherman Oaks*	Barr, Eugene
San Diego	Manni, Patricia L	*Sherman Oaks*	Doss, Douglas H
San Diego	Marquez, Liane	*Sierra Madre*	Howard, Nolie
San Diego	Matthews, Jack E	*Solana Beach*	Austin, David
San Diego	McGuire, Hilary	*Solvang*	Laver, Rod
San Diego	McPherson, Robert	*Spring Valley*	Sarten, Randall
	B	*Stanford*	Van Der Linden,
			Dirk

Stockton	Andrews, Rich
Studio City	Hampshire, Karen Leigh
Suisun	Cello, Philip C
Summerland	Rurac, Vini
Sunnyvale	Kop, Rodney A
Sunnyvale	Newman, Richard B
Sunnyvale	Stever, Sherman R
Sunnyvale	Sunderland, Dexter
Sunnyvale	Young, Jan K
Tahoe City	Kohlmoos, John
Tahoe Paradise	Barnes, Thomas R
Tarzana	Sepel, Martin Van
Tarzana	Xanthos, Paul J
Thousand Oaks	Alm, Mitchell C
Thousand Oaks	Baer, Erick
Thousand Oaks	Mardyks, Harvey
Tiburon	Houston, Dave
Tiburon	Weston, John P
Topanga	Marsten-Shapiro, Margo
Torrance	Yonex
Tustin	Christofferson, Mark
Tustin	Luttrell, Howard M
Tustin	U.S. Sports Equipment
Twain Harte	Barbera, Felix
Vacaville	Hansen, Mark
Vancouver— V6J2P6	Bardsley, Tony
Van Nuys	Kleiman, Zachary
Van Nuys	Piper, Deborah
Van Nuys	Sie, Niesi
Van Nuys	Stoner, Michael
Visalia	Hofer, Doug
Visalia	Holm, Bob
W. Covina	Cianchetti, Bob
Westlake Village	Brown, Robin M
Westlake Village	McCarthy, Melinda (Mindy)
Woodland Hills	Byrne, Thomas M
Woodland Hills	Curtis, Phillip
Woodland Hills	Dawson, Dick
Woodland Hills	Jacobson, Herbert L
Woodland Hills	Mullen, Jean
Woodland Hills	Wagner, Dick
Woodside	Lowell, Jim
Woodside	Triolo, Jim M
Woodside	White, John
Yorba Linda	Lloyd, Hank

COLORADO

Aspen	Grinnan, Lew
Aurora	Loeb, Larry S
Aurora	Oakes, William G
Boulder	Bodam, C D
Boulder	Brown, David A
Boulder	Scott, Rob
Boulder	Walters, Terence E
Boulder	Williams, John C
Castle Rock	O'Brien, Boots
Colorado Springs	Bartz, Kenneth
Colorado Springs	Cuadra, Luis E
Colorado Springs	Heinicke, Victoria
Colorado Springs	Kono, Art H
Colorado Springs	Moll, Joe
Colorado Springs	Scott, Bob
Colorado Springs	Standiford, Larry D
Commerce City	Garcia, Ben
Denver	Brading, Carey
Denver	Flater, Roald H
Denver	Hall, Michael C
Denver	Lays, James E
Denver	Monahan, Thomas T
Denver	Moyle, Mark
Denver	Nelson, Jay B
Denver	O'Connell, John M
Denver	Phelps, Ward
Denver	Ray, David A
Denver	Smith, Scott
Dillon	Petter, Karl
Durango	Horvath, Gary
Durango	Peeples, Michael
Englewood	Courtney, Judy
Englewood	Pulver, George
Englewood	Romberg, Dave
Ft. Collins	Dragoo, M Alan
Ft. Collins	Lewis, Larry J
Ft. Collins	Sergi, John V
Golden	Brown, J Mark
Golden	Thompson, Joseph
Grand Junction	Stettner, Richard
Greeley	Cochran, James
Greeley	Ford, Scott A
Lakewood	Buchholz, Cliff
Lakewood	Jenkin, John
Littleton	Holt, Scott K
Littleton	Lance, Dawn Kimberly
Littleton	Ross, Randy
Littleton	Rupp, Ken
Littleton	Schwimmer, Alan
Littleton	Thomson, Arthur R
Longmont	Dawkins, Hardy
Parker	Hodsdon, Geoff
Westminister	Schumacher, Gregg
Wheat Ridge	Esmail, Dean O
Wheat Ridge	Loehr, James E

CONNECTICUT

Avon	Jutras, Peter
Bethany	Wilson, Praveen
Bethel	Donofrio, Rosaly M
Bloomfield	Slobin, Gerald L
Bridgeport	Carey, Tom
Bridgeport	Davis, Charles R
Brookfield	Stuart, J Michael
Canton	Taylor, Joel N
Cheshire	Caine, Daniel
Cheshire	Houle, Arthur E
Collinsville	Zysk, Robert
Cos Cob	Hayes, Leo V
Danbury	Abraham, Michael
Danbury	Bouquin, Joe
Danbury	Burns, Susan M
Danbury	Donofrio, Carrie
Danbury	Moran, Greg R
Danbury	Tierney, James E
Danbury	Waidelich, Alan W
E. Hartford	Bishop, Ben
Ellington	Kennedy, Daniel
Ellington	Uthgenannt, Ernie
Fairfield	Kraus, James
Fairfield	Sergio, Thomas
Fairfield	Shapiro, Jack M
Glastonbury	Arnold, Jeffrey H
Glastonbury	Bosworth, Warren
Greenwich	Ewing, Sheila
Greenwich	Rosengarten, Susanne Brody
Greenwich	Sobek, Joseph G
Greenwich	Stephens, James R
Hartford	Sutherland, George
Manchester	Casalino, Thomas
Manchester	Castleman, Bonnie
Manchester	Darling, Gloria
Meriden	Crone, Paul R
Meriden	Felix, Lois
Meriden	Stanton, Richard
Meriden	Walsh, Betty
Milford	Kindley, Catherine G

Mystic	Foster, Donald B
New Canaan	Callaway, Robert G
New Canaan	Gagon, Paul D
New Fairfield	O'Connor, Daniel F
New Hartford	Germer, Albert E III
New Haven	Felske, Peter
New Haven	Willinger, Steven
New Milford	McLean, George
Newington	Vieira, Peter T
Newtown	Fowler, David H
Newtown	Freeman, Betsy
Newtown	Sargeson, Richard J
Norwalk	Coyle, Doug
Norwalk	La Marche, Robert J
Norwalk	Pierce, Joseph
Norwalk	Scudder, Buddy
Norwalk	Tennis Magazine
Orange	Beers, Gary
Orange	Lufler, Henry S
Orange	Schweitzer, Jerry
Pawcatuck	Faulise, Jacques A P
Plantsville	Lapane, Leo H Jr
Ridgefield	Bengston, John A
Ridgefield	Dukes, J Terry
Riverside	Leon, Roberto
S. Windsor	Redmond, Jack
Simsbury	Berry, Eileen Kelly
Stamford	Harring, Donald M
Stamford	McHugh, Vincent
Stamford	Seminoff, John A
Stamford	Zermani, Gloria F
Stratford	Van Beverhoudt, Edward
Torrington	Werner, Dean
Wallingford	Russell, Richard W
Waterbury	Sims, Forrest W
W. Hartford	Billington, John R
W. Hartford	Garrett, Gene
W. Hartford	McClellan, W E Jr
W. Hartford	Smith, Sidney J
Westport	Baruch, Sanford
Wethersfield	Hutnick, Larry
Windsor	Reid, Timothy E
Windsor Locks	Crapo, Eric
Winsted	Swanton, Ray
Woodbridge	Flint, Ann
Woodbury	Frew, Peter A

DELAWARE

Bethany Beach	Kozlowski, Dave
Newark	Van Allen, Bruce
Rockland	Bennett, Robert C
Wilmington	Attinger, Stephen S
Wilmington	Harwick, Stephen
Wilmington	Tharp, F Scott

DISTRICT OF COLUMBIA

Washington	Grubbs, Ann C

FLORIDA

Altamonte Springs	Brennan, Laura
Altamonte Springs	DiFlumeri, Lucille
Altamonte Springs	Grasha, Ronald
Altamonte Springs	Horn, Jeffrey
Altamonte Springs	Stock, Robert
Apollo Beach	Apollo Racquets
Apollo Beach	Maharaj, Janet R
Apollo Beach	Maharaj, Saisnarine
Atlantic Beach	Jones, Gordon P
Bal Harbour	Buchko, Gregory W
Bartow	Burrus, Harry

Bay Harbor Island	Patrick, Charles
Bay Harbor Island	Walker, Herb
Belleair Bluffs	Obrakta, Donald
Belleair Shores	Kaiser, Donald G
Belleair Shores	Letzring, Howard
Boca Raton	Bezecny, Dagmar
Boca Raton	Booth, James
Boca Raton	Boutin, Robert Jr
Boca Raton	Brooke, Joseph E
Boca Raton	Cheeswright, Gregory A
Boca Raton	Fawcett, John
Boca Raton	Fischer, Alex R
Boca Raton	Fischer, Ineke V (Mrs.)
	Friedman, Mike
Boca Raton	Grammen, Michael S
Boca Raton	Gurney, Kenneth W Jr
Boca Raton	Hanley, Sue
Boca Raton	Kane, Jerry
Boca Raton	Kenny, Robert F
Boca Raton	Kerbis, Don
Boca Raton	Kraft, Whitney T
Boca Raton	Kraus, Edward W
Boca Raton	Latos, Steven D
Boca Raton	Merles, Elliott
Boca Raton	Miller, Elizabeth
Boca Raton	Nolan, Gene
Boca Raton	O'Brien, Jim
Boca Raton	Ocampo, Luis Carlos
Boca Raton	Petra, Craig
Boca Raton	Poske, Carl
Boca Raton	Ross, Mary
Boca Raton	Silver, Erik
Boca Raton	Sinett, Arthur
Boca Raton	Verzaal, Richard
Boca Raton	Withall, Ted P
Boca Raton	Woodcock, Warren
Boynton Beach	Brenner, Hank
Boynton Beach	Olenik, Dennis
Boynton Beach	Smith, Rhea D
Bradenton	Avilies, Samuel
Bradenton	Barr, Donald
Bradenton	Bolivar, Carolina
Bradenton	Bollettieri, Nick
Bradenton	Brandi, Andres V
Bradenton	Brooks, Chip
Bradenton	Cabrera, Cesar
Bradenton	Denyes, Lawrence W
Bradenton	Duncan, Michael D
Bradenton	Hart, C W (Chip)
Bradenton	Henderson, Michael
Bradenton	Jerome, John
Bradenton	Kelty, Timothy E
Bradenton	Knox, John Jr
Bradenton	Koechlein, Donald F
Bradenton	Moros, Julio
Bradenton	Olson, Daniel
Bradenton	Owens, Steve
Bradenton	Patrick, Michael
Bradenton	Phillips, Milton
Bradenton	Shoenberger, Del L
Bradenton	Thanas, Tony
Bradenton	Yokomatsu, Hisashi
Brandon	Maharaj, Sewsankar
Brandon	Maharaj, Wanda
Brandon	Seiferd, Mary E
Cape Canaveral	Tarry, Richard W
Cape Coral	Funk, Thomas H
Cape Coral	Robinson, Fred
Clearwater	Alloco, Dennis
Clearwater	Ekers, John A
Clearwater	Murray, Richard S
Clearwater	Wroten, Karen Meares

City	Name	City	Name
Clearwater Beach	Presti, Louis E	Ft. Pierce	Elwing, James R
Cocoa Beach	Heiss, John	Ft. Walton Beach	Evans, Leo
Coconut Grove	Gilmore, Rich	Ft. Walton Beach	Spears, Teri
Cooper City	Moussette, Gregory	Gainesville	Beeland, Steve
Coral Gables	Barry, Alan	Gainesville	Daglis, Tom
Coral Gables	Beauchamp, David N	Gainesville	Oransky, Michael
		Gainesville	Purs, Vija
Coral Gables	Cahill, Thomas	Grenelefe	Macci, Rick
Coral Gables	Cook, Jack E	Gulf Breeze	Cobia, George
Coral Gables	Hart, Doris		Clinton
Coral Gables	Heacock, Jim	Gulfport	Cobourn, Carol
Coral Gables	Kurtz, David B	Haines City	Baker, Benny
Coral Gables	White, Ray	Hallandale	Silverman, Al
Coral Springs	Boylan, Skip	Highland Beach	Howell, Robert
Coral Springs	Coyne, Betty Anne	Hollywood	Cooper, Martin
Coral Springs	Knauer, Michael P	Hollywood	Cooper, Robert E
Coral Springs	Madison, Dolly	Hollywood	Hunter, Scot L
Crystal River	Katz, Leo	Hollywood	Lewis, William (C W)
Dade City	Crosby, Thomas J	Hollywood	Markley, William N
Davie	Hoosty, Andreae K	Hollywood	Smithyman, Dan
Davie	Hoover, Richard A	Hollywood	Weinstein, Michael
Daytona Beach	Fasick, Marian C	Holmes Beach	Browne, Roger
Daytona Beach	Loy, James K	Indialantic	Basey, Lee
Daytona Beach	Meik, Colvin	Indian Harbor	
Daytona Beach	Summerfield, Sidney	Beach	Blanchette, Bud
Daytona Beach		Inverness	Barnes, Steven L
Shores	Maloney, Loraine	Islamorada	Harris, Gary P
Deerfield Beach	Centerbar, Richard	Jacksonville	Aguero, German J
Deerfield Beach	Ketterer, Ken S Jr	Jacksonville	Benjamin, J P III
Deerfield Beach	McFee, Anne Joffre	Jacksonville	Cox, Daniel
Deerfield Beach	Shapiro, Ron	Jacksonville	Hatfield, Mike
Deland	Heard, Jean A	Jacksonville	Lague, Ronald E
Deland	Oescher, Jim	Jacksonville	Lee, W Sperry Jr
Delray Beach	Bynum, William F	Jacksonville	Shattuck, Thomas
Delray Beach	Cunningham, Robert	Jacksonville	Spiller, Chip
Delray Beach	Foster, Ed	Jacksonville	Sprengelmeyer, Roy
Delray Beach	Foster, Michael E	Jacksonville	Vorwerk, Leo
Delray Beach	Goodman, Susan	Jacksonville	Voyles, Patrick
Delray Beach	Hahn, James	Jacksonville Beach	Kramer, Raphael W
Delray Beach	Lofgren, Bill	Jupiter	Smoliak, Rick
Delray Beach	Newman, Ken	Jupiter	Ullman, Mark W
Delray Beach	Olingy, Nancy	Key Biscayne	Apey, Patricio
Delray Beach	Overton, Wendy	Key Biscayne	Blanco, Carlos
Delray Beach	Rankin, Elizabeth W	Key Biscayne	Schwarte, Gisa
Delray Beach	Suurbeek, Astrid L	Key Largo	Ecuyer, Robert E
Destin	Guarachi, Fernando	Key West	Mager, Lloyd S
Englewood	Durham, Mark	Kissimmee	Kidd, Scott
Englewood	Rodgers, Robert A	Lake Wales	Smith, Cy Mitchell
Fernandina Beach	Bean, Scott D	Lake Worth	Buerkle, David
Ft. Lauderdale	Appelbaum, Michael	Lake Worth	Esser, William L III
Ft. Lauderdale	Brandt, David	Lake Worth	Jahn, Les
Ft. Lauderdale	Burns, Patti	Lakeland	Beerman, Dave Jr
Ft. Lauderdale	Craig, Shawn	Lakeland	Chambers, Betty
Ft. Lauderdale	Crawford, Thomas E	Lakeland	Jeffries, Ed
Ft. Lauderdale	Dempsey, James G	Largo	Betancur, Alvaro
Ft. Lauderdale	Doddridge, Bob	Largo	Brandi, Jane
Ft. Lauderdale	Dyser, Joseph	Largo	Burpee, Claude M
Ft. Lauderdale	Evert, James A	Largo	Hopman, Harry
Ft. Lauderdale	Floyd, Don	Largo	Hurtado, Jose
Ft. Lauderdale	Focus on Competition	Largo	Pettis, Leroy
		Largo	Rainville, Charles T
Ft. Lauderdale	Hanks, Benjamin	Lauderhill	Alvarado, Carlos
Ft. Lauderdale	Hoag, William D	Lauderhill	Golin, Robert H
Ft. Lauderdale	Kadera, Dean C	Lauderhill	Kesl, Gary
Ft. Lauderdale	Katterfield, Jim	Lauderhill	Lawrie, Don
Ft. Lauderdale	Krukiel, Thomas	Luaderhill	Martin, Douglas
Ft. Lauderdale	Narvin, Chuck	Lauderhill	Miller, Gary A
Ft. Lauderdale	O'Neal, Kathy	Lauderhill	Sassano, Robert
Ft. Lauderdale	Pierce M Kent	Lauderhill	Watson, Robert L
Ft. Lauderdale	Pleva, Richard L	Lauderhill	Webb, D Randy
Ft. Lauderdale	Prochaska, Arthur J	Lighthouse Pt.	Barr, Scott
Ft. Lauderdale	Rabinowitz, Robert	Lighthouse Pt.	Bernal, Jorge
Ft. Lauderdale	Rolley, Grant	Longboat Key	Eken, Bill
Ft. Lauderdale	Romanus, Fred	Longboat Key	Leary, Don J
Ft. Lauderdale	Sposa, Edward	Longboat Key	Sutherland, Becky
Ft. Lauderdale	West, Tony	Longwood	Fogarty, Ron
Ft. Lauderdale	Zieba, Sygmunt	Loxahatchee	Davidson, Richard Jr
Ft. Myers	Beardsworth, Jak	Lutz	Shannon, Robert L
Ft. Myers Beach	DeRitis, Anthony	Maitland	Meyers, Mrs. Mickey

Marco Island	Varoski, Albin Jr
Melbourne	Dickens, Mike
Melbourne	Holmes, Norman J
Merritt Island	Hilburn, Ronald
Miami	Alder, Beverley Ann
Miami	Allen, Jeffrey Eric
Miami	Amaya, Jim
Miami	Castillo, Francisco
Miami	Colina, Tomas A
Miami	Colson, James Frederick
Miami	Fales, Donna F
Miami	Garcia, Andy
Miami	Gardner, Lorraine E
Miami	Gonzalez, Emilio
Miami	Greenwood, Gabriel N
Miami	Gustafson, Thomas
Miami	Harbett, E John
Miami	Johnson, Merlin
Miami	Kuykendall, Anna
Miami	Lender, Karel Charlie
Miami	McDonald, James
Miami	Miller, Robert O Jr
Miami	Montana, Francisco
Miami	Moore, Girard W Jr
Miami	Moore, John W
Miami	Mulloy, Gardnar
Miami	Off, Roger Scott
Miami	Parks, William
Miami	Ponton, Stephen
Miami	Porter, Pat
Miami	Stamm, Dave
Miami	Stubbs, Robert D Jr
Miami	Van Bylevelt, H C
Miami	Wycoff, Norman Douglas
Miami Beach	Calhoun, Guy R
Miami Beach	Mignolet, A J
Miami Beach	Szucs, Joseph
Naples	Beale, Eddie
Naples	Brandon, James
Naples	Cabiness, Gregory
Naples	Devendorf, John J
Naples	Eddy, Christine
Naples	Eisenberger, Charles
Naples	Gibbons, Dale
Naples	Kerstetter, James
Naples	Levy, Edgar
Naples	Lewis, Walter J
Naples	Martin, Don
Naples	Mass, Igor
Naples	Minarich, Peter
Naples	Norris, Ted L
Naples	Payne, Griff
Naples	Vines, Jean B
Naples	Watson, Gordon
Naples	Welsh, Candace
Naples	Welsh, Doug
N. Miami	Flanagan, Philip Alan
N. Miami	Keighley, Michael
N. Miami	Paradise Island, Ltd
N. Miami	Snelling, Jeff
N. Miami	Tennis Industry National
N. Miami Beach	Brown, Geoffrey
N. Miami Beach	Buxby, Martin
N. Miami Beach	Deming, Richard
N. Miami Beach	Eddy, David
N. Miami Beach	Greenberg, Jacob
N. Miami Beach	Herman, James
N. Miami Beach	Rakusin, Ben
N. Miami Beach	Stolle, Fred
N. Palm Beach	McCutcheon, Robert D
New Smyrna Beach	Holley, David E

Newport Richey	Lufler, William C
Ocala	Stephens, Todd
Oldsmar	Harner, Mark
Oldsmar	Kirsten, Denis
Oldsmar	Kirsten, Nancy
Orange Park	Aragon, Leon
Orange Park	McDaniel, H Joseph
Orlando	Csandli, Joe
Orlando	Hayes, Linda C
Orlando	Meyer, Chris
Orlando	Rountree, John
Orlando	Tantalo, Victor
Orlando	Tietjen, William H
Orlando	Whitaker, Larry
Orlando	Whitehouse, James
Ormond Beach	Braunstein, Barbara
Ormond Beach	Janovsky, Dale
Ormond Beach	Poort, Douglas
Palm Beach	Hemingway, Peter R
Palm Beach	Thaxton, King
Palm Beach Gardens	Boggs, David C
Palm Beach Gardens	Faulkner, Patricia R
Palm City	Baldwin, Michael B
Palm City	Grossman, Bob
Palm City	Noel, Kenneth
Palm Coast	Grimes, Gregory V
Palm Coast	McClain, Leslie
Palm Coast	Vidamour, James H
Palm Harbor	MacDonald, John R
Palm Springs	Sloan, Bob
Panama City	Palafox, Gustavo
Pembroke	Mason, Mark P
Pembroke Pines	Mason, Patrick Lee
Pembroke Pines	McMahon, Mark
Pembroke Pines	Murphy, Jerry
Pembroke Pines	Revman, Abe
Pensacola	Alvarez, Mario H
Pensacola	Balfour, Elizabeth
Pensacola	Booth, Douglas W
Pensacola	Boyette, Nancy E
Pensacola	Carson, Ralph
Pensacola	Grafton, Charlene
Pensacola	Leatherwood, David
Pensacola	Reimer, Victor
Pensacola	Robinson, Martin E
Pensacola	Sakey, Brian
Pineland	Fitzhugh, Ed
Pinellas Park	Wolf, Bill R
Plantation	Adler, Paul
Plantation	Coffman, Lowell
Plantation	Glassman, Phil
Plantation	Hoffner, Scott K
Plantation	Kay, Joel
Plantation	Poindexter, Robert A
Plantation	Zwetchkenbaum, Peter M
Plantation Key	Dunham, Jack
Pompano Beach	Deege, Al
Pompano Beach	Katz, Marilyn
Pompano Beach	Kenney, William M
Pompano Beach	Swanson, Charles E
Pompano Beach	Tierney, James
Pompano Beach	Walker, Harry
Pompano Beach	Kirk, J F Jr
Pompono Beach	Valanos, Constantine
	Walters, Jerry L
Ponte Vedra	
Ponte Vedra Beach	Mincek, Zdravko
Port Charlotte	Jones, Ted E
Port Richey	Durrance, Gary
Punta Gorda	Cross, Jennie O
Riviera Beach	Horne, Jimmie H
Royal Palm Beach	Hall, Christopher
Royal Palm Beach	Ross, Stan
Ruskin	Davis, Anne W

S. Miami	Sanchez, Carmen	Titusville	Ouellette, Ken
S. Miami	Solow, Jon	Treasure Island	Lester, Kenneth S
Sanford	Maliczowski, Doug	Treasure Island	Wray, Donald W
Sanibel	Kridle, James R	Venice	Baker, Phillip W
Sanibel	Parker, Gregory L	Venice	O'Connor, Paul X
Sanibel Island	Scheb, Paula S	Vero Beach	Calhoun, James R
Sarasota	Guerin, Artie	Vero Beach	Cole, James Allen
Sarasota	Harrington, Chris	Vero Beach	Horizon
Sarasota	Harris, Rodney R		Sportsystems of Fl
Sarasota	Herschel, A J Bob		Inc
Sarasota	Houssein, Sayed A	Vero Beach	Jarvis, Mally
Sarasota	Jones, J Gregory	Vero Beach	Layton, Steven L
Sarasota	Jones, Martha S	Vero. Beach	McCarthy, Kevin P
Sarasota	Koutras, Christine	Vero Beach	Rahaley, Michael
Sarasota	Langer, John H	Vero Beach	Robb, Bayard Van R
Sarasota	Lawrence, John R	Vero Beach	Roup, Donna S
Sarasota	Luxembourg, Bob	Vero Beach	Schwartz, Roger A
Sarasota	Maharaj, Gewan	W. Palm Beach	Bochte, James W
Sarasota	Maharaj, Susan	W. Palm Beach	Erbe, Kevin F
Sarasota	McNichols, Robert J	W. Palm Beach	Garo, Spence
Sarasota	Morgan, Jay	W. Palm Beach	Gornto, Mitch
Sarasota	Morlock, Thomas R	W. Palm Beach	Macbeth, Ted
Sarasota	National Tennis	W. Palm Beach	Paganini, Thomas
	Academy	W. Palm Beach	Spiller, Ernie
Sarasota	Richards, Robert A	W. Palm Beach	Stiff, Judith A
Sarasota	Richardson, Daniel	W. Palm Beach	Walters, Shelley
Sarasota	Sheesley, Brian		Cabell
Sarasota	Simonetta, Joseph	Wesley Chapel	Heckler, Tim
Sarasota	Towner, Wesley C	Wesley Chapel	Saddlebrook Resort
Sarasota	Vieira, G Luiz	Wilton Manors	Allshouse, Susan E
Sarasota	Wagstaff, Kenneth	Wilton Manors	Le Vant, Dixon J
	R	Windermere	Harris, Todd L
Sarasota	Weldon, Michael	Winter Haven	Beeland, Maggie M
Sebring	Arner, Robert	Winter Haven	Fitzpatrick, Jim
Sebring	Lesh, Lona M	Winter Park	Copeland, Norman
Seminole	Serban, Costel		N
Sorrento	Harned, Russell W	Winter Park	Eschbach, Philip
Spring Hill	Weinheimer, Fred	Winter Park	McCarthy, Kevin W
St. Augustine	Craig, Sheryl S	Winter Park	Schunk, Sandy
St. Augustine	Scott, Peter L	Winter Springs	Anderson, Timothy
St. Augustine			
Beach	Swope, L Franklin		
St. Petersburg	Austin, Bill		
St. Petersburg	Beem, David M	**GEORGIA**	
St. Petersburg	Sullivan, Dan J	Alpharetta	Brenner, William M
St. Petersburg	Trombley, Alice	Alpharetta	Jones, Cynthia
St. Petersburg	Zinn, Michael Dean	Alpharetta	Ouellette, Lucia
St. Petersburg		Athens	Magill, Dan
Beach	Barrancotto, Jim	Atlanta	Amaya, George
St. Petersburg		Atlanta	Bator, Zachry M
Beach	Payberg, Sally	Atlanta	Bodin, Rick
St. Petersburg		Atlanta	Cohen, Natalie
Beach	Thiele, Frank H III	Atlanta	Cooper, Deborah
	(Trey)	Atlanta	Fuller, Thayer S
Stuart	Bowman, Dr. P I	Atlanta	Grant, Bitsy
Stuart	Butchee, Joseph K	Atlanta	Hardcastle, James
Stuart	Elliott, Dan S		R
Stuart	Falkenburg, Tom	Atlanta	Hoblitzell, Woody
Stuart	Froehling, Frank	Atlanta	Howell, Peter D
Stuart	Harper, Brian	Atlanta	Hunt, James P
Stuart	Henderson, Scott	Atlanta	Jarvis, Paul
Stuart	Jenkins, David	Atlanta	Johnson, Walter R
Sunrise	Rowntree, Hardy D	Atlanta	Kelly, Julia
Tallahassee	Eckhardt, Peter F	Atlanta	Laughlin, James S
Tallahassee	Long, Allen R	Atlanta	Letts, Michelle
Tallahassee	Zolin, Jonathan R	Atlanta	Lowe, Jack
Tampa	Barrett, Tim	Atlanta	Newman, Fran
Tampa	Bedingfield, Sherry	Atlanta	Phelan, Joseph P III
	Ann	Atlanta	Sherby, Martin G
Tampa	Crowne, Jeffrey S	Atlanta	Troy, Wendell Jr
Tampa	Diaz, Juan	Atlanta	White, Charles A
Tampa	Jannone, Michael	Atlanta	Witten, Erik
Tampa	Pero, George T	Augusta	Ellis, Charlie
Tampa	Posada, Emilio A	Augusta	Ramsay, Helen G
Tampa	Taylor, Spafford	Canton	Evans, Pride A
Tampa	Williams, B Marsha	Clarkston	Snyder, Kathy
Tequesta	Cikigil, Bertran	College Park	Sasseville, Robert
Titusville	Hoctor, Michael J	Columbus	Banaszak, Henry J
Titusville	Knatz, Gerard A	Columbus	Dow, Robert A

Columbus	Scott, Terry	Honolulu	Somerville, John W
Cornelia	Robinson, William W	Honolulu	Thompson, Fred B III
Covington	Smith, Duane		
Dalton	Valleriano, Gary	Kahului	Maushardt, Rhonda J
Decatur	Campbell, Jeff		
Decatur	DeCubas, Carlos	Kailua	Fanning, Richard L
Decatur	Wilmot, Garry	Kameulo	Bondallian, Dina
Dublin	Martin, J T	Kaneohe	Skillicorn, Mark
Duluth	Powell, Beverly	Kihei, Maui	Van Steen, Tony
Duluth	Whitworth, Pat	Lahaina, Maui	Montez, Tony
Dunwoody	Stanfield, Andrew	Lahaina, Maui	Anderson, Wayne
Dunwoody	Waid, Richard L	Lahaina, Maui	Bard, Donald G III
Dunwoody	Waters, Jack	Lahaina, Maui	Powell, Nick G
Fortson	Hatfield, Archie E	Lihue, Kauai	Blacke, William F
Gainesville	Bernard, Randy E	Miliani	Briston, William D
Gainesville	Primrose, Graham	Molokai	Neils, Herbert
Jasper	Stotz, Jonathan	Pearl City	Kraesig, Jerry
Lithonia	Sutter, Mark A		
Macon	Benner, James W		
Macon	Earnhart, Ramsey		
Macon	McClure, Ken	ILLINOIS	
Macon	Payne, Gloria A	Addison	Anderson, Randy
Macon	Peek, Leslie H	Arlington Heights	Anderson, Judith A
Marietta	Baskin, Jerry C	Arlington Heights	Kust, Robert N
Marietta	Carter, E V	Barrington	Dickenson, Diane S
Marietta	Gardner-Reese, Pat	Barrington	Doessel, James
Marietta	Harvey, Michael A	Barrington	McKenna, Donna
Marietta	Hunt, Anthony	Barrington	Morgan, H Steve
Marietta	Neugebauer, Dunn	Barrington	Shogren, Carol Ramsey
Marietta	Wrege, Julia B		
Nelson	Cook, Thomas D	Barrington	Talbot, Lynne D
Norcross	Lyon, Lynn M	Belleville	Huffman, Dr. Joseph Jr
Norcross	Peavy, Jim		
Peachtree City	Bristol, David N	Blue Island	Muir, David A
Peachtree City	Davis, James J	Broadview	Sorensen, Bob
Rome	Carver, Nell	Broadview	Zak, Tom
Roswell	Brady, Cindy	Brookfield	Lehotsky, William A
Roswell	Daffin, Robert C	Buffalo Grove	Breckenridge, Bob
Roswell	Grover, George	Burr Ridge	Jedlo, Thomas S
Roswell	Raby, Clark D	Carbondale	Le Fevre, Dick
Roswell	Sheffield, John B	Champaign	Groppel, Jack L Ph.D.
Roswell	Smolenski, Harold		
Roswell	Stephens, Randy	Champaign	Kraft, Robert
Savannah	Coggins, Paul W	Chatham	Sipka, Andrew
Savannah	De'Lettre, Daniel M	Chicago	Amato, John T
Savannah	Hunt, Howard L	Chicago	Baladad, Raymond
Savannah	Norwich, Wallace J	Chicago	Blackburn, Les
Savannah	Ouzts, Bill	Chicago	Cahnman, Ray
Savannah	Stone, William J (Bill)	Chicago	Chenoweth, Christie Jo
Sea Island	Anderson, Richard	Chicago	Cummings, Kevin J
Sea Island	McLean, David S	Chicago	Dlugie, Perry S
Smyrna	Edenfield, Jim R	Chicago	Draska, Steven C
St. Simons Island	Maharaj, Vishnu	Chicago	Edwards, Helyn M
St. Simons Island	Sapp, Norman S	Chicago	Flesch, James H
Stone Mountain	Ramey, Garry	Chicago	Fortino, Joe
Tucker	Brocksmith, Jack	Chicago	Fotinos, Antoinette
		Chicago	Gallagher, Steve
		Chicago	Grant, Angela I
		Chicago	Hodgskin, Donald R
		Chicago	Huang, Bob
HAWAII		Chicago	Imala, Immanuel E
Ewa Beach	Beyster, Ed	Chicago	Jackson, Wilbert
Honolulu	Alexander, Berk	Chicago	Kersjes, Thomas
Honolulu	Bartlett, James	Chicago	Kutzen, Marilyn
Honolulu	Burwash, Peter	Chicago	Lott, George
Honolulu	Cundall, Ann	Chicago	Maytnier, Chris
Honolulu	Cunningham, Phil	Chicago	Meredith, Simon
Honolulu	Graham, Sue	Chicago	Moore, Charles W
Honolulu	Hakman, Doris	Chicago	Ratliff, Bill D
Honolulu	Hall, Larry B	Chicago	Rodriguez, Phillip R
Honolulu	Hubbard, Jerry	Chicago	Scott, Christopher C
Honolulu	Kawada, Henry H	Chicago	Seiffert, Jane M
Honolulu	Knappmann, Karl	Chicago	Simms, K W
Honolulu	Mauch, Thomas	Chicago	Skurdall, Barbara
Honolulu	Moon, Barney	Chicago	Stiltz, Matt
Honolulu	Peter Burwash International	Chicago	Susz, Paul
Honolulu	Prior, Tim	Chicago	Walker, Tommie L
Honolulu	Schwitters, Jim	Chicago	Watkins, Michael F

Clarendon Hills	Sartore, Jack	Northbrook	Maxwell, Barry S
Crestwood	Alletto, James	Northbrook	Schwartz, Ronald J
Crystal Lake	Herrick, Walter Jr	Northbrook	Shockley, Helen
Crystal Lake	Johnson, William C (Bill)	Northfield	Anderson, Keith
Crystal Lake	Pasco, Stephanie J	Oak Forest	Rimkunas, Grazina E
Crystal Lake	Schunk, Chuck	Oak Forest	Stearns, Pete
Danville	Simpson, N Scott	Oak Park	Moosbrugger, Rev. Ed
Darien	Ceranec, Martin		
Darien	Dunlap, Tom	Orland Park	Villarete, Jose C
Deerfield	Cisneros, Carlos	Palatine	Greene, Robert L
Deerfield	Davis, W Hughes	Palatine	Greer, Lewis M
Deerfield	Gluck, Geoffrey S	Palatine	Nyquist, Rex
Deerfield	Morrison, Charles	Palos Heights	Wideikis, George
Deerfield	Sheftel, Charles L	Park Forest	Gothard, Sylvia A
Deerfield	Smith, J Matt	Park Forest	Peterson, E Glen
Deerfield	Stap, Jake	Park Ridge	Farrell, Michael E
Deerfield	Wild, Stephen	Park Ridge	Lathrop, Donald S
Deerfield	Zalinski, Stephen J	Park Ridge	Thompson, Edwin J
Downers Grove	Enge, Charles	Peoria	Duboff, David L
Downers Grove	Kramer, Jay	Peoria	Greenwood, Geoff
Elmhurst	Barry, John W	Peoria	Price, Mike A
Elmhurst	French, Janet	Peoria	Vaughan, Kenneth
Elsah	DeLaney, Lyn Gerber	Peru	Hibben, Stephen M
		Prospect Heights	Ball, Jean
Elsah	Gerber, E Lawrence	Richton Park	Newberry, Mark
Evanston	Carvell, Allan C	River Grove	Shafer, Robert
Evanston	Robbins, Ralph	River Grove	Wilson Sporting Goods
Evanston	Sacks, Franklin A		
Flossmoor	Larned, Gardner	Rockford	Miller, Mike
Fox Lake	Gordon, Edward T	Rolling Meadows	Association Group Admn.
Glen Ellyn	Heidron, Patti Lee		
Glencoe	Harris, Miles	Rolling Meadows	Karasick, Arlene
Glenview	Birnbaum, David A M.D.	Rolling Meadows	McKenna, Patrick
		S. Holland	Martin, Karen
Granite City	Rusick, William A	Savoy	Kernodle, Michael Wayne
Gurnee	Torricelli, Paul		
Hazel Crest	Hayne, Webb	Savoy	Pecore, Linda D
Highland Park	Bozzo, Barbara	Schaumburg	Bearby, Mark J
Highland Park	Bushala, Joseph	Schaumburg	Gordon, Theodore R
Highland Park	Fink, George C	Schaumburg	Kennedy, Owen
Highland Park	Horwitch, Linda (Mrs.)	Schaumburg	Morgan, Jay S
		Schaumburg	Smith, Warren
Highland Park	Kammann, James L	Skokie	Baer, Michael
Highland Park	Tilsch-Eastman, Susan	Skokie	Carvell, Cale
		Springfield	Bauer, Dennis J
Hinsdale	Aldworth, Peter	Springfield	McCain, Dave
Hinsdale	Head, James R	Springfield	Morse, Glenn
Hinsdale	Henry, Kathe	Sterling	Wolens, Marc
Hinsdale	Stocker, James H	Streamwood	Musgrave, James
Hoffman Estates	Doerer, Nancy Lee	Streamwood	Von Boeckmann, William
Hoffman Estates	Marchese, Fred		
Homewood	Moe, Linda E	Tinley Park	Munson Floyd
Homewood	Muskievicz, Wayne	Urbana	Lilienthal, Jeffrey
Joliet	Gillman, Kit P	Vernon Hills	Johnson, Richard M
Joliet	Weitendorf, Holly	Vernon Hills	Kaplan, David Tai
Lagrange	Love, James R	W. Dundee	Miller, Lewis R
Lake Bluff	Iftekaruddin, Syed	Wauconda	Steiner, Charles
Lake Forest	Banford, Mark A	Waukegan	Laverty, Lance
Lake Forest	Felipez, Rick	Waukegan	Pregracke, Celeste
Lake Forest	Ferguson, Friedel	Westchester	Kolis, Timothy
Lake Forest	Ferguson, Thad	Western Springs	Nemecek, Paul M
Lake Forest	Lyden, Joseph A	Westmont	Cote, Richard
Lake Forest	Stap, Susan	Westmont	Prado, Manuel
Lake Forest	Swenson, Kathryn H	Wheaton	Sember, Michael D
Lake Forest	Workman, Rick	Wheeling	Chapman, Steven R
Libertyville	Wu, Frank Ph.D.	Wheeling	Cisneros, Oscar
Lincolnshire	Wilde, Mark	Willowbrook	Callahan, Bill
Lincolnwood	Schroeder, Rod	Wilmette	Golden, Abe
Matteson	Ventress, Andy	Wilmette	Levis, Walter
Matteson	Ventress, Tena Ann	Winnetka	Birnbaum, Asher J
Melrose Park	Lincoln Standard	Winnetka	Buerger, Carlton F
Moline	Hollander, Jack	Winnetka	Foreman, Frederick L
Morton Grove	Grant, Patrick A		
Mt. Prospect	Bachmann, Raymond	Winnetka	Olson, Dan
	Brown, Marcia	Zion	Buksa, David M
Naperville			
Normal	Whitman, James		
Northbrook	Leighton, Charles H		

INDIANA

Anderson	Hammel, Kendel
Anderson	Scott, Galen
Bloomington	Greer, H Scott
Carmel	Power, Bill Jr
Elkhart	Richter, Karleen
Evansville	Fane, Kevin M
Evansville	Weber, John P (Chip)
Evansville	Yahia Gregory
French Lick	Blankenbeker, Bill J
French Lick	O'Connell, Michael
Ft. Wayne	Heathman, Ron
Grandview	Hazlett, Anna
Highland	Granger, Mary L
Indianapolis	Brown, Scott P
Indianapolis	Brune, Edward I
Indianapolis	Gill, David M
Indianapolis	Gill, Paul D
Indianapolis	Lowe, John W (Jack)
Indianapolis	Mattingly, Thomas
Indianapolis	Phipps, Tyra
Indianapolis	Thomas, Paul M
Kokoma	Hobbs, William Paul Jr
Merrillville	Primer, Charlotte
Michigan City	Brooks, Ronald A
Muncie	Shull, James D
Munster	Peoples, Shirley
New Albany	Endris, Lou Ellen
New Albany	McCorkle, David
Newburgh	Cash, Douglas R
Rockville	Rowe, Doug
South Bend	Doyle, Monica
Terre Haute	Hopkins, John Daniel
Valparaiso	Manigault, Juan A
Valparaiso	Mesches, Bruce
Winona Lake	Beeson, Joseph E
Zionsville	Petticrew, Paul Scott

IOWA

Burlington	Murphy, Randall
Cedar Falls	Vandeventer, David
Cedar Rapids	Loomis, James
Davenport	Smallfield, John
Des Moines	Bauer, Ted P
Des Moines	Goplerud, John B
Des Moines	Hamilton, Scott A
Dubuque	Bissell, Fred
Dubuque	Gallas, Dennis
Dubuque	Sprengelmeyer, Bob
Iowa City	Klotz, Don
Okaboji	Regan, Bruce W

IDAHO

Boise	Alexander, George E
Boise	Chandler, Barbara
Boise	Haggerty, Leslie
Hayden Lake	Nosworthy, Kathleen M

KANSAS

Fairway	Guilfoil, Bridget
Hutchinson	Bietau, Steve
Kansas City	Clow, Ken P
Lenexa	Muir, Robert
Manhattan	Snodgrass, Stephen E
Overland Park	Bregin, John J Jr
Overland Park	Dickinson, Roscoe
Overland Park	Guilfoil, Bill
Overland Park	Haas, Charles (Chuck)
Overland Park	Hansen, Christopher
Overland Park	Waltz, John
Prairie Village	Hamilton, Sara L
Shawnee	Thies, David
Shawnee Mission	Pekich, Steve Jr
Shawnee Mission	Silbersher, Paul C
Topeka	Smith, Frederick B Jr
Topeka	Van Winkle, Rick
Wichita	Luoma, John R
Wichita	Morrison, Sam
Wichita	Moxham, Tony
Wichita	Snyder, Darrel L
Wichita	Webster, Mervyn

KENTUCKY

Benton	Dotson, Jamie K
Crestwood	Hart, Pamela S
Dayton	Prigge, Nick
Highland Heights	Klein, Roger
Hopkinsville	Bilotta, Vincent
Lexington	West, Thomas R
Louisville	Cooper, Charles R
Louisville	Davis, Howard
Louisville	Garner, James F
Louisville	Love, Bob
Louisville	McGraw, Tom G
Louisville	Olins, Andris
Louisville	Saacke, Charles W (Chuck)
Louisville	Stephenson, Greg
Louisville	Walker, Wm Carr
Murray	Purcell, Bennie
Murray	Purcell, Del A
Owensboro	Ramey-Ford, Joan
Paducah	Heflin, Larry J
Paducah	Rowton, Paul E

LOUISIANA

Alexandria	Stephenson, Douglas W
Baton Rouge	Albertine, James G Jr
Baton Rouge	Anders, Ray
Baton Rouge	Carter, Steve
Baton Rouge	D'Aquin, Thomas L
Baton Rouge	Higgins, Michael F
Baton Rouge	Layman, Joe
Baton Rouge	Longmire, David A
Baton Rouge	Pendergraft, B J
Baton Rouge	Shapter, Allen
Baton Rouge	St. Martin, Eugene C Jr
Baton Rouge	Weber, Diana
Bossier City	Bradshaw, Robert D
Gretna	Daugherty, Steven M
Hammond	Clark, George
Kinner	Durham, Andrew H
Lafayette	Driscole, Al
Lafayette	Fenasci, Ronald F
Lafayette	Hoge, Robert
Lake Charles	Chamberlain, Randy
Metairie	McGrath, Clay
Metairie	Schmidt, John R
Metairie	Streeck, Elliott
Monroe	Marks, Peter
Natchitoches	Paz, Walter W
New Iberia	Klear, Pete
New Orleans	Apffel, Rick
New Orleans	Campbell, Harvey D
New Orleans	Partridge, Wade

New Orleans	Sack, Lester M Jr	Davidsonville	Zeller, Brent
New Orleans	Schweppe Depaolo, Sally	District Heights	Davis, Eddie
		Easton	Hertelendy, Barbara L
New Orleans	Smith, Jeffrey L		
New Orleans	Sutherland, Susan	Easton	Mars, George N
New Orleans	Weiss, Dr Juan	Federalsburg	Meenan, David B
New Orleans	Whaley, Thomas Lee III	Gaithersburg	American Court Service
Ruston	Bruley, Duane	Gaithersburg	Anderman, Robert
	Frederick	Gaithersburg	Dann, Shari
Shreveport	Brown, Chris	Gaithersburg	Howe, Glen M
Shreveport	Bunn, Stewart	Gaithersburg	Iriarte, Raul A
Shreveport	Bunn, Susan E S	Gaithersburg	Ruel, William
Shreveport	Higgins, Billy	Greenbelt	Harvey, Timothy R
Shreveport	Jantz, Kenneth W	Hagerstown	Har-Tru
Shreveport	Krause, Lynn	Hebron	Travers, C J
Shreveport	Livesay, Jimmy	La Plata	Worcester, Francis J
Shreveport	McCarter, Helene	Linthicum	Konigsberg Janie
Shreveport	Montgomery, Jerry	McDonogh	McKibbin, Marty
Shreveport	Pham, V Quan	Ocean City	Turner, Rennie T
Shreveport	Varela, Luis Fernando	Odenton	Borman, William R
		Potomac	Castillo, Gustavo
Slidell	Hunter, James	Potomac	Ehrenreich, Richard
Starks	Smith, Felix	Preston	Moldoch, William Jr
		Randallstown	Meng, Harry G
		Rockville	Babitz, Ed
		Rockville	Dichiara, Susan R
		Rockville	Killen, Terence James
MAINE		Rockville	Plaisance, Steven A
Bangor	Byram, Kenneth A	Rockville	Watson, Dan
Brunswick	Reid, Edward T	Rockville	Zatman, Eric
Gorham	Bearce, Chan	Salisbury	Burroughs, A Dean
Lewiston	La Rochelle, Ron	Silver Spring	Drilling, Fred W
Waldoboro	Cross, Hugo H	Silver Spring	Feldman, Sylvia
Waterville	Osbourne, Kendall	Silver Spring	Henkin, Mitchell
Yarmouth	Fleury, David G	Silver Spring	Mullen, Dean V
		Silver Spring	U.S. Handicap Tennis Assoc.
		Timonium	McGurrin, Joseph M
		Towson	Morrell, Lynn
MARYLAND		Towson	Van Middlesworth, Charles
Annapolis	Bayliss, Robert E		
Annapolis	Kiefer, Sheila Job	Williamsport	Deitchler, Joe
Annapolis	Quigley, Dennis S	Williamsport	Myers, Suzanne
Baltimore	Chazen, Sheldon		
Baltimore	Daniels, R Bruce		
Baltimore	Greenberg, Morton		
Baltimore	Hoffman, Adrienne		
Baltimore	Scheuermann, Lenny	**MASSACHUSETTS**	
		Agawam	Fein, Paul S
Baltimore	Schloss, Leonard	Allston	Hess, Daryl K
Baltimore	Smith, Larry	Allston	Yosinoff, Andrew
Baltimore	Syvrud, Knute	Amherst	Serues, Edward Joseph
Beltsville	Tompkins, George J		
Bethesda	Addie, Pauline Betz	Amherst	Spinek, Thomas R
Bethesda	Beeson, Thomas	Arlington	Canole, James W III
Bethesda	Hatten, Frank C	Arlington	Maskell, Sheryl
Bethesda	Mayer, Michael S	Beverly	Frost, William N
Bethesda	Pass, Robert N	Beverly	Martineu, Richard J
Bethesda	Ritzenberg, Allie	Beverly	Tiberio, Henry
Bethesda	Tidball, Steven	Boston	Coard, Errol I
Bethesda	Weise, Stephen W	Boston	Dubois, J Wesley
Bowie	Schweitzer, Don	Boston	Monroe, Donald L
Capitol Heights	Giles, Samuel L	Boston	Offner, Henry
Cheverly	Davis, Robert E	Boston	Pryce, Geoffrey
Chevy Chase	Adams, A Lee	Brewster	McDonald, Lloyd G
Chevy Chase	Adams, John A	Brighton	Lederman, Morton S
Chevy Chase	Henkin, Gary	Brighton	Raws, Beverly G
Chevy Chase	Ornstein, Suzanne	Brockton	Footjoy, Inc.
Chevy Chase	Washington Tennis Service	Brookline	Rodman, Franklin H
		Brookline	Rogers, Albert P
Coceysville	Batz, Clifford	Cambridge	McCarthy, John
Colora	Miller, Dusty (Ralph)	Cambridge	Royer, Candace
Columbia	Alexander, William W Jr	Cambridge	Welsh, Deborah K
		Canton	Dorsey, Paul B
Columbia	Broderick, Daniel	Canton	Powell, Alan D
Columbia	Salmon, Richard	Chelmsford	Boucher, Therese
Columbia	Sittig, Greg	Chestnut Hill	Coulter, Cheryl S

Chestnut Hill	Glenn, Thomas B
Chestnut Hill	Sims, Benny Joseph
Clinton	Prinos, Dennis C
Cohasset	Parks, Gail
Concord	Higgins, Gerald C
Concord	Lee, Jeffrey W
Cotuit	Maloy, John L
Framingham	Farricker, Myke
Framingham	Hamilton, William A
Framingham	Jordan, Mark
Framingham	Orr, Charles C
Framingham	Ratner, Steven
Framingham	Weinstock, Sheila
Franklin	Karoghlanian, Janice
Franklin	Karoghlanian, Robert
Georgetown	Hebert, Don
Gloucester	Murray, Avis R
Gloucester	Usher, Donald K Jr
Hanover	Mahler, L Bruce
Holden	Mott, Bill
Hyannis	Stening, Roger
Lee	Perry, John
Leominster	Mascitti, Samuel R
Lexington	Brown, Arnold
Lexington	Harvey, Geoffrey
Lexington	Lewitt, Michael A
Lexington	Thomas, Adolph
Lincoln	Barnaby, John M
Longmeadow	Griswold, Anne B
Longmeadow	Stephens, Carlene D
Longmeadow	Thorne-Thomsen, Roger
Lowell	Bodor, Steve J
Manchester	Chase, Neil
Manchester	Leduc, Edward
Marlborough	Campbell, Peter
Marlborough	Waintrup, Daniel
Marshfield	Gundlach, Wallace
Mattapan	Paige, Henry E
Medfield	Chambers, Ralph E
Middleboro	Renfrew, Charles M
Milford	Leclerc, Maurice
Millis	Graham, John (Jay)
Millis	Karoghlanian, Aram
Milton	Saul, Albert
Montague	Roberts, Manuel P
N. Amherst	Williams, Steven C
N. Dartmouth	Gilkey, Bob
N. Easton	Bridges, Robert A
N. Easton	Dunmead, Jack
Natick	Olson, Larry
Natick	Wall, Beverly R
Needham	Drake, William S
Needham	Sanders, Richard A
Newton	Brass, Sydney Dr.
Newton	Caycedo, Simon G
Newton	Volpe, A George
Newtonville	Sharton, Richard T
Northampton	Knox, David S
Norwell	Lavanchy, Stephen J
Peabody	Winer, Steven M
Provincetown	Busa, Christopher
Randolph	Goldman, Stephen
Rockland	Roach, James P
S. Dennis	Friend, Buzz
Salem	Maitland, Barbara
Scituate	Lynch, Jack
Scituate	Lynch, Peggy
Seekonk	Clarke, Paul F
Sheffield	McKenna, Jack (Edward)
Sherborn	Taylor, Clark R
Somerville	Johnson, Donna Jaquith
Springfield	Hughes, John P
Stockbridge	Ogden, Elliott
Sudbury	Hammel, Laury

Swampscott	Foley, John L
Swampscott	Reagan, R Joseph
Topsfield	Lechten, Robert
W. Roxbury	Blake, Richard A Jr
W. Roxbury	Chenell, Herbert Jr
W. Roxbury	Van Nostrand, Marion M
Walpole	Baldassari, Dominic
Watertown	Scianna, Joanne
Watertown	Swan, John E
Wayland	Izdebski, Paul
Wayland	Levitan, Walter M
Wellesley Hills	Fish, David R
Wellesley Hills	Howard, Evelyn
Weston	Gummere, Barbara
Williamstown	Sloane, Sean
Winchester	Corf, John R
Winchester	Thomas, Lloyd H Jr
Winchester	Totman, Bryan
Woburn	Baldassari, James
Worcester	Power, William P
Worcester	Gunterman, Peter S

MICHIGAN

Adrian	Gale, Mark K
Ann Arbor	Fischer, Jonathan E
Ann Arbor	Ware, Michael C
Battle Creek	Horton, James R
Battle Creek	Maddock, William J
Belleville	Wilke, Jeff L
Big Rapids	Schultz, Scott R
Birmingham	Brown, Donald Kenneth
Birmingham	Cullen, Keith A
Birmingham	Hainline, Jon S
Brighton	Hines, Chad
Cadillac	Taylor, Thomas R
Canton Twp	Hlady, Kerry
Cedar	Buck, James K
Dearborn	Berkheimer, Gerry
Dearborn	Schad, Mickey
Detroit	Graves, Louis
E. Lansing	Balasis, Taty
E. Lansing	Rutz, Earl Jr
Galesburg	Spann, Linda A
Grand Rapids	Hoffman, Mike
Grand Rapids	Marcus, Brian
Grand Rapids	Swidwa, Paul
Grosse Point Woods	Gelina, Marc R
Grosse Point Woods	Guastella, Aggie
Harbor Springs	Lester, H W
Holland	Anderson, Kirk
Holland	Japinga, William H
Huntington Woods	Simcina, Mark
Jackson	Perkin, Peter R
Kalamazoo	Webb, Andrew
Kentwood	White, Roy C Jr
Lansing	Ferman, Richard Jr
Lansing	Frew, Scott D
Lansing	Selke Susan V
Lapeer	Rincon, Gilberto
Livonia	Snyder, Dean
Madison Heights	Brady, R Todd
Madison Heights	Dombrowski, Anthony P
Midland	Cook, Steven C
Midland	Margoni, Dennis D
Oak Park	Karabell, Charles
Oak Park	Tookes, Allison K
Okemos	Struck, William B
Pontiac	Veillette, Jodi S
Portage	Tilma, Timothy P
Rochester	Gadoua, Richard E
Roseville	Steiss, Dale M
Royal Oaks	Storey, Stephen

Sanford	William, Glenn
St. Clair Shores	Sohaski, Anita Yvonne
St. Joseph	Harbert, Stephen D
Sylvan Lake	Maxson, Randy B
Troy	Pezold, Roland G
Union Lake	Geelhood, Lawrence
W. Bloomfield	Trump, John
Wyoming	Flemming, Mark
Wyoming	Flynn, Mike

MINNESOTA

Apple Valley	Mathews, David M
Apple Valley	Wheeler, Kathryn
Bloomington	Biernat, Brian R
Bloomington	Broin, Tracy Scott
Bloomington	Johnson, Jan
Bloomington	Powell, William T
Bloomington	Schissel, Janet A
Brainerd	Boland, Bruce
Burnsville	Oaster, Patricia Ann
Chanhassen	Kotsonas, Thomas M
Crystal	Ebbitt, James
Deephaven	Johnson, Howard
Deerwood	MacKay, John G
Duluth	Laiti, Phillip R
Eagan	Nipper, Jeffrey H J
Eagan	Smith, Melvin R
Eagan	York, Ron
Eden Prairie	Allar, Patricia L
Eden Prairie	Babcock, William L
Eden Prairie	Danielson, Scott
Eden Prairie	Manning, Jackie
Edina	Ehlers, Steve
Edina	Greer, Ted
Edina	Hatch, John T
Edina	Noyce, Jerry
Edina	Warner, Ted E
Excelsior	Hensel, Pamela W
Grand Rapids	Alstad, James
Hopkins	Fish, Tom
Hopkins	Reier, David
Lakeville	Amis, Robert W Jr
Mahtomedi	Barr, Ellen B
Mankato	Pettengill, David
Maple Grove	Brekken, Scott
Maple Grove	Sears, Blair W
Marshall	Curtler, Hugh
Minneapolis	Anderson, Charles B
Minneapolis	Anderson, Dana
Minneapolis	Burke, Timothy
Minneapolis	Curtiss, Todd
Minneapolis	Desmond, John
Minneapolis	Dorson, Jeffrey
Minneapolis	Drolson, Paul
Minneapolis	Halvorsen, Daniel K
Minneapolis	Hardman, Jon D
Minneapolis	Kiewel, Bob
Minneapolis	Lappin, Gregory R
Minneapolis	Madson, Robert G
Minneapolis	Olson, Michael D
Minneapolis	Pappas, Nick
Minneapolis	Paul, Clyde
Minneapolis	Peden, Ellie
Minneapolis	Prendergast, Mary E
Minneapolis	Ritter, Susan L
Minneapolis	Roach, Jack
Minneapolis	Stryker, Susan
Minneapolis	Swanson, Warren
Minneapolis	Westrum, Bruce
Minneapolis	Wicklund, Greg P
Minneapolis	Ylinen, Kevin
Minneapolis	Zachman, Gary R
Minneapolis	Zimmerman, Charles
Minnetonka	Halverson, Roy
Minnetonka	Martinson, Richard

Minnetonka	Peterson, Dave
Mound	Plowman-Hahn, Becky
Mound	Stearns, Dave
N. Mankato	Boyer, Roger
Plymouth	Mueller, John H
Rochester	Butorac, Tim
Rochester	McGill, David L
Sauk Rapids	Zittlow, Eileen B
Shoreview	Kridle, Bill
St. Cloud	Black, Jeffrey Lee
St. Cloud	Gilchrist, Jane
St. Louis Park	Mall, Julie A
St. Paul	Abe, Babatunde
St. Paul	Caine, Clifford J
St. Paul	Dixon, James P
St. Paul	Filstrup, Ronald A
St. Paul	Greene, Ernie A
St. Paul	Hickman, Christopher
St. Paul	Johnson, Kim
St. Paul	King, John P
St. Paul	Klinger, David W II
St. Paul	Macias, Jose Z
St. Paul	McCoy, Brian R
St. Paul	Shelander, John T
St. Paul	Stephens, Nancy
St. Paul	Yates, Richard G
St. Paul	Young, Jamie B
St. Peter	Wilkinson, Steve
Tonka Bay	Ofstehage, Gail
Victoria	Muesing, Paul
Virginia	Prittinen, Jim
Wayzata	Mahin, Brian J
Wayzata	Myers, Claudia
Wayzata	Voigt, Frank O
Wayzata	Yorks, David
White Bear Lake	Morin, David
White Bear Lake	Steinhauser, Paul E

MISSISSIPPI

Biloxi	Avdoyan, Alan
Brandon	Toler, Susan
Greenville	Brien, Robert C
Greenwood	Craig, Mary F
Greenwood	Dunn, James R
Hattiesburg	Covington, J Dennis
Jackson	Chadwick, Barney
Jackson	Griffith, Jack W Jr
Jackson	Henry, Carolyn G
Jackson	Hester, W E Jr
Jackson	White, Joan P
Long Beach	Dauro, Samuel A
Natchez	Peabody, Jean H
Ocean Springs	Cantrell, Jim
Oxford	Chadwick, Billy
Pascagoula	Pennington, Steven R
Shaw	Atkinson, Asa B Jr

MISSOURI

Chesterfield	Huetteman, Candace
Chesterfield	Klein, Lawrence D
Columbia	Vargas, Jaime E
Florissant	Beer, Terry G
Florissant	Benne, John H
Florissant	Johnston, Teeter
Florissant	Rauch, Richard T
Hazelwood	Claywell, James J
Hillsboro	Brown, Lloyd
Imperial	Riley, James R
Independence	Allee, Doug
Kansas City	Cox, Robert G Jr

Kansas City	Dorzweiler, E Joseph	Portsmouth	Ruel, Kay
Kansas City	Hannas, Jake	Waterville Valley	Gross, Thomas R Jr
Kansas City	Kane, Kevin	Wolfeboro	Brookes, Donald K
Manchester	Browne, Reggie C	Wolfeboro	Fraser, Barbara K
Manchester	Price, Bill		
Raytown	Rockhold, Jerry		
Springfield	Holbrook, Bruce H	**NEW JERSEY**	
St. Louis	Bell, William T	Atlantic Highlands	Allan, Denise M
St. Louis	Brant, Bailey	Augusta	Bain, Ann G
St. Louis	Caldwell, Sheldon	Bergenfield	King, Thomas Stuart
St. Louis	Frederick, Ian R	Bernardsville	Tourdo, Joseph C
St. Louis	Furman, Roger A	Beverly	Singer, Stanton J
St. Louis	Hughes, Richard P	Bloomfield	Lundgren, Charles G
St. Louis	Lewis, Jack	Branchville	Malmstrom, Dick
St. Louis	Muenz, William G	Bridgeton	Amaranto, Sophie M
St. Louis	Salzenstein, Richard	Bridgeton	Cossaboom,
St. Louis	Salzenstein, Skip		Constance
St. Louis	Schmidt, Charles A (Skip)	Cherry Hill	McCaffrey, James E
		Cranford	Moffat, Carol
St. Louis	Sports Pal Company	Cresskill	Sachs, Jana J
St. Louis	Stroble, Mathew Edward	Edison	Weston, Andrew
		Elizabeth	Oppenheim, Michael
St. Louis	Toburen, Brad	Essex Fells	Ellis, Sharon
St. Louis	Williams, Gene	Fair Lawn	Sengun, Asim S
Warrensburg	Reed, Lori	Flemington	Powers, Claris R
Webster Groves	Rogge, Chuck	Flemington	Sturgess, Bill
		Franklin Lakes	Cerelli, William
		Freehold	Goldberg, Marc
		Ft. Lee	Thompson, Dick
MONTANA		Glassboro	Fox, John D
		Hackensack	Guiney, Pat
Billings	Holmes, Maurice L	Hackensack	Reiss, Robert
Florence	See, Terry	Haddonfield	Laverson, Albert
Great Falls	Cham-A-Koon, Winston	Hammonton	Caruthers, James L
		Haworth	Gregor, James Lawrence
Whitehall	McKie, James K		
		Hawthorne	McGuire, Michael
		Hawthorne	Oricchio, Dennis
		Kinnelon	Vigneri, Ron
NEBRASKA		Lake Hiawatha	Hilsinger, Alan
		Lakewood	Rupp, Frederick G
Grand Island	Halpine, Richard	Lawrenceville	Dillon, Dickie
Lincoln	Garnett, Sigurd	Lawrenceville	Rothstein, Jeff
Nemaha	Cade, Terry	Leonia	Dumansky, John
Omaha	Arnette, Grigsby	Lindenwold	King, David Wayne
Omaha	Borland, Doug	Linwood	Birnbaum, Philip
Omaha	Greenwald, Douglas H	Long Valley	Perkins, Robert
		Maple Shade	Radler, Irene
Omaha	Hubbs, Deborah	Maywood	Montenegro, Walter
Omaha	Hubbs, Edward	Medford	Smith, Stephen A
Omaha	Petersen, Milton	Medford Lakes	Trach, Mark H
Omaha	Roach, Bill	Middletown	Reid, Dee
Omaha	Sloboth, Susan A	Montclair	Raju, Ramu V
Omaha	Weber, David L	Mt. Laurel	Hoffmann, Harry R Jr
Papillion	Ovici, Toma R		
Wilber	Travnicek, Robert G	Neptune	Wright, Richard W
		Normandy Beach	Allen, Ronald H
		Northfield	Antonio, Rudolph
		Nutley	Dumansky, Jeffry B
NEW HAMPSHIRE		Oakland	Russo, John
Dixville Notch	Professional Tennis Services	Ocean City	McCone, Henry
		Orange	Wallace, Charles W
Exeter	Bailey, David W	Paramus	Lucas, Warren
Exeter	Henderson, James W	Park Ridge	Madan, Nausher K
		Pennsauken	Subaru
Exeter	Tyrell, Charles	Pennsauken	Subaru of America, Inc.
Gilford	Hatfield, Richard		
Goffstown	Richer, Don	Plainfield	Lob-ster, Inc (W J Balka)
Hanover	Hamilton, Jeffrey		
Hanover	Kinyon, Charles M	Plainsboro	Brzoska, Michael J
Manchester	Wilson, Andrew	Princeton	AMF Head Division
Milford	Miller, David	Princeton	Brewer, Lewis
Nashua	Daugherty, John W	Princeton	Conroy, John
Nashua	Harkins, W Cary	Princeton	Frazer, Claude R
Nashua	Trowbridge, Rob	Princeton	Kraft, Eve F
Newbury	Huber, John M	Princeton	Long, Robert S
Newfields	Burnett, Howard	Princeton	Prince
Newton	Herbert, Gregory		Manufacturing

Princeton	Prince Manufacturing
Princeton	Prince Manufacturing
Princeton	Prince Manufacturing
Princeton	Tabak, Lawrence
Princeton	Wishingrad, Amy
Princeton Junction	Benjamin, David A
Princeton Junction	Vroom, Larry
Rahway	Manhardt, Hilda
Ridgefield	Edgeroy Company
Ridgewood	Benzing, Marvin P
Ridgewood	Fusco, Tony
Ridgewood	Loguidice, Philip
Rockleigh	Versfeld, Berry
Rumson	O'Shea, John M
Somerville	Korda, Mary-Louise
Spring Lake Heights	Torres, Edward A
Springfield	Leite, Frank Manuel
Stratford	D'Alessandro, Michael A
Succasunna	Lovi, Elliot A
Summit	Hannas, Joan F
Summit	Poling, Jim
Tinton Falls	Cuming, Thomas W
Tinton Falls	Stam, Allen G
Trenton	Cramp, Art
Trenton	Mennel, David W
Union	Diamond, Steve
Upper Greenwood Lake	Covie, Frank P
Vernon	Yanes, Manuel
Vineland	Madden, Patrick
Vineland	Steinour, Sidney B
W. Orange	Spiegel, Caroline
W. Orange	Stafulli, Robert
Westfield	Bacso, George
Westfield	Singer, Stanley
Westfield	Watts, Daniel H
Westwood	Eoff, Jane
Woodbridge	Annesi, James
Woodcliff Lake	Ingis, Gail

NEW MEXICO

Albuquerque	Dellinger, Dennis
Albuquerque	Dorato, Alex
Albuquerque	Felice, Joseph T
Albuquerque	Geatz, David
Albuquerque	Horn, Helen H
Albuquerque	Johnson, Richard R
Albuquerque	Kelly Sissy (S B)
Albuquerque	Long, Joe
Albuquerque	MacCurdy, Doug
Albuquerque	Ochoterena, David
Albuquerque	Powell, Ray B
Albuquerque	Stansifer, Gary
Albuquerque	Vogl, Mike
Albuquerque	Wheeler, Gary
Gallup	Archuleta, Ruben
Las Cruces	Fry, Mary
Las Cruces	Worski, Sally J
Mesotta Park	Nicholas, Richard E
Nogal	Burkstaller, Herman
Nogal	Crouse, James U
Roswell	Jimenez, Alberto
Santa Fe	Gray, Bo
Santa Fe	Heldman, Gladys
Santa Fe	Light, Dale
Santa Fe	Martinez, Julian
Santa Fe	Mechem-Light, Adrienne
Santa Fe	Moss, James A
Santa Fe	Raedisch, Bob
Santa Fe	Romero, Deborah M
Santa Fe	Schmid, Lloyd (Bud)
Santa Fe	Schmid, Susan
Taos	Edelbrock, Kurt

NEVADA

Las Vegas	Arceneaux, Pierre
Las Vegas	Boone, Keith W
Las Vegas	Cole, Charmaine
Las Vegas	Gurovsky, Tony
Las Vegas	Harrell, Jerry
Las Vegas	Hennessy, Martin E
Las Vegas	Kellogg, Chuck
Las Vegas	Kuhle, Michael A
Las Vegas	Lane, Johnny
Las Vegas	Lavis, Jay S
Las Vegas	MacCall, George R
Las Vegas	Prisock, Jim E
Las Vegas	Rapp, Herb M
Las Vegas	Rockwell, Ann
Las Vegas	Schwikert, Jo
Las Vegas	VanCronkhite, Janice
Reno	Buell, Scott
Reno	Stewert, Robert B
Reno	Whitehurst, John E III

NEW YORK

Albany	Sykes, Marion
APO New York City	Schwanz, Verlon D
Astoria	Ferrara, R Armand
Astoria	Van Trigt, Eduard
Baldwin	Seligman, Betsy
Bayshore	Forsythe, Bruce J
Bayside	Funk, Bruce
Bayside	Goldstein, Bernice
Bayside	Seewagen, George
Beacon	Browne, William
Belle Harbor	Callaway, Ken
Bellerose	Graham, Carlos
Brentwood	Bustamante, Andrew
Bronx	Del Prete, Michael
Bronx	Koenigstein, David
Bronx	Ross, Gloria
Bronx	Sylva, Donald Gene
Bronxville	Barnes, Ronald
Bronxville	Decarvalho, Jaime
Bronxville	Meyers, C Alan
Brooklyn	Benjamin, Arnold
Brooklyn	Carberry, Stephen
Brooklyn	Cataldo, Robert
Brooklyn	Cerato, Joseph
Brooklyn	Cowan, Raymond
Brooklyn	Eisenstadt, Murray
Brooklyn	Goldsmith, Barry
Brooklyn	Kripanidhi, Biligere R
Brooklyn	Lempert, Robert
Brooklyn	Mitchel, Anthony
Brooklyn	Musial, Mark
Brooklyn	Myerson, Robert R
Brooklyn	Pittaluga, Luciano
Brooklyn	Rubell, Phil
Brooklyn	Solway, Kenneth
Brooklyn	Tucker, Raymond
Brooklyn	Wisoff, Lloyd
Brooklyn Heights	Weiss, Robert L
Buffalo	Crispell, Russell E
Buffalo	More, W Philip
Cornwall on Hudson	Holmberg, Ron
Carle Place	Lynner, Paul K
Chappaqua	Quinn, Hank
Commack	Pisciotta, Frank Jr

Location	Name	Location	Name
Copiague	Brandine, Bill	*New York City*	Giuglescu, Florin
Copiague	Spiegel, Jodi	*New York City*	Grill, Stephen C
Cortland	Cahill, Peter J	*New York City*	Hacohen, Avner
De Witt	DeHoog, Rosemary L	*New York City*	Hartman, Lewis H
		New York City	Kaufman, Richard
Dobbs Ferry	Kosloff, George	*New York City*	Lebow, Lawrence
Douglaston	Hoopes, Peter	*New York City*	Letteron, Edward H
E. Meadow	Cohen, Steven	*New York City*	Loomtogs
E. Quogue	Bass, Thomas J Jr		(Schoenfeld A M)
Ellenville	Rubin, Fred		MacNutt, Dawn M
Elmhurst	Levy, Stanley	*New York City*	McNamara, Paul
Elmira	Levkanich, Philip	*New York City*	Rowlands, Scott T
Fairport	Lynett, Michael J	*New York City*	Russell, Douglas
Farmingdale	Politzer, Milan	*New York City*	Ryland, Robert
Floral Park	Ballato, Lou	*New York City*	Schobel, David E
Flushing	Goodall, George A	*New York City*	Seewagen, Butch
Flushing	McCollum, Catherine	*New York City*	Tennis Week
Flushing	McQuillin, Edward D	*New York City*	USTA National
Forest Hills	Liebman, Rick		League Admn.
Forest Hills	Nash, Joseph	*New York City*	Wilensky, Gary
Gansevoort	Stearns, Stewart P	*New York City*	Zelman, Gary
Garden City South	Scainetti, Jack	*Newburgh*	Hoyt, Hubertus G
Glen Cove	Freeman, Ed	*Newburgh*	Silvestri, Al
Great Neck	Luper, Alan	*Northport*	Graham, Mark F
Great Neck	Rebhuhn, Ronald	*Patchogue*	Nowak, David
Hauppauge	Tom, Richard	*Peekskill*	Zawiski, Michael
Haverstraw	Sanders, Charles E Jr	*Penfield*	Clarke, David T
		Pittsford	Ritchie, Gwendolyn
Hensonville	Spear, Jonathan C	*Pleasantville*	Klipstein, Jeffrey
Hicksville	Galasso, Anthony P	*Port Washington*	Shore, Sam
Honeoye Falls	Saetta, Richard	*Poughkeepsie*	Capolino, P A N
Honeoye Falls	Scorza, Francis (Skip)	*Pound Ridge*	Aarts, Jeffrey
Honeoye Falls	Strebel, David	*Riverdale*	Greene, Dr. Robert Ford
Honeoye Falls	Weymuller, Carol	*Rochester*	Borysko, Jerry W
Honeoye Falls	Weymuller, Frederick	*Rochester*	D'Emilio, Greg
		Rochester	Derry, Elizabeth A
Huntington	Korolczuk, Stefan	*Rochester*	Gohagan, Linda
Huntington	Poirier, Harvey	*Rochester*	Gonzales, Spike G
Huntington	Schmidt, Bob	*Rochester*	Lyman, Peter
Huntington	Zeese, Herb	*Rochester*	Miller, Barbara C
Hyde Park	Smith, Timothy D	*Rochester*	Nealon, Ann
Katonah	Lane, Alan J	*Rochester*	Perlman, Richard L
Katonah	Sampson, Lydia Jane	*Rochester*	Rehbach, Bruce
		Rochester	Schwarz, Nancy
Kew Gardens	Sokolowski, Renie	*Rochester*	Wiseman, Doug
Lake Placid	Coffey, Bill	*Roosevelt Island*	Ginsburg, Dale (Mrs.)
Lake Placid	Stevenson, John H	*Roslyn*	Becker, Stewart
Lake Ronkonkoma	Bustamante, Richard	*Roslyn Heights*	Wagner, Robert
Latham	Negri, Bruce	*Rush*	Perlman, David E
Little Neck	Glickman, Robert	*Rye*	Balun, Dale
Lockport	Shambach, David N	*Rye*	Schrank, Daniel
Long Island City	Castaldini, Frank A	*Saratoga*	Levine, Bruce A
Lynbrook	Bailin, Stuart	*Saratoga Springs*	Whalen, Rodney N
Mahopac	Rosen, Sherwin	*Sayville, Long Island*	Kubelle, Otto J
Mamaroneck	Bauska, Gunnar	*Scarsdale*	Ehlermann, Dieter F
Mamaroneck	Vinokur, Martin	*Scarsdale*	Olson, Vincent
Manhasset	Rurac, Magda	*Scarsdale*	Ross, Joel
Manhasset	Schmidt, Edward	*Schenectady*	Kuzman, Stevan P
Marion	Perkins, Robert	*Scottsville*	Carter, Dave
Massapequa	Rogers, William	*Setauket*	Fortuna, David
Melville	Wenzel, Clarence E	*Setauket*	Grauer, Cynthia
Merrick	Webber, James	*Somers*	Barta, Judy
Mt. Kisco	All American Sports	*Southhampton*	Degroot, Douglas
N. Babylon	Reid, James T	*Spencerport*	Malnati, Robert P
Nanuet	Mounkhall, Thomas	*Springfield Gardens*	Lynn, Arnold E
Neponsit	Cowan, Arthur M	*St. James*	Miller, Donald C
New City	Mitchell, William A	*Staten Island*	Barton, James
New York City	Barnard, Phillip A	*Syosset*	Tyras, Conrad W
New York City	Beitler, Steve A	*Syosset*	Wolfarth, Ed
New York City	Bird, Stephanie	*Syracuse*	Pepiot, Jack
New York City	Blackwell, Chuck	*Syracuse*	Romeo, Alfred
New York City	Dealy, Robert	*Utica*	Pfisterer, Michael F
New York City	Doyle, Al	*Utica*	Zebiak, Stanley
New York City	Estrin, Yale	*Valley Cottage*	Pinho, Fernando (Fred)
New York City	Fenton, Hank		
New York City	Ford Tennis		
New York City	Fuentes, Rafael		

Valley Cottage	Rogers, Patrick A	Fargo	Kapaun, Steven F
W. Islip	Gerdts, William	Grand Forks	Wynne, J Tom
Wantagh	Jaklitsch, Thomas	Grand Forks	Wynne, Timothy J
Webster	Mayer, Doris M	Jamestown	Whalen, Marnie
White Plains	Bouyer, Tommy		
White Plains	DeGray, Robert		
Williamsville	Mack, Robert J		
Woodbury	Harjes, Robert W	**OHIO**	
Woodmere	Kasoff, William A	Akron	Aleman, Dallas R
Woodmere	Miller, Larry	Akron	Bradford, Lois J
Woodmere	Nielsen, Stan	Akron	Dinie, Joanne
Yonkers	Kalpak, Berj B	Akron	Marias, Frank
Yonkers	Schwab, Walter (Tex)	Akron	Patton, Vicki L
Youngstown	Johnson, Arthur W	Aurora	Richey, Gary
		Bay Village	Engelke, John Beyer
		Berea	Krueger, Robert C
		Canton	Bird, Robert A
NORTH CAROLINA		Canton	Hurley, Michael
Ashville	Brown, Buster	Canton	Kerchner, Linda
Boone	Otto, Wayne	Centerville	Cook, John H
Brevard	Beehler, C E (Clarence)	Chagrin Falls	March, Jack
		Chillicothe	Parks, Guy
Brevard	McGuire, Kevin J	Cincinnati	Contardi, Steve
Brevard	Parker, James	Cincinnati	Crawford, Geoffrey
Carrboro	Schroeder, Howard	Cincinnati	Daggett, John K
Cashiers	Bowen, John	Cincinnati	Foley, Joseph
Chapel Hill	Rauchbach, Marvin	Cincinnati	Friedlander, Jerry
Chapel Hill	See, Michael J	Cincinnati	Geraci, Tim
Charlotte	Coombes, Karl	Cincinnati	Jacobs, James R
Charlotte	Loughlin, Terry J	Cincinnati	Kiessling, Roy C
Charlotte	Ralston, Len	Cincinnati	Morgenstern, Michael
Concord	Cline, Donald R		
Durham	Cole, Hugh W	Cincinnati	Power, Dave
Durham	Cox, Robert E (Bob)	Cincinnati	Turman, Stephen
Durham	Harrison, Katherine	Cincinnati	Weil, Philip John
Durham	Oehler, Bill	Cincinnati	Zaeh, Howard Charles
Fayetteville	Monroe, Zan		
Gastonia	Eppinette, Charles	Cleveland	Adams, Bernice
Gastonia	Fender, Dale	Cleveland	Dempsey, Tom
Greensboro	Corthum, Kenneth Jr	Cleveland	Lahl, James Russell
Greensboro	Ray, David C	Columbus	Alexander, Gary
Greensboro	Rives, Edwin Earle Jr	Columbus	Lathrop, James
		Columbus	Mueller, Barbara
Greensboro	Winstead, Jim	Columbus	Walton, Ralph
Hendersonville	Lynn, Laurie M	Columbus	Wookey, Wayne H
High Point	Bolick, Herb Jr	Dayton	Babolat Maillot Witt
High Point	Ray, Ed	Defiance	Costello, Michael
Lattimore	Corn, Jim	Delaware	Becker, John E
Morganton	Naylor, William C	Findlay	Safipour, Fred
New Bern	Mack, Al	Geneva	Bradshaw, Arnold
New Bern	Norfleet, Tom	Granville	Tooley, Dr. Fay V
Pineville	Brown, Gary S	Hamilton	Joos, Tim
Raleigh	Blackburn, Debby	Hamilton	Manring, Tom
Raleigh	Burke, Kathleen B	Lexington	Schaub, Ronald
Raleigh	Daugherty, Kevin O	Lima	Dredge, Ronald B
Raleigh	Emmons, James T	Louisville	Parrish, Gregory
Raleigh	Happer, Marshall III	Malvern	Shaffer, Ryan
Raleigh	Heald, Robert S	Mansfield	Lorentz, Gerald
Raleigh	Henderson, Richard	Massillon	Najdovski, Krste (Kris)
Raleigh	Keller, Rick		
Raleigh	Rothschild, Keith R	Maumee	Preston, Judy E
Rocky Mount	Easter, Ken	Medina	Risteen, Jeff
Rocky Mount	Richardson, Keith F	Medina	Rubenstein, Bryan
Wilmington	Harris, Barry E	Milford	Luecke, Craig
Wilmington	Sauer, Ron	New Philadelphia	Black, Neal
Wilmington	Sauer, Virginia	Painesville	Hach, Marlene
Winston-Salem	Barker, Francis Boyer	Painesville	Young, David J
		Parma	Bethlenfalvy, Jack
Winston-Salem	Blackwelder, Philip	Perrysburg	Carr, C James
Winston-Salem	Crookenden, Ian	Richfield	Maynor, Walt
Wrightsville Beach	Kraly, Harry L	Shaker Heights	Thomas, Gwyneth
		Shreve	Nelson, James V
		Solon	Walker, Paul A
		Springfield	Beach, David Lee
		Stow	McCardle, Jeffrey
NORTH DAKOTA		Stow	Stine, Muriel M
Devils Lake	Smith, David B	Strongsville	Stofey, Kristine
Fargo	Gavin, Deborah	Sunbury	Nelson, Thomas R

Tallmadge	Jeffries, Pam
Toledo	Cabanski, Patricia White
Toledo	Davis, James E
Toledo	Hollingsworth, Rusty
Urbana	Dredge, Greg
Vienna	Vens, Keith Allan
Vienna	Vens, Warren
Warren	Vens, Ray
Westchester	Stanis, Elizabeth A
Woodmere	Jetli, Arun K, Ph.D.
Wooster	Frey, Kirk
Wooster	Schilling, Hayden
Youngstown	Keil, John
Youngstown	Thompson, Robert J
Zanesville	Arnold, Richard

OKLAHOMA

Ardmore	Kelly, Raymond T
Bethany	Van Der Wal, Ronald
Broken Arrow	Daniel, Andy
Broken Arrow	Witzel, Raymond E Jr
Edmond	Cabato, Rodrigo S
Enid	Williams, John R
Jenks	Richison, Brad
Miami	Coppedge, Donald L
Oklahoma City	Battad, Fortunato M Jr
Oklahoma City	Bender, Kim K
Oklahoma City	English, Tommy
Oklahoma City	Fernandez, Michael
Oklahoma City	Gilkey, Dick E
Oklahoma City	Jack, Roger
Oklahoma City	Lease, Sharon
Oklahoma City	Mears, Marcus
Oklahoma City	Mikysa, Ivan
Oklahoma City	Murphy, Mark A
Oklahoma City	Robertson, Colin
Oklahoma City	Rompf, William James
Oklahoma City	Ryan, Sharon Rose
Oklahoma City	Short, Arnold
Oklahoma City	Wright, Lee
Piedmont	Rathway, Alice Ann
Shawnee	Sharp, Ronald
Tulsa	Batchelor, Janan E
Tulsa	Cobb, Lillian Galloway
Tulsa	Eberhardt, Betsy
Tulsa	Morton, Ainslie P
Tulsa	Price, Cliff
Tulsa	Straney, Lindsay
Tulsa	Young, Colleen S

OREGON

Albany	O'Hearn, Julie
Corvallis	Quandt, Gary M
Eagle Point	O'Neal, Tim
Eugene	Bassett, Brice
Eugene	Cosgrove, Greg
Eugene	Koffler, Kenneth
Eugene	Sterett, Barry
Florence	Simpson, James E
Lapine	McCartney, Bill
Medford	Inn, Frank Jr
Portland	Ball, Shaun D
Portland	Brouhard, Wayne
Portland	Dibbins, Samuel A Jr
Portland	Goldstein, Karen
Portland	Johnsen, Mary P
Portland	O'Connor, Geoffrey
Portland	Rudholm, Doug
Salem	Engle, Bruce
Sunriver	Carlson, Ted H

PENNSYLVANIA

Abington	Alexander, John
Alliquippa	Fodor, Ron
Allison Park	Budd, Barry
Allison Park	Ruzanic, Robert G
Ambler	Ferguson, Edwin E Jr
Ambler	Hyde, Lawrence W
Ambler	Renner, Dale A
Bala-Cynwyd	Jessup, Robert B
Berwyn	Hassell, Terry
Bethlehem	Smith, Arthur W Jr
Bethlehem	Zajac, Helen P
Bridgeville	Dilettuso, David N
Bryn Mawr	Harrity, William F
Bryn Mawr	McMullen, Jim
Camp Hill	Shipp, Richard Edwin
Carlisle	Smith, Patrick
Carnegie	Moss, Peter H
Chadds Ford	Bogard, W Carl
Chadds Ford	Righter, John F
Chalfont	Easi, Michael D
Chalfont	Gatter, Sharyn C
Clarks Summit	Steege, William
Clarks Summit	Weiss, John A
Clarks Summit	Yablonski, Edward J Jr
Coatesville	Poltrone, Joseph A
Collingdale	Siano, Joseph A Jr
Danboro	Wright, Douglas R
Devon	Warzycki, John
Downingtown	Desmond, Rebecca
Downingtown	Gilliford, William J Jr
Downingtown	Himes, David M
Downingtown	Waltz, Paul M
Drexel Hill	Bates, H John
E. Stroudsburg	Duran, Gilbert A
E. Stroudsburg	Hanlon, Richard R
Easton	Walters, Jeffrey S
Erie	Pizzat, Joseph
Erie	Pizzat, Michael E
Erie	Rice, Mont D
Erie	Simon, Jerome F
Erie	Yost, Ray
Exton	Scott, Le
Finleyville	Carper, Kirk L
Flourtown	Coyle, Joseph
Fogelsville	Chassard, Albert
Ft. Loudon	Kegerreis, Douglas A
Gilbertsville	Powell, Dick
Glen Mills	Schmidt, Arthur
Greensburg	Kilgour, Doug
Greensburg	Schunck, Fritz
Gwynedd Valley	Carleton, Frank H
Haverford	Bramall, Norman B
Haverford	Leary, Catherine Collins
Haverford	Leary, H Michael
Hershey	Rice, Richard N
Hollidaysburg	Genter, Steve
Horsham	Garabedian, Alan
Kennett Square	Kropf, Dorothy
King of Prussia	Castelli, Adrian C.
King of Prussia	Krinsky, Julian
Landenberg	Garcia, Eduardo S
Landisville	Talbot, Donald P
Langhorne	Binns, Adrian S
Lansdale	Daub, Peter
Lansdale	Daub, Ruth L
Landsdale	Jeffers, Jimmy

Lebanon	Ruhl, Suzette L	Yardley	Mooney, Mike
Lehighton	Cohen, Julian H		
Library	Provence, David P	**RHODE ISLAND**	
Lima	Grubb, James		
Lititz	Epps, Patricia W	Ashaway	Crandall, Steven J
Malvern	Clark, Charles H	Barrington	Hecht, Janet
Malvern	Palmer, Richard L	Cranston	Howe, Stephen R Jr
McKeesport	Zatek, Don	Cranston	Moretti, Jamie
Mechanicsburg	Hains, Jonathan	Cumberland	Majkut, Henry S
Mercersburg	McNamee, Daniel	E. Providence	Gray, Spencer E
Monroeville	Antaki, Charlotte A	E. Providence	Henson, Don
Monroeville	Penn Athletic	Hope	Gordon, Marvin
	Products	Kingston	Marcus, Alan S
Monroeville	Penn Athletic	Mapleville	Manville, Michael N
	Products	N. Kingstown	Clarke, Ronald S
Monroeville	Penn Athletic	N. Kingstown	Connerton, Tad
	Products	N. Kingstown	Jordan, Lester
Monroeville	Pierce, Jeanne	Narragansett	Golden, Edward M
Mountville	Witmer, Jeff S	Newport	Howard, Charles W
Mt. Lebanon	Nichols, William H		II
N. Wales	Weaver, Joseph A	Newport	Kenney, Frank J
Narberth	Feise, Frank C	Pawtucket	McPhillips, John
Narberth	Friedman, Bill	Providence	Feinstein, Stephen
Newtown Square	Young, Robert A	Providence	Roach, Phyllis R
Norristown	Cook, Jeffrey	Providence	Robertson,
Norristown	Dormagen, Robert		Alexander (Sandy)
	(Bobby) L	Riverside	Anelundi, Edmund
Paoli	Mellor, Edward L	Woonsocket	Gaylorde, Michael
Philadelphia	Bailey, Lee		
Philadelphia	DeGray, Richard E	**SOUTH CAROLINA**	
Philadelphia	Dillon, Albert W		
Philadelphia	Gregory, Russell	Aiken	Ashhurst, Fred
Philadelphia	Hupka, Kenneth	Aiken	Davidson, William B
Philadelphia	Laveson, Alan	Aiken	Hull, Jeffrey
Philadelphia	Montgomery, Rubel	Aiken	Philson, Bob
Philadelphia	Oliver, Charles W	Camden	Morris, Don G
Philadelphia	Pogonyi, Andrew	Charleston	Barth, Roy
Philadelphia	Schwarzman, Seth J	Charleston	Brockman, Lee
Philadelphia	Thomson, Mark	Charleston	Hane, Diane Gilruth
Phoenixville	Coyle, Daniel F Jr	Charleston	Hane, Mark C
Pineville	Debaise, Miki	Charleston	Heffernan, Butch
Pittsburgh	Adams, William N	Charleston	Hosick, Scott
Pittsburgh	Bennett, Robert E	Charleston	Moran, David W
Pittsburgh	Fechter, Leonard F	Charleston	Silcox W A
Pittsburgh	Gillespie, John T	Chester	Whitesides, Joel W
Pittsburgh	Henry, Walter L	Clemson	Johnston, Andrew
Pittsburgh	Rath, Mark G	Clemson	Kriese, Charles P
Pittsburgh	Sciorilli, Frank C	Columbia	Denoon, James J
Pittsburgh	Surampudi,	Columbia	Elkins, Arlo
	Sudershan	Columbia	Kefalos, Jeff
Pittsburgh	Tenex	Columbia	Marshall, Mary G
Pittsburgh	Tenex	Columbia	McGuire, Bernie
Pittsburgh	Whittington, Richard	Columbia	Niemann, Bruce
Pottstown	Bartlett, John	Columbia	Riley, Roy
Pottstown	Weeber, Bruce C	Easely	Mahanes, Dr. James
Prospect Park	Brown, Richard K		R
Quakertown	Osipower, Robert	Florence	Smith, Archie III
Rochester	Lemmon, William D	Florence	Sprengelmeyer,
	Jr		Mike
Southampton	Sunderlin, Drew	Fripp Island	Trellue, Edwin D III
Springtown	Serues, William S	Greenville	Holliday, Darelyn M
Wayne	Faber, Rick	Greenville	Scarpa, Paul
Wayne	Gilliford, Winifred	Greenville	Spears, Frank H Jr
Wayne	O'Brien, Bill	Greenwood	Rearden, Mark
West Chester	Buchanan, Michael	Greenwood	Smith, Allen D
	R	Greer	Haddox, Bud
West Chester	Butler, Judy	Hanahan	Maurer, Heinz
West Chester	Kline, George	Harbor Island	Mears, Graylin
West Chester	Sember, William A		(Sam)
West Chester	Tapper, Russell J	Hilton Head	Gage, Ben C
West Chester	Welsh, Jeffrey M	Hilton Head	Oliver, Kenneth C
West Chester	Woods, Kathy S	Hilton Head	Reichel, Rob
West Chester	Woods, Ronald B	Hilton Head	Riggins, Paul R
Westlawn	Motacki, Bill	Hilton Head	Wehunt, Johnny
Westtown	Gaebel, Herbert W	Hilton Head Island	Barnes, Jefferson T
Willow Grove	Chambers, Stanley	Hilton Head Island	Kamperman, Kurt
Winwood	Mackin, Harold J	Hilton Head Island	Page, Patrick Q
Worcester	Reilly, Michael G	Hilton Head Island	Van Der Meer,
Wormleysburg	Mathias, Craig K		Dennis

Isle of Palms	Tinkey, Michael	*Nashville*	McDonald, Allen C
John's Island	Goffi, Carlos	*Nashville*	Robinson, Carl B Jr
John's Island	Lake, Robert	*Nashville*	Sheehan, Thomas J Jr
Mt. Pleasant	Berryman, David W		
Mt. Pleasant	Cooke, Frank G	*Sewanee*	Kalkhoff, Norman E
Myrtle Beach	Johnson, Loren S		
Myrtle Beach	Tessier, Ralph		
Pawley Island	Wynn, Corey		
Pickens	Barthelmes, John A	**TEXAS**	
Rock Hill	Hendrick, Gerald	*Abilene*	Barrett, Dean
Rock Hill	Lacrosse, Donald P	*Abilene*	King, Max C
Shaw AFB	Grifol, Rene	*Abilene*	Meyers, Rick
Surfside Beach	Rizzo, Larry	*Addison*	Matthieson, Creig
Taylors	Harvey, Etta	*Amarillo*	Crowell, Dennis
Walterboro	Nelson, Bobby	*Amarillo*	King, Dick
		Amarillo	Nichols, Dave
		Amarillo	Wood, Eddie
		Arlington	Grantham, Cindy Ann
SOUTH DAKOTA		*Arlington*	Grassanovits, Robert
Rapid City	Paluch, Daryl		
Sioux Falls	Johnson, Marty	*Arlington*	Manning, Gregg
Sioux Falls	Kopren, Ted	*Arlington*	Seymour, Garry
Sioux Falls	Volin, James (Jamie)	*Arlington*	Vieira, Armando
		Austin	Baker, Madalyn
		Austin	Behne, Sheryl
TENNESSEE		*Austin*	Egeberg, Duane E
Antioch	Kacian, James M	*Austin*	Freer, W T (Billy)
Ashland City	Weiss, Lawrence	*Austin*	Gould, Bruce F
Brentwood	Van Lingen, Peter	*Austin*	Gregorio, Renee
Bristol	Helton, Bob	*Austin*	Hill, Larry M
Bristol	Risner, John J	*Austin*	Ingram, John H III
Brownsville	Petrolini, Mickey	*Austin*	Ingram, Thomas S
Chattanooga	Bartlett, Tommy	*Austin*	Johnson, Jerry D
Chattanooga	Gouvitsa, Gus K	*Austin*	Ketelsen, Kimm
Chattanooga	Guerry, Alex	*Austin*	Lusson, Brian C
Chattanooga	Leach, Elizabeth G	*Austin*	Oxley Paul
Clarksville	Martin, Michael B	*Austin*	Schwartz, Geraldine
Daisy	Bartlett, William L	*Austin*	Shields, Susan Kurz
Elizabethton	Austin, James G	*Austin*	Sivertson, Dave
Franklin	DeHart, Kenneth	*Beaumont*	Griffin, Ian A
Gallatin	Ammons, Timothy	*Beaumont*	McDonald, David
Germantown	Cadwallader, Rob	*Beaumont*	Nelson, Barb Porter
Hixson	Jones, James B	*Bedford*	Green, Kevin
Hixson	Kigongo, Eustace	*Belton*	Linden, Karen
Hixson	Sanhueza, Poncho	*Bryan*	Connell, Thomas V
Hixson	Strang, Thornton	*Bryan*	Turek, Lynette
Hixson	Swafford, Donald T	*Carrollton*	Riley-Hagan, Maggie
Hixson	Tym, Wanda	*Carrollton*	Ross, Judy
Jackson	Locke, Sean	*Carrollton*	Velasco, Fernando M
Johnson City	Warner, Dan		
Johnson City	Zannis, Peter	*Carrollton*	Coyne, Rick
Kingsport	Toney, Reedy	*Clifton*	Robinson, Jim F
Knoxville	Bales, Michael A	*College Station*	Baldwin, Jan
Knoxville	Clapp, Thomas (Mike)	*Conroe*	Frazier, Aubrey III
		Coppell	Kaskow, Christopher
Knoxville	De Palmer, Mike	*Corpus Christi*	Casey, B H
Knoxville	Mozur, Tom	*Corpus Christi*	Castorri, Robert
Knoxville	Polte, Gunter F	*Corpus Christi*	Dekoning, Ken
Martin	Madrey, William Jr	*Corpus Christi*	Kuykendall, Joe
McDonald	Tym, Alice	*Corpus Christi*	Mapes, Bob
Memphis	Barton, Billie	*Corpus Christi*	Rumfield, Leroy D
Memphis	Barton, Derrick W	*Corpus Christi*	Torrance, Dr. Shelby F
Memphis	Berryhill, Patricia Ann		
Memphis	Chamberlain, Philip	*Corpus Christi*	Torrance, Susan Shelby
Memphis	Hankins, Jerry M	*Corpus Christi*	Wilder, Roy
Memphis	Mansour, Stephen Kelly	*Corpus Christi*	Woods, Ron
		D/FW Airport	Lee, Steve
Memphis	Mille, Donna Joy	*Dallas*	Bass, Martha Ann
Memphis	Risser, Sarah	*Dallas*	Bohrnstedt, David
Memphis	Walker, Ina	*Dallas*	Booziotis, Kathy
Memphis	Wilson, Mark	*Dallas*	Bos, Bill
Memphis	Young, Robert H	*Dallas*	Bourne, Stanley
Morristown	Miller, Jamie	*Dallas*	Brewer, Don
Nashville	Anderson, Dave Jr	*Dallas*	Coleman, Brad R
Nashville	Butchee, Thay	*Dallas*	Cooper, Daniel
Nashville	Kelly, Joe G	*Dallas*	Dobbs, Danny
		Dallas	Ellis, William R

Dallas	Foust, Arthur L	Grand Prairie	Franklin, Steven E
Dallas	Geyman, Jerry D	Grand Prairie	Landers, Jo Delle
Dallas	Hagerman, Betty Sue	Grapevine	Goodwin, L Gaines
		Harker Heights	Jenkins, Beth Ann
Dallas	Hagerman, Bobby	Harker Heights	Tenney, Weston
Dallas	Hammett, William C	Harlingen	Ehlers, Timmy Dean
Dallas	Kindred, Gary B	Henderson	Phenix, James N
Dallas	Kirwan-Rinehart, Nancy	Houston	Alexander, Brice
		Houston	Barbeau, Terry L
Dallas	Lacouture, Cary F	Houston	Bearup, Jeffrey T
Dallas	Laing, Barry C	Houston	Bennett, Donald
Dallas	Laing, Doug	Houston	Bond, Kent W
Dallas	Landenberger, Richard	Houston	Burrmann, John E
		Houston	Cahill, Dennis J
Dallas	Lipp, Billie Louise	Houston	Christian, Paul
Dallas	Mabe, Dixie	Houston	Cliffe, Timothy
Dallas	Martin, Mickey L	Houston	Courson, Daniel C
Dallas	Martindale, Judy	Houston	Early, Desmond
Dallas	McGowan, William L	Houston	Eastman, Susan
Dallas	McHaney, Owen	Houston	Elmore, Rex
Dallas	McKenna, Bob	Houston	Everett, William
Dallas	Mooty, Robert T	Houston	Fineman, Paul
Dallas	Newman, Butch	Houston	Flack, Albert E (Al)
Dallas	Pampell, Sue	Houston	Giammalva, Sam
Dallas	Rains, Andrea	Houston	Godwin, Martin B
Dallas	Raphael, Ken	Houston	Greco, Karen G
Dallas	Richardson, Ron	Houston	Hadi, Jeanette Monica
Dallas	Ruday, Jeffrey		
Dallas	Sharshan, Richylee A	Houston	Holladay, John
		Houston	Holmes, Charlie
Dallas	Unger, Jeffry S	Houston	Howell, Richard C
Dallas	Valentincic, Dan	Houston	Hudson, Shelly
Dallas	Verde, John	Houston	Johnson, Helen M
Dallas	Wade, Wm H Jr	Houston	Jones, Ruth E
Dallas	Weyman, Carol	Houston	King, Robert C
Dallas	Wiegand, Paul B	Houston	Ladig, Debbie
Dallas	Wood, Vicki	Houston	Land, A Glenn
Denton	Miller, Allie I	Houston	Lawrence, Toni
Duncanville	McMillan, Ken	Houston	Leclear, Clarence G (Lee)
El Paso	Alvarez, Louis		
El Paso	Ball, Donald R	Houston	Maxa, Donald J
El Paso	Crossland, Damon Scott	Houston	McAllister, Ken D
		Houston	McCue, Phil
El Paso	Hall, Brett	Houston	Mills, John D
El Paso	Rainey, Matt	Houston	Mitic, Dragutin
El Paso	Walker, Ross	Houston	Munks, Herbert
Euless	Miller, M Rex	Houston	Owens, Michael J
Euless	Pasquale, C C (Tom)	Houston	Parker, Jim
		Houston	Parten, Harry S
Ft. Worth	Bartzen, Bernard (Tut)	Houston	Rathkamp, Dave
		Houston	Rose, James
Ft. Worth	Costello, David J	Houston	Sanchelli, Chuck
Ft. Worth	Crawford, Randy	Houston	Schmidt, Jim
Ft. Worth	Davis, Gordon S	Houston	Schulz, Mark
Ft. Worth	Elfassy, Allan	Houston	Sochor, Irena
Ft. Worth	Fuller, Don A	Houston	Swiggart, James M
Ft. Worth	Gage, Jeffrey D	Houston	Thomas, Linda Rupert
Ft. Worth	Johnson, John B		
Ft. Worth	Mattingly, Randy	Houston	Thomas, Timothy J
Ft. Worth	Matyastik, Bill	Houston	Thompson, Edward H
Ft. Worth	McMillan, Warren K		
Ft. Worth	Van Zandt, Earl	Houston	Turner, William R
Ft. Worth	Williams, Glenn	Houston	Turville, Larry
Galveston	Bryant, David	Houston	Wilson, Craig R
Galveston	Garcia, Shelton H	Houston	Wright, James
Garland	Farley, Harry	Hurst	Hopkins, Cal
Garland	Green, Bob	Irving	Bristol, Scott Jr
Garland	Heimberg, S R (SRHE)	Irving	Dawson, Tony
		Irving	McKeown, Denis K
Garland	Meyers, Jay	Keller	Foote, Karissa (Kris)
Garland	Neal, Edward C	Kerrville	Jennings, H Lee
Garland	Sartori, Patrick	Kerrville	Parish, Henry L
Garland	Tejeda, David	Kerrville	Perry, Richard
Garland	Zimmerman, Gary	Kerrville	Seidel, Jon
Georgetown	Henderson, Marvin J	Kerrville	Sutherland, Beau E
Georgetown	Peterson, David Alan	Killeen	Lopez, Omar S
		Kingwood	Gross, Ruth
Granbury	Dobbrow, William (Sandy)	Laredo	Widener, T Perry

League City	Hughes, Marilynn	*Waco*	McCleary, Charlie
League City	Weber, Gideon	*Waco*	McCleary, Lee
Lubbock	Allen Gaylen B	*Waco*	Sheehy, Jack
Lubbock	Conaway, Robert W	*Waco*	Trogolo, Robert
Lubbock	Dadich, Rich	*Waxahachie*	Howe, Jack G
Lubbock	Damron, Ronald	*Wharton*	Smith, Travis Jr
Lubbock	Van Zandt, Barbara	*Wichita Falls*	Brotherton, Jon P
Mansfield	Seybold, Mike	*Wichita Falls*	Davis, Mark
Marble Falls	Herrington, Charlie M	*Wichita Falls*	Hickey, Mike
		Wichita Falls	Lynds, Jayne
McAllen	Donnalley, Mary Jane	*Wichita Falls*	Sargent, Robbie
		Wichita Falls	Simmons, John
Midland	Barizon, Peter Paul	*Wichita Falls*	White, Jody Ann
Midland	Bobbitt, Terry	*Windcrest*	Koth, Alan L
Midland	Edmonds, Derek J	*Yorktown*	Packard, Frances C
Midland	McClung, Neill		
Midland	Pierce, Gary L		
Midland	Williams, Joe		
Mission	Gates, William S		
Missouri City	Avera, Don	**UTAH**	
Missouri City	Bovett, Chris	*Ogden*	Cox, R Keith
Missouri City	Moriarty, David W	*Salt Lake City*	Jones, Larry J
Missouri City	Rhodes, Eugene	*Salt Lake City*	Rohrbacher, Thomas T
Montgomery	Eichenbaum, Larry		
Montgomery	Lewis, Michael A	*Salt Lake City*	Simmonds, Carol
New Braunfels	Fann, Robert		
New Braunfels	Mabry, Clarence		
Odessa	McBeth Joe Dan		
Orange	Dorrell, James V		
Pasadena	Calderon, Ron	**VERMONT**	
Pearland	Wrigge, Bill	*Burlington*	Hoehn, Ted
Plano	Bunn, Robert	*Burlington*	Merritt, Robert
Plano	Glaze, Dale	*Johnson*	Witherell, Charles F
Plano	Sumrow, Kenneth W	*Lyndonville*	Bell, Dudley S
Richardson	Eby, Kevin	*Manchester Center*	Gunterman, Kelly
Richardson	Eckel, Katherine	*Mendon*	McEwan, Kenneth
Richardson	Guion, Bud	*Morrisville*	Yerrick, Charles E
Rockwall	Austrew, John Paul	*Quechee*	Crocker, Edward A
Rockwall	Moreland, Jill	*Stowe*	Gervickas, Steven N
Round Rock	King, M Kent	*Stowe*	Moriarty, Marvin
Rowlett	Moen, Susan M	*Waitsfield*	Abrams, Larry
San Angelo	Hamilton, Kevin R	*Waitsfield*	Carlson, Richard
San Antonio	Chew, Edgar Jr	*Wallingford*	Stout, Barry L
San Antonio	Conway, Bryan J	*Warren*	Kern, Thomas D
San Antonio	Derk, Timothy	*Winooski*	Goldberg, Roberta
San Antonio	Folks, Harold		
San Antonio	Folks, Michael		
San Antonio	Geraghty, Walter Jr		
San Antonio	Grammen, Robert		
San Antonio	Mayo, Sarah S	**VIRGINIA**	
San Antonio	McCabe, James W Jr	*Alexandria*	Fiske, Stephen C
		Alexandria	Hublitz, Martin
San Antonio	O'Bryant, Bill	*Alexandria*	King, Harold B (Chip) Jr
San Antonio	Oxford, Larry		
San Antonio	Reblin, Dennis	*Alexandria*	McCollom, Robert
San Antonio	Reygadas, Tom	*Alexandria*	Ranney, Peter C
San Antonio	Samuelson, Saundra A (Sandy)	*Alexandria*	Wald, Mitchel A
		Annandale	Drake, Betty
San Antonio	Shirley, Louis (Chip)	*Annandale*	McGettigan, Timothy G
San Antonio	Smith, Bohn W	*Arlington*	Ahrendts, Harry G
San Antonio	Soliz, Paul Norman	*Arlington*	Dillard, Kim Z
San Antonio	Walthall, Richard	*Arlington*	Dulany, Rod
Sherman	Menton, Charles	*Arlington*	Lamkin, Griffin
Sherman	Northcut, Bob	*Arlington*	McDonald, Ron
Spring	Collins, Mike	*Arlington*	Meyer, Henry (Ted)
Spring	Mauldin, Janis M	*Arlington*	Nozick, Melvina
Spring	Roush, Neil D	*Charlottesville*	De Long, Bob
Spring	Symonds, Jacquelin	*Charlottesville*	Leavell, Mary H
Sugarland	Averett, J E Cynthia	*Charlottesville*	Rogers, Philip C
Sugarland	Moellering, Jim	*Danville*	Clark, Martha L
Terrell	Samuels, Dessie	*Falls Church*	Clark, Johnathan H
Texarkana	Ward, Craig	*Falls Church*	McClure, Ann E
The Woodlands	Dinoffer, Joseph	*Falls Church*	Stilwell, Graham R
The Woodlands	Engel, Brian E	*Fredericksburg*	Vander Berg, Paul
The Woodlands	Harris, Joy E	*Ft. Eustis*	Horney, Gail W
Tyler	Kniffen, Fred	*Glen Allen*	Shipstedt, John D
Tyler	Nikolic, Sima	*Great Falls*	Snauwert
Tyler	Smith, Stephen M	*Hampton*	Screen, Dr. Robert M
Waco	Herr, Jefferey N	*Hampton*	Tysinger, Nancy

Hot Springs	Morgan, Thomas W	Redmond	Whitney, Marceil L
Martainville	Cooper, Kelly	Richland	Phan, Nguyen
McLean	Becerra, R A Jr		Thanh
McLean	Carey, Sally S	Seattle	Albrecht, Eric
McLean	Delton, Mark	Seattle	Behrens, Robert C
McLean	Eikenberry, Mike	Seattle	Brown, Jacquelynn
McLean	Graham, Robert W III	Seattle	Chauner, Michelle
McLean	Morrison, John H Jr	Seattle	Hawkins, Jodene D
McLean	Ryan, Anne H	Seattle	Knutsen, Jane K
Midlothian	Bard, Eva	Seattle	Ranney, David
Midlothian	Cummings, John	Seattle	Ratte, Jeffrey J
Newport News	Miller, Thomas E	Seattle	Thompson, William
Newport News	Shivar, Col. William		Rork
Norfolk	Brunson, Mason C	Seattle	Verdieck, Douglas L
Norfolk	Steingold, Andy	Seattle	Yee, Amy W
Oakton	DeGregorio,	Tacoma	Simpkins, Robert
	Anthony J		(Bob)
Richmond	Anderson,	Tacoma	Smith, Gregory L
	Christopher	Woodinville	Delay, Mary D
Richmond	Burrows, Hal	Yakima	Lockwood, Arthur
	(Harold)		
Richmond	Doeg, Bill		
Richmond	Hamilton, Ward		
Richmond	Heffner, James	**WEST VIRGINIA**	
Richmond	Koechlein, Fred E	Bluefield	Sarver, Mark S
Richmond	Leovey, Steven T	Bluefield	Sarver, Stephen C
Richmond	Mid Atlantic Tennis	Charleston	Pilsbury, Skip
Richmond	Sylvia, Dell R	Granville	Fleming, Mark
Richmond	Waters, Hugh	Morgantown	Ganahl, Gary
Roanoke	Lineberry, Larry C	Shepherdstown	Bell, Andrew J III
S. Boston	Cage, Robert	Slaty Fork	Owen, Michael
Salem	Foxworth, Mark B	War	Jones, Anne
Salem	Gibbs, Thomas	War	Jones, Lynne
Springfield	Sanders, Fred	White Sulphur	
Springfield	Shaw, Patricia	Springs	Bohrnstedt, Ron
Vienna	Bishop, Arthur H		
Vienna	Russo, Eugene		
Vienna	Statton, Philip J	**WISCONSIN**	
Virginia Beach	Benjumea, Jose F	Altoona	Morse, Robert A
Virginia Beach	Cole, Marjorie	Appleton	Luedtke, Robert J
Virginia Beach	Colvin, Richard B	Appleton	Neuman, Karen
Virginia Beach	Ellis, Hal R III		Marie
Virginia Beach	Flohre, Ralph A	Appleton	Van Lieshout,
Virginia Beach	Howell, David		James R
Virginia Beach	Ives, Dean	Bristol	Moffat, Andrew
Virginia Beach	Kamrad, Joseph G	Brookfield	Bergmann, Guenter E
Virginia Beach	Sholes, Russell	Cable	Henderson, William J
Warrenton	Baisden, H Monroe	Germantown	Martin, Donald J
	Jr	Glendale	Buckley, Robert J
Waynesboro	Blackburn, Lois H	Glendale	Kilian, Mary Beth
Williamsburg	West, Mildred B	Green Bay	Luedtke, Robert E
Woodbridge	Westebbe, Bruce	Green Bay	Medow, Mark B
		Hartland	Mashaw, David J
		Hartland	Sowersby, Sara
WASHINGTON		La Crosse	Devoll, Cliff
Aberdeen	Lind, Larry	Madison	Holgerson, Laurel
Bainbridge Island	Kringen, Gus R	Madison	Kourim, Adi
Bellevue	Adkisson, Janet H	Madison	Schackter, Denny
Bellevue	Doerrer, Steve	Madison	Schaefer, Lyle P
Bellevue	Harper, Bill	Marshfield	Feirer, Thomas M
Bellevue	Strang, Jerry	Mequon	Vetter, Rick
Bothell	Sennett, David	Milwaukee	Bachman, J Cary
Edmonds	Buren, Richard W	Milwaukee	Bronson, Walter
Edmonds	Sayrahder, Edward	Milwaukee	Burns, Dennis B
FPO, Seattle	Tempel, Victoria	Milwaukee	Cakans, Vilis
	Dianne	Milwaukee	Giles, Upton W
Grandview	Latham, Forrest F	Milwaukee	Lenard, Mark
Issaquah	Grobler, Charl	Milwaukee	Matheny, John
Kennewick	Hopp, Allen L	Milwaukee	Rocheleau, Michael J
Kirkland	Bard, Steve	Milwaukee	Schield, William H III
Kirkland	Loucks, Thomas R	Milwaukee	Scott, Valerie
Mercer Island	Adams, Brian L		Eveline
Mercer Island	Vozenilek, Elizabeth	Mukwonago	Saxe, Dave N
	Harrison	Neenah	Francart, Donald
Mercer Island	Vozenilek, Tom	Neenah	Lingelbach, Joanne
Olympia	Eisendrath, John	Neenah	Rotzenberg, George J
	(Bris)	Neenah	Tembelis, James J
Redmond	Knight, Dick	New Berlin	Janikowski, James L

Oconomowoc	Mueller, Roland F	*Waukesha*	Recknagel, David
Oconomowoc	Stuckey, Sharon	*Wausau*	Johnston, C Eugene
Oconomowoc	Wasserman,	*Wauwatosa*	Eiff, Timothy
	Kenneth P	*West Bend*	Sprinkman, Ted
Onalaska	Uglem, Wayne S	*Whitefish Bay*	Banzhaf, Sharon
Oshkosh	Adelman, Paula Brill		Pritula
Oshkosh	Van Lieshout,		
	William	**WYOMING**	
Racine	Libby, Lee J	*Casper*	Thayer, George
W. Allis	Drutowski, Joseph K	*Laramie*	Kroupa, Steven
Waukesha	Carpenter, Steve	*Rawlins*	Gibson, Robert W
Waukesha	Plaushines, Peter J		

International Members

USPTA Members Residing Abroad or in Areas Not Included in Regular 17 Divisions

AUSTRALIA	Hammond, Tony
	Hatt, Mrs. Pamela H
	Marshall, Arthur
AUSTRIA	Maslowski, Mark
CANADA	Nicholls, Peter
	Cysneiros, Miguel
	Senn, Lise
	Senn, Benita
CHINA	Brielmaier, Tim
COLUMBIA	Leal, Anibal D
	Molina, Ivan
DENMARK	Ohlsen, Bengt A
ENGLAND	James, John
FRANCE	Avril, Jean Luc
	Guessoum, Kamel
	Moszkowicz, Stephan
	Noel, Bernard
	Marconnet, Philippe
	Barcessat, Philippe
	Bouthelier, Karine
	Labout, Jean Claude
	Lando, Georges
	Labout, Christian
GERMANY	Dietsche, Thomas
	Nurnberger, Helmutt
	Gilg, Ralph
	O'Malley, John
	Huber, Wolfgang
	Iflinger, Rudi
	Van Oyen, Petra
	Beck, Rainer
	Dacruz, Sergio
	Sommer, Paul
	Baumgartner, Sepp
HOLLAND	Suyk, Dick
INDONESIA	Gondowidjojo, Mien
ITALY	Huber, Herbert
	Vetturelli, Federico
JAPAN	Kimpara, Kiyotaka
	Matsueda, Rei
NEW ZEALAND	Woolcott, Kevin
	McEachran, Gordon
	Sims, Graham Scott
SOUTH AFRICA	Rufus, Nel
SWITZERLAND	Sette, Pasqualino (Nino)
USA	Edwards, David R
	Coronado, Baudilio
	Vielma, Jesus
	Acevedo-Porto, Ricardo
VENEZUELA	Andrew, Jorge

AUSTRIA	Borowicz, David J
BRITISH WEST INDIES	McField, Richard L
CANADA	Sloan, Ron
	Cramer, Charles (Corky)
	Mitha, Ash
	Kaemmle, John
CHINA	Holsinger, John
COLUMBIA	Colbert, Kim C
COSTA RICA	Soto, Gustavo
DENMARK	Donahue, Edward
	Butler, Hayward
	Cooper, Larry
GERMANY	Ehrhardt, Kurt W
ISRAEL	Weisman, Allan D
ITALY	Kobleur, Richard
JAPAN	Breunich, Gregory
	Smith, Frank M
KENYA	Davies, Jane
LESOTHO	O'Connell, Daniel T
NETHERLANDS	O'Sullivan, Frances M
OMAN	Hament, John M
PHILLIPINES	Bacani, Jacinto
	Navarro
PUERTO RICO	Murray, Ted J
	Spilman, Bob
	Hauser, Tom
QATAR	Bickford, R Janet
SAUDI ARABIA	Daniels, Michael
SWITZERLAND	Hewitt, Ross
USA	Hunt, Marcella
	Parish, Pat
	Sharp, Cathy
	Renuart, Gene
	Provoteaux, Henri
	Ebbesen, Victor L Sr
	Kelman, Sandy

South East Asia

Japan Professional Tennis Association

MALAYSIA

SOUTH EAST ASIA

Anchant, Jim

Anchant, Roy
Boon Hock Soon, John
Chan Alphonsus, Joseph
Fadillah, Ghani
Ho, Nelly
Koh, Albert
Loh, Patrick
Lye, Doreen
Ng, Chee Seng
Ong, Kah Beng
Oon, Desmond
Tan, Chye Hui

Adachi, Hideo
Akashi, Goro
Akita, Naoki
Amano, Masahito
Aono, Akira
Araki, Kenjiro
Asano, Akira
Azami, Satoshi
Baba, Koji
Chiba, Toshihiko
Chikazawa, Yoshimi
Chino, Tokiharu
Dohkan, Yoshiki
Doi, Hiroshi
Doi, Takashi
Endo, Tomiharu
Eshima, Hideo
Fong, Kuang Ming
Fujii, Yasuo
Fujishima, Toshiyuki
Fukushima, Makoto
Furukawa, Shoji O
Furuta, Yoshifumi
Hagiwara, Toshio
Hamada, Kunio
Hao, Toshiji
Haraguchi, Hiroshi
Hashimoto, Hiroshi
Hatano, Kimitsugu
Hatano, Tetsuji
Hayashi, Kenichi
Hayashida, Michihiro
Higaki, Yasuaki
Hirano, Miki
Hiratsuka, Kazuo
Horiba, Nashiki
Houda, Kazuo
Ichikawa, Masato
Ichinose, Nobuharu
Igarashi, Akira
Ikeda, Kazumasa
Ikeshiro, Masafumi
Inohara, Mashiro
Inoue, Noriyuki
Ishida, Fumio
Ishida, Masakazu
Ishiguro, Osamu
Ishikawa, Hisao
Ishizaki, Yoshiro
Iwamoto, Akihiko
Iwamoto, Masao
Iwata, Katsuji
Kabasawa, Kohichi
Kai, Tateki
Kamiwazumi, Jun
Katimansah, Eddy
Kato, Hirokazu
Kato, Takumi
Kawakatsu, Hideaki
Kawakita, Shinichi
Kawano, Koji
Kawasaki, Yuji
Kawazoe, Minoru
Kikuchi, Senichi
Kojima, Kazuhisa
Kondoh, Takeshi

Kono, Teruo
Kotsuka, Hisayuki
Kounsosu, Atsushi
Koyama, Toshiyuki
Kudo, Toshio
Kumagai, Toshiharu
Kumakura, Yukiko M
Kunisaki, Hisao
Kuriyama, Masanori
Maeda, Keiichi
Maruta, Teiji
Maruyama, Kohichi
Masuda, Kenji
Matsuda, Shuichi
Matsuda, Yoshio
Matsuda, Yoshiomi
Matsui, Sadataka
Matsumoto, Hiroshi
Matsuoka, Shosei
Mimura, Akira
Misawa, Shuken
Mitsuhashi, Tamotsu
Miyoshi, Masato
Mori, Jiro
Mori, Ryoichi
Morikane, Kemji
Morimoto, Shudo
Morioka, Kiyoshi
Morita, Tsuneki
Moriwaki, Shigeru
Moriyama, Hiroshi
Motooka, Ryo
Murakami, Yoshiyuki
Nagahama, Takao
Nagai, Katsumi
Nakajima, Yasuhiro
Nakamura, Osamu
Nakanishi, Yasuyoshi
Nakano, Yoshitaka
Nakashima, Yoshiaki
Niina, Shoji
Nishi, Masato
Nishikawa, Kazuichi
Noda, Hitoshi
Nogichim, Koji
Nukariya, Hiroyuki
Obata, Atsushi
Ochiai, Saburo
Ogata, Kimio
Ohashi, Chihiro
Ohmori, Koji
Ohmori, Yoshio
Ohta, Kozo
Ohtani, Yohsuke
Ohtomo, Toshiyuki
Okada, Tadaaki
Okada, Takahiko
Okanoto, Toshinari
Osamura, Haruyuki
Oshibe, Nobuto
Otsudo, Mitsuo
Saitoh, Kaoru
Sakasai, Akira
Sakuma, Tsuyoshi
Sakurai, Takashi
Sango, Junichi

Sasa, Akira
Sato, Hitoshi
Sato, Kazuhiko
Sawada, Makoto
Shibata, Kazuyuki
Shibatsuji, Akira
Shibatsuji, Hikaru
Shimano, Kyoichi
Shimizu, Hiroyuki
Shoji, Kuniyasu
Suga, Toshihiko
Sugaya, Yuji
Sugita, Shunpei
Sugiura, Akira
Suzuki, Keiko
Suzuki, Kuniaki
Suzuki, Michimasa
Suzuki, Yoshihiro
Takahashi, Yasuo
Takano, Osami
Takasawa, Katsumi
Takase, Yuji
Takayama, Hideki
Tamura, Kenji
Tamura, Noaki
Tamura, Nobuya
Tanaka, Fumiyoshi
Tanaka, Toru
Tanaka, Toshimitsu
Tani, Kaoru
Taniura, Keiji
Tatsumi, Makoto
Tezuka, Yuji
Tomioka, Shinya
Tomita, Hitoshi
Touyama, Hiroshi
Tsuyuki, Toshiyuki
Uchida, Kazumi
Ueda, Masahiro
Usui, Masanori
Wantabe, Isao
Wantabe, Tsutomo
Yagisawa, Kyoji
Yamada, Hiroshi
Yamaguchi, Takayoshi
Yamaki, Hiroshi
Yamamoto, Ichiro
Yamamoto, Yashikata
Yanagi, Keishiro
Yasukawa, Shiro
Yasuno, Kiyoshi
Yazawa, Toshio
Yogo, Toshihiko
Yokochi, Hideo
Yokoyama, Kazuo
Yoshida, Nobuyuki
Yoshida, Yoichi
Yuasa, Shogo

ATP Members

Acuna, Ricardo
Adams, Egan
Aguilera, Juan
Alexander, John
Allan, Trevor
Amaya, Victor
Amritraj, Anan
Amritraj, Vijay
Andrade, Juan
Andrews, Andy
Arias, Jimmy
Arraya, Pablo
Ashe, Arthur
Aubone, Guillermo
Austin, John
Avendano, Juan

Ball, Syd
Bailey, Joel M.
Barr, Mike
Bauer, Mike
Benavides, Ramiro
Becka, Jaromi
Betancur, Alvaro
Beutel, Hans-Diete
Birner, Stanislov
Blocher, Woody
Bohrenstedt, Dick
Boileau, Bernard
Borg, Bjorn
Borowiak, Jeff
Bourne, Lloyd
Brawley, Sean
Brown, Jimmy
Brunnberg, Mike
Buehning, Fritz

Cain, Tom
Cahill, Mike
Cano, Ricardo
Canter, Jonathan
Carnahan, Scott
Carter, David
Casa, Christophe
Casal, Sergio
Case, Ross
Cash, Patrick
Castellan, Carlos
Chappell, Rory
Cortes, Alejandro
Courteau, Loic
Curren, Kevin

Damiani, J L
Davis, Martin
Davis, Scott
Dell, Dick
Dent, Phil
Denton, Steve
DePalmer, Mike
Derlin, Bruce
Dibbs, Eddie
Dibley, Colin
Dickson, Mark
Dowdeswell, Colin
Dowdeswell, Roger

Dowlen, David
Doyle, Matt
Drewett, Brad
Drysdale, Cliff
Dunk, Chris
DuPasquier, Ivan
DuPre, Pat
Dyke, Broderick

Eberhard, Klaus
Edberg, Stefan
Edmondson, Mark
Edwards, Eddie
Elter, Peter
Emerson, Roy
Estep, Mike
Evett, Rand

Fagel, Rick
Fancutt, Charlie
Farrow, Juan
Fassbender, Jurgen
Feaver, John
Feigl, Peter
Fillol, Alvaro
Fillol, Jaime
Fitzgerald, John
Fleming, Peter
Forget, Guy
Frawley, Rod
Freeman, Marcel
Fritz, Bernard
Fromm, Eric
Fukui, Tsuyoshi
Frawley, John

Gandolfo, Michael
Ganzabal, Alajandro
Garcia, Jose
Gattiker, Alex
Gattiker, Carlos
Gehring, Rolf
Giammalva, Sammy
Giammalva, Tony
Gilbert, Brad
Gildemeister, H.
Gimenez, Angel
Gitlin, Drew
Glickstein, Solomo
Gomez, Andres
Gonzalez, Francisco
Gorman, Tom
Gottfried, Brian
Graham, Tony
Granat, Jiri
Grant, Mike
Gullikson, Tim
Gullikson, Tom
Gunnarsson, Jan
Gunthardt, Hans
Gurfein, Jimmy
Goven, Georges

Hampson, Wayne
Harmon, Rodney
Hayes, John W.

Hewitt, Bob
Hightower, Ron
Higueras, Jose
Hjertquist, Per
Hlasek, Jakob
Hocevar, Marcos
Hogstedt, Thomas
Holmberg, Ron
Holmes, Greg
Holroyd, Glen
Hooper, Chip
Hoyt, Hubertus

Iskersky, Erick
Ismail, Haroon

Jarrett, Andrew
Jarryd, Anderson
Johnston, Chris
Joubert, Gideo

Kamawazumi, Jun
Kandler, Hans-Pete
Kary, Hans
Kelaidis, Nicki
Keller, Ney
Keretic, Damir
Kirmayr, Carlos
Kleege, R. B.
Kley, Ivan
Kohlberg, Andy
Korita, Eric
Krickstein, Aaron
Kriek, Johan
Krishnan, Ramesh
Krulevitz, Steve
Kuharszky, Zoltan

Lapidus, Jay
Leach, Mike
Leconte, Henri
Lendl, Ivan
Leonard, Tom
Lewis, Chris
Lewis, Chris
Lewis, Richard
Lloyd, John
Lofgren, Bill
Lopez-Maeso, Jose
Luna, Fernando
Lutz, Bob

McCain, Scott
McCurdy, John
McEnroe, John
McMillan, Frew
McMillan, Ken
McNamara, Peter
McNamee, Peter
McNair, Fred

Malin, S. Gene
Manson, Bruce
Martin, Billy
Martinez, Mario
Masur, Ian Walter

Maurer, Andres
Mayer, Gene
Mayer, Sandy
Maynetto, Fernando
Mayotte, Chris
Mayotte, Tim
Maze, Bill
Mecir, Miloslav
Meiler, Karl
Meister, Steve
Menon, Sashi
Meyer, Ricky
Michibata, Glenn
Miller, Craig
Mir, Miguel
Mitchell, Matt
Mitton, Bernie
Montano, Emilio
Moor, Terry
Moore, Ray
Moretton, Gilles
Motta, Cassio
Mottram, Buster
Murphy, Pender
Mustard, David
Myburg, Mike

Nastase, Ilie
Navratil, Jarosla
Newcombe, John
Nunez, Juan
Nunna, Bhanu
Nystrom, Joachi

Ocleppo, Gianni
Odizor, Nduka
Okker, Tom
Orantes, Manuel
Osta, Eduardo
Ostoja, Marko

Palin, Leo
Panatta, Adriano
Panatta, Claudio
Pasarell, Charlie
Pate, David
Pattison, Andrew
Pecci, Victor
Perez, Diego
Pfister, Henry
Piacentile, J M
Pierola, Alejandr
Pils, Bernhard
Pimek, Libor
Pinner, Uli
Pirow, Brent
Pohmann, H.
Portes, Pascal
Potier, Jerome
Prajoux, B
Puncec, Frank
Purcell, Mel

Ralston, Dennis
Ramirez, Raul
Rebolledo, Pedro

Reininger, Robert
Rennert, Peter
Rheinberger, Robert
Richey, Cliff
Riessen, Marty
Rinaldini, G.
Rodriquez, Pato
Roger-Vasselin, Christophe
Rosewall, Ken
Roverano, Hugo
Royer, Rocky
Ryan, Torry

Sadri, John
Sanders, Louk
Sauer, Freddie
Saviano, Nick
Scanlon, Bill
Schapers, Michiel
Schneider, David
Schwaier, Hans
Scewagen, Butch
Segarceanu, F
Shiras, Lief
Simonsson, Hans
Simonsson, Stefan
Simpson, Jeff
Simpson, Russell
Singh, Jasjit
Slozil, Pavel
Smid, Tomas
Smith, Jonathan
Smith, Stan
Soares, J A
Solomon, Harold
Stadler, Roland
Stansbury, Cary
Stefanki, Larry
Stewart, Sherwood
Steyn, Christo
Stockton, Dick
Stoller, F.
Strode, Buzz (C)
Strode, Skip (M)
Sundstrom, Henrik

Tanner, Roscoe
Taroczy, Balazs
Tarr, Derek
Taygan, Ferdi
Teacher, Brian
Teltscher, Eliot
Testerman, Ben
Theissen, Harald
Tidemann, Magnus
Tiberti, Gustavo
Torre, Paul
Tous, Alberto
Tulasne, Thierry
Turner, Steve

Ulrich, Torbin
Urpi, Gabriel

Van Der Merwe, Schlk
Van Dillen, Eric

Van Patten, Vince
Van't Hof, Robert
Velasco, Jairo
Venter, Robbie
Vines, Mark
Visser, Danie
Vizcaino, Roberto

Waltke, Trey
Walts, Butch
Warwick, Kim
Westphal, Michael
Whitecross, Greg
Wilander, Mats
Wilkison, Tim
Windahl, Jorge
Winitsky, Van
Wittus, Craig

Ycaza, Ricardo
Youl, Simon

Glossary of Tennis Terms

Ace An unreturnable serve.

Ad court The side of the court in which the second point of each game begins, also called the left court or the backhand court.

Alley The area on each side of the singles court that enlarges the surface area for doubles play.

Approach shot A shot used from inside the baseline to enable a player at or near the baseline to attain position at the net.

Australian doubles formation A serving formation in doubles wherein the server and server's partner are initially positioned on the same side of the court.

Australian grip A grip midway between the Eastern and Continental, so named because it was developed in Australia to facilitate serve-and-volley play on grass.

Backcourt The area between the baseline and service line.

Backhand For a right-hander, the stroke played on the left side of the body; the reverse for a left-hander.

Backspin or underspin The reverse or backward rotation of the ball in flight.

Backswing The initial portion of the swing, so called because it involves bringing the racket back before swinging it forward; it can be straight-back or loop.

Badminton Another racket game, played over a net with a lighter racket and by striking a light fluffy shuttlecock.

Ball toss The action of lifting the ball into the air with the non-racket arm when initiating the serve.

Baseline The line which demarcates the legal length of the court.

Block volley A volley produced by holding the racket firmly in the path of the oncoming ball and "blocking" it back with almost no motion.

Bounce-hit technique A method of reducing tension and increasing concentration; the hitter says "bounce" aloud when the ball lands on his or her side of the net and "hit" when he or she makes contact.

Cannonballs Very fast, hard serves, hit with little spin.

Centerline Refers to both the line dividing the service boxes and the smaller hashmark that bisects the baseline.

Challenge ladder Vertical listing of players, arranged like a ladder, which allows players in lower rungs to challenge players above them and move ahead of them if they win.

Changeover The time after every odd game when players change ends of the court; they have 90 seconds to make the changeover.

Checkpoints Specific spots or places to stop and examine to be sure one's grip or swing is correct.

Chip shot A soft dipping shot with backspin that just clears the net, forcing the net player to volley up; often employed to return serve.

Chop shot A stroke with heavy backspin, hit with a chopping motion.

Circular backswing or loop backswing Taking the racket back high, so that a graphic illustration of the swing would resemble a loop, or a circle; alternative to straight-back backswing.

Closed face When the face of the racket is inclined slightly forward, tilted towards the oncoming ball; opposite of open face.

Conditioning Exercise schedule to prepare one physically for tennis.

Consolation A separate tournament for those who lose in the championship tournament.

Contact point The place where and when the racket meets the ball.

Continental grip A grip which is the same for forehand and backhand, so called because it was developed on the "continent" of Europe; favored by serve-and-volley players.

Counter-force bracing A mechanical means of protecting against and/or lessening the effects of tennis elbow and other tennis-related injuries.

Coupling effect When two body segments are utilized in immediate succession during the swing their cumulative effect (impact) increases.

Court conditions The state of the court itself or, more generally, the impact of sun, cold, wind, and other weather factors.

Court maintenance Maintaining the court for play; procedures vary according to the type of surface.

Court surface The material that covers the court; it ranges from grass to soft granules to wood.

Court tennis The progenitor of tennis as we know it; an indoor game developed by French royalty prior to the French Revolution.

Court zones Imaginary areas of the court that lend themselves to offensive, defensive, and neutral tactics.

Critical games Games that are more important than others, such as the first and seventh games of a set.

Critical points Points that are more important than others, such as the first and fourth points of a game.

Crosscourt shot A ball hit diagonally across the court, as opposed to one hit straight down the line.

Cross slice A shot hit with underspin, or backspin, and sidespin at the same time.

Davis Cup An international team competition between nations, begun in 1900.

Defensive lob A high, deep lob played from a defensive position which allows the defender time to recover court position and forces the offensive player away from the net; almost always hit with underspin.

Deuce court The side of the court in which the first point of each game begins, also called the right court or the forehand court.

Dink shot A soft dipping shot that just clears the net; used often in doubles, especially on return of serve. See also Chip shot.

Double-fault Failing to place either of two serves in play.

Doubles A match between two teams, each team consisting of two players.

Down-the-line shot A ball hit straight down the line, as opposed to one hit diagonally across the court.

Drag volley A volley hit with the racket face slightly open, producing some backspin; used for control.

Drift or intercept A doubles tactic wherein the receiver's partner moves into the middle to intercept server's first volley.

Drilling Practicing in set patterns.

Drive A hard-hit groundstroke, forehand, or backhand.

Drive volley or swing volley Playing the ball in the air with a longer swing than the normal short volley movement.

Dropshot A delicate shot that barely clears the net and falls short in the opponent's court.

Drop volley Same as the dropshot, but hit off a volley, usually from a position close to the net.

Eastern grip A strong groundstroking grip, so called because it was developed in the eastern United States, that employs separate hand positions for forehand and backhand.

Error Failure to return the ball legally.

Face The hitting surface (strings) of the racket in relation to the ball; the face can be open, closed, vertical, or flat.

Fast courts Court surfaces, such as wood and grass, that allow the ball to bound faster and lower than others.

Finish The end of the swing; also called the follow-through.

First volley The first ball played by a server rushing the net after serve; usually played at or near the service line and before it bounces.

Fitness The product of conditioning, and the level of physical readiness to play tennis (and other sports) well.

Flat backswing Taking the racket straight back in preparation for the swing, as opposed to a loop or circular backswing.

Flat face When the strings of the racket are perpendicular to the ground and the racket meets the ball squarely, with little spin.

Flat serve A serve hit with little or no spin, usually it is hit with great speed and power.

Flat shot Any shot hit with little or no spin; usually it is hit with great speed and power.

Follow-through The finishing motion of the swing after the ball has been hit.

Footwork The art of moving the feet in such a way that one's body is correctly positioned to execute the best possible stroke.

Forcing shot Any shot that forces one's opponent into a defensive position.

Forehand For a right-hander, the stroke played on the right side of the body; vice versa for a left-hander.

Forward swing The movement of the racket forward into the ball; opposite of backswing.

Frame The portion of the racket that contains the strings or, more generally, an unstrung racket.

Game A unit of scoring. A game is won by a player who outscores his or her opponent by two points, while scoring at least four points.

Game point The point that will win a game if the player who is ahead in the score wins it.

Grand Prix circuit A year-long succession of professional tournaments linked by an overall sponser, a bonus pool for participants, and a final Masters tournament.

Grip The way in which one holds the racket; also the handle of the racket itself and/or the material covering the handle.

Grip change The shifting of one's hand on the racket to facilitate the next shot; usually from forehand to backhand or vice versa.

Grip size One of many sizes in which the handles of rackets are made for smaller and larger hands.

Groundstroke Hitting the ball after it has bounced, usually from the area of the baseline.

Groundstroke slice A groundstroke hit with an open-faced racket producing backspin or underspin.

Gut A responsive string, made from animal intestines, used to string rackets; it is expensive.

Hairpin backswing A backswing whose arc describes a hairpin; a compromise between the straight-back and loop backswing.

Halfcourt The area of the court midway between the baseline and net, also called midcourt.

Half-volley Playing the ball just after it bounds with a very low, short stroke.

Hard approach shot A shot used to approach the net, but hit very hard.

Hard or composition courts A court surface that is hard to the touch and on the feet; it requires very little maintenance.

Head The area of the racket containing the strings.

Hip rotation Movement of the hips during a swing.

Hitting deep Keeping the ball near the opponent's baseline.

Hitting on the rise Playing the ball before it has reached the peak of its bounce.

Hitting short Hitting the ball near the opponent's service line.

Jump-smash An overhead, or smash, hit while jumping in the air.

Junior tennis Competitive tennis, usually referring to tournaments played by boys and girls 18 years of age and under.

Kill To put the ball away and end the point.

Ladder play See Challenge ladder.

Lawn tennis Original name for tennis, alluding to the fact that the game was invented for play on grass.

Lob A high-arcing shot, usually hit from behind the baseline to regain position.

Match A contest between two or four tennis players, usually the best of three sets but sometimes the best of five sets.

Match point A point that will end the match if the leading player wins it.

Midcourt The area around the service lines, halfway between the net and the baseline.

Mixed doubles A match involving two teams, each team consisting of one male, one female.

Moon ball A very high lob mixed into a baseline exchange, primarily used to change the tempo.

Net The netting placed across the middle of the court.

Net player In doubles, the partner of the server when he or she takes a normal doubles position at the net.

Net rusher A player who aggressively moves forward to a position at the net.

Net skimmer A ball which barely clears the net.

"No-man's" land The area near the service line, also called midcourt.

Offensive lob A lob played from an intermediate or offensive position, usually hit with a lower trajectory than the defensive lob, and intended to win the point; often hit with topspin.

One-handed backhand A backhand hit with one hand on the grip, as opposed to a two-handed backhand.

One Up One Back doubles formation Doubles positions wherein one player of a doubles team remains at the baseline while the other takes the net.

Open face When the face of the racket is tilted away from the oncoming ball, or "open" to the ball, as opposed to "closed."

Open stance Any hitting stance in which the back foot is closer to the path of the ball than the front foot.

Open tennis Play that allows amateurs and professionals to compete together.

Out Applies to any ball that lands outside the playing area.

Overhead smash A stroke played above the head with a service-type action, usually from near the net and in response to a lob.

Passing shot A groundstroke that passes a net player on either side.

Paume, Le Jeu du The French racket game that evolved into court tennis, which inspired tennis. (In English, "the game of the palm.")

Percentage tennis Shot selection according to the position of the ball and the opponent, the physical dimensions of the court, the opponent's strengths and weaknesses.

Placement Placing a shot so that it cannot be returned.

Poach In doubles, a tactic in which a net player leaves his or her area and moves into partner's territory to attempt a kill at the net.

Point The smallest unit of scoring. (Four points win a game, as long as the player is ahead by two points or more.)

Punch volley A volley marked by a very short "punching" movement of the racket.

Putaway volley A volley hit beyond the opponent's reach.

Rally Play exchange between two or more players.

Rating A point value that expresses a player's skill level; part of the National Tennis Rating Program (NTRP).

Ready hop A hop used just before an opponent serves or hits the ball; helps facilitate a quick response.

Ready position A preparation for any shot; weight slightly forward, knees slightly bent, racket up and in front of the body.

Referee The tournament official who is responsible for the tournament draw and supervising all aspects of play.

Round robin A type of tournament in which all members of a group play each other in turn.

Run-around forehand A forehand hit from the backhand side, i.e., a player runs to his or her backhand side in order to hit a forehand instead of a backhand.

Semi-circular backswing A backswing that approximates a semi-circle, i.e., the racket does not complete a full circle or loop.

Semi-Western grip A grip midway between the Western and Eastern grips.

Serve Putting the ball into play, usually with an overhead motion.

Serve-and-volley A style of play that involves rushing toward the net immediately after the serve, in order to volley the return.

Service box The area on the other side of the net in which a serve must land in order to be legal.

Service break When one player wins a game while the other player is serving; also called "a break."

Service line The line near midcourt that marks the boundaries of the service boxes.

Set A unit of scoring; a set is won by the first player to reach six games by a margin of two, or by the player who wins a special tie-break game at 6–6.

Short-radius backswing Very short preparation for the swing; most appropriate when returning serve.

Sidelines The lines on each side forming the boundaries of the court.

Side slice Moving the racket across and under the ball at impact, imparting both backspin and sidespin at the same time, also called sidespin.

Sidespin shot See Side slice.

Sideways stance Standing in neither a closed nor an open stance, also referred to as a "square" stance.

Singles A match between two players.

Slice shot A shot hit with slice, or backspin.

Slow courts Courts that grab the ball on impact, slowing the bounce.

Smash See Overhead smash.

Snap volley A volley hit with some wrist action at impact, used for more power.

Soft courts Courts that give under the feet, i.e., clay and Har-Tru.

Specialty shots Shots other than the basic serve, volley, and groundstrokes, i.e., dropshot, approach, half-volley, lob, and overhead.

Sphairistike The name first given to tennis by its inventor, Major Wingfield.

Squash A racket game played in an enclosed room with a small rubber ball.

Stand in When receiver stands inside the baseline to return serve, intending to play the ball early.

Standard doubles formation Positions for the serving team, server stands at baseline with partner at net; for the receiving team, receiver stands near the baseline with partner on the service line.

Straight-back backswing Taking the racket straight back, as opposed to a loop or circular backswing.

Strategy A general plan of play.

String The nylon, gut, or synthetic that forms the hitting surface of the racket.

"T" The midcourt area formed by the junction of the center service line and the service lines.

Tactics The specific implementation of a general strategy, i.e., your strategy is to tire your opponent, so you utilize the tactics of dropshot and lob.

Taking the net Moving from the baseline position to the net position.

Tear-drop backswing A backswing whose graphic illustration would resemble the shape of a tear-drop.

Tempo The time between shots and/or between points; tempo can be fast or slow.

Tennis elbow Pain in the elbow caused by too much play and/or improper technique.

Tension The degree of tautness in the strings of a racket.

Throat The area of the racket immediately beneath the head, joining the head to the handle.

Tie breaker A special game played to decide the winner of a set when the score is tied at 6–6. The winner of the tie breaker game is the first player to reach seven points, by a margin of two.

Topspin or forward spin Forward rotation of the ball in flight.

Tournament A meeting of many players in a format that leads to a champion.

Two-handed backhand A backhand hit with two hands on the grip.

Vertical face When the hitting area of the racket is at a right angle to the ground or "on edge," as opposed to an open or a closed face.

Volley Playing the ball in the air before it bounces.

Volley lob Hitting a lob off the volley before the ball bounces.

Western grip A grip developed on hard courts in California, allowing a player to hit high-bouncing balls with power and promoting topspin.

Wide An out ball that is hit wide of the sidelines, as opposed to one that goes out over the baseline.

Wimbledon A suburb of London that lends its name to "The Championships," acknowledged by tennis players as the number one tournament.

Winner A ball hit beyond the opponent's reach; an unreturnable shot.

Index

CREDITS

PHOTOGRAPHS

Tennis World
Michael Cole
Western Mail and Echo
Sports and General Press Agency
Australian Information Service
Eiichi Kawate
Akio Matsumoto

DRAWINGS:

Osamu Nagumo
Shinichi Yamashita
Makoto Murata